Business Power

The Power-Book Library

Its Aim

NOT Training in the well-known Arts, Sciences or Businesses, but Cultivation of the Real Personality for Successful Living in any Art, Science or Business.

Its Philosophy

The Highest Human Science is the Science of Practical Individual Culture.

The Highest Human Art is the Art of Making the Most of the Self and its Career.

One Science-Art stands Supreme: The Science-Art of Successful Being, Successful Living, Successful Doing.

Its Eight Highways of Power

The Highway of Bodily and Mental Health.
The Highway of Dauntless Courage-Confidence.
The Highway of the Controlled Whirlwind.
The Highway of Symmetrically Great Will-Power.
The Highway of Variously Growing Mind-Power.
The Highway of Physical and Psychic Magnetism.
The Highway of Expanding Practical Ability.
The Highway of the Arthurian White Life.

Its Double Goal

Supreme Personal Well-Being and Actual Financial Betterment.

Its Method

Exactly What to Do and How to Do Exactly That.

The Volumes

"Power of Will," (Travels Seven Highways).
"Power for Success," (Travels Eight Highways).[1]
"The Personal Atmosphere," (Suggests all Highways).
"Business Power," (Travels Seven Highways).[1]
"The Culture of Courage," (Travels Four Highways).[1]
"Practical Psychology," (Travels Six Highways).[2]

You are invited to enter one or more of the Eight Highways and to share in the labor and rewards of many now on the path of personal betterment.

2 In preparation.

BUSINESS POWER

A PRACTICAL MANUAL
IN FINANCIAL ABILITY.

By FRANK CHANNING HADDOCK.

Founder of THE POWER-BOOK LIBRARY.
Author of "THE PERSONAL ATMOSPHERE," "POWER OF WILL."
"POWER FOR SUCCESS," "THE CULTURE OF COURAGE,"
"PRACTICAL PSYCHOLOGY," &c., &c.

In Four Parts:

THE PERSONAL FACTORS, ECONOMIC LAWS AND BUSINESS
MAXIMS, PSYCHOLOGY IN BUSINESS,
BUSINESS IN FACT.

Foundation:

Vital Education is the Evolution of Consciousness.

SEVENTH EDITION.

1914
THE PELTON PUBLISHING CO.,
MERIDEN, CONNECTICUT.

L. N. FOWLER & CO.
7 Imperial Arcade, and 4 & 5 Imperial Buildings,
Ludgate Circus, London, England.

PRESS OF
THE HORTON PRINTING CO.,
MERIDEN, CONN.

To

George Russell Eager

Unwavering Friend, Magnetic Leader,
Master of Initiative Energy,
At Home with Large Men and Important Affairs;
One Whose Lasting Works Perpetuate the Outlasting Man
In the Demonstration of Practical Success;
And More—A Great Soul, Free, Independent, Tolerant,
Who Exemplified, Above All Financial Achievement,
The High Intrinsic Value of a Chivalrous Heart,
A Growing Mind
And a Perennially Helpful Life.

"*Success, success, success. Nothing could be of more importance. Its attainment argued a man's efficiency in the Scheme of Things, his worthy fulfilment of the end for which a divine Providence had placed him on earth. Anything that interfered with it,— personal comfort, inclination, affection, desire, love of ease, individual liking,— was bad.*" — "The Blazed Trail," Steward Edward White.

PREFACE.

PRINCIPLES BASIC TO BUSINESS.

I. The most fundamental fact in human activity is the push of personality seeking the gratification of desires.

II. There are three general methods by which such gratification may be realized: (A) By appropriation justified by discovery; (B) By force equivalent to war; (C) By adjustment creating business.

III. In its permanent phase, business founds in adjustment contributing equally (more or less) to the welfare of all engaging parties. Every phase not so contributing exhibits either the monopoly of discovery or the monopoly of war, and, in the long run, therefore, is necessarily temporary.

IV. The broadest foundation of permanent business is that personal intelligence which operates by skill rather than by force, for community benefit in part rather than for individual interest solely, and for long-run development rather than individual success.

v

V. The two central factors which infallibly make for these ends are personal integrity and practical ability.

VI. Since permanent business is mutual adjustment for gratification of desires, the element of personal integrity must both exhibit and create courageous confidence and confident courage, and the element of practical ability must demonstrate persistent personal address to the end that desires may be gratified, and yet stimulated, or even created, with the most satisfactory completeness.

VII. The requirements of this permanent complex transaction in adjustment are: what to adjust for; to whom to adjust; and how to secure and maintain adjustment as thus decided.

VIII. These requirements resolve into *Magneto-Practical Personal Adjustment, applied with Confident Courage to Continuing Gratification of Developing Community Desires, to the end of a Satisfactory Balance of Self-Interest with Other-Interest, the two great polar forces of financial success.*

These eight statements constitute my preface, and indicate the ideal sought in all the following pages. Not instruction in the conduct of your business, but suggestion in the practical psychology of business power. The foundation and the edifice of business are first of all psychic, and the art of business psychology is the art of personal masterhood in practical affairs.

It is hoped that the author's aim may not be overlooked in the study of the book. You are invited to "make good" the reader's implied contract: The multiplication of self into the studies solely for the aim indicated — business power.

"A stimulus to nervous matter effects a change in that matter by calling forth a reaction in it. This change may be exceedingly slight after the first stimulus, but each repetition of the stimulus increases the change, with its following specific reaction, until by constant repetition a permanent alteration in the nervous matter stimulated occurs, which produces a fixed habitual way of working in it. The gray matter layer of our brains need not be left with only the slender equipment of functions which Nature gives it at birth. It can be fashioned artificially, that is, by education, so that it may acquire very many new functions or capacities which never come by birth nor by inheritance, but which can be stamped upon it as so many physical alterations in its proplasmic substance."—"Brain and Personality," W. H. THOMSON.

INTRODUCTION.

IN a certain old book, "*Elements of Logic*," by Richard Whately, may be read the following significant remarks: "But many who allow the use of systematic principles in other things, are accustomed to cry up Common Sense as the sufficient and only safe guide to reasoning"— let us substitute "to business." "Now, by Common Sense is meant, I apprehend, an exercise of the judgment unaided by any art or system of rules; such an exercise as we must necessarily employ in numberless cases of daily occurrence; in which, having no established principles to guide us,— no line of procedure, as it were, distinctly chalked out,— we must needs act on the best extemporaneous conjectures we can form. He who is eminently skilful in doing this, is said to possess a superior degree of Common Sense. But the generality have a strong predilection for Common Sense, *except in those points in which they, respectively, possess the knowledge of a system of rules; but in these points they deride any one who trusts to unaided Common Sense.* A sailor, e. g., will, perhaps, despise the pretensions of

ix

medical men, and prefer treating a disease by Common
Sense, but he would ridicule the proposal of navigating
a ship by Common Sense, without regard to the maxims
of nautical art."

The old logician was right, and his remarks are
applicable to every department of life. Common
Sense is, after all, merely the crystallized wisdom of
ages, and, contrary to being in opposition to rules, is,
if good for practical purposes, made up of rules, which
gradually have been absorbed by the general mind.
The new and the difficult are always being worked
over into the universal consent of common sense.

The business man, especially the young business man, perhaps, may feel that common sense, together with what technical training he possesses, can
alone be relied upon to guide him in the ways of financial success, and emphatically may hold that business
instruction scarcely will be expected outside of a
counting-room or a factory office — unless we except
the commercial college. The present book should
not be misunderstood as making any pretension as a
teacher of business methods, *per se*; nevertheless, it
is hoped that the attempt of these pages will neither
contradict common sense nor fail in demonstrating
a reasonable degree of practical usefulness. It would
seem to be a common-sense view that even a general
survey of qualifications and methods essential to
success must prove valuable to the reader, if the survey stick to the theme and all along aim to be directive
in certain respects as well as suggestive in others.
And this is the aim of the present pages: to set forth,
not beautiful theories about success, but downright
practical suggestions for the development of sure
business power.

It has been thought best to divide the work into four parts: The Personal Factors, Economic Laws and Business Maxims, Psychology in Business, Business in Fact. The first, second and fourth parts will speak for themselves, but the third part invites a word at this point because the theme is altogether modern. In older days the combination, Psychology and Business, would have received scant courtesy outside the class-room of some speculative college instructor. To-day, the psychology of business life is gaining attention from the higher schools, and more and more, the subject will make its way into counting-room and office. We shall, therefore, essay a brief study of certain mental abilities which are in daily use in all business with the view of suggesting to business men a completer investigation and mastery of their own well-worn but not always understood instruments. Every business person employs psychology every hour during his work. Why should not serious attention be given the science he must bring into action, and why should not all advantage be sought from an intelligent application of the science to commercial effort? The more a man knows, the more confident he ought to be in his own field. "It is the self-confident man who compasses the finest wreck," you will say with Henry Seton Merriman in "*The Velvet Glove;*" but that variety of self-confidence is due to ignorance or a refusal to learn. Surely a better knowledge of one's own mental powers — a knowledge constantly related, as here, to actual business — invites the man who understands the value of the right sort of self-confidence, the sort that is based on conscious personal competence. Thousands of men would undoubtedly get on more successfully had they a completer knowledge

of their own common powers and greater skill in
handling themselves. In these evident facts arises
the justification of a brief excursion into the science
of mind in which we shall later indulge. For a more
exhaustive examination reference is made to a future
work now in preparation, "*Practical Psychology.*"

Professor Elmer Gates once said: "In the first
place, beyond all other factors in importance, I consider as foremost the knowledge which I have of my
own mind. It is the mind which makes every discovery, every invention; which originates every new
idea; which formulates every plan; which directs
every series of volitions; which acquires all knowledge.
Therefore, a knowledge of the mind, and the application
of this knowledge to the art of better using the mind,
I consider to have been the chief element in my success."

Take, for example, the one act of mind called
Attention. The power to put forth this act and to
hold it differs greatly among different people. Here
is a tool, say, like a carpenter's bit, which is dull or
sharp, weak or strong, short or long, boring small or
large, as the case may be. Surely a knowledge of the
tool itself,— of the good and bad qualities of the attention as you employ it,— and of correct methods for
improving it and its handling and usefulness — all
this must be of very practical importance.

If, now, the reader has accepted the illustration as good, it is evident, nevertheless, that he does
not understand attention after all, for, as a matter
of fact, the "bit" is any ability of mind, while *attention is merely a way the man has of using that ability.*
I have given the illustration this rather abrupt twist
to show that it may be well to ascertain precisely
what the familiar "power" which we call attention

really is. It is not a "faculty" of the "mind"; it is rather and simply the self in a given use of its power. And the mind's *power* is just the self in action.

Or take the so-called power of imagination. *All practical foresight involves the imaginative ability.* It is useless to expect imaginative planning from a mind deficient in the power. Even if you possess some talent in this direction, its usefulness depends upon its kind. Imagination is not all one. You cannot see how the new store is to look if you have no visualizing imagination — no mind's eye, so to speak. A medical lecturer exhorts his students not to commit to memory, but to secure mental pictures of the bodily organs. Some of the students are utterly unable to do this: they have no visualizing mental power. What then? The student must discover what kind of imagination he does possess, and use that variety, as he may, to equally practical effect.

"A mole, having consulted many oculists," says an ancient fable "for the benefit of his sight, was at last provided with a good pair of spectacles; but, upon his endeavoring to make use of them, his mother told him that, although they might help the eye of a man, they could be of no use to a mole." The moral is: A little study in practical psychology *invites you to the discovery of the right kind of glasses.*

And thus with regard to all those mental phases of practical ability referred to in the third part of this work. No mechanic will content himself with ignorance of the tools which he employs. Shall a business man be satisfied with a species of ignorance which must discount his effort from start to finish?

The labor suggested in these pages may seem considerable. The book would be worthless other-

wise. The literature about success is to-day an ocean,
but the books that tell you what to do and how to do
it in order really to succeed are mountain springs found
only here and there in high places. There is absolutely no smooth road to efficiency. Success always
means downright hard work. Nevertheless, this work
employs the common abilities which we all possess.
Any scheme promising miracles through some "occult"
means may safely be ignored at the start.

A foreigner, who had traveled extensively, was
asked whether he observed that any one quality could
be regarded as a universal characteristic. He answered, "Me tink dat all men lofe lazy."

But the labor a man puts into the study of himself for practical handling of his abilities inevitably
pays immense interest in the end. "In nations," remarks Guizot in his *"History of Civilization,"* "as
well as in individuals, the good fortune to have all
the faculties called into action, so as to secure free
and full development of the various powers, both of
mind and of body, is an advantage, not too dearly
paid for by the labor and pain with which it is attended."

Precisely the same remark may be made concerning the unknown things for which a man may turn
out to be adapted. "You never can tell." Anticipative imagination, with good hard work making steadily
toward a goal, may lift a ditch-digger to a mountain
tunneller, from inferiority to superiority of almost any
variety. Every man has his natural limitations, perhaps,— I am inclined to doubt,— but who is there to
disclose what they are? *The poorest act any person
can perform is the setting of his or her limit-stake anywhere in the universe.* Let the limit take care of itself,

as it will. Meanwhile, attend you to the business of putting the ambition stake constantly just a little further on. This means work, of course, but when work goes out of the world, we may as well follow.

"It is a good rule to endeavor hour by hour and week after week to learn to work hard," said President Eliot. "It is well to learn to work intensely. You will hear a good deal of advice about letting your soul grow and breathing in without effort the atmosphere of a learned society or a place of learning. Well, you cannot help breathing and you cannot help growing; those processes will take care of themselves. The question for you from day to day is how to learn to work to advantage."

There was a common man, says a little story, who had got it into his head that work was really the right thing in the right place. He was a big, burly, awkward fellow, with nothing significant in his face except square jaws; and all who saw him called him a "dub." He applied for a position as clerk in the shipping department of a large concern. In this position he failed; "his work was too poor to hold him the job," and the head remarked: "Why, you 're not fit to be a clerk. You 're to be trucking barrels around down in the stock-rooms." "Will you give me a job there, then?" he asked. "And then when I 'm able to do this kind of work here I want you to give my job back," he persisted. "Oh, very well," said the head, not knowing his man yet. In six months the Dub returned with a commendation from the superintendent of the stock-room, and received the old job again. He did his work well now. "When did you learn to figure since you were here last?" the head queried. "Nights," said the Dub. "I practised

nights and noons." At the end of the year everybody still called him Dub, but a checker left and he
clumsily approached the head with the words, "I can
do it." "You!" the head and the chief clerk gasped.
"Surely," said the Dub. "How did you learn it?"
"Nights," replied the stupid man. "I practised
nights." "Give him the job," said the head. He was
checker for a year. Then the truckmen, on a Saturday
afternoon, struck, with the last car in the train only
half loaded. Everyone else had gone home but the
man who knew no better than to work hard. He went
on with the loading alone. The nice truckmen, who
desired doubtless to advance from the ranks of the
"down-trodden," pelted him with various articles,
until a brakeman called in the police. The Dub
stolidly finished the work. "You Dub, you might
have been killed and no good done by it," said the
head on the following Monday morning. But he offered to take the Dub out of the invoice department and
give him an assistant superintendency in a certain
part of the plant. "But I hain't had no chance to
learn that work yet," said the unconquerable man,
"I'd sooner stay here till I can practise some more
kinds of work." "Come to me when you're ready,"
the head assented to the gloriously stupid soul. "And
the Dub eventually got ready, and if you happen to
visit *Going & Co.'s* nowadays, you will find him walking around the plant, dressed as roughly as ever, and
still looking much like a dub. But if you wish to get
a position in the plant, you must go and ask the Dub
for it." This bit of realism is taken from "*How a Dub
Won Success*," by Allen Wilson. The Dub possessed
brain-cells which had never been used and a pair of
jaws which drove him to their discovery. He knew

how to work; he felt that he could do better things;
but the quality of his make-up that impelled him to
"practise nights and noons" in order to acquire rules
and ability was that supreme digester of all practical
things — Common Sense Applied in a Common-Sense
Way.

"The man who controls himself is usually able
to control just so much of his surrounding world as
may suit his purpose." This statement signifies the
common meaning of control — and one other: that
masterly handling of self which results from discovery
and training of the powers which make up the self.
That means "practising" all the "nights and noons"
you can get.

This Dub had mastered many kinds of work and
so had made himself independent of employment in
any particular direction. He could lose one position,
yet hold his relation to the concern by ability to fill
another. In brief, he had adapted himself to more
than one form of labor because he has conquered all
that he had undertaken.

John L. March, in "*A Theory of Mind,*" illustrates adaptation by using the life-history of the
lobster. "The lobster, as is well known, is armed at
its forward part with two large claws or nippers.
These claws are not alike, the right one being provided with fine sharp teeth, the left with blunt rounded
ones. If, now, this right claw be amputated, the
lobster remains deformed until it next casts its shell
and secretes a new one. Meanwhile it makes constant
use of the left claw which remains. When, now, it
casts its shell the lost claw is regenerated, but this
new right claw is not a right claw in shape, but has
blunt teeth; and the much-used claw on the other
side is found to have gained sharp teeth."

You can only become independent of one kind of work by learning how to do another kind. And the sure method for making yourself able to learn that other kind of work consists in doing the first kind to the best of your ability.

Unless you fill the place you now occupy, you cannot expect to fill a more important one. Life, be it physical or mental or financial, should be a series of moultings. The lobster casts its shell because its soft body has become too large for the house. You can never get a better position than the one you now have unless you grow too large for the latter. Or, if you secure that better position, you can only keep it because you have somehow grown to that size.

CONTENTS.

"*The earliest relationship that ever existed, was the relationship between buyer and seller, creditor and debtor. On this ground man first stood face to face with man. No stage of civilization, however inferior, is without the institution of bartering. To fix prices, to adjust values, to invent equivalents, to exchange things — all this has to such an extent preoccupied the first and earliest thought of man, that it may be said to constitute thinking itself. Out of it sagacity arose, and out of it, again, arose man's first pride — his first feeling of superiority over the animal kingdom world. Perhaps our very word man (manus) expresses something of this. Man calls himself the being who weighs and measures. In the ancient Sanskrit the word from which 'man' comes meant 'to think, to weigh, to value, to reckon, to estimate.'*"— FRIEDRICH NIETZSCHE.

PART I.
THE PERSONAL FACTORS.

Success-confidence must be energy-charged, like compressed steam, yet controlling, like the steam chest. It must concentrate on self: "I am the man! I can achieve!" Power, dynamic, controlling, now avers all reasonable things possible. This expresses the one majestic phase of the nature of things, Suggestion. Such confidence, concentrated on self, expands exactly as intuition directs. Infallibly it finds, in time, its decreed highway. The man intuits—knows. Outsiders counsel; he is sure he can accomplish. That assurance is compulsion. Inevitably the thing will be taken up and carried through. The nature of things, which makes no mistakes, has issued its command in such assurance, and it now enlists itself to fulfil its own prophesy

BUSINESS POWER

CHAPTER I.

ACTION AND THE UNDERGROUND MIND.

THE German physicist, Nerst, discovered that the longer the electric current flows through a filament of the oxide of magnesium the greater becomes its conductivity. Precisely the same law holds good with reference to the human brain. The longer the "current of thought" flows through this organized protoplasm, the greater becomes its "conductivity" to thought. Regulated use increases its facility in thinking and the resulting power of light. Well may the analogy introduce the work of this book.

§ 1. Your body requires Air, Fuel, Water, in exactly right proportions. The outcome of a perfect arrangement in this respect is *Physical Health*.

§ 2. Your mind requires Inspiration, Truth, Purpose, in equally perfect proportions. Too much inspiration, with scant truth or purpose, means insanity or lack of common sense. Too much truth, with scant inspiration or purpose, means the pedant or the mere theorist. And purpose, without truth, gives the world its pure dreamers, who achieve nothing, however earnestly they may toil, or hair-brained adventurers who set "the street" agog with Mississippi Bubbles. But the infallible outcome of *inspiration*, *truth* and *purpose* duly compounded in adequate amounts by the Hand of Work, is *Personal Power*.

SPECIAL REQUIREMENTS.

§ 3. The Hand of Work requires certain other factors if it is to win considerable success: *Will-Power*, *Personal Magnetism* (defined as you wish for the present), *Courage-Confidence, and Practical Ability*. Here, also, the proportions must be right or difficulties will multiply. Mere Will-Power may be "mulish" obstinacy; mere Magnetism may be superficial attractiveness; mere Confidence may be repellent egotism; and Practical Ability may be mere mechanical handiness. *Ability is practical when it understands the relative value of things and accomplishes that which is really worth while.* Everybody has some practical ability, but the highest form of the talent is shown by the kind of achievements which it brings to pass. If Will-Power is magnetic, if Magnetism is backed by strong and intelligent Will, if Confidence goes with a high order of Practical Ability, if Courage means self-knowledge, and if all these elements are duly combined, the inevitable outcome in the nature of things must be personal and financial success. I assume that Purpose is morally right.

§ 4. Yet one other factor is necessarily implied in the above combination, for Health, Power, and Success depend always upon the kind, amount and address of *Action*.

§ 5. In a drop of water placed under the lense of a microscope was observed a bit of searcely organized, but living, protoplasm—*Amœba.* It was wearisome work watching for long this low form of life—"never once still from its birth." Nevertheless, in all its incessant movements an activity revealed itself which had lifted chemical elements to the plane of the psychic existence, and which, elsewhere throughout the world, has for countless centuries been engaged in elevating those same elements higher and higher in the scale of being, from *Amœba* to Man, from slime-ooze to modern civilization, from simple barter to the great financial mechanisms of New York and Paris and London. *Action!* That is the giant factor of a world's evolution—lying always back of all the values of Brawn and Brains and Banks.

Inaction Spells Ruin.

§ 6. What does the destruction of action mean? It means the annihilation of being. *Things are, only because action is.* "Assume that every physical process in the world should suddenly be stopped, so there should be no change. That would mean that all motions were stopped. There would at once be neither day nor night, for these are due to the earth's rotation; no light, for light is a wave motion; there would be no heat, for heat is a vibratory motion; there would be no chemical changes, for they depend upon heat; there would be neither solid nor liquid nor gas, for each depends upon conditions of temperature, that is, of heat, which is assumed to be absent; there would be no sight, for that implies wave-motions; nor sound, for that implies air-waves; nor taste, for that implies chemical action; nor smell, for like reason; nor touch, for that implies pressure—the result of motion. The heart would cease to beat, the blood to flow, and consciousness would be stopped. Every one of the senses would be obliterated or annihilated; nothing would happen, because there would be no change anywhere."

§ 7. *Inaction spells ruin.* It is incessant action that builds and sustains the Universe. And such a dire picture as Professor Dolbear has here portrayed ("*Matter, Ether and Motion*") would inevitably be realized in the world of human life were financial activity everywhere to cease. Money would decay and rust, grass would grow in now busy streets, buildings would crumble, schools and churches, stores and banks, would no longer exist, the arts and sciences would die, man would slowly and surely revert to ancient barbarism. The success of the world and the secret of that success are merely magnified forms of the success and secret of *Amœba*. Without Action, the approach of death is a whirlwind.

VALUE OF VARIETY.

§ 8. But the value of Action springs from its *variety*. All force is one, we are told, yet how different its manifestations! The world has marched on a million highways. The pyramids of Egypt sacrificed armies of "earth-toilers," and modern success employs absolutely all the known forms of human activity, from ditch-digging to prayer and government and truth-finding. If any of these forms be curtailed, life turns back to sameness. What is true of the great world is equally true of the individual. Everlasting action is the price of success in every case. In all cases must that action take on the greatest possible variety. *Financial success*, as well as every other kind, *demands all the talents which a man possesses acting in all legitimate ways.*

§ 9. "Suppose," says Ribot in "*The Diseases of Memory*"—"though the hypothesis is one that cannot be realized—suppose an adult human being placed in such conditions that he has *no more new states of consciousness*—no new sensations, ideas, concepts, sentiments, or desires: the different series of states of consciousness which constitute each form of psychic activity would at last become so well organized as to make him a hardly conscious automaton. Narrow minds that always move in the same ruts reduce this hypothesis to a reality in some degree. Restricted within a narrow sphere, they have very little contact with what is new and strange, and hence tend toward the state of perfect stability; they become mere machines; so far as the greater part of their lives is concerned, consciousness is superfluous."

SUCCESS-ACTION.

§ 10. There are multitudes who do not "get on," and never will "get on," because they have surrendered so many of the possible forms of activity of which they are capable in a life that is lacking in ambition and given over to mere routine. They are *machines for others*. Were they to insist on the full action of all their powers, they would discover many which are unused, now and

it is easy to see that they would necessarily advance
very greatly in actual success.   The remedy for
much of the present " down-on-my-luck " condition,
then, is here, *in Action—Greater Action—a Larger
Variety of Action*, and the forced discovery of new
and untried activites in every direction.

§ 11.   *Mere fussiness*, however, is not synonymous with business action. There are many people
who are always fearfully busy, but their activity
analyzes into pure commotion. They are "all over
the place," but somehow they fail to "saw wood."
The difference between this sort of action and that
which builds business is a matter of controlled self-
direction and purpose that is worth while.   Right
action means the bit as well as the spur. A young
hound will follow every scent in the field and
become frantic in his mad chase here and there;
but the old dog ignores ten thousand allurements
and sticks to the one trace which unerringly runs
to game.   It is just this difference between mere
fussiness and the activity of practical ability which
keeps thousands on the level of mediocrity.

§ 12.   Returning, now, to a somewhat smaller
field of thought, let us say that the action required
for success is—*Exercise*.   The thing thus immediately in hand becomes *Action for the sake of Power*,
—applied life-action in the interest of any and all
achievements.

This book concerns the exercise-action indicated with reference to the several results: Health,
Power, Will, Magnetism, Assurance, Courage,
Practical Ability.   You can carry its principles and
methods directly into the applied life-action of your
work and your business for the obtaining of these

values. Our aim is, not pleasing theories, but actual practical conduct, in the gymnasium of the
present pages, but also on the field of life and in
the "game" of business, always endeavoring to tell
the reader exactly what to do and how to do exactly
that for business power.

EXPERIENCE.

§ 13. Assuming that you are a practical person, you greatly believe, of course, in the *School of
Experience*, and you depend yourself upon actual
experience for your improving knowledge of business life. And you are right in this regard. No
book was ever written, no school was ever founded,
superior to the book and school of the world's
every-day conduct—if only one could always have
at one's command the whole fund of experience
which man has demonstrated, (See Chapter 15,
Section 28).

§ 14. Now, as Thomas Carlyle said, experience is "teacher good and true, but he demands
dreadful wages." In the first place, no one may
always command the whole fund of experience
which the world has demonstrated. Some of the
most valuable of our experiences are covered up,
intentionally, and "not all the king's horses" could
draw their secret from us. Moreover, most people
borrow their neighbor's experience whenever they
can do so. And experience never comes to us twice
in the same way. Finally, what does experience
say when it appears? We are not always sure. In
any event, it would seem wise to take advantage in
advance of all possible suggestion, living or written,
which the other man's experience may offer on any

given subject. That is precisely what business
people are doing who study incessantly men and
methods, books and events. Common sense advises:
Take all the advantage offered to betterment. You
can lessen the expense and inconvenience of your
own experience by resorting to the accumulated
teachings of centuries. This book attempts putting
together a number of those teachings. It stands,
within its scope, for two things—*Action and the
Right Kind of Action*—and for these in the interest
of the three B's of the business world, *Brawn,
Brains, Banks.*

THE SUBJECTIVE SELF.

§ 15. The activities of the self, your self, are
Objective, those of the familiar life; but also *Subjective*, those of the deeper and greater personality.
The action involved in success must,—simply must,
—and always does, begin in the less evident
recesses of individual human nature. Every person who achieves anything on a grade above that
of sheer manual labor has a more or less powerful
subjective self. The other self, the self we ordinarily know, the objective "mind," is, so to speak,
the captain on the steamer's bridge, but the moving personality is the engineer down in the hold.
Or, better, the objective self may be compared to
the wheel, or the rudder, while the subjective self
takes the place of the propellor driven by the
steam—for it is the Will that drives us, subjective
as well as objective. If it be said that the subjective self is simply obedient to some Will, the reply
is that the self could not obey without Will, and
the assertion that it acts only in obedience to

another's Will is not shown by the facts of life.
The individual's Will is always the supreme
psychic factor in his life, superior even to what we
call mind. What you make of your life depends
upon Will compelling objective and subjective self
to do its bidding.

§ 16. That subjective man who wore Napoleon's uniform without the Emperor's conscious
knowledge of the fact, won all his battles ere the
plans thereof had slowly emerged in his upper
consciousness, but took wrong suggestion working
havoc when he invaded Russia. The subconscious
self made Napoleon—and it also dethroned him.
History holds that the "man of destiny" defeated
himself. Edison broods over his problems until
the common matters, eating, drinking, sleeping,
are forgotten, and the subconscious self wrings
secrets from Nature by guesses or convictions,
while the outer man is sunken in the bottomless
well of concentration's lacklustre eye. *All great
successes are prefigured and born in the underground
mind.*

§ 17. I hold to the *single personality* of man.
The above statements do not indicate that any
person is two minds. As well speak of ten minds
as of two. Each human being is one person: the
objective self is that which is commonly known and
knowingly used; the subjective self represents
latent possibilities and unconscious activities of
thought, feeling and Will. The subjective self is,
perhaps, the primitive man-self possessed of powers
which the primitive man more or less felt and
employed before he had, through the utilization of
experience, developed the particular objective self

known to history, yet the primitive self improved
by just the fact and experience of the later objective self. The latter is the first evolution product
of age-long processes leading up from instinct and
other remarkable activities to reason, judgment and
self control.

§ 18. The process of human evolution seems
to have involved *three great stages:* First, development of the merely animal kingdom, in which the
law of psychic activity is, reaction to external
stimuli; second, development of a psychic factor
capable not only of responding to stimuli but also
of directing and controlling such reactions and of
originating willed action; third, development of
masterful powers, meanwhile, which are capable of
utilizing Nature's forces by direct methods of control rather than alone by the well-known indirect
methods now apparently limiting human power.
The first stage contained at the start prophesies of
the last. The second stage is devoted to the
unfolding of the distinctively human self—this self
coming to real personality by incessant reaction to
the Not-self, or Nature. The third stage is exhibited in all the great men and achievements of
life. It shows the real self trying to assert its
essentially deific powers. I cannot here enter this
subject for lack of space, but I hope to treat
the third phase of human nature in "*The White
Life*," the crowning volume of the present Library.

§ 19. The subjective mind responds to *suggestions*, because it is automatically true to itself
or the laws which constitute it. The one individual
mind acts according to the law of economy, carrying on underground activities, of itself, and so

leaving open a larger field for free conscious action at the least expense of known effort. *Economy of conscious effort is one of the greatest laws of our nature.* It is willed action that tires muscles and wears out nerves. Activities which run automatically do not have such results. Human personality, therefore, seeks constantly to transfer consciously willed activities to the sphere of unconsciously conducted activities, in order that the great work of life, development, may go on at least expense and not be too constantly stopped for rest and repairs. It is precisely here that the value of self-suggestion appears. *We can commit a very great deal of work to the subjective mind.*

§ 20. *This underground mind is one of the chief factors in a successful career.* It is vital to all the business world, for it solves many problems, obviates many defeats, and leads to many achievements—if properly educated. During the "rush of trade" it is busy, "mulling things over," deciding propositions, "sensing" men and situations, preparing new campaigns.

§ 21. "Our judgment of things depends on our past experience, the particular instances of which we may be unable to recall, but which undoubtedly have their effect in determining the result at which we arrive," says David Kay in *"Memory."* "A merchant can test a piece of goods and declare its quality and value with the greatest accuracy from having previously examined numerous examples of the same kind, none of which may be consciously before the mind at the time, but many of which must have unconsciously aided him in coming to a decision. 'What is termed Common

Sense,' says J. D. Morell, 'is nothing but a substra-
tum of experiences out of which our judgments
flow, while the *experiences themselves are hidden
away in the unconscious depths of our intellectual
nature.*'"

"In a curious case mentioned by Carpenter
("*Diseases of Memory*," Ribot), a man was vaguely
cognizant of the work going on in his brain,
without having distinct consciousness. A business
man in Boston, having an important question under
consideration, had given it up for the time as too
much for him. But he was conscious of an action
going on in his brain which was so unusual and
painful as to excite his apprehensions that he was
threatened with palsy, or something of that sort.
After some hours of this uneasiness, his perplexity
was all at once cleared up by the natural solution of
his doubts coming to him—worked out, as he
believed, in that obscure and troubled interval."

§ 22. All this may seem mysterious, and
possibly, rather "occult," but the action of mind
indicated is really an every-day affair. You have
simply to *look to your deeper self for your best problems and your best solutions*, some of which come
because you seek them, but many of which come
when you are not seeking them. In educating the
underground mind and in depending upon its help,
you merely place responsibility upon it, demanding
that it remember and act as you will—suggest—it
shall do. In a way, these are the things you
always have done. Undeliberated reliance should
now be consciously brought to bear on your work.

§ 23. Action, constant and varied, *builds
brains*. "We can make our own brains, so far as

special mental functions or aptitudes are concerned," remarks Dr. William Hanna Thomson in *"Brain and Personality,"* "if only we have wills strong enough to take the trouble. By practice, practice, practice, the Will stimulus will not only organize brain centers to perform new functions, but will project new connecting, or, as they are technically called, association fibres, which will make nerve centers work together as they could not without being thus associated. Each such self-created brain center requires great labor to make it, because nothing but the prolonged exertion of the personal Will can fashion anything of the kind. A person, therefore, acquires new brain capacities by acquiring new anatomical bases for them in the form of brain cells, which he has trained, and of actively working brain fibres, which he has himself virtually created."

§ 24. In all this work the great General of Action is the Will. "We have already demonstrated the mighty work of the Will in dealing with brain matter as the potter does with clay (in establishing brain areas and centers for hearing, vision, power to distinguish sounds, music, words, and to form thought and speech, etc.), and that it is the Will alone that has this power. But on the same account we are now to show that in thus making an instrument for the mind to use, *the Will is higher than the Mind,* and hence that its rightful prerogative is to govern and to direct the mind, just as it is the prerogative of the mind to govern and direct the body. * * Here we come to the highest illustration of that great principle in nervous development, Discipline, for it is the Will, as the ranking official of all in man, who should now step forward to take the command. * * A mind always broken in to the sway of the Will, and therefore thinking according to Will, and not according to reflex suggestion, constitutes a purposive life. * * That majestic endowment constitutes the high privilege granted to each man apparently to test how much the man will make of himself. It is clothed with powers which will enable him to obtain the greatest of possessions— self-possession. Self-possession implies the capacity for self-restraint, self-compulsion and self-direction; and he who has these, if he live long enough, can have any other possession that he wants."

§ 25. The chief purpose of the above considerations concerns, of course, the present study. *The subjective self may be trained* to perform work which would otherwise be impossible. The compactness of this volume and the details of directions given may appear to call for more time and labor than an active business man can control. A remedy for this lies in referring much of the work to the subjective self. You can "bed down" in the deeper mind the fixed purpose of carrying on the study and of putting into actual practice the suggestions given. It needs but an emphatic exercise of the Will for a little time, and a fair measure of confidence, possessed or assumed, to make your intelligent subconscious self a most faithful servant. A sea captain wrote of certain directions which he had read in "*Power of Will*": "I found myself time and again calling to mind the practical rules of that book, much to my advantage." Here, then, is the Golden Law of subjective personal development, one of the highest factors in human life:

Educative auto-suggestion educationally and unconsciously unfolds the self.

A large part of our life is conducted by habit. You tend to act along the line of least resistance; constant action in any given way develops habit because that way becomes the easiest way. Right education is the development of habits that are conducive to personal welfare. Right habituated actions are accomplished with the least effort— when established. Meanwhile, all sorts of new or first-time activities are going on in your life which are in part spontaneous and in part deliberated or chosen. You carry on, then, habituated activities almost automatically, with least effort, but you are also always engaged in the first-time or the new non-habituated activities. If, now, you have acquired a large number of right habits, you have greater freedom in the "new business" requiring especial attention. It has been our object here to suggest methods by which the subjective self may acquire by habit the feeling and elements of power.

In other words, we are constantly engaged in accumulating material for the mind, working it over into new forms, and utilizing the old and the new in the active life. Max Müller, in *"Biographies of Words,"* briefly sketches Aristotle's analysis of the mind as follows: "After stating that all animals possess sensation, he divides them into two classes—those whose sensations remain and those whose sensations do not remain. Those whose sensations do not remain possess no knowledge beyond sensation, while those whose sensations do remain are again divided by him into two classes according as they are able or not to gather the permanent sensations which remain. The process, therefore, by which, according to Aristotle, thought arises is first sensation; then permanence (memory). Then from repeated acts of memory comes experience; and lastly, from experience arises both art (technical skill) and knowledge." It is varied action which increases the mind's supply of material, and the things that remain are worked over and made permanent in the deeper self. Business is always engaged in precisely this sort of work. The business mind has the great principles of commercial transactions at the instant command of the Will, and is forever storing in the mind's stronghold the details which must be held and the lessons therefrom which must be acquired, and not only so, be kept continuously available—like the funds demanded for the running expenses.

§ 26. If you are really resolved on the possession of Will-Power, Magnetism, Courage-Confidence, and Practical Ability, all essential to business power, remember, now, the imperative need for Action, Larger and more Varied Action, and that training of the deeper mind which makes the objective self freer for the opening of greater and richer opportunities in the struggle for the highest success.

CHAPTER II.

ACTION: ATTACK AND MAINTAIN.

ALL action is a display of energy. "Matter is but a stepping-stone, to energy," says Professor R. K. Duncan; "here and away through one form to another and from one body to another, infinitely restless, constant only to one thing,—its total quantity." It is so in human life. Restlessness moves the world. Man's action, however, just as in the physical sphere, must be guided if the vast energy of the brain and the body is to achieve the greatest results. The highest human power is that of thought: even the Will is a form of thought. Our problem, then, is action brought to highest efficiency and held to that level.

§ 1. The *value of Action* is determined in part by its outcome, in part by its purpose. If the outcome is good, the action leading thereto is usually good. But a good outcome may be accidental, or merely incidental to the action, and then the phrase, "a fool's luck," indicates the high estimate we always place on purpose. The complete value of action is only realized when a good outcome is the sure result of a good intention.

§ 2.   Now, incessant, intelligent and varied activity, while it builds brains of some kind, does not necessarily build business brains. It is *purpose* and outcome, of a certain nature, which determine business action.   The purpose is accumulation of "economic goods."   The outcome depends upon the application of such purpose to existing financial conditions.   *Business is the product of action multiplied by purpose into the sum of the conditions one can more or less command.*   The process of multiplication is itself a result—a result of faith adequate in kind and amount to make business a "live proposition."

BUSINESS ACTION.

§ 3.   Business,—the professions, art, science, —is a proposition making various appeals to us, and succeeding in winning allegiance according to the fundamentals of our likes and dislikes.   *If we have a "leaning" to business, into it we should go.* There is Nature's call.   In that event, business becomes, not a mere possibility, but a "live proposition."   Nature has now "made the circuit," and has connected the man with the great business world, inspiring within him purposed action, and alluring him with possible, probable, or "dead certain" outcome.

§ 4.   But business as a proposition is complex, composed of ten thousand subordinate propositions. These propositions incessantly shift and change, day by day, year after year.   At one time they are "live," and then again they are "dead."   Hence, *business activity knows no rest*, and cannot tolerate merely "ancient" methods, but must *forever adjust*

to new conditions. However "live" all sorts of
propositions may be, if the man himself is not
equally alive, and if his methods have no "electricity" in them, his action in relation to such
propositions is simply non-effective. It is this
incessant pull of things, this everlasting demand
of changing propositions, that tests men in the
business world and uncovers the fact whether or
no they are really business men. The successful
men and businesses are those which keep themselves at the top pitch of aliveness as propositions
in the financial world. However it may have been
in the era of wooden shoes, to-day this test requires
the very utmost of two indispensable qualities, *the
quality of courage and the quality of confidence.* It
is not enough to have the old-time plodding merchant's faith, nor to exhibit the courage which
ventures a traditional policy under commonplace
conditions. The faith must be electric enough
to vitalize half a state, and the courage great
enough to travel a discovered highway against a
Universe.

COURAGE AND CONFIDENCE.

§ 5. "Business," said Andrew Carnegie, "is
a large word and in its primary meanings covers
the whole range of man's efforts. The same principles of thrift, energy, concentration and brains
win success in any branch of business from
medicine to dry goods." That is an "electric"
sentence: in each of the quality-words you see
courage-confidence: "Thrift" (courage — faith);
"Energy" — (courage — faith); "concentration"
—(courage—faith) ; "brains" — (courage—faith);

the whole expressive of grim *determination vitally courageous.*

§ 6. Inasmuch as a live man puts courage and faith or confidence into a proposition which is alive to him,—and, indeed, cannot throw the one into it without the other,—I combine the qualities into that dynamic compound of power which has always driven the world on and up; *Courage-Confidence*, or confident courage—self-reliance, belief in one's self, faith in one's business, a vigorous, undoubting, unfearing assurance of success in the business life.

§ 7. In a symposium of English merchants appears the following: "There are two physical qualifications which are of extreme importance for success in life: the first, a good set of teeth—in these days easily acquired—and secondly, a good stomach. A combination of these should endow a man with a good temper and a spirit of perseverance which will triumph over all obstacles."

If we make these references figurative, they give us a good description of business action—*Attack and Maintain.* The good set of teeth is needful for the attack; the good stomach is required to maintain attacking power. These are the functions of courage—to attack in many ways the problems of business exchange; and of confidence—to maintain the attack to a successful finish.

§ 8. Now, courage and confidence are of differing grades, physical, mental, moral; spasmodic, lasting; native, compelled; and the grade of a man's courage may not always go equal with his grade of confidence. Some men are courageous in a particular extremity, yet are devoid of long-run confidence, or assurance of triumph, whether on the whole or in a specific undertaking. A man may, again, possess great mental courage and little physical, or the reverse; or great physical and no moral courage; or fickle courage of one or more varieties, yet be lacking in long-run courage of any given grade. Similarly with confidence. *Your order of confidence should be "on the level" with your order of courage, grade for grade—and every grade should be of the highest possible.* When these qualities cross, more or less of failure is apt to follow. This important combination is analyzed for practical application to life in the author's second volume of The Power-Book Library, *"Power for Success,"* and can only briefly be considered in the present chapter.

§ 9. All this means "that the whole of the man must have responded in real life to every particle of experience which he uses in his work," as John Jay Chapman remarks in *"Causes and Consequences,"* "and that *anything that the whole of him does is right.*" The interpretation for our present purpose is this: Your courage-confidence need never be shaken by obstacle or defeat if the whole of you has gone into your work. The immov ability of the obstacle is often no fault of yours, —it is a downright impossibility for any man,— and meanwhile your effort to move it has made a better man of you in the long run. So also, on the same supposition, your defeats in particular instances are very frequently no real defeats, for you can trace to them many an aftercoming success.

§ 10. When the whole of a man has gone into an undertaking, he always exhibits the qualities

before us. Lack of courage-confidence accounts
for a large per cent. of apparent or real failures,
and is greatly due to a lack of dynamic Will send-
ing the whole man into his life work. No great
success can be won without that ingo of a man's
bigness which infallibly breeds confident courage.
Even if you are born with the combination, itself
is required for its own use. It takes courage to
use courage. It requires faith to throw what faith
one has into any venture. If these facts seem to
make success more difficult, however, they are offset by others which declare one of the most useful
laws of our nature, to-wit: the *law of increase by
exercise*. The more you call into action the courage and faith you have, the more of these qualities
you possess.

How to Acquire Courage-Confidence.

§ 11. For the development of this vastly
important double power, reference may be had to
the whole of this book, but our particular methods
for the present chapter are briefly indicated in
three words set over against the quality desired—

Assumption
Assertion } of Courage-Confidence
Ascension

This formula is really a theoretical statement
of the one only practical method by which any
desirable quality or goal may be reached. Let the
goal be courage or faith, education or a fortune;
you *assume* that you have it—that is, you think of
it always as though yours already; you *assert* the
possession against all opposition; and you *ascend*,
both yourself and your practical conduct, to *the*

level of assumption and assertion. The arrangement of our thought may seem rather artificial, but it nevertheless involves the fundamentals of the whole psychology of success. You are therefore invited specifically to transfer into your personality the spirit and principles of the following régimes.

§ 12. FIRST RÉGIME: ASSUMPTION OF COURAGE-CONFIDENCE. The rediscovered law of auto-suggestion assures us that the incessant assumption of a fact as true within the self tends to make that fact actual. We all know that men sometimes become possessed of a notion of fault or weakness and defeat, and practically themselves make good the notion in the final outcome. As a matter of fact, it costs just as much to win a defeat as it does to win success. Think that over. *It is just as expensive to build up a wrong idea as a right one.* Thought, of any kind, is creative and transforming —every kind in its own way. If you long enough assume, insistently and with all the energy you possess, that you are full of sound, red-blooded courage and are vitally confident in yourself and your business, you will in the end actually possess these splendid qualities.

§ 13. The work before us is a matter of *brain-cell discipline and education.* You have already taught your brain cells to see, hear, taste, smell, touch, think, distinguish words, objects, sounds, and to utter speech, etc., etc. You can therefore teach your brain cells to think "courage" and "confidence" so repeatedly that the ideas and feelings associated will become "natural" and inevitable through cell activity responding with just that effect to all the influences of life.

§ 14. At the outset of any important work, *two alternative attitudes* present themselves: *uncertainty of success, and compelling confidence.* Uncertainty of success is one of the ways in which we permit brain cells to act, and is therefore never a merely negative *attitude;* it is really a positive action of brain and mind, and is a breeder of defeating personal conditions. Compelling confidence is always something more than an attitude toward a venture; it is an *attitude* of the man toward himself, and it thus creates a host of success-bringing qualities—if, of course, the man's best reason run with it.

In Hall Caine's story, "*The Deemster,*" the positive evil of a negative attitude is thus illustrated. "A man does something, and some old woman sneezes. Straightway he thinks himself accursed, and that what is predicted (by the woman) must certainly come about. (It is precisely so with the old women of your doubts and uncertainties.) And it does come about. Why? Because the man himself, with his blundering doddering fears, brings it about. He brings it about himself—that's how it is! And then every old woman in the island sneezes again." When a man brings about the prophesy of any one of his fears, every other fear-element in his nature gathers in his soul and holds a witch-dance about the struggling, dying form of his courage-confidence. And the "last estate of that man is worse than the first." *He said that he would—and he did not.*

§ 15. The second attitude, that of confident courage, is finely shown in words of Professor William James. "*If you only care enough for a result, you will almost certainly attain it.* If you wish to be rich, you will be rich; if you wish to be learned, you will be learned; if you wish to be good you will be good. Only you must, then, really wish these things, and wish them with exclusiveness, and not wish at the same time a hundred other incompatible things just as strongly."

Of course my reader prefers the latter attitude. Well, then, let us combine these suggestions in one electric declaration of independence:

Down with doubt and up with assurance!

This means that you always, with never a moment's weakening—

§ 16. *Treat Yourself as a Live and a Surely Successful Proposition!*

I had ulcers on the right eye-ball, and then iritis. These facts and their possible consequences I knew; but not for an instant, night or day, during a month of darkness and pain enough, did I in the least fear blindness or fail to claim a cure. At the end of the treatment my physician remarked: "Most people say, as you said, that they respond readily to treatment, and most of them are mistaken, but you are one of the exceptions."

§ 17. SECOND RÉGIME: ASSERTION OF COURAGE-CONFIDENCE. The first régime involves also an immense amount of assertion by way of assuming that one even now possesses the qualities desired, but the present régime concerns the attitude assumed with reference to the outside world of business. *Auto-suggestion becomes an incessant discharge of power into the man himself by just so much as he asserts what he assumes before the whole earth.* Between assumption and assertion there is a play and a reaction which result in development of the quality in hand. If you do not assert, you deny assumption. If you do not assume, you have nothing to assert. This back-and-forth play of the two activities is always evident in positive, successful people.

§ 18. It should be understood, however, that assertion does not consist in mere proclamation of faith and courage. A man should, of course, at the proper time and in a manner dictated by common sense, indicate in his language both fearlessness and confidence, but beyond all expression by mere words, the idea of assertion is here the *exhibition of dauntless courage against all odds and boundless confidence in face of all doubts and difficulties.* These qualities are *assumed* as *of* the self and *asserted to* the self, so that in time the brain cells habitually influence the general consciousness and the muscular activities to exhibit in a courageous and confident external manner.

"Who gains promotions, boons, appointments, but the man in whose life they are seen to play the part of live hypotheses, who discounts them (as at a bank), sacrifices other things for their sake before they have come, and takes risks for them in advance? His faith acts on the powers above him as a claim, and creates its own verification."

If, therefore, you wish to create courage-confidence, you must, for one thing, think the quality until it becomes an habitual mood with you, and then bring the mood into evidence before the world of business activities. This is the king's coat: you weave and wear it as altogether your own.

§ 19. THIRD RÉGIME: ASCENSION TO THE
LEVEL OF ASSUMPTION AND ASSERTION. No matter
how strenuously one assumes and asserts courage-
confidence, if conduct does not "make good," the
law of auto-suggestion largely fails, because the
want of action corresponding to thought indicates
to the subjective self that you do not really mean
what you assume. If you wish to build courage,
you must *think* courage and *act* courage. If you
wish to build confidence, you must *think and act
confidence.* Similarly with the compound quality :
*you must throw courage-confidence into your actual
business.* This practical "making good" of assumption and assertion may be conducted along two
lines, the one artificial, the other involving actual
affairs in business. You are emphatically urged
to go into the suggestions which follow "for all
you are worth."

§ 20 (A). *The Artificial Line of Discipline.*
The method here suggested is given in a quotation
from "*Talks to Teachers,*" by Professor James.
"Keep the faculty of effort alive in you by a little
gratuitous exercise every day. That is, be systematically heroic in little unnecessary points, do
every day or two something for no other reason
than its difficulty, so that, when the hour of dire
need draws nigh, it may find you not unnerved and
untrained to stand the test. Asceticism of this sort
is like the insurance which a man pays on his
house and goods. The tax does him no good at
the time, and possibly may never bring him a
return. But, if the fire does come, his having paid
it will be his salvation from ruin. So with the
man who has daily inured himself to habits of

concentrated attention, energetic volition, and self-denial in unnecessary things. He will stand like a tower when everything rocks around him, and his softer fellow mortals are winnowed like chaff in the blast."

§ 21. The value of this advice may not appear to a busy man. He is always taking "gratuitous exercise." Yet such a man would find himself all the more fitted for his work if he would follow the suggestion in ways a little aside from the direct line of his ordinary efforts. *By so much as one rightly varies his accustomed effort, even in matters not immediately connected with business, by so much will one find his general fund of power increased.* No man knows when that general power, or the results of such gratuitous exercise, may prove the one thing needful for promotion or for some great financial achievement.

§ 22. The chief purpose of introducing the quotation from Professor James, however, is its applicability to the work of the present book. The book is just a manual for such exercise, in the line of business, and yet preliminary or aside from any specific commercial effort. I do not know how to run your business; *I know how to build power.* If you will make the contents of these pages your own, and apply them in every-day business transactions, you can no more fail to discipline yourself to a finer courage and confidence than you can fail to maintain health by observing the laws of health.

§ 23 (B). *The Practical Line of Discipline.* It probably does not occur to one business man in ten to analyze and represent to himself the business qualities embodied in his business.   The business man knows, of course, (a) his own business, (b) its various departments, (c) the kind of methods employed in any department or throughout the whole; but (d), the *qualities represented by the entire outfit* are usually known rather vaguely and hit-or-miss.   There is a quality-atmosphere in one place which you will not find in the other place.   I prefer to trade with A because of this intangible something, and I will not trade with B because that something he and his people know nothing about. Mark your business, departments, and methods as A1: the qualities of personal action behind these three factors may be good, bad or indifferent.   So, also, the qualities may be A1, while the three factors are mediocre.   In other words, let the gun be perfect: an important question now is, What about "the man behind the gun?"   It is there that you find the quality or characteristic that makes or unmakes, in the action of clerks working individually, in that of superintendents and managers handling the clerks as group-units, in the head himself, who stamps the whole company with the quality which he determines upon.

§ 24.   Now, one compound quality that is all-important in any man's life is courage-confidence. Does the clerk, or the truckman, or the manager, or the agent of the establishment carry the courage-confidence-atmosphere into and through every day's business?   If any of these people are to succeed, they must do precisely that.   Does the head "make good" the courage-confidence-attitude in and toward his business?   If he does, other things being reasonably equal, that is the quality the whole place presents to the business world. *He is Faith, with a Will and a full-blooded Heart behind it.* These factors breed confidence, if the business stands for the "square deal," and confidence is the creator of financial achievement.

§ 25. Business power, then, means courageous faith put into business action and held up to "concert pitch" by assumption, assertion and the ascension of conduct "making good." The suggestive injunction may be made to read thus:

Act with judgment but boundless faith, and, assured that you are right, fear nothing—neither deity, devil nor man.

§ 26. The limits of the present chapter forbid any elaborate unfoldment of this injunction, so that I can here merely indicate how the quality of courage-confidence as a success-factor may be made to educate certain other main-line qualities confessedly indispensable in any business. The following analysis indicates the application required. Its observance in practical business will "make good" your assumption and assertion of courageous faith.

(The letters S, P, and J, stand for "steady-going," "particular," and "judgment" demanded in the use of the qualities indicated.)

THROW YOUR

Courage into	*For Confidence*
(Cut Timidity out)	(Cut Doubt out)

(1) Your business and methods; S.

(2) The thought of your final success; S.

(3) Your action in emergencies; P. J.

(4) Initiative: new things; daring and doing; P. J.

(5) Branching out, and taking hold of large propositions; P. J.

(6) Facing competition; S. J.
(7) Confronting changes, and prevision concerning them; S. P. J.
(8) Maintaining commercial honor; S.
(9) Building-up the confidence of others; S.
(10) Standing and waiting; self-control under financial strain; S. J.
(11) Independence: going into business for yourself; J.
(12) Finding the right people, and trusting them; P. J.
(13) Assuming responsibility; P. J.
(14) Investments and outlays; P. J.
(15) Suffering drawbacks and sacrificing for a goal; S. J.
(16) Making the most of defeat and disaster; S.
(17) All details and particular propositions; P. J.
(18) The general atmosphere of the place; S.
     Etc.,   Etc.,   Etc.

PRACTICAL OUTCOME: COURAGE-CONFIDENCE.

§ 27. The object of the analysis is definite investigation of yourself and your people in your business, definite discovery of opportunities for improvement, and the immediate application of courage-confidence (assumed and asserted) to every detail of every day and week and year.

§ 28. The force of the analysis will be seen if the words (at the top of the list) "courage" and "confidence" are replaced by "timidity" and "doubt." In the latter case you prophetically analyze defeat. In the case as I have outlined it, you spell success almost to a certainty. Said Andrew Carnegie: "I would not give a fig for the young man in business who does not already see himself a partner or at the head of an important firm. Do not rest for a moment in your thoughts as head clerk, a foreman, or a general manager in any concern, no matter how extensive. Say to

yourself, 'My place is at the head.' *Be king in
your dreams.* Vow that you will reach that position
with untarnished reputation, and make no other
vows to distract your attention." And Orison
Swett Marden remarked: "I know a man in New
York who worked for others until he was thirty
years of age and ever received but a small salary.
It always chafed him to think that he must be
dependent on the Will of another, although he had
never made any exhibition of power or executive
ability while in a subordinate position. *But the
moment he started out for himself he seemed to grow
by leaps and bounds,* and in a comparatively few
years he had become a giant in the business world.
He has developed a tremendous passion and ability
for doing things; his executive ability comes into
play when he makes his own programme; he is also
strong in carrying out his own ideas, whereas he
was comparatively weak in trying to fit his individuality into another's programme."

A young man held a subordinate position in
the greatest concern of its kind in the world.
After a while, his employer began to throw out
hints in regard to a certain independent opportunity with which the young man might grapple,
if he would, going so far as even to suggest that
the required capital to start with might, in some
mysterious (?) way be found. The big man's efforts
to induce the little one to launch out for himself in
a venture which, at the worst, could only fail,
leaving the latter still young, but which in human
probability would not fail, were all in vain. The
older business man said afterward: "I wanted him
to have it, for I had enough myself, and we would

have seen him through; but he preferred connection with a big concern to independence in a small
one capable of being made an indefinite success. I
made up my mind that if he wouldn't take broad-
axe hints, we'd let it go." Courage-confidence in
this case would have switched the current of success into a main line.

Courage-confidence is business electricity.

§ 29. Of course both courage and faith are
always questions of *judgment.* In sound commercial judgment business power is bulked. But there
are various kinds of judgment, one extreme being
that of the old-line conservative who always follows
the procession, the other extreme being that of the
mere "plunger." This chapter assumes a reasonably happy medium. And that medium is a question of—mere judgment, or,—judgment electrified
by courage-confidence. Some minds hold judgment
only to be good when it decides, "The thing can't
be done." But judgment is still judgment when it
declares: "Be thou of a stout heart! The thing
can be done because I will it!"

My friend, the business man who had always
been restless unless handling big things, determined to put a railway through a wilderness of
mountains, forests and swollen streams, to be used
by a population altogether ignorant of cook-stoves
and bath-tubs. Wall Street laughed at him. He
began operations notwithstanding. He got his
money by miracles. Then his partner died, and
capital fought shy. But, since this man had to
have more money, his bonds coerced purchasers.
The work was slow, with all sorts of delays constantly coming up. My friend somehow built

road-bed and made up for delays. Then legislation
got in his way, and he camped down among friends
who cried "Impossible!" and enemies who sneered.
This man told them all precisely what they would
do—and did.   Then came the threat of bonds
lapsed if the road failed to get into its terminus at
a certain date.   The fighter had so conducted his
war that a neighboring road actually gave his construction material right of way and precedence
before all other business. The man won, of course,
for he had never for an instant doubted or feared.
On the completion of the whole line, he went over
it in a special car, and judgment now declared that
the actual thing was an impossibility, and courage-
confidence oozed out of his soul, so far as feeling
was concerned, at every mile.   Still, there was the
road—a vindication of that kind of judgment on
which the whole fabric of human life to-day is
built, and a monument to that courageous faith
which has always put values where once there
were none.

§ 30.   This is the everlasting word of business:
"Put values where now are none!"   The director-
general in that work is the Will, but the power
to achieve is Courage-Confidence, and the skill
demanded to make director and power effective is
Practical Ability.

CHAPTER III.

HIGHEST personal power results from an inner attitude, which is aptness with reference to men and situations, meaning: "I am able! I draw to myself whatever I will!" and energetic yet controlled action forced to correspond with the assertions—*continuously*.

§ 1. The highest efficiency of a machine or a tool depends on two things: the condition of the instrument, and the skill of the man who handles it. In building business power we have regard, then, to precisely the same factors—*personality as an instrument, and skill in its use*. Among the many tools or machines which the business man constantly employs is himself, and among all the varieties of commercial and financial skill brought into play in business life not one particular kind is so important and so difficult of attainment as the skill with which he handles his own person and powers.

UNFOLDING POWER.

§ 2. I have suggested the value of incessant and varied action, together with unfailing courage

37

and faith, in power-building. We need also to
remember that the creation of power demands the
use of existing power to start with. Force comes
out of force; power breeds power. This law holds
good in the business world as surely as elsewhere,
but the fact need suggest no discouragement, for
we are here dealing with human power rather than
the merely material.

*Any man now possesses all the power he will
ever have, if he could but discover the fact and draw
upon his own resources.*

We do not create power; we merely unfold
power from within. And the process of unfoldment is very simple, so far as analysis goes. You
assume and assert that you have power, and you
"make good" by courageous and confident action.
The process, then, is plain enough; but its practical realization involves the whole man in business.

§ 3. Now, *the manner of the assumption and
assertion is a very important thing*. If the manner
is weak, the power will be weak. If assumption
and assertion are vigorous and constant, power
will correspond. But when the man is possessed
by a mighty passion for assuming, asserting and
rising to the level of power, he will be invincible.

"A man fleeing for his life, with death in pursuit, will bound over a stream into which in less
stimulating circumstances he would fall and
perish," says Dr. James McCosh in "*The Emotions.*" "I have known students, at a competitive
examination, by a gathering and concentration of
force, doing as much intellectual work in a few
hours as they could have done in as many days
without the combined stimulus of fame, rivalry and

profit." It is precisely so in business. Successful business is a boundless passion. Here we find the driving power of action and the feeder of courage and confidence—in a tremendous passion to win the fight and accumulate wealth.

"The ruling passion, as a center, aggregates a crowd of associations, and it moves on like a marshaled host, with the combined strength of the whole, bearing down the obstacles which oppose."

§ 4. You can develop the business passion by assuming, asserting and courageously and confidently acting on the basis, "This one thing I do." You can so steep the subconscious self in the thought and feeling of power as possessed that the whole personality will respond and unfold its resources incessantly and almost without limit. If we disregard the nature of the physical body, since it is not yet in man's progress fully under the sway of the self, we may remove even this modification. *"There is no limit to the knowing of the self that knows,"* the Hindus have said. *There is no limit to the developing of the self which steadily and vigorously wills to unfold.*

§ 5. The winning personality in business has always back of it a fund of actual power. A weak man or woman is never magnetic. It is true that mere personal force is not in itself an attractive thing; nevertheless, it is equally true that the right kind of power properly handled constitutes personal magnetism, one of the most vital of business qualifications, however surely charlatanry and nonsense have been connected with it. This variety of power is, of course, peculiar to itself, but it is

always associated with some degree of general
power familiarly indicated in the phrase, "a person
of power." It is this necessary background of
general personal power which is just now before
us. That general, personal, business power may
be developed, and out of such development genuine
magnetic ability may be caused to issue.

How to Unfold Power.

§ 6.   The methods for developing a powerful
personality are not complex. They are difficult
enough, of course; yet they are perfectly simple,
as already suggested. We need but to apply the
directions of the preceding chapter to find power
unfolding infallibly. Thus—

§ 7.   First Method For Developing Personal
Power—Assumption of Power. This method consists in *assuming the present possession of all the
power one now needs.* If we examine the assumption, "I have no power; I am a person of no
consequence," we see at once that the thought
must surely confirm and increase actual weakness.
Our method, then, is exactly the opposite. The
man now assumes that he already *is* power, thinking, "I am power—power—power," day in and day
out, and always trying to sense and increase the
power-feeling by attending to it as within himself,
by *imagining himself full of limitless power.* A
talismanic sentence is this:

*"I am power! I am equal to anything that may
come up in my life. I will unfold personal power.
I make real within dynamic business power!"*

Let not this talisman be slurred over as nonsense. To do so will be to betray ignorance. I

know that unremitting assumption of power means ultimate unfoldment of power, and of the most valuable kind, if only the remaining methods are similarly observed.

§ 8. SECOND METHOD FOR DEVELOPING PERSONAL POWER—ASSERTION OF POWER. Two attitudes we are always assuming: one toward self, and one toward the business world. Assumption of power is an attitude of self toward self *as* power. *Assertion of power is the attitude of self as power toward business men and affairs.*

I had an appointment to meet one of my agents at a railway station, and, at the moment agreed upon for our meeting stepped away from the designated place, and waited with some curiosity, for I had not as yet any sight acquaintance with him. When he entered the depot he did not at first discover my presence. He passed me like a healthy breeze, his whole manner vigorously expressive of action, courage, confidence, and a sense of ability. It was good to see him breathing power to right and left. Privately he frequently reveals the mood of modesty and a reasonable knowledge of personal defects, like an ordinary human being, but in business he is dynamic and confident. This is the attitude of assertive power. The picture should be taken as a direction for imitation. A talismanic auto-suggestion may be given as follows:

"*I am power! My manner, and my personal atmosphere (a sphere of space around you—see "The Personal Atmosphere") vigorously express active and courageously confident personal power. It is my way. It's my attitude—just enough to win confidence and respect.*"

§ 9. THIRD METHOD FOR DEVELOPING PER-
SONAL POWER. Always important is the "make-
good." If an engineer who has followed the
preceding régimes fails to take his chance at a bad
emergency-run, his assumption and assertion turn
out to have been mere bluster. He has hurt himself with other people, but more, he has deceived
his subjective self. *You must never, under any
circumstances, fail to keep your word with the subjective self.* We assume and assert for the sake of
an unfolding consciousness of power, and the
subjective self is exactly like an outsider: he
discovers bluster on the instant, and that moment
loses confidence in the blustering objective man.
The subjective self infallibly knows the absolute
truth about the man above. Thought and feeling
are vastly important in self-education and development, but demonstration alone makes them real
creators. I am not dealing in miracles. People
pay their money for instruction in which the
"New Thought," as it is called, plays so large a
part, glance it over, drop it, and fail, of course, to
realize adequate returns. Human thought is
omnipotent—but only on the basis of incessant
demonstration by corresponding conduct. I know
how to build business power, but I do not know
how to get it at any price less than the hard work
which consists in throwing creative thinking incessantly into every-day life. The first two methods,
then, must be demonstrated by constant use of
power,—assumed, asserted, realized.

§ 10. It is here exactly as it is in gymnasium
work of a modern character. You attend to various muscles or members of the body while exercis-

ing them; you put your mind right there; you think power as in the part in action; you take the attitude of vigor; and you use the power you have, persistently, with determination—in the gymnasium and out of it. Thus you develop strength. And thus only can power for business be unfolded: by thinking it, taking its attitudes, using it without fear or doubt.

Our talismanic declaration is now: *"All the power called for goes now into this work. All the power I possess I demonstrate by using it in business life. None to waste; all for success!"*

UNFOLDING MAGNETIC POWER.

§ 11. The second paragraph of this chapter contained the following sentence: "Among the many tools or machines which the business man constantly employs is himself, and amid all the varieties of commercial and financial skill brought into play in business life not one is so important and so difficult of attainment as the skill with which he handles his own person and power." The man himself must constitute the power-house or the storage-battery. *And success in business depends on the skill of the man in the use of his own ability.* This skill involves two factors: the one consisting of dealing with things, situations, conditions, and events, and the other consisting of dealings with human personalities. Skill in regard to the first factor is an outcome of the knowledge and use of the laws of business; skill in regard to the second factor issues from recognition of latent magnetism in the self and the practice of régimes designed to unfold the force, together with the application to human contact of attractive ways and manners.

§ 12. All men and women are endowed with
some degree of *latent magnetism*. Many people
possess it unconsciously, some of whom use it well
without knowing the fact, while others employ it
unintelligently and poorly. The degree of magnetic efficiency in different people varies according
to original personal endowment, even when developed and properly handled. Thousands fail in
business because of either its lack or its misuse. In
every human it may be unfolded to a degree. No
one possessing it is beyond improvement in regard
to it. It is at least *one* of the great success-factors
of the business life.

§ 13. For a full treatment of the magnetic
personality reference may be made to the author's
work on the subject, *"Power for Success."* The
limits of the present book permit only the briefest
discussion of the power, and I cannot take up at all
the essential exercises without which magnetism
can never be developed in any person, but must
content myself with the indication of some of the
more superficial aspects of the force in general
operation.

MAGNETIC CHARACTERISTICS.

§ 14. NUMBER ONE: PHYSICAL ATTRACTIVE-
NESS. Successful business encounter usually calls
for the absence of repelling physical defects and
traits. To-day stature may be increased, wrinkles
may be smoothed out, the nose reformed, the
breath sweetened, the hands manicured, unnecessary movements and unpleasant mannerisms
removed, and, indeed, nearly all the common
defeating characteristics of the body overcome, if

only one is determined on the best possible personal appearance. Such improvements, however, although of the greatest importance, are really negative in character. Positive improvements look to a similar goal—a physical personality void of repellent traits and brought up to all-round attractiveness in every respect. This condition involves the body wherever visible, together with carriage, walk, use of arms and hands, gestures, poise, attitudes, and general action. Failures often hinge on matters of such seemingly trivial nature. Success has frequently no other start than that of the attractive physique.

§ 15. Back of the improvements thus indicated should live and breathe, as it were, in consciousness of attracting power, the thought of *magnetism and magnetic feeling*. The action of such thought and feeling is like that of light pouring out of a clear source, or that of heat radiating from a good fire. If you desire such action, you are urged to think of your body as a marvelous and mightily choice instrument through which you may express yourself to, and successfully influence, the business world. The meaning of the injunction is this: *Think of your body with a nice feeling, as you would of some delicate and prized instrument which has cost you much and which you highly value, and put into that thought a fine sense of valuation and care.* These thoughts and feelings will come in time to act upon the body itself, and will then unconsciously pass from it as an attracting force felt by others. A talisman may be suggested as follows: [Observe! Avoid fussiness and self-babying.]

*"I am in love with this my body, and I will give
it the finest thought and treatment in all my daily
work and use it as a delicate machine for the greatness of life."*

§ 16. NUMBER TWO: THE FREE AND OPEN
MIND. The motto of such a mind must be: *"All
the truth there is, all the facts in the case, all the
evidence to be had,—and every mind to its own honest opinion!"* That attitude alone is immensely
magnetic, for it attracts not only by force of its
sincerity, but as well by its spirit of toleration. No
one would hesitate to appreciate such a mental
characteristic, yet probably few people understand
any method by which it may be developed. I
suggest, therefore, the following, taken from Dr.
Thomson's *"Brain and Personality"*—an infallible
direction for the acquisition of sure knowledge, and
in action a perfect creator of openmindedness.

*"First, begin by finding out all you know on the
(any) subject. Then be sure that you do not pass to
the consideration of the unknown except along lines
definitely connected with that which is certainly
known."*

The sentences for auto-suggestion would read
in harmony with this direction: *"I meet you at
every point with the friendly and tolerant mind. In
business the right thing and the true thing are the
only things worth while."*

§ 17. NUMBER THREE: THE RIGHT INNER
CHARACTER. The chief factor now is the evident
right intention. Nevertheless, the intention must
practically realize in "good business." Most people
accept at par—at the start—the appearance which
indicates: "My honest intention is right;" but

if the concrete variations are repeated too often, there comes a time when intention is discounted, and the man who "means well" is voted incompetent or a fool, as the phrase actually signifies, *non compos*. Modern business is too strenuous and rapid to waste much time in finding excuses for unbusinesslike character. While the winning personality in the business world is not a drawing-room factor, the "square man" *is* a counting-room factor and a real asset, because human magnetism acts and is responded to along "right" lines. The talismanic principle, then, may be called the

Crystal Palace of Brains, Brawn and Banks: *"I win you by the truth that you will never find the facts other than exactly as I show them—and no 'explanations' required."*

§ 18. NUMBER FOUR: MAGNANIMITY IN TRADE. This means a large attitude of "live and let live." Business is competition, of course, but good business is never robbery. Self-interest is the law of life, from that of a jelly-fish to that of a Cæsar, yet nothing is more unbusinesslike and unmagnetic than raw selfishness. The moment people detect this vice in a man, that moment he ceases to be the winning personality. *Business is absolutely a matter of mutualism.* Magnanimity is a commercial asset. The best standing-ground in finance is satisfied customers and active trade all-round. Hence, we may make the present talisman read as follows:

"Because I want your trade, I desire your business to succeed."

§ 19. NUMBER FIVE: CONSCIOUSNESS OF BEING WORTH WHILE. Old John Graham, in *"Letters*

From a Self-made Merchant," remarks on "superiority" that it "makes every man feel its equal. It is courtesy without condescension; affability without familiarity; self-sufficiency without selfishness; sympathy without snide." When a man feels "worth while," it only remains to inspire in the other person a similar feeling to establish at once magnetic relations. This is not difficult, of course, on your own grade or level, but the magnetic art calls for such inspiration when you meet a person who naturally "belongs" on a different grade. In such event, you must inspire the feeling, either in yourself, if the man you meet seems above you, or in the man himself if he seems below you. The practical method consists in *acting a part*, thus—

The First Case: Assumption of Personal Worth in Self: "I assume and assert that I am really worth while—and I conduct myself, I will conduct myself, on exactly that basis."

The Second Case: Assumption of Personal Worth in Others: "I assume that you are of course entirely worth while. Pray be at ease. I am now acting toward you on that assumption."

It needs scarcely be said that these affirmations are for one's own private thought only. If they seem rather simple and, perhaps, foolish, you are invited to remember that as a matter of fact there are millions of people on this earth to whom even such simple directions would prove godsends for down-on-the-ground practical life.

§ 20. NUMBER SIX: TACT. This characteristic has been described as "the knack of keeping quiet at the right time; of being so agr--eable yourself that no one can be disagreeable to you; of making inferiority feel like equality. The tactful man can pull the stinger from a bee without getting stung." For the practical acquisition of tact you are invited assiduously to observe the thought:

"It is my immediate and special business to please you here and now."

§ 21. NUMBER SEVEN: RESOURCEFULNESS. The following instance is just one link in a chain that runs around the world every twenty-four hours. "A lady once went into an emporium and asked for a powder. The assistant who had the privilege of attending to her wants at once asked: 'Gun, face, or bug?'" This was non-magnetic (except in its humorousness), even if due to ignorance. If said bluntly, it was poor salesmanship. If said impertinently, it was an enemy to business. Impertinence builds nothing but its own monument. *The small matters of life are the great things in business.* Such incidents as that just related have been large enough to send nations to war. The winning personality is never guilty of such gross blunders. You are on this earth, so far as business goes, to please the buyer—or seller, and you never can tell what thing in the human shape may turn up with vastly important matters on hand.

The talisman is now: *"Just the right thing and word in just the right place. My wits are here, alert and equal to the occasion."*

§ 22. NUMBER EIGHT: ADJUSTMENT, OR ADAPTABILITY. Some men are born with this quality. They are naturally "good mixers." With others the trait is not native, and must be acquired. In order to the attainment of ability to adapt oneself to all sorts and conditions of people, reference may be

had to preceding suggestions, but the main thing
is the discovery of what kind of address the other
person likes, together with his hobby, or fad, or
pleasures, or books, or admirations, and the adjustment of yourself, in a natural and honest manner,
to any of these items in his life and character. The
work indicated is, of course, considerable, and
much must be learned from experience, which is
itself a costly affair, but if you are really to turn a
business man your way you've got to "cog-in" with
the cogs of his nature, whatever the difficulty may
be. *A business is a matter of inter-relations;* it is
merely international diplomacy on a lesser scale.
The man who can "gear his wheels" the most
accurately with the intricate machinery of the
commercial world, has solved in large part the
problems of success.

Our suggestion may now seem a little like
sycophancy, but it presumes the preceding régimes
as necessary associates, and if these lie back of it,
can never be other than perfectly sincere and
genuine: *"All that you wish in honorable business,
precisely that I am in the present transaction—for
mutual benefit!"*

§ 23. Number Nine: Avoidance of Clash.
Adaptability involves the following negative particulars—affirmative enough, however, in the effort
required and the attitude essential. It strenuously
seeks avoidance of all interference with other
people's hobbies, beliefs, tastes, political affiliations,
friendships, fads, ideas of life, business or happi-
ness. This negative attitude does not mean, let it
be noted, that the winning personality is to cater
to every variation of the mind, or to stand indif-

ferent to the whimsicalities of human nature, but it does signify that in *business* a man's chief duty is to do *good business*, which may best be effected by refraining from running amuck of mere individual peculiarities. A practical motto would be:

"Peace, for the sake of business, and all present minor things sacrificed for the long-run goal!"

§ 24. NUMBER TEN: ATTRACTIVENESS OF MANNER. We have here a very magnetic quality. Boorishness, brutishness, roughness, uncouthness, vulgarity, profanity, haughtiness, slovenliness, arrogance, opinionativeness, sarcasm, impertinence, joking at another's expense, ridicule, depreciation, hot temper, the loud voice, the hard eye, the violent gesture, and all the elements of the "witch's cauldron" called "the natural man," have never yet conducted successful business.

§ 25. The desirable quality consists of a fine combination of the exact opposites to the above. That complex bit of magnetism ought to be and surely may be cultivated in every department of the business world. I know no suggestion to self more infallibly a builder of attracting power than the determination, bedded down in the subconscious mind:

"Nothing to repel, everything to win, the people I meet in the financial world."

§ 26. NUMBER ELEVEN: GENUINENESS. This quality is everywhere in great demand. The business arena interprets honesty in various ways, and that it means genuineness is more and more insisted upon. When you pass light through a prism, the ray is decomposed into many colors. Genuineness, passed through a real man, yields magnetic qualities of the first importance. You see the result in

—honesty, largeness of feeling and thought, a sense of personal dignity neither stiff nor egotistic, politeness born of true interest, and never mere society attitudinizing, companionableness, accessibility, frankness, confidence, straightforwardness, reliability, and the like through a long and attractive list. More and more the business world wants that kind of people in its army. You see its appreciation of the value of such qualities in the current phrases: "true blue," "all wool and a yard wide," "a square man," "a straight proposition," "all O. K." etc. The talisman, then, might be given in this manner:

"I know exactly what I am—just what I seem to be; and you know it as well as I."

§ 27. NUMBER TWELVE: SELF-CONTROL. The factor of magnetic self-control eliminates the usual faults of personal intercourse, such as blunders in personal allusions, the loss of temper, indulgence in the "quick" word, the unpleasant manner, and so on; but it particularly embraces a certain balance between reserve and expression, power and outgo, a poise and sure handling of the whole man which invariably inspires respect and confidence. The every-day thought that will surely create the power of magnetic control if carried out in action, expression and language, is this:

"I have myself perfectly in hand, and release only as and what I will."

§ 28. NUMBER THIRTEEN: MAGNETIC PHYSICAL CHARACTERISTICS. The winning personality carries the following high values: A good voice well trained, a friendly eye, sometimes compelling, now and then revealing deep fires not to be played with but surely to be trusted, an adaptive touch and grasp of the hand, an erect carriage and the evidence of controlled internal energy (see Chapter XIII Section 35). With these qualities should also go a responsive power of listening. One gained admission to the presence of Thomas Carlyle, the English essayist, and uttered scarcely a word during the entire interview, while Carlyle talked a torrent of thought and reminiscence. When the visitor had left, the great man remarked that the other was one of the finest conversationalists he had ever met. *If you really wish to interest people, get them to do or talk in regard to matters pertaining to their own worlds.*

The qualities mentioned in the above paragraph are sometimes natural gifts, but in the vast majority of cases they must be acquired if possessed at all. You are invited, then, to observe the following suggestions:

(1) For the good voice the services of a competent instructor will return great dividends on your investment.

(2) For the magnetic eye it is suggested that you practice putting kindness and genuineness into the look.

(3) For the eye of power it will be of great value to cultivate a sense of personal superiority backed up by conduct, and to seek to develop within a feeling of intense, masterful energy (see Chapter XIII).

(4) For the adaptive touch and grasp, one should study lightness and firmness of contact, together with heartiness and vitality of grasp, always devoid of roughness and the crushing grip,

putting the hand squarely into the other person's
clasp, but never in such a way as to offend or pain.
The society finger pick-up on a level with the nose is
inane—in a male. No "live man" shakes hands in
that manner; the "live" woman is privileged. In
addition to these suggestions, it may be added that
the use of the hands upon various objects or in moving articles about may contribute to general personal
attractiveness. Some hands fall on objects like
stones; some swoop down like beasts of prey; some
crawl around like reptiles. But others go to objects
handled unerringly yet evenly and with perfect touch
like a bird that knows how to alight, and when these
hands move things from place to place the inert
matter seems endowed with life. None of these items
is too trivial for magnetism. They are among the
factors that make good gunners, artists, lovers,
drivers. And the hand of power may just as well
smoothly make its way through life as run a swath of
disaster through the cut glass and sèvres china of
existence.

§ 29. NUMBER FOURTEEN: PERSONAL POISE.
The following, taken from "*The Personal Atmosphere*," by the author, may well close this chapter:
"In contact with other people, maintain in your
Peronal Atmosphere a perfect and constant calm.
Bring your will to the centre of your field (a certain
space extending beyond your body), and maintain
absolute self-control. Let this be so complete that
it may not betray the effort to secure it, either in
disturbed ether-waves, or in movements which the
other person's subconsciousness will recognize as
coolness or suppressed hostility.

"*Avoid all excitement! Send out no antagonisms.*

"Banish absolutely all thought-waves of *fear for persons with whom you are dealing.*

"Banish all thought-waves of *distrust as to success with such persons.*

"Maintain a Personal Atmosphere that is surcharged with the dynamic force of confident expectancy of good desired."

Victor Hugo, in "*Ninety-Three,*" describes Gauvain, a hero: "He was thirty years old; he had a Herculean bust, the solemn eye of a prophet, and the laugh of a child. He did not smoke, he did not drink, he did not swear. He carried a dressingcase through the whole war; he took care of his nails, his teeth, his hair, which was dark and luxuriant. During halts he himself shook in the wind his military coat, riddled with bullets and white with dust. * * * He was a heroic and innocent soul. The sabre in his hand transfigured him."

Every one who was really human loved Gauvain. He usually had his own way. The picture suggests the very heart of magnetism—the magnetic intention.

§ 30. It is always to be remembered, now, that no mere reading of these pages will yield more than a passing value. The directions should vigorously be worked into practical life and sunken deeply by such effort into the subconscious self. The matters enumerated are common enough, to be sure, but they are vastly more common in the *fault* than in the excellence. If people were to act intelligently on what they already know, there would be no call for power-books. Success in life consists not in the things that you are aware of, but in the things which you actually use in the every-day

life. Magnetism is a growth, and it follows the
law of growth in all things: *Unfoldment is Right
Action.*

"I looked up," said the hero of "*The Crossing*,"
"and my eyes were caught and held with a strange
fascination by fearless blue ones that gazed down
into them.   I give you but a poor description of
those blue eyes, for personal magnetism springs
not from one feature or another."   It is rather the
whole personality itself, in which pulsates a power
that draws as the pole star for effective action and
is like the sun for value.

CHAPTER IV.

PRACTICAL ABILITY: THE HAND OF POWER.

A WRITER has said, with large appreciation of our common nature: "We may believe there is not a superfluous man—one who, if he consults his aptitudes instead of his inclinations, will not find that he has a call," and it may be added—to some particular kind of work in the world. The word *aptitude* is derived from the Latin *aptare*, "to fit or join together." Your aptitude, therefore, is your ability to fit a situation or task, to join practical skill to a practical requirement. There is nothing demanded in our life for which some person has not the requisite ability, and there is no normal person on this earth who is not able to do more things than he believes himself capable of. This chapter advises: Find the one thing that you can best do, then multiply that one thing into other things equally practical.

§ 1. A fourth element essential to successful business is *Practical Ability*. This qualification is of course always before us in the present work, and can here receive but the briefest treatment; nevertheless, certain aspects of the value demand emphasis as being what may be called "main things" in all our study.

PRACTICAL ABILITY.

§ 2. *Practical ability is power efficiently applied.* It accomplishes things that are worth while from a business standpoint. Remembering, now, that any man possesses at present all the power he will ever acquire, needing only to discover the fact and draw on his own resources, it is evident that the development of the power, and the applying skill which demonstrates efficiency, call for three things: ascertainment of *aptitude, unyielding persistence,* and time-consuming *patience* in practical effort.

§ 3. If your *aptitude* is decidedly not for business, the axiom, "power to be had is now possessed," may demonstrate in some one of many careers, but will not be realized in financial matters. If your aptitude runs to business dealings, it may exhibit (a) executive ability, (b) a capacity for leadership, (c) fidelity in reliance upon others, (d) or just mechanical efficiency. *The kind of power a man is to unfold is largely determined for him in advance*—but only by his endowment.

§ 4. But I wish, now, to lift into bold relief the following proposition: *No man knows what the aptitude of his native power is until patient persistence has had a chance to demonstrate.*

I have immense faith in the average mind, and do not for a moment believe that the common individual brain is ever limited to just one kind of achievement. Concentration of effort is essential to success, of course, but evidence of aptitude in some particular line of action does not necessarily deny aptitude in other lines. A man may "get away" for his life career at the start and stick to the "one thing" to the end; yet it is exactly as true that at the first there may be a good deal of wobbling and backing and filling with other men before the best thing to do is really discovered. Young business people should never for an instant doubt their ultimate success, nor yield to any feeling of uncertainty of discouragement arising from such inability at once to decide what they are good for. Only practical effort can determine the question of aptitude, and no man in the world may know exhaustively the kind of power determined for him by original endowment until trial, patient and persistent, has demonstrated the facts in his case.

§ 5. One of the laws of business success, then, is this: *The highest achievement depends upon practical effort made with determination to move up from demonstration of aptitude on the Marble Stairway of Applied Power*, as follows: (This analysis I find, after writing it, precisely agrees with the division of business men as given by Dean Johnson, of the School of Commerce, Accounts and Finance, New York University—Read up).

To....Leadership with executive ability.

To....Leadership without executive ability.

To....Fidelity in dependent superior positions.

From....Mere Mechanical efficiency.

§ 6. You are invited to think this process over with reference to your own aptitude thus far discovered, referring to Section 28 of Chapter II for its exact significance. The talismanic sentence is this:

"I shall never know my own undiscovered power until I mightily try for better things, and at least one step higher I will certainly climb. I aim for the top stair, but if my ability is precisely and only what it seems, then I will give that power the utmost efficiency—for the sake of my personal betterment."

§ 7. The demonstration of the kind of power a man possesses, if it is to manifest in a large way, *demands unyielding persistence and time-consuming patience.* Modern business lacks not in rewards, but it is an exacting master. Modern business is just law—the law of the nature of things at work in the exchange of goods and the achievement of wealth. As is true in the case of every law, then, the whole man must go into the utilization of the laws of business while he is engaged in business effort.

In "*The Westerners,*" by Stewart Edward White, Lafond, the half-breed, conceives the idea of revenge by killing. Then a chance-met traveler said, during an over-night camping on the open plains: "Listen, my friend. Life is a little thing. Any man can take it who has a gun, or a knife, or even a stone. But the true revenge is in finding out what it is that each man prizes the most, and then taking it from him. And that requires power! power! power!" For two hours the scantily clothed half-breed sat brooding over the fire. "From the potent reflections induced by these one hundred and twenty minutes it resulted that Michail Lafond became civilized and a seeker for wealth in the development of the young country. In wealth he saw power." The history of the revenge-seeker engulfed fifteen years of absolutely tireless effort and dogged patience. Take out the element of crime, replacing it by honor, and this episode incarnates three factors indispensable to success— patience, persistence, power. There is just one method for the development of these qualities: *the immediate and continued application of the Will to be patient and presistent to the little things and the great of every-day life right here and now.*

§ 8. Assuming, then, the kind of power one possesses to have been already discovered, and taking for granted persistence and patience in its unfoldment, certain related considerations now appear which are of immense importance. *Practical ability measures out power with judgment according to demand in any given case.*

Some men always over-use the power they possess, in the main thing, or in getting ready for an undertaking. Washington Irving tells of a Dutchman who had a ditch to leap, and who went so far back from it in order to make a run and secure momentum that when he reached the edge he was completely fagged and had to sit down and recover breath.

Some men exhaust power in developing schemes which are utterly devoid of real value. I once knew an inventive person who devised a sure-enough mechanism for locking hotel bed-room doors from the inside. The thing worked perfectly, but I said, "Why not get up something for fastening the door from without and making it secure while you are absent? You already have the key for the inside, and, besides, you are there yourself and can barricade the entrance." Of this consideration he had not thought. *He never used hotels himself.*

Some men are immensely talented in working up schemes and planning all the detail methods essential thereto, but when this labor is completed to their satisfaction, not a factor being omitted, their interest immediately diverts to some second interesting theory. These people may be very practical thinkers, but *they are not practical doers*.

Then again the thinking of others is mere dreaming, and fantastic chimeras forever dance before their eyes with never-ceasing allurement. But *nothing comes of the dreaming*.

There are business men who really understand the science of business, theoretically, who nevertheless do not seem able to succeed in business practice. The best writers on political economy have not been the great financiers. Some writers of law-books have wisely drifted away from the actual conduct of their profession. In ancient Greece there were subtler rhetoricians than Demosthenes, the most eloquent man of his time. It is not the artists, statesmen, generals, of first rank, who give us the standard works on æsthetics, government and military tactics. The man who is a genius in the theory of commerce and finance may prove to be the poorest sort in every-day business life.

§ 9.   But the business man, if he is to succeed in his profession, must be able to carry out the completed theory of his own field of effort. Without practical ability, a man may well enough plan a beautiful craft, but some other worker must build the boat in order that the plan may float. We may imagine a shipbuilder who is so fussy about timbers and tools and clean yards, and so superstitious and conservative in his notions and methods of doing things, that moss would grow all over any vessel on the ways before she could be got off; the real marine craftsman is he who has his mind's eye on the boat alaunch, the best for the money, in the quickest time, largely disregardful of all relatively unimportant matters, and forever working straight-away for finest results. It is precisely so in business affairs. *The way to do a thing in a practical way is to get right after it and do it in a practical way.*

§ 10. *Practical ability*, therefore, may be summarized roughly as follows:

Item 1. It is bed-rocked in *good judgment* or plain common sense;

Item 2. It has the *financial vision* well developed;

Item 3. It knows how to profit by *past experience;*

Item 4. And to seize quickly *all advantage* coming its way;

Item 5. It is, hence, ability of *every available sort;*

Item 6. But ability to *do something* on the earth and now;

Item 7. And to do things *that pay*—and to *keep right on;*

Item 8. Moreover, it is ability to do things *rapidly and well;*

Item 9. And a little *better than other people* can do the same things;

Item 10. Practical ability has the knack of *maintaining advantage* secured and positions gained;

Item 11. Or of *letting them go* for better;

Item 12. And of *holding values* created or possessed;

Item 13. It has the secret of *overcoming* or getting around or destroying obstacles;

Item 14. It knows how to *control and use various kinds of men;*

Item 15. It has an eye that *sees values* and *appreciates situations;*

Item 16. It develops *intuitions* for dangers and for opportunities;

Item 17. In some way it manages to *shape events.* The only method for doing this is by shaping human beings ("He was a born leader"—Kosmoroff, in *"The Vultures"*—"an organizer not untouched perchance by that light of genius which enables some to organize the souls of men");

Item 18. And other people—other kinds of people—call the results of practical ability "luck;"

Item 19. It is an error to deny the reality of luck; but the *men who make it do not give it that name* (If you are sure that luck is a fiction, you are lucky);

Item 20. *Practical ability is action, swift, insistent, and compelling.* A young man talked with the representative of people who had a new kind of steam packing. He wanted the agency for his house in Honolulu, but the representative stated their policy to be that of sales to any customer anywhere. When the steam-packing man had left, the young pusher took steamer for San Francisco, the headquarters of the representative, arrived before the latter, convinced the house that specializing on their goods would be vastly better than depending on hit-or-miss deals, went home, and straightway sold eighteen hundred dollars worth of the packing.

Practical ability is no matter of the kind of luck some men are always charging up against the successful worker. It is the deposit in a man's nature and character of centuries of evolution. The single-cell animal had to get it in some degree or die a violent death, and from *Amœba* to the wealthiest millionaire, hard work has been engaged in building it up in the human brain, toiling, age-long for a little here and age-long for a bit there, until the modern business world climaxes the mighty process.

§ 11. You are invited to force each one of the above items into your life as a student of Business Power. If you merely read these pages, you infallibly miss their most vital values. If you multiply yourself into them and work the suggestions in with your character, as the ink-maker thoroughly mixes colors and basic material, you will find yourself unfolding more and more that indispensable factor of financial success: business ability. It cannot be too strongly emphasized that deliberated concrete action alone can be relied upon in development of the power we seek.

POWER OF WILL.

§ 12. Now, the thing that is, and creates, human power, is the Will. Theoretically the Will is the man. Practically, *the Will is just a way the man has of being and doing*. The Will is man's inherent nature-tendency to act—to do something. This tendency to act in some way must act on itself—take itself in hand—in order that it may

act intelligently, continuously and with steady
purpose. Will is itself power; but unfolded, controlled and directed power in man is Will self-
mastered, not man-mastered. The man-mastered
Will goes with the motive or impulse which is
strongest. The self-mastered Will goes with that
motive which it makes (he makes) greatest, and
with mere impulse in very slight degree so far as
the life of intelligence is concerned.

§ 13. *The first evidence of real personal power
is the self-mastered Will.*

The self-mastered Will can do anything—within reason; and reason in this connection should be
conceived in its highest human sense. "The man
who, outside of pure mathematics, pronounces the
word Impossible, lacks prudence," said Arago. No
one knows what the human Will cannot achieve.

In Pedro A. de Alarcon's Spanish story, "*The
French Horn,*" Don Basilio, who knew nothing of
music, became master of the horn in fourteen days,
because his own life and that of a friend depended
upon the feat. "What shall I tell you further? In
fourteen days (ah, the power of will!), in fourteen
days, with their fourteen nights, (I did not sleep
for half a month)—yes, you have cause to be astonished—in fourteen days I learned to play upon the
horn! Had I been dumb, I should have learned to
speak; if lame, to walk; if blind, to see—because
it was my will to do it. Ah, the will, that is the
greatest power on earth."

§ 14. The function of Will is like that of
steam. It must be powerful, under control (self-
mastered), and properly directed. The *power* may be
developed, but only through controlled and directed

action. The *control* may be acquired, but only through willed and directed action. The *direction* may be determined, but only through willed and controlled action. *When Will is self-developed, self-mastered, self-directed, it only needs proper application to become practical ability incarnated.*

§ 15. Thus, *"it is all with the man."* The man is just the Will using all sorts of instruments for practical success. If one instrument, or method, or plan, or road fail, the man-Will declares for others, and continues its efforts, and never yields, and always flames with assurance of success. The Will says to the man: "You must win out; you must play the horn!" When a man really must, he can. He then assumes the big end of the contract for achievement. There are no excuses—if a man must. There are no fits of weakness—if a man actually must. Does the man want "pull"? The Will says, "Get it!" Opportunity? The answer is, "Make it!" Business? The last order is, "Create it!" Sales? And the Will shouts, "Go after them!"

§ 16. There are, however, *two prevalent errors* in the common idea of the Will. The Will is sometimes defined as a "faculty" of the mind; it is really one of various ways the "mind" has of being and doing, as the "mind" is simply the whole of such ways considered in one word for the sake of convenience. When the Will acts, it is the man who acts. Hence, there are as many kinds of Will as there are kinds of persons. The right Will for any person is just the best way he *can have* (not has) of being and doing. Will-power is therefore never to be confused with sheer personal force. *A man's personal force is the product of his Will mul-tiplied into his personality;* it is that which exhibits when he throws himself into work or against an obstacle. The Will is the man's *ability* to throw himself into action—either action of the inner self or action of the physical powers. Personal force may be mere brute force. The highest type of Will is farthest removed from that plane. The Will, again, is sometimes referred to as though it were a simple element in our nature. As a matter of fact, it is always as complex as the individual. "The Will is the man." What he is, that is his Will. He, and therefore, the Will, may be obdurate, obstinate, headstrong, stormy, crafty, perverse, and so on. Every such type has some discount in the business world. *The ideal Will is—courageously confident magnetic power in self-mastered and self-directed action practically applied to matters that are actually worth while.* That kind of Will is achieving power.

§ 17. If we define the Will as *the man's power of choice, adhesiveness and control of conduct,* we shall have before us all the Will-elements essential to business. It only needs, now, the demonstrating application of such ability to business affairs, to discover the *Hand of Power.*

THE HAND OF POWER.

§ 18. The hand is the mind's executive physical instrument. To a certain extent, character stands revealed in the hand. I do not mean by this statement to indicate approval of palmistry, but I suggest merely that hands do more or less betray personality. The human hand has literally

lifted man out of the plane of the apes. Or, man
has built his hand by the process of rising above
the apes. A successful man grips things with a
strong hand. It was so with John Godfrey in *"The
Trail of the Grand Seigneur:"* "His shoulders
were broad and powerful and his huge hands,
gnarled and knotted with muscle, like the wrists
above, indicated a terrible strength." Such a hand
is but an index of that power which manifests in
equally significant hands of a totally different form.
Witness the hands of Raphael's Michael, of the
finest mould, and those of the vanquished fiend
beneath the angel's feet—mere digital protuber-
ances. Whatever its shape, the hand of power

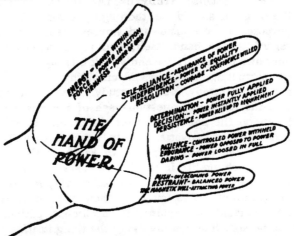

indicates the masterful achieving Will. On analysis, it reveals at least the following qualities, given
in the diagram above, every one of which is absolutely essential to business.

§ 19.   This is the outline of a successful business man's hand—a real hand. Well may it be called the Hand of Power!

§ 20.   The practical utilization of the diagram on page 69 calls for certain labor on the part of the earnest student. Kindly remember that the object of this book is the development of power, and that the only method by which power can be developed consists in intelligent, directed and persistent effort, the self using the self and driving the self to action.

You are now invited to the study of the following régimes:

Régime One: Study of the Hand.   First, the diagram should be thoroughly examined for purposes of criticism and improvement (a) in regard to the hand itself, and (b) in regard to your own character. Secondly, original suggestions for correcting, training and unfolding will-power should be gotten out of that study. If you will put into the following question each of the qualities given on the hand, one after the other, you will make some discoveries surely worth the while: *What is the nature, degree, and habitual efficiency of my* (each quality in turn), *and how may I secure improvement in the directions indicated by my self-examination?* The only method for securing improvement in *anything* is intelligent, patient, and persistent action involving the thing itself.

Now the answer to the latter part of the above question embraces two things:

§ 21.   Régime Two: Development of Will-Power in General.   A strong Will in one respect may be a strong Will in all other respects, but such is not usually the case. For example, the will to overcome present tangible difficulties is frequently prominent in men who are unable persistently to endure inactive waiting. Nevertheless, the headstrong worker may surely cultivate the ability to wait in utter inactivity. Any kind of personal discipline affects brain cells neighboring those brought directly into action in any Will-area, and the secondary influence induces reaction in the self for Will-culture in general; while the very fact of such effort suggests to the whole mind ambition and conduct leading to a powerful Will. You are, therefore, invited to bed down in your subconscious self a deep determination (not mere intention) to acquire the Will of developed power. Remember, "in trying it's the second half that brings results." In furtherance of this resolution, you should proceed to invent and apply various methods for culture of power of Will. For a full gymnasium (mental as well as physical) on this subject, the author's work, *"Power of Will"* (second edition) is referred to as scientific and practical.

§ 22. RÉGIME THREE: THE TRAINING OF THE WILL. Practical people study to improve, no less than to employ, tools, machinery, their line of business. The Will is an instrument, and it ought to be trained by intelligent methods additional to those of every-day affairs. The present chapter itself may be taken as a genuine, though limited, instructor in the matter, and for our immediate purpose the following will prove of value:

(1) You are invited to commit to memory the Hand of Power, and from memory to draw the same diagram, all the Will-elements and definitions

written in place, with increasing concentration upon the Hand as a whole and in its details, until every feature is absolutely and permanently embedded in mind. When sure that this is the case, you will find frequent reviews of great value. You should then be able to use the Hand of Power in your own hand, say, the right, as a constant reminder, and to think the elements on your thumb and fingers, exactly as given in the diagram.

(2) You are invited to ascertain your peculiar characteristics of Will, and to compare results with the analysis of the Hand of Power. You are urged to proceed to and persist in (a) a knowledge of the general characteristics of your own Will, (b) the discovery of your weak points, or the qualities in which you are lacking, (c) resolute and persistent strengthening and development of the same, (d) indomitable equalizing of the latter, (e) the culture of your entire Will-personality up to the highest level of power and efficiency. For success in these efforts you require merely memory and adhesiveness. If you will go on, and "stick," the end is certain.

§ 23. Régime Four: Development of Practical Ability. This involves the whole of the present work, and all there is in the man and his life. Nevertheless, certain brief suggestions may now be noted.

Returning to the consideration of the Hand of Power, the diagram should be studied, further, and applied along the following lines:

(1) Investigation of your own practical ability:

(2) Testing various financial theories and schemes with the questions in mind: (a) is the matter worth while from a business point of view? (b) is it, not only practical, but practicable? (c) will it probably succeed?

(3) Testing of instruments, inanimate and human, deemed necessary, with regard to economy, speed and efficiency;

(4) Testing of lines of action in regard to possibility, directness, economy of effort, and best results;

(5) Testing of methods suggested in precisely the same respects.

The above numbered paragraphs are not mere chance writing, and it will avail little simply to read them. They are boiled-down suggestions having actual utility for the development of practical ability. You are invited to bore into them and to get at their hard-money value, but especially to apply the tests with rigid impartiality to yourself as a business man and the business, in its various aspects and details, in which you are now engaged.

I knew an otherwise intelligent man once who spent days and money in rigging up a small windmill inside a boat, expecting thus to secure adequate motor power. That might have been worth while had the power been possible under the law that action equals reaction. And an old boat-builder once tried to sell me a boat containing a hand mechanism for turning the propellor blades. I said: "What is the difference between pumping your machine and pulling the oars?" Practical ability always knows that what it undertakes is worth while, practicable, on the best line, using the most economical and efficient instruments, following the surest, cheapest and most promising methods. It prefers oars at $1.25 the pair to hand-machines for power at $50.00 the "sale."

The tasks thus far indicated need not seem formidable to the determined Will. Well said David Ritchie, in *"The Crossing:"* "The next vivid thing in my memory is the view of the last barrier Nature had reared between us and the delectable country. It stood like a lion at the gateway, and for some minutes we gazed at it in terror from Powell's Valley below. How many thousands have looked at it with sinking hearts! How many weaklings has it turned away! Nothing in this life worth having is won for the asking; and the best is fought for, and bled for, and died for."

CHAPTER V.

BUSINESS is organized when its elements are brought into relation for a financial end—the accumulation of wealth. The word *organ* springs from a Greek word meaning "to work," and signifies an implement or *instrument*. The elements of business are various, but they become financially instrumental when they are *organ*-ized into such mutual relations as to contribute to the one end—gain. The relation of all the elements is important; it is, however, the personal element which gives effectiveness to their organization. This chapter deals with the relation of person to person in organized business. Such business is a system, the outcome of which, as in any system, involves all personal relations at their best.

§ 1. This chapter does not deal with business relations in the law-sense of rights and obligations, nor in the sense of the structure of business associations, as seen in partnerships, trusteeships, and the like, except by way of illustration. Our theme is development of power for all business, not instruction in the conduct of some one or more

75

kinds of business, and hence we eliminate the legal and structural aspects of the idea of relations and confine our treatment of the subject to this question: *How to acquire power in the study and use of relations which run through the whole financial world.*

§ 2. A *relation* is "the character of a plurality of things;" "the condition of being such and such with *regard to something else.*" For example, goods are values only when related to sales, at least in the active business life. Certain kinds of goods are related in substance, quality, price, purpose, salability, and so on. Money is related to business as a medium of exchange. Business is related to society as a mechanism for activity, sustenance and accumulation.

FOUNDATIONS OF BUSINESS RELATIONS.

In actual life men and women are related in ten thousand ways through beliefs, interests, likes and dislikes, pursuits and purposes, and the like.

§ 3. Every business man stands over against or opposite the whole mass of the people. He is related to all as a business man because all desire, sooner or later, something which he can furnish by way of goods, labor or skill, or some direct or indirect result of the disposition of utilities affected by his effort. Here is seen the broadest business relationship possible.

§ 4. This truth—that *all men want your business in some way*—should be magnified in your thought because it really is a fact, because it is the great justifying foundation of the business world, and because such a broad conception, if it is vitally present with you, cannot fail to give you larger respect for your life-work, and so inspire in your thought courage, hope, confidence and the will to succeed.

§ 5. The fact that all the people, standing, so to speak, opposite you, are related to your business through immediate direct or ultimate indirect satisfaction of wants, *splits up the mass of the people into all sorts of groups*, the kind of group in each instance depending upon the nature of the wants to be satisfied. The idea of wants is here used in a very broad sense, and the grouping process thus comes to include every other person in the world who now has or in future may have some business dealings with yourself. From the standpoint of desired success it is not safe to treat or think of any human being as not likely to become a business proposition in your own affairs. Many people err in precisely this respect. One of the fundamental maxims of successful trade relations is this:

I treat and I think of every kind of human being as though I knew each individual to be important to my business. "You can never tell." Business relation with any living person is always a possibility. "All your birds sooner or later come home to roost."

§ 6. In its general aspect, therefore, business relation divides all the rest of humanity somewhat as follows: Relations Depending on Wants, and Relations which are Personal.

RELATIONS DEPENDING ON WANTS.

§ 7. In supplying wants you are serving those who receive your labor, your skill, or your goods, and hence the things corresponding to your service, given in one or more of these ways, constitute their wants. Thus we may tabulate business relations either for "wants" or for "services," because the word "wants" indicates the side of relation oppo-site to yourself, while the word "service" indicates your own side of the relation. The relations, expressed in terms of wants and service, then, are

Wants=Nourishment———Satisfied by service in goods, labor and skill.

Wants=Housing———Satisfied by service in sales or rents.

Wants=Warming———Satisfied by service in goods, labor and skill.

Wants=Clothing———Satisfied by service in goods, etc.

Wants=Adornment———Satisfied by skill, etc.

Wants=Attendance———Satisfied by service in labor and skill.

Wants=Assistance———Satisfied by service in mutual labor and skill.

Wants=Amusement———Satisfied by service in skill and labor.

Wants=Personal Vanity———Satisfied by goods, labor and skill.

Wants=Instruction———Satisfied by service in labor and skill.

PERSONAL RELATIONS BASED ON ABOVE.

§ 8. In these "services" you are addressing yourself to the people in various ways, a compre-hensive understanding of which is important to large business ability. The relations involved are in the main as follows (*Outline of Business Relations*):

I.—BUSINESS MAN RELATED TO PEOPLE:
  (1) Whole mass of the people.
  (2) Groups wanting your goods, labor or skill directly.
  (3) Groups wanting results of sales, labor or skill.
  (4) Groups reached by your business.
  (5) Groups yet to be reached by your business.
  (6) Sellers directly to you.
  (7) Sellers indirectly to affect your business.
  (8) Others: bankers, attorneys, physicians, special people.

II.—EQUALS RELATED TO EQUALS:
  (1) Partners.
  (2) Incorporators.
  (3) Co-operators.
  (4) Directors.
  (5) Trustees.
  (6) Stockholders.
  (7) Members of Associations.

III.—BUSINESS MAN'S RELATION TO EMPLOYEES:
  (1) Presidents.
  (2) Superintendents: General; Limited.
  (3) Fully Executive Agents: Foreign Heads, Factors, etc.
  (4) Partially Executive Agents: Traveling Salesmen, Brokers, etc.
  (5) Managers: General; Departmental.
  (6) Commission Merchants.
  (7) Superior Dependent Positions not enumerated above.
  (8) Inferior Dependent Positions, but regular.
  (9) Casual Laborers.

IV.—RELATION OF EMPLOYEES TO EMPLOYERS:
  (1) The Employer.
  (2) The Superintendent.
  (3) The Manager.
  (4) Associates in General.
  (5) Associated Groups of Employees as Groups.
  (6) Associates in Your Own Group.
  (7) The Public Group you immediately serve.

The above outline will be referred to again under the heading, "Personal Adjustment" (see Section 13, present chapter). The immediate purpose of the outline here is merely to suggest a general survey of business relations by way of introduction and for the raising of certain questions having a practical bearing on the development of business power.

§ 9. The greatest importance attaches to this idea of personal business relations and the practical application of knowledge covering the relations. When we analyze the idea of relations, all sorts of suggestions arise involving the right attitude and address toward those with whom we come into business contact. You are, therefore, urged carefully to examine the outline with regard to the following sets of questions:

Set the First. (1) Where am I in the outline? (2) Where might I be therein? (3) Where am I determined to be? In a position superior or inferior?

Set the Second. (1) How can I more surely maintain my present place in the outline? (2) How can I advance one or more places in the outline? (3) How may I improve my attitude toward the people and my associates or employer for the betterment of the business I am now engaged in?

Set the Third. (1) Where is my business properly to be placed in an outline of the world's business, I being one member of a relation, and any listed group or groups out of the whole total of groups in near or remote ways affected by my business constituting the other member of the relation? (2) How can I make my business more completely and directly affect those ascertained groups? (3) How can·I improve my attitude toward, and hence my relations with, all these groups regarded as (x) buyers, (y) sellers, (z) competitors?

It may be felt that this is a rather vague piece of work and not very useful for practical business. I suggest, however, that it is eminently practical because it involves three desirable things: Larger thought concentrated on your business, the improvement of your present business, and expansion of its scope and effectiveness. These three ideas are always being considered in every great railway system, in every great journalistic plant, in every huge department store. *The big men ever relate themselves in thought to at least a whole continent*, and they bend all energies to put themselves practically in touch with all the want-groups of all the people. The suggestions here offered will repay a very careful and persistent study and a thorough application of results to your actual business.

In the meantime we pause a moment to indicate

THE DEVELOPMENT OF THE PSYCHIC MEANING OF RELATIONS.

§ 10. Psychologically speaking, the general analysis of relations may be expressed as follows: "There are four great stages in the progression through which the psychic meaning attaching to *relation* has to pass," as Professor James Mark Baldwin, of Johns Hopkins University, remarks in "*Thoughts and Things.*"

"First, there is the mere *altogetherness of parts* of any cognized object as such." Examples of this altogetherness would be, all people on the earth, or in a state, or in a family, or in a store, and the like.

Secondly, there is the *relation expressed in the group idea :* the *world-human* group, the *state* group, the *family* group, the *store* group, and so on. In this idea the vague idea of altogetherness has given way somewhat to a definite thought about the people involved, as, "composing a group."

Thirdly, there is, not only the vague group-idea because of some kind of altogetherness, but a recognition of *specific group-membership in individuals*, as, say, in a department store====the managers, the floor-walkers, the book-clerks, and so on. That is to say, we have now not only togetherness, not only group-associations, but perception that certain individuals are being what they are with regard to definite work and purpose, such as, all the managers, or, all the clerks, or, all the trustees, etc., considered as such.

Fourthly, we have the *abstract idea of relationship*, worked out from altogetherness, group, and membership. You are related in your business as head, superintendent, manager, trustee, director, clerk — as any particular function. Here the thought, however, is not that of position or office; it is the *relation into which the position puts you.*

We now gather up preceding considerations for what (to use a rather ugly word) I may call the practicalization of business relations.

PRACTICALIZATION OF RELATIONS.

The above progression by which we get the psychic meaning of relation is pure theory for our present purposes unless we apply the analysis to practical affairs. When we practicalize the idea of relation in business we secure pretty nearly the whole of the all-essential of business success.

§ 11. *For business is simply human relations adjusted to a financial end.* The successful business man is never satisfied in his thought with the mere altogetherness of things or people. Instinctively he gets things and people into groups of various sorts, so far as they may come within the scope of his commercial effort. And the scope of the big man's effort measures an attempt to group all mankind into differing sections in relation to his own business. This, indeed, discloses the outlook for possible improvement. Practically considered, it means the questions—*How can I supply the wants, or a greater number of wants, of more people in the groups I am already dealing with? What other groups can I add to the list which I now affect?*

§ 12. Even for men who do not yet claim pronounced greatness in practical business comprehension or reach, the practicalization of relations is altogether important. There is no law compelling one to reject the big-department-store idea of commercial activity for the country-cross-road idea— although the man who is realizing the latter idea may be filling his field perfectly. The work here suggested may well be taken up by men lesser than the greatest, and especially, perhaps, by those who deal with the public in the interest of employers. As an employee one might profitably ask: *How can I more efficiently satisfy the people who belong to my public group? How can I increase the number of patrons in that group? How can I add to this group one or more unusual groups?*

6

You are manager, let us say, of a department
in a great establishment.   Your department has so
many groups of clerks: if it is the gentlemen's
furnishing department it has the collars-and-cuffs
group, the necktie group, the shirt group, and so
on through your list.   These groups simply represent so many groups of the people, and the question
now is, What do these patrons buy elsewhere that
I do not yet furnish of articles related in some way
to my department? Higher-priced goods? Lower-
priced goods? Odd colors and styles? Foreign
fashions? When you find a distinct thing your
people want along with your general kind of goods,
you have an *opportunity to come into relation with
another group of purchasers* and add them to your
list.

Space forbids, of course, an elaborate extension
of the suggestion here given.   The illustration is
designed merely to indicate the immense scope and
the practical nature of our analysis of relations.

Thus much for one phase of the practicalization of the outline of business relations through
attempted satisfaction of a greater variety and
number of distinct wants.   Our next question concerns the same process brought about by a study of
personality.

PERSONAL ADJUSTMENT.

§ 13.   Business is, of course, always a matter
of personal adjustment. But this involves not only
the items, labor, skill, goods, and the abstract
group-relation idea; it brings up prominently the
question of *right personal attitude and its practical
realisation in business conduct*. You cannot success-

fully deal with people unless you remember that
you are always dealing with human types and
variations of the same in individuals,—unless, therefore, you ascertain in some way (a) What kind of
persons you are handling, (b) What their wants are,
either necessary or special, and (c) How they prefer the satisfaction of these wants.

§ 14. In your business you are always dealing
with a common human nature, and at the outset we
may begin our present work with certain *assumptions which are universally true* and essentially
important in the business man's relation-attitude
toward the people.

(1) *All the People are Human.* None of them
is a perfected saint; none of them is a mere animal—at least for business. It is never good business to think of them with contempt, or to treat
them like cattle. Business wants them, all of them,
every day of the year. It is no favor on your part
to the people that you are in business. It is exceedingly favorable to you that you have the people to
do business with. You cannot get along without
them, but they can get along without you, for
they can put some other man in your place. Do
you know that an immense bulk of business is
based on *personal liking, or liking for a place?*

Business power respects the people. On the
other hand, every sort of human has some fault or
"out," and this is precisely as true of the business
man himself as of any individual among the people.
The fact that every person is open to criticism calls
for adjustment on the part of the business man to the
foibles and disagreeable traits of the people for the
sake of his business. A first practical method for

right adjustment consists in schooling the mind to the fact itself—in establishing a reasonable recognition of common, imperfect human nature. The business man must expect to meet with disagreeable things, he must count flaws in the character of others as inevitable parts of the situtaion, and the wiser business man will take the people *with* their faults, *for* their virtues, *and as better than they are.*

(2) *All the People Want the "Square Deal,"* whether the business relation lies between buyer and seller, or associate and associate, or employer and employee; and they want the "square deal" all the time. This truth involves an interesting consideration in business life. *Every business trnasaction consists only of itself,* and when it closes it is closed completely. The real business transaction tolerates neither friendship nor enmity nor memory of the past nor discount against the future. There is no *moral virtue* in the "square deal" *regarded as business,* although it may be dictated by the moral business man whose act is then a virtue. The non-moral character, the purely commercial nature, of a business transaction, surely calls for the "square deal," but it can never pile up any credit against which a future dealing less than "square" can properly be discounted. Any affair must stand by itself, for every affair is an exchange of values—goods, labor, skill—agreed upon between the parties interested at the time. Every new transaction between the same parties implies a new agreement of such exchange at such and such values—so much goods or labor or skill for so much cash or equivalent consideration. The people, therefore, demand that the mutual understanding

be carried out in each case, and fully. The square
deal is just that: a transaction in which an agreement which is explicit or must in mutuality of
interest be assumed, is completely realized.
Because the people understand this law of agreement in any business dealings, they see that it can
earn no other credit than reputation, and that it
must never be discounted. The people are sometimes unduly rigid and exacting in this respect.
They frequently require *more* than the square deal
—as for instance, an *unjust* "make-good" of a
guaranty. But business is not a court in session
weighing up exact justice with finicky distinctions;
it is activity for accumulation, and hence, to be
good business, must be reasonably willing to
"make good" beyond level justice for the sake of
business itself.

My friend, the business man, guarantees his
goods. Now and then a customer demands the
make-good on articles which he knows are perfect,
and his inside people are inclined to resist the
demand and "talk back." This is what he says:
*"Make your guaranty good first ; then find out what
the trouble is."* Sometimes, after the guaranty has
been made good, he dictates a letter which reads
like this: "We are sorry our goods do not please
you, but return your payment on last order, and
respectfully request the discontinuance of your
trade."

(3) *All the People Want Courtesy All the
Time.* This is true, but some of them forget that
you are a part of the people. It is good business to
ignore that lapse of memory. If you fail to ignore
it, you simply hurt yourself, for discourteous

buyers or sellers (the other-side people) can go elsewhere. Sometimes business associates forget their own demand for courtesy; nevertheless, good business ignores this also, for if two associates fall out, the last one to yield is invariably hurt the most. As between the business man and the people, be he head, or agent, or clerk, long-run courtesy fills long-run wants. The man on the outside knows only what he sees, and if you fail in courtesy that is all he sees: he certainly cannot get into your personality and understand why you so fail. For example, he doesn't perceive your physical condition, for you are able to stand on your feet, and his mind is preoccupied. Does he care that you are being slowly killed by trouble or disease? Not if you forget courtesy. But if he detects sheer effort to be courteous with a fierce headache, or the tired-to-death illness, or some home grief, then he cares, and he is one out of a million who would not help you if he could. He expects, however, invariable courtesy, and will "put up" with nothing less. When he fails to receive it, you are the one who is hurt.

All the people want courtesy, especially after they have offered courtesy. I saw a young woman clerk laugh when a gentleman who had given her simple, hearty consideration had turned away. *This is the sort of thing that keeps salaries down.* He who ridicules or sneers at the politeness of any individual in business dealings, betrays the punk order of brains.

§ 15. With these assumptions affirmed, we may now proceed to the further practicalization of business relations. This involves two kinds of indispensable effort: (A)—*Study of Human Nature;* and (B) — *Successful Application of Results to Adjustment.* In either case the first requirement covers

A REASONABLE KNOWLEDGE OF SELF.

§ 16. Now, this knowledge of self is a stupendous matter. It is so great, not because the subject is vast, but because of the processes involved and the significance of those processes. We begin first with a vague awareness of things with which we are confusedly mixed. Then, after long, there comes a feeling of self as different from the things. Then, following a period in which consciousness of the instruments of the self—body and mind—slowly develops, a time arrives in which we set these instruments over against the self for study and investigation. All through these periods *three goals* are coming toward us: *the entering of the self into relation with its mind, the entering of the self into relation with its body, and, through the approach of these two goals, the final entering of the self into relation with itself.* The outcome of all is mastery of self-personality. The "entering into relation" means that we discover body and mind as in each case a something which we have made for ourselves, which have become "wrong" or imperfect because we have ourselves, by inner self-activity, fashioned them incorrectly, but which we may just as surely fashion as we will, according to our ideals and the closeness of the relation into which we enter with body or mind. In business, then, the necessity of self-knowledge is based on the fact that your body and mind are instruments *right now in your hands*, so to speak, which you have made as they are, and which you can bring to larger efficiency by remembering that they are your self-made instruments and can be made to be and do about as you will. This truth you will not at first see or accept; you will be influenced by the ideas of heredity and traditional science, but in time the underlying philosophy will begin to work over your entire theory of life. In order to this, I ask you to remember as follows: *our present ideal of self-knowledge is not a mass of information about yourself, but is the turning of your self upon body and mind as instruments of your own creation, and by so much, the direction of all of your self, body and mind and ego, as self-fashioned, into business for the success which surely belongs to you.*

§ 17. Every business man may be regarded as possessed of two selves—the Static Self and the Dynamic Self. These terms will be defined.

§ 18. *The Dynamic Self is the man in action.*

§ 19. The Static Self is the man *capable* of action, also the man who *throws himself into action.*

§ 20. That this division is real may be indicated by reference to many facts and occurrences in common experience. There is a something within us which seems to continue on and the same during all personal changes and through all the activities of life. I do not care in this connection whether we call this abiding self a sum-total of states of consciousness, a sum-total of physiological activities, a purely material or a purely non-material reality, or a mixture; the thing I wish to indicate is the fact that there is in the idea of *an individual* an abiding something which seems to

lie behind its manifestations. On reflection we are
able to distinguish this phase of the self, or to
infer it as distinct from the self as manifest in a
given action-experience. Here we have, then, the
self *expressing*, and the self *expressed*. At other
times the *quality* of the expressing action seems to
surprise us, and we say: I really did better than I
supposed I knew. Then again, the reverse is true,
and we deny that the manifested self was the real
self. And always with the active man, when he
stops to reflect, is the feeling that not the whole of
himself, even at his best, goes into an act—lets go
fully—drains all off—but that *a* self, his fundamental reserve, is always left behind, so to speak,
on the throne, to direct all other possible activities.
This at least is my own experience—unless I am to
be classed with the "naive" people so frequently
referred to by the psychologists as not really knowing their own minds. I am always, *so to speak*, two
persons when in action: the Static Self capable of
various things; the Dynamic Self expressing the
capability.

§ 21. Now, this static self stands behind the
dynamic, and thus the *dynamic self always reveals
exactly the quality* (not of the static self) but of the
static self's relation to the human world. If we
refer to the outline of business relations given in
Section 8 of this chapter, we shall see, therefore,
that a third factor should be introduced in the outline, the first two being the static self and the
world. The dynamic self is the third factor, and
without such a third factor I do not see how we
could make out any of the relations indicated. If
you had never known other than two colors, black

and white, you could not determine their color-
relation to one another. Any two things are in
some way related; the relation between no two
things can be determined in terms of the things
without a third. If you stand before the human
world with all its groups of people, divisible
millions of ways, merely as a static self, your relation to whole or groups can never be made out in
your own thought. As a matter of fact, if you do
not become dynamic, if you never *do* anything, you
have no relation to that world on your part. You
are then a mummy. The moment you *do something the circuit of relation closes :* the world has
become related to you and now is related, and you
are thus in conscious relation to the world. *The
study of self in business relations is,* therefore, *a
study of self static and self dynamic.*

§ 22. The study of the static self cannot be
carried on independently, however, of the dynamic
self, for *you can only know yourself through self-
action made a subject of observation.* The media for
such observation are your sensations, your consciousness and its changing contents, or the
sum-total of your mental activities and their
changes, and what we call your own powers, as the
senses, memory, imagination, reason, will, feeling,
intelligence, etc., together with certain general
characteristics, as habits, tendencies, temperament,
and the like. The aim here is suggestiveness
rather than perfect analysis.

§ 23. All these media are simply ways you
have of doing, and it is the doing—within and as
revealed within—which discloses the static self.
that is, induces the inference that the latter truly

exists. You cannot see the static self, feel it, objectively touch it or hear it, know it directly in any manner. What you know about it directly is action of various kinds. Nevertheless, the expressing ways that action takes furnish opportunity for study of the self which acts. This is vastly important. If one in business must understand other people with reasonable clearness, he must certainly understand in a similar way what manner of person himself is. *There can be no intelligent adjustment of self to others unless the self is in some fair degree understood in its own apprehension.*

§ 24. It is the static self—the self acting upon the self and so acting within rather than objectively —which must deliberate on the matter of adjustment and decide the same, and it is the dynamic self that must carry out such decision in the actual adjustment. If you think of the self within as a theatre for all sorts of activities and as controlling, eliminating, choosing these activities and determining which of them shall express in action, manifesting the latter outwardly, you will have the idea suggested at the beginning of this paragraph. *Business adjustment means the legitimate mastery of others for the sake of business.* But how shall a man master others who cannot master himself? And how can one master himself if he knows not the general character of self?

§ 25. You are therefore urged to discover what manner of person your static self really is. This end is accomplished through persistent study of the dynamic self—the self in action, or the self as acting outwardly, engaging, of course, such inner activities as you can detect. The purpose of such

study is practical, involving not only knowledge of
your own abiding personality with regard to its
business worth, but also its improvement for
greater value in your business capacity.   In a
general way the work may be outlined with various
tables, such, for example, as are given below.   The
tables will illustrate what one can do in the field of
self discovery and improvement, and of course have
no value unless the reader endeavors to put himself into them, or uses them as suggestions stimulating effort on his own part.

TABLES FOR STUDY OF SELF.

Table A.   Fundamental Conditions and Kinds of—

(1) Body as House........Ideal....Faults..Improvement
(2) Body as Instrument..Ideals... Faults..Improvement
(3) Mind as Instrument..Ideal....Faults..Improvement
(4) Temperament.........Ideal....Faults..Improvement
(5) Disposition.... ....Ideal....Faults..Improvement
(6) Tendencies ....Ideals... Faults..Improvement
(7) Habits................Ideals... Faults..Improvement
(8) Tastes....... ....Ideals... Faults..Improvement
(9) Morals................Ideals... Faults..Improvement
(10) Will ....Ideals... Faults..Improvement
(11) Emotions....... ....Ideals... Faults..Improvement

It is suggested that the table just given be
drawn out on a large sheet of paper and filled in
by the reader to show his conception of the ideals,
his faults in the respects indicated, and items of
possible improvement.   And let it be remembered
that the work I seek to inspire is exactly the kind
of work which the successful business man desires
to accomplish in his own establishment—a study of
ideals, of faults and of improvements thus suggested.   It is surely as important to devote the
same sort of effort to the main function in your

business, yourself, as it is to expend thought and energy upon the business itself. As examples of what may be done with the table, certain pertinent questions are now supplied:

Questions. Is your *body* in sound health? Is your thought concerning health a constant assumption of vigor and harmony, and does your care of the body correspond? Is the body, regarded as an instrument, sufficiently muscular, supple, alert, enduring, and efficient? Are your *senses* keen, swift, skilful? Is your *memory* retentive and comprehensive? Is your *imagination* large and vivid? Are your *logical powers* rapid and correct? Is your *temperament* master of you, or do you mould it by your *will?* Is your *disposition* cheerful, hopeful, courageous, confident? Are your *tendencies* ideal or indifferent or bad? Are your *habits* conducive to health of body, soundness of mind, elevation of morals, and expansion of business? Are your *tastes* refined but not finicky, ideal and yet practical? Are your *morals* open to the noblest friends you have? Is your *will* reasonable and strong and symmetrical? Are your *emotions* wild horses or controlled activities of a person whose ideals are elevated above his ambitions and so modify the latter? *Business power banks on highest human character.* I repudiate the notion that business is to be conducted merely as business, with every other value in life to go to the dogs. But, whether or no, the above questions have downright importance to pure business.

It is, moreover, heresy against self that a man must not frankly acknowledge his own virtues. It is a worse heresy against self when one will not squarely confront his own faults. Your business wants more power. Why not get it?

§ 26. *Table B. Basic Thought-Attitudes Toward*

(1) Man in General...Critical?...Indifferent?...Friendly?
(2) Any Named Groups Recalled
                Critical?...Indifferent?...Friendly?
(3) Specific Groups Touching Your Life
                Critical?...Indifferent?...Friendly?
(4) Any Named Individuals......Indifferent?...Friendly?

Questions. Does the habit of *criticism* give you a successful relation to people for business? Does it add to your comfort and welfare? Is not the attitude of *indifference* a postively negative thing in business? Is not *friendliness* better for blood and business in every nameable way? Do you know that your *thought-and-feeling attitude* toward people, groups, individuals, sooner or later telepathically (in some way) reveals itself to others? Do you know that the *habit* of criticising people tells them at last through an unseen telephone line what you think about them? Do you know that friendliness carries to them from time to time messages which are great business-getters? Do you know that a great bulk of the world's business is directed by purely personal likes and dislikes? Are your attitudes toward people inspired by mere personal motives or conditions, or by down-on-the-ground business principles?

§ 27. *Table C. Expression of Attitude in Business Action. The Opposite Poles.*

(Attitude)	(Attitude)
(1) Vigorous?	(1) Weak?
(2) Calm?	(2) Nervous?
(3) Controlled?	(3) Spasmodic?
(4) Even?	(4) Fickle?
(5) Rapid?	(5) Slow?
(6) Decisive?	(6) Uncertain?

(Expression)		(Expression)	
(7)	Agreeable ?	(7)	Repelling ?
(8)	Confident ?	(8)	Doubtful ?
(9)	Courageous ?	(9)	Fearful ?
(10)	Faithful ?	(10)	Unreliable ?
(11)	Honorable ?	(11)	Tricky ?
(12)	Practical and large ?	(12)	Small and destructive ?

Observe. The list is a set of interrogations directed toward the reader, and meaning: Is your manifested attitude in action toward people any or all the characteristics on the left or on the right hand of the page? If you represent in any way the right hand of the page, you are surely lacking in business power.

§ 28. You are invited, now, to subject Table A to the criticism of Table C. In Table A we have the great factors of the static self,—the real self,— while in Table C we have the qualities of action and personality through which the static self dynamically expresses. Table B also expresses the static self—your own private attitudes toward people, and Table C represents a choice which the reader is to make in regard to the expression of those attitudes.

§ 29. Now, one can always wear a mask, and so conceal the real self, but this is not necessarily the best business method. It is infinitely preferable to cultivate those qualities of the static and dynamic self which one would willingly blazon before the world. Business to-day knows that such qualities really make for better business. *The thing a business man should be, first, middle, and last, is just—a great, splendid man.* This book does not belittle the function of business in the world's life. You are therefore invited to give the above tables genuine and practical attention.

Knowledge of Human Nature.

§ 30. Having worked our way thus far
through an immense subject, business relations,
we have now graphically to portray the divisions
indicated in Section 8 of this chapter. What I
have said about the static self and the dynamic
self must again be brought to the fore. The static
self, we remember, always stands behind the
dynamic self, and the latter always stands *between
the static self and individuals and groups of the
people.* To show this fact, and to indicate how
surely every human is in some way related to all
others, variously, directly or indirectly, I have
drawn the following diagrams. These illustrations
are not mere curiosities; they are designed for the
closest study, with the view always of understanding your business relations, and of improving your
personality and action in such relations.

Diagrams of Business Relations.

§ 31. We may first suggest the subject in
general by the universal diagram.

I. *Diagram of the Universal Relation:*
(The order of thought is—static self—dynamic self—
people.)

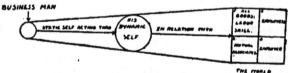

Thus, the business man adjusts the static self
through the dynamic self to—

(1) *All the people,* directly or indirectly, for
service by labor, skill and goods;

(2) *Mutual associates* in equal *superior* positions;

(3) Various other *employees;*

(4) Various employers or *superiors.*

The problem of adjustment is always individual, either in the sense of individual groups or in that of single persons. This important fact will be brought out specifically in later sections.

With such general survey in mind, we now proceed to its particular analysis.

§ 32. II. *The Business Man Related To—*
(The order of thought is—static self *through* dynamic self *to* people.)

(1) Whole *Mass* of People;

(2) *Groups* Wanting Your *Goods* (service) Directly;

(3) Groups Wanting *Results* of Your Service;

(4) Groups *Reached By Your Business;*

(5) Groups *Yet To Be Reached;*

(6) Sellers *Directly* To You;

(7) Sellers *Indirectly Affecting You;*

(8) Others: Bankers, Attorneys, Physicians; all specialists.

SERVICE BY GOODS, LABOR, SKILL.
ALL THE PEOPLE.

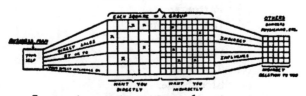

Larger+ =groups you reach.
Larger ☐=groups to reach.
Smaller ☐=groups to affect you.

Questions. The significant questions are three: How to increase the number of individuals in the sales-groups marked $+$? How to reach and affect groups not buying, or not in direct relation with you, and bring the nearer groups more completely into relation with your business, and the remoter or less affected groups more directly into such relation ? How to make the qualities listed on the left-hand of the page in Section 27, "*Expression Of Attitude In Action,*" tell more perfectly in the endeavor to answer the above questions?

§ 33. The only method by which the diagram and these questions may be practicalized is that of study of yourself in your own business relations, and heroic persistence in seeking sure personal improvement. I can visit Boston any business day and in two hours list a score or more of people in business to whom the resolute application of the diagram No. II, would mean absolutely certain promotion or greater success. It is just a question of the *Alert-Initiative-Magnetic Personality multiplying self, work and business into any situation.*

§ 34. III. *The Business Man Related To—*
(The order of thought is—static self *through* dynamic self *to* people.)

    (1) Partners;
    (2) Incorporators;
    (3) Co-operators;
    (4) Directors;
    (5) Trustees;
    (6) Stockholders;
    (7) Members of associations, etc.

§ 35. In this diagram we have *conditional equality;* that is, if you are a partner, or a co-operator, or a director, or a member of an association, say of a business man's association, or of an exchange, and so on, your equality with any other

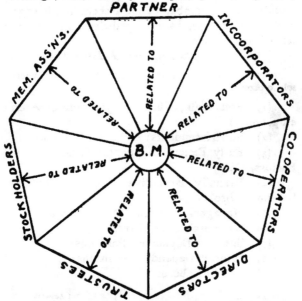

person in your group depends on your investment, duties, agreed privileges, appointment, and any similar item. But, whether or no, *your dynamic self stands between you and all other persons in the group you represent, and your dynamic-partner-self, or dynamic-trustee-self, or dynamic-director-self, stands between your static self and all people outside of your group whom you in your function or business affect*. These are the business relations which you now sustain as an occupant of one of the given positions. Here again, then, appear the meaning

and value of *"Expression Of Attitude In Action,"*
(Section 27).   The ideal business partner, incor-
porator, co-operator, director, associate, trustee,
stockholder or member of an association, is represented, of course, by the qualities listed on the
left of that section.

§ 36.   IV. *The Employer Related To—*

(The order of thought is—static self *through* dynamic
self to people.)

(1) Presidents; (The employer is one of several
employers.)

(2) Superintendents: General; Limited;

(3) Fully Executive Agents: Foreign Heads,
Factors, etc.;

(4) Partially Executive Agents: Traveling
Salesmen, Brokers, etc.;

(5) Managers: General; Departmental;

(6) Commission Merchants;

(7) Superior Dependent Positions;

(8) Inferior Dependent Positions;

(9) Casual Laborers.

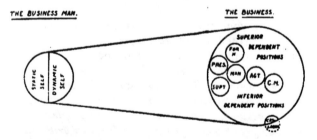

This diagram represents business relations of
various kinds as follows (put *yourself* in small
circle. Think of any one—P.—F.H.—S. etc., there):

(1), The business man as an employer related to any of the functions indicated—Presidents, Managers, Etc.

(2) The business man in any function related to his " Head."

(3) The business man in any function related to various associates,—equal, superior, inferior.

But always business power calls for the great qualities listed at the left in Section 27 under the heading, *"Expression of Attitude in Action."* When the static self embraces those qualities and expresses them in a very high degree in the dynamic self, we have the executive who knows how to handle free men and retain them in his own interest because he successfully appeals to their personal interests. In the measure in which this ability is exhibited are you graded in the business world, from casual laborer possessing none of the ability (that is, in that function), through inferior dependent people exhibiting little of it, through managers, agents, and the like, more largely capable, and on to the great executive leaders in world-covering finance. You are invited to look into the diagram and run over the listed positions, having in mind these.

Question. How can I develop and employ the qualities on the left of Section 27 for the purpose of advancement to a superior rank? And if you are an employer in the relations indicated, remember that your static self must possess the qualities suggested and must manifest them in action toward those whom you employ and the general public in order to the greatest and most permanent success. If this be so, the question, *How*, is again pertinent.

§ 37.   V.   *The Employee Related To—*
(The order of thought is—static self *through* dynamic
self to employer.)

- (1)   The Employer;
- (2)   The Superintendent;
- (3)   The Manager;
- (4)   Associates in General;
- (5)   Associates in Groups of Employees;
- (6)   Associates in Your Own Group;
- (7)   The General Public;
- (8)   The Public Group You Serve.

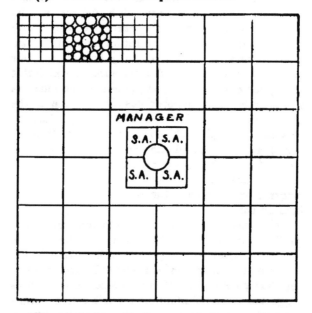

The circle in central square is any employee—
yourself—in your work. The four-framed square
is your particular department. The next square

inclosing this is any head employee as head above you. The larger outside squares are groups of employees. The small squares and circles are associates in departments. Squares in the central square are your immediate associates; that is, associates in your group: special associates indicated by S. A.

The further treatment of this phase of business relations must be deferred to the next chapter, as it demands altogether too much space for the present. We can here merely revert again to the list of qualities given in Section 27, left hand, as absolutely indispensable to business power and success. As an employee, then, you are invited to make sure that your attitudes toward the people named in the above diagram manifest in action all those golden characteristics to which attention is now called. They stand invariably for golden power.

We come, now, to the most important phase of the practicalization of business relations—

ADJUSTMENT TO HUMAN NATURE.

§ 38. The task of personal adjustment is great and imperative, and it is one which is frequently left to the chance of vague impressions and haphazard experience. The study before us should be taken intelligently in hand by every man or woman engaged in business of any sort. Business is a matter of relations, and relations are realized by practical attitudes. The right attitude toward any person requires a knowledge, first, of his peculiar type, and secondly, of his individual variety as exhibiting weaknesses, strong points, tastes, tendencies, habits, etc. (see Section 25). I do not know any work on human science in general. There are works on Phrenology, Physiognomy, Graphology, Palmistry, and the like, but I rather question their actual practical value—unless one can make them pronounced specialties. Still, a study of such works can do no harm, perhaps, and may suggest many important considerations if mental balance is preserved meanwhile. In the main, however, one must trust to thoughtful observation and observed personal experience for knowledge of men and women and the best adjustments to their countless peculiarities. Some people are good intuitive readers of human nature, while to others every specimen is a brand new problem. Business power takes advantage of the native talent, but just as surely seeks to develop a power of understanding which is not given by natural endowment. For our present purposes the following suggestions are offered:

A—First Suggestion in Character Reading: Determination of Individual Cases. As every business transaction is complete in itself, so in every business transaction you are dealing with an individual who must be selected out of all general human nature and be regarded as a specific instance, to be dealt with, so far as possible, on that basis. It will not do to assume anything of a broad human character concerning him, nor to deal with him on general principles, for he is not a general principle, but is rather a *specific variation of some type*. A knowledge of human nature is, of course, vastly useful here, but, so far as it is possible, every man in actual or prospective relation to your business must be studied individually and handled for what he happens to be at any moment. This rule is universal and fundamental.

§ 39. It should always be remembered that the scheme of personal adjustments involves certain processes of determination. Our question is, How to address self through the dynamic phase of it to all sorts of people in all sorts of business relations under all sorts of circumstances? *The fundamental principle is that of constant and particular appeal to individual self-interest.* This and the subordinate principles will now be stated. It is impracticable to go more minutely into details.

FUNDAMENTAL PRINCIPLE OF PERSONAL ADJUSTMENT (1) UNCEASING AND INTELLIGENT APPEAL TO SELF-INTEREST.

Subordinate Principle—(2) Each person means to you a self, static and dynamic, which controls its life in the same sense and more or less with the same ability which are true in your own case. In other words, each individual is a human being. He must be treated as such.

Subordinate Principle—(3) Each individual has certain characteristics peculiar to his race. He is, let us say, an American, and of the United States; or he is an Englishman, or a Frenchman, and so on. You have to deal with him on that basis.

Subordinate Principle—(4) Many individuals manifest certain traits peculiar to a section or a state or a country. The man is, say, a New Englander, a Bostonian, a New Yorker, a St. Louisian, a Devonshire man, and thus on. Some New Englanders prefer the round-about method in business dealings; some Westerners wish to come directly

to the matter in hand; some Bostoners insist on
deliberation; some New Yorkers decide questions
on the instant; some Devonshire men are frankly
pernickety or insistent on particulars for the general good.   All sections represent favorite idols and
prejudices.   You have to ascertain these factors
and adjust to them—on the basis of the individual's
self-interest.   Always is it law that your own self-
interest must not appear to override the other self-
interest.

Subordinate Principle—(5) Each individual is
peculiar to himself.   No two of us are alike.   The
items given in Section 25 are broad lines in which
personal characteristics exhibit.   The individual
must not be handled merely as human, or an
American, or a New Englander, etc., but as one
special individual, precisely as you, whatever you
are in larger aspects, are one specific individual
requiring treatment as such.   Your man must be
treated as exactly the person before you—quick,
slow, easy, irritable, honest, crafty, having this or
that strong point, weakness, fad, identifying trait,
and so on, and so on.

Subordinate Principle — (6) Each individual
varies from time to time in his moods, and the
man who presented no difficulty yesterday may
seem impossible to-day.   All the above principles
now come in play, together with the present—that
the man must be dealt with, not as he ought to be,
not as he has been or is likely to be, *but precisely
as he is just here and now.*   You can reach him only
through self-interest (in business), and you must
come to that through your knowledge or intuition
of what he is at the present moment, *through* his

present mood, in *spite* of it, or by *changing it* to normal or better.

Subordinate Principle—(7) Each business situation is unique, just itself, and dealings with the same individual under conditions which in general duplicate others must frequently confront unexpected variations in circumstances. Some such variations in the usual situation make immediate business impossible, and attempted adjustment now means friction and failure. In other cases, you must adjust to the individual through the present situation, in spite of it, or by changing it.

Of course, any adequate *specific* directions are here impracticable, demanding, in fact, a library on human science, and we must content ourselves with general suggestions only. Nothing can take the place of personal experience and observation.

Subordinate Principle—(8) Every business transaction involves immediate adjustment to the peculiar individual before you—as he now is, under the present circumstances, in the present peculiar situation. The thing is like a game of chess, in which the pieces constantly shift, and *every identical move must be made for itself with reference to the goal.*

For a graphic presentation of these principles, I append the following diagram:

DETERMINATION FOR DIRECT PERSONAL ADJUSTMENT.

You get the case to its lowest present terms.

B—Second Suggestion in Character Reading:
Serving Yourself Through Self-Interest of
Others. You are invited to re-examine Section 25,
and to fix the idea in mind that human nature
expresses its greater characteristics along certain
main lines. You stand, the static self, confronting
the people, and the question of business is, How
shall I adjust or address myself toward each individual with whom I come in contact for successful
business transactions? You are seeking self-interest,
but not selfishness. Every person you meet is also
seeking self-interest, and, perhaps, selfishness as
well. You must address yourself to the individual
in such a way that *your self-interest* (or the interest
of the business you are in) *shall be served by his
self-interest, or his selfishness.* These factors in
him may at the time be specifically active—he may
want something; or you may need to awaken the
factors in some definite form in his thought or feeling. When both of you want in regard to some
one thing, the adjustment required is an agreement.
To bring about this adjustment in agreement, you
must know your man. Since you cannot put
people into glass cases for leisurely study, you
must cultivate the ability to get at men and women
on the instant. This demands a general understanding of human nature and the power to "size
up" individuals as you meet them. Hence the
further suggestions.

C—Third Suggestion in Character Reading:
Observation of Personal Characteristics. It is
impossible, of course, to indicate all the chief
characteristics of human nature. The following
points, however, are offered as a study in practicali-

zation of business relations. The main things to be noted would seem in part at least to be about as given below.

§ 40. *Main Lines for Study and Adjustment.*

(1) *Body:* Health. Size and Weight. Appearance. Soul.

(2) *Carriage:* Erect. Limp. Alert. Sluggish. Steady, Jerky. Etc.

(3) *Organs:* Eyes. Hearing. Hands. Touch. Etc.

(4) *Dress:* Ordinary. Careful. Slouchy. Wealthy-Feeling. Etc.

(5) *Mind:* Weak. Mediocre. Strong. Educated. Uneducated. Etc.

(6) *Temperament:* Dull. Decided. Shrewd. Narrow. Broad. Critical. Etc.

(7) *Disposition:* Commonplace. Poetic. Practical. Happy. Morose. Etc.

(8) *Tendencies:* Health. Rush. Dally. Absent-Minded. Worry. Close. Etc.

(9) *Condition:* Prosperous. Medium. Poor. "Down."

(10) *Habits:* Good. Bad. Careless. Peculiarities.

(11) *Tastes:* Refined. Quiet. Coarse. Showy. Particulars.

(12) *Strong Points:* To coincide with or avoid.

(13) *Weak Points:* To take legitimate advantage of.

(14) *Hobbie and Fads:* To use in a legitimate way.

(15) *Positive Faults:* To ignore or pass around (in business).

(16) *Likes and Dislikes:* To cater to honorably ; not to disturb.

(17) *Connections:* Not to criticise ; to make concessions to.

(18) *Politics:* Not to antagonize ; to make concessions to.

(19) *Religion:* Not to antagonize ; to respect ; to use honorably.

The above outline of trait-pointers is suggestive only. You are urged to improve it.

§ 41. In the meantime it will be helpful to make a list of the people one knows, and to write their names and the trait-pointers on large cards, then proceeding to fill in the outline according to the facts. Such a method cultivates definiteness of knowledge and stimulates the mind to further discoveries. But a danger connected with this study should be avoided. Many people are satisfied with what may be called practical knowledge without making application of it to every-day affairs. *The practicalisation of the instruction here given requires persistent attempts to bring the suggestions to bear actually upon the business in which you are engaged.*

D—Fourth Suggestion in Character Reading. It will prove of great value if you will observe the above suggestions with yourself as subject—divided as the static and the dynamic self: the self you feel behind all expression, and the self as manifested.

E—Fifth Suggestion in Character Reading. Adjustment, to be of utility, must be practical. Knowledge of the people may be all theory, in which case it has no business importance. Its practical application to life requires some imaginative prevision for practice and a good deal of thought and concrete action in real affairs. The present suggestion, then, is two-fold:

§ 42. (1) You are invited to practice imagining the best thing to do under given conditions when meeting such and such known people. This effort will assist in developing adjusting ability for unforeseen and all sorts of other conditions.

(2) You are invited to *cultivate* the following characteristics in yourself under all circumstances, with the purpose of getting on the "good side" of people—legitimately and for right business ends:

(a) Agreement with opinions and tastes in some possible respects.

(b) Tactful change of conversation when you cannot agree.

(c) Self-possession under all circumstances.

(d) Patience with the most irritable.

(e) Calmness of manner free from provoking elements.

(f) Quietness of voice and body.

(g) The friendly smile and the frank look.

(h) Respectfulness of attitude toward all classes and kinds.

(i) Interest in the person now dealt with.

(j) The countenance controlled always.

(k) The spirit of fair (not overdone) conciliation.

(l) Appeals to self-interest as entirely legitimate.

(m) Sympathy, indicated if not expressed, where called for.

(n) A feeling that you are sure to please the other person.

(o)   Commendation, of those met, and of their friends.

(p)   Tolerations for opinions, tastes, errors, etc.

(q)   Intuitive knowledge of the self under appearance.

(r)   The atmosphere of unostentatious equality.

(s)   Confidence in bringing the other person your way.

(t)   The business atmosphere of assured business.

(u)   Specific attention to the person and thing in hand.

§ 43.   You are invited to study *avoidance* of the following characteristics in yourself under all circumstances, with the view of keeping as well as getting on the " good side " of people—legitimately and for right business ends:

(a)   Agreement so constant as to awaken suspicion.

(b)   Sudden and provoking conversational changes.

(c)   The calm patience which suggests the wearied superior person.

(d)   The kind of patience that advertises the martyr.

(e)   Quietness and calmness indicating indifference.

(f)   Undue friendliness, or familiarity too free.

(g)   Close and prolonged inspection of the person.

(h)   Attention so close and persistent as to suggest watching.

(i) The countenance controlled with evident effort.

(j) Conciliation excessive, indicating weakness or a desire to influence.

(k) Egotistic assurance that the other person must be pleased.

(l) Obstreperous attempts at pleasing.

(m) Commendation overdone, and of your man's enemies.

(n) The appearance of make-believe sympathy.

(o) Excessive appeals to self-interest inspiring suspicion.

(p) The toleration which suggests insincerity.

(q) Obsequiousness and respect only veiling contempt.

(r) Affectation of equality of the other man in an irritating way.

(s) A business atmosphere intolerant of anything else.

(t) Attention to one so close that others feel neglected.

§ 44. And now we bring our study, altogether too great for adequate treatment, to a close with the following:

GOLDEN LAWS OF BUSINESS ADJUSTMENT.

Law of Confidence. So adjust yourself to all whom you meet in business relations that you infallibly win the respect, confidence, and friendliness of every reasonable mind.

Law of Business Influence. So adjust yourself to all who come into practical relations with you that you surely influence them your way for business purposes in their own interest and your own.

Law of Continuity. In all business relations and adjustments remember the high requirements of the long-run business. You want every person to come your way as often and for as long as may be possible for mutual benefit.

Law of Mutuality. In all business adjustments to individuals or concerns, make your business self-interest really conducive to at least the proper self-interest of those whom you serve.

Law of Business Character. In all adjustments make the personal methods of your business conducive to the assured honor of your own character.

Law of Individuation. In all adjustments with concerns, treat them as individuals according to these laws.

Law of Business Inter-dependence. In all adjustments to the business community or world, remember that to destroy any legitimate business is to hurt the field of your own effort. Recent (1907) financial developments and social movements are demonstrating the truth of this law, notwithstanding the complacency and assumed wisdom with which it has been violated by great magnates whose selfishness has surely blinded their business vision.

Law of Business Humanity. All business adjustments to human nature should be conducted on the basis that you and your friends and competitors are altogether human. Business is never war save when it is " hell." And I respectively submit that hell is not business.

CHAPTER VI.

PERSONAL REQUIREMENTS.

OUR goal in this chapter is Psychic Income. "We define subjective (psychic) income as the stream of consciousness of any human being," remarks Professor Fisher. "All his conscious life, from his birth to his death, constitutes his subjective income. Sensations, thoughts, feelings, volitions, and all psychical events, in fact, are a part of this income stream. All these conscious experiences which are desirable are positive items of income, or services; all which are undesirable are negative items, or disservices." The business man should keep two sets of books, one for the physical income, and one (in his self-observing mind) for the psychic income. The physical income of highest value is *net*; and the real income, psychically considered, is also *net above all personal disqualifications*. You are invited to study this chapter with the thought thus presented incessantly in mind. Remember the net psychic income!

§ 1. In every phase of practical life certain personal requirements, in addition to the main considerations already given, become imperative if

effort is to be crowned with success. These requirements concern body, dress, personal style, language,
character, self-mastery, business conduct, and
savings or increase of capital.

§ 2.   The factors enumerated represent, on the
one hand, success-assets, but imply, on the other
hand, all the handicaps of a lack of capital.   If you
were to capitalize yourself, so to speak, that is,
try to ascertain your capital worth, or your income
worth, the items would be (a) your static self, (b)
the acting expression thereof through your dynamic
self, which means simply the factors named above
in Section 1, (c) your experience, with corresponding judgment (practical ability), (d) the
probability of your life-term, and (e) the money
you can now command.   But the capitalization
would take into account the weakness of your
static self, the faults of your dynamic expression (the
personal faults), the impractical character of your
judgment, the likelihood of failure of your experience to instruct, and the opportunities you have
had.   Capitalization of self, in the sense here indicated, asks : *What kind of business man ought this one
to be, at his time of life, with his experience, with the
opportunities he has had, with the money he has used,
with such and such abilities as he evidently possesses?*
And invariably the man as he actually is comes
into comparison with the answer.   The business
world is forever weighing—What is the man's
present worth?   But always, in this weighing process, personal requirements appear imperative and
insistent.

§ 3.   Now, this matter of personal requirements brings into play in our thought what may

well be called *psychic bookkeeping*. Ordinary bookkeeping, in representing a firm's financial condition,
takes into account the assets and the liabilities,
setting down for the assets the capital, surplus,
and undivided profits, and for the liabilities noting
the debts and other obligations owing to others. In
an exhaustive statement of capital summation, the
assets ought to include the business man himself, for
oftentime, when capital is wholly swept away, the
assets of the man to himself are so greatly estimated
by the public that the capital he needs is immediately
placed at his disposal. This capital element, the
man, calls for the psychic bookkeeping referred to
above.

PSYCHIC BOOKKEEPING.

§ 4. In this form of capital account we have
psychic capital and its increase on the one hand, and
what may be called *psychic charges*, including faults,
weaknesses, various tendencies, and habits of all
sorts. The business man should summarize his
condition psychically considered by offsetting
against his "capital" all "liabilities" or charges of
a psychic nature.

§ 5. In regard to ordinary bookkeeping, "the
object of a conservative business man in keeping
his books is not to give mathematical accuracy,"
says Professor Irving Fisher, of Yale University,
in "*The Nature of Capital and Income*," but to make
so conservative a valuation as to be well within the
market, even in times of financial stress. He is
more interested in safety than in precision, and in
maintaining his solvency even in the face of heavy
shrinkage of market values than in meeting the
requirements of ideal statistics."

§ 6. But any general capital account of a concern will be made up from two points of view: That of the concern, giving the actual bookkeeper's figures, and that of the public, based on outside estimate of the concern's "earning power." Professor Fisher illustrates: "The Second National Bank of New York had, at a recent statement, a total capital, surplus and undivided profits, of $1,295,952.59, of which the original capital was only $300,000. We should expect, therefore, that the stock certificates, amounting to $300,000, would be $1,295,952.59, or, in other words, that each $100 of stock certificates would be worth $432. The actual selling price, however, is found to be $700." The difference in figures represents the public estimate of the concern's earning power.

§ 7. In psychic bookkeeping the business man, whether clerk or employer, messenger boy or president, estimates the capital value of himself and his abilities as he may. But there is usually some discrepancy between this estimate and that of the public. The latter may be less or greater than the former. If less, the fact is evident in one way or another, and can be discovered. The man who keeps books with himself ought to ascertain why the public estimate of himself is less than his own. He will find the trouble somewhere among "personal requirements." If the public estimate is greater than the man's, it is a psychic law of financial success that the individual must keep his own counsel in the matter and permit the public ignorance to continue. *Do not belittle yourself in confidence with others.* He who in thought discounts his abilities suggests to the subjective self depreciation of value as a fact. He who insists on his own worth and tries to "make good," inspires self and breeds confidence in others. But if the public estimate of a man's business value is really greater than that of the man himself, the fact will almost always, if not quite always, come out in advancement to positions of larger responsibility. It does not seem that one need entertain very refined scruples in the matter.

§ 8. Remembering, now, this difference between the world's psychic account of yourself and your own account, *it is the public estimate which must be kept constantly in mind*, so far as business success which depends on the public is concerned. Your psychic *assets* are what *you are*, with what the *people think you are*, so that your great task consists in making others think you are tremendously worth while to them. There are three ways of doing this: (a) by *being* worth while, (b) by conscious deception, (c) by deception unconscious. The first method is safe, and it insures financial reward and your own psychic satisfaction. The second method is always in the long run discovered, and means financial defeat and psychic distress. The third method is harmless so long as it signifies honest effort to be of real value in business. If the effort fails, or if it lags, the public eventually uncovers the actual facts in the case. In the final outcome we are all fairly estimated by those who know us. The first method, then, is alone safe and soundly bankable.

THREE GREAT PRINCIPLES IN PSYCHIC BOOKKEEPING.

§ 9. Psychological bookkeeping with self reveals three interesting features:

First Feature. In many instances a *single wrong factor*—fault or deficiency—*more than offsets a sum-total of assets which would otherwise insure success.* Always do the former items count more rapidly in the long run against a man than items of the better nature count for him,—unless it is evident that he is genuinely striving to overcome the offset. If such is the case, the psychic capitalization may remain uncertain for a time; the improving effort must demonstrate itself; then a period follows in which present worth tends to rise; and finally it reaches a pretty steady level.

§ 10.   Psychic bookkeeping works itself out in this way. On the left hand of the page we in imagination place the items, *labor, time, discipline, weariness and pain* of the self considered within the sphere of self; on the other side we place the *work accomplished,* and a *score or more of additional values.*

Second Feature. Now, in this account you *do not credit any improvement with labor,* etc.; *you charge yourself with such items*—although people are constantly engaged in doing exactly the reverse: they give themselves credit for labor, discipline, pains endured, and so on. But these items are all outgo, and should be charged to Improvement or to Life. Moreover, in this account you *do not charge Improvement with work,* for work is a psychic income; but *you credit the item as an asset.* It is an error to confuse labor with work. Labor is effort, weariness, etc., so far as self is concerned. Work is what is done by the effort, so far as the world is concerned, and, by so much as it is efficient, does it become an asset to self as well as to the world. If you dig a ditch for hire, you are paid, not for your labor, but for your work. When you pay the ditch-digger, you are not paying him for his labor (for what is his labor to you as an employer—in a business sense?), but for *the thing accomplished*. The man might labor most strenuously with hands and feet for a day or a week, and dig no ditch—do no real work. Only as his self-effort is projected into the world of actual values does it have pecuniary worth to you. Then it becomes work. Business means to pay only for work—and is quite indifferent to mere labor. This explains the fact that one man receives more pay for his "labor" than another: he does more real work (it may be, with less labor), accomplishes more of value, and is worth a larger remuneration. Precisely so is it in bookkeeping with self-improvement. Your labor, weariness, and the like items, merely concern effort, and are all outgo; while what you do, your work, concerns improvement, and is income. This brings us to the third interesting feature in psychological bookkeeping.

§ 11. *Third Feature.* When the account is made up in regard to the items indicated, we have, on the side of charges, labor, time, discipline, self-denial, weariness, and so on, and, on the side of credits—thus far—just work. But so far as efforts for improvement are concerned, *the work is always at least equal in value to all its cost*, because the charged items mean precisely the struggle for improvement. If, however, there has been no striving for improvement, the self-action in labor, and the pains and weariness, may have been very great, and the work is simply what it is, but that item is not as a matter of bookkeeping equal in value to the labor in cost, and may be considerably less. It is a psychic law that *practical determination for self-improvement offsets all cost of labor, pains and weariness in the multiplied returns which it insures.*

DEBITS AND CREDITS WITH SELF.

§ 12. The principle here suggested has an enormous inspirational value, and it is practically applicable to all departments in life. A good business illustration might be given in the following manner:

Any Successful Business.

DR.		CR.	
To Goods Bought in	x	By Goods in Stock	x
" Labor, time, skill	x	" Work	xy
" Running Expenses	x	" Gross Returns	xyz
	3x		3x2yz
		Credit Balance	2yz

In such an account, expense for goods is offset by goods added to stock (with sales value to appear in gross returns); labor, etc., are offset by work,—what is accomplished,—with an indefinite credit entry; and running expenses are offset by gross returns, with an indefinite surplus entry. The account shows success.

§ 13. *This surplus cash* and *psychic advance* on the completion of any period of business effort, *depends*, of course, *on business skill.* The goods-account item, for example, will not on the credit side offset the charge of cost if you have paid too much for the goods, or if the work-item has had less value in money than the labor-item in money, or if for any reason the market will not permit sales beyond goods-cost in money. In such a case the psychic credits drop, first in work, and secondly in satisfaction: both being negative, or *minus*. This fact shows how intimately the psychic factor is blended with the financial. Indeed, if there were no elements of psychic satisfaction concealed under the credit items of ordinary bookkeeping, business would fail out of the world. The expression: "I'm not in business for fun," is a curious misstatement; that is exactly what you *are* in business for—the "fun," the psychic satisfaction, defined in one way or another among ten thousand possibilities.

§ 14.   The simple axioms of business are thus assumed in our first bookkeeping illustration: *Buy the cheapest best goods; sell at a profit over all; look out for waste and leaks; hit your markets right; see to it that work always more than offsets labor and discipline.*

§ 15.   Let us expand the idea involved by representing the psychic account in the case of the divisions of business relations suggested in Section 8 of the preceding chapter. Take, for example, the account of employer with regard to services rendered by employees. This would stand, briefly stated, as follows:

Employment.

DR.		CR.	
To Labor & Expense		By Work	2x
(pains, etc.)	x	" Improvement	y
" Right Attitude Toward	x	" Spirit of Loyalty	z
		" Personal Advertise-	
		ment	&
	—		———
	2x		2xyz&

The psychic income is here blended with indefinite financial values, as, improvement, loyalty,
personal advertisement, but is necessarily a gross
income the value of which may be approximated by
asking the question: "What would I give for the
business with labor expense cut so and so and personal attitude toward employees reduced to lowest
terms?"   The expression, frequently heard, "I
wouldn't run my business as he does, wages and
treatment of his people, for twice his net income,"
tells the story.   If your business is successful, the
item of work cancels that of labor-expense, and the
remaining items on the right give you an indefinite
surplus over attitude toward your people. In other
words, you always have, or ought to have, work
over against labor-expense, and *all the psychic
values of the best handling of your employees as
credits against all charges*, which values are more
or less of a money return ultimately, if you are a
successful business employer. It is well to remember that the employer's handling of his people, to
their reasonable satisfaction, is as truly an evidence
of success as is any item of cash surplus on the
books.   The psychic factors cannot be kept out of
the account.   If the employer's attitude toward his
people is of a contrary character, he is actually
placing the psychic items on the wrong side of the
ledger: he is charging (weighing) his business with
an outgo that ought to be an income. This method
of illustration shows in the strongest manner the
value of purely personal factors in business.

§ 16. Or, take the case of the employee in
relation to the employer. The account will now
be stated in this fashion:

Self—Employee.

DR.			CR.	
To Item: Labor	x		By Work	3x
" Time	x		" Use of Skill	y
" Weariness	x		" Utilization of Time	z
			" Freedom from Responsibility	a
			" Improvement	b
			" Opportunity	c
			" Expectation	d
	3x			3xyzabcd

If the employee is striving to be worth his remuneration, as well as to receive the same, his wages or salary cancels labor, time, weariness, when he is fairly paid, and the remaining items on the right (which are here merely samples) are all "to the good" indefinitely. And the employee who declines to see the fact is simply mistaken. If he is not fairly paid, the fault is either his own or that of his employer, in which latter case the account stated in the preceding section needs correction by the employer, the principle still remaining true that the balance of psychic bookkeeping is always on the credit side if business is really successful or the worker is of the right sort, and from the psychic as well as the financial point of view. Assuming, however, that the inadequate wage or salary is the employer's fault the employee must take the responsibility either of insisting on better pay or of leaving the employ, or of compelling increased remuneration by improved service. As a general rule the business world does not underpay valuable men. The only person who can make you more valuable is yourself. When your value reaches a certain level, you can bring any employer to reasonable terms—but not until you really reach that level. The process by which such increase of value is secured is one which invariably *multiplies the credit* items, or intensifies them, in the above account. Look it over—on the right hand side of the statement. There is your opportunity. Here again personal requirements become imperative.

§ 17. Or, take the case of one who is engaged in a superior, or more or less independent, position, as, say, a superintendent, a manager, and the like. We have now a psychic account as illustrated below:

Superior Department of Service.

DR.			CR.	
To Item:	Time	x	By Work	6x
"	" Skill	x	" Occupation	y
"	" Labor	x	" Superior Position	z
"	" Weariness	x	" Confidence and Honor	a
"	" Responsibility	x	" Use of Skilled Ability	b
"	" Results of		" Large Ways of Living	c
	Hazard	x	" Society	d
			" Surplus over Expenses	e
			" Growth	f
			" Salary	xg
			" Expectation	h
		6x		7xyzabcdefgh

Here also we see that work alone—what one accomplishes—offsets all the items on the debit side, because work is the thing paid for,—paid for on the part of self by the debit items, and on the part of employer or public by salary. The assumption is, of course, that the work is worth the salary. When the salary is too large, that fact depreciates in psychic value every item on the credit side. When the salary is inadequate, the fault may be that of employer or public, but is usually one's own, in either of which cases the *psychic income to him who is striving steadily for greater improvement steadily advances in one way or another*, and the remedy consists in resigning for some other position, insisting on larger salary, or lifting value of self to a higher level compelling increase of remuneration. Always, however, whatever the *financial phase of the matter may be, within reason, the psychic income more than cancels the physical and psychic outgo when the individual persists in multiplying the best of himself into his work in the best improving way.* The man always has himself to reckon with on the credit side of the account. Personal requirements thus again come to the fore.

§ 18. If we desire to represent a general application of the principle given in Sections 9, 10 and 11, and just above, italics, a form like the following may be used:

Our Successful Business.

DR.		CR.	
To Item		By Work	5x
" Time of Self	x	Gross Returns	4x
" Labor, Weariness, etc.	x	Use of Skill	y
" Skill Given	x	Occupation	z
" Wear and Tear of Body	x	Sustenance	a
" Responsibility	x	Accumulation	b
		Development of Power	c
		Realized Ambition	d
" Investment	x	Enjoyment of Business	e
" Interest	x	Reputation	f
" Insurance	x	Growth of Self	g
" Other Expenses	x	Growth of Business	h
	9x		9xyzabcdefgh

(Personal: Time of Self, Labor Weariness etc., Skill Given, Wear and Tear of Body, Responsibility. Financial: Investment, Interest, Insurance, Other Expenses.)

Work (accomplishment of results) ought to be

worth what it costs in personal debits. The financial charges are more than offset by profits in the successful business. The success of business depends on personal requirements of the character to conquer environment. The psychic income is thus an indefinite surplus over all charges.

APPLICATION OF THE ILLUSTRATIONS.

§ 19. And thus with all other phases of business relations. The general principle indicated always obtains. It is understood, of course, that the illustrations do not pretend to precise accuracy in the use of symbols or in listing all items suggested by the bookkeeping, but that the design is merely to unfold the principle that psychic income is a real business factor dependent on fulfilment of, among other things, personal requirements of a peculiarly business character.

In Owen Wister's "*The Virginian*," the "hero" very aptly remarks: "It may be that those whose pleasure brings yu into this world owes yu a living. But that don't make the world responsible. The world did not beget you. I reckon man helps them that helps themselves. As for the Universe, it looks like it did too wholesale a business to turn an article out up to standard every time.

"The money I made easy that I *wasn't worth*, it went like it came. I strained myself none gettin' or spendin' it. But the money I made hard that I *was worth*, why, I began to feel right careful about that. And now I have got savings stowed away.

"Take my land away to-morrow, and I'd still have my savings in bank. Because, you see, I had to work right hard gathering them in. I found out what I could do, and I settled down and did it. Now you can do that, too. The only tough part is in finding out what you're good for."

Underneath[3] the words, "The money I made easy that I wasn't worth,"—"The money I made hard that I was worth," and—"Finding out what you're good for,"—we have one of the ideas involved in psychic bookkeeping. In this the question is always one of *personal worth offsetting all costs of attaining that worth.* "The money I made easy that I wasn't worth" represents a bad credit side opposite the debit side of labor, etc., while "The money I made hard that I was worth" represents a long list of psychic values accruing because of desire and determination for improvement. That is to say, the latter statement of the Virginian uncovers attention to valuable personal requirements which are absolutely indispensable to successful business.

I desire that the general principle of the foregoing account-illustrations may be given a very wide application. I am writing for young men and women who are determined to succeed, for clerks and employees of all sorts, but also for people in superior positions, for heads of concerns, co-partners, co-trustees, and so on. The principle is good for the whole business world. Personal qualifications are imperative, on the part of financial magnates no less than on the part of messenger boys and agents, and the psychic income by way of the development of such qualifications, together with many other credit items of a personal or psychic nature;—*this income always more than offsets all debit items,* if *the man and the business are really successful, each for each, and each* in *its own way.* This is simply a method for exhibiting the imperative necessity of a constant attention to the personal elements in the business man's life. And the greater the man, the more readily will be seen the pertinency of the attempts here given to illustrate and instruct.

PERSONAL REQUIREMENTS IN DETAIL.

Having suggested, then, the idea of debits and credits in account with self, always with a sharp eye on a surplus of some kind on the credit side, that is, on personal requirements essential to successful business effort, we now proceed to consider the latter factors in some detail.

§ 20. THE FIRST REQUIREMENT—BODY AT ITS BEST. Your body is your most important material machine, and, like all productive machinery, is subject to "wear and tear," and decay, and should be brought to and maintained in its best possible condition. One phase of "wear and tear," in the commercial sense, is "the depreciation of an article due to the fact that the services left for it to render gradually diminish." This depreciation may not be altogether due to physical injury by use, but may result from other causes decreasing value, as, for example, from the threat of better devises. *Your body's utility to you is measured by its approach to perfection, its enduring power, and the ease and completeness with which it responds to your will, all of which means, its actual efficiency and its ability to stand against the threat of other better bodies.* The call for merely younger bodies does not, as a general rule, I think, displace older men, having equal physical efficiency, and if it does in any case the crime is that of some fool business men. In order to maintain efficiency and hold the place which your body, in part, now secures you, the laws of physical health must be observed. Extended suggestions for health treatment cannot, of course, be here given, but what I may call the Ten Diamond Rules and the Ten Subjective Brilliants are absolutely imperative. These two sets of rules would have saved thousands of business men from physical disaster had they but given the body-instrument the indicated care that they insist upon for other machinery.

The Ten Diamond Rules.	*The Ten Subjective Brilliants.*
(1) Breathe Deeply.	(1) Eliminate Fear.
(2) Cleanse Channels.	(2) Conquer Worry.
(3) Drink Water Freely.	(3) Avoid Anger.
(4) Exercise Systematically.	(4) Omit Depression.
(5) Keep the Flesh Sweet.	(5) Shun Hate.
(6) Sleep Regularly.	(6) Study Cheerfulness.
(7) Live Simply.	(7) Cultivate Hope.
(8) Maintain Buoyancy.	(8) Develop Courage.
(9) Control Self.	(9) Exhibit Confidence.
(10) Think Health Yours.	(10) Assume Success.

Patience, persistence, and faith in self will in time give you full realization of the Diamond Rules and the Subjective Brilliants. If you compel your thought to co-operate with your practice, you will discover your mental sovereignty for best physical results. The world to-day has come into a great secret, *that mind exercises controllable power over body*, and the business man should hasten to take advantage of the new régime of suggestion, good cheer and conquering courage.

§ 21. If, now, we put the matter of physical values in the form of psychic bookkeeping, the sense of instruction or directions will be preserved, and at the same time our old principle will remain prominent: *to him who strives, credits are always greater than charges.* Thus, for the business man's body, we have an account as given below:

Physical Health.

DR.	CR.
To food, drink, clothing, shelter	By Renewal and Protection.
To Care of Body as a Machine.	By Improvement of Machine.
To Honor in Thought of Body.	By Psychic Uplift.
To Discipline of Sense Organs.	By Increased Abilities.
To Muscular Exercise.	By Physical Endurance.
To Preservation of Nerve Tone.	By Nervous Self-control.
To Attention to Carriage.	By Attractive Carriage.
To Sense of Physical Dignity Held.	By Personal Satisfaction.
To Physiological Purity.	By Psychical and Physical Power.
To Psychic Factor in Labor.	By Thought Command in Work.

A careful study of this account will indicate personal requirements of great importance, together with "income to the person" of immense value both to the individual and to all others in business relations with him. The question here is not merely one of health; it concerns personal assets to be estimated and paid for by the man himself and by others—in effort and in wages or salary. Whatever your business position may be, you must keep your body "good for *work*"—not merely labor;—and keeping it good for the very best kind of work means something more for you than it can mean for a horse or a made machine. You are a human, and your success depends on how efficiently you handle your machine, the body, in a first-class condition. Hence, it is psychic law that—

(1) You must honor your body by making habitual a sense of *personal dignity* too great for carelessness or immorality;

(2) You must bring your *muscles* to adequate efficiency in strength and suppleness for the work you have to do;

(3) You must secure the *nerve-tone* of perfect self-control;

(4) You must put thought of perfection into your physical exercise—by *putting your mind into the part exercised* when you exercise and maintaining at the same time the *idea of perfection;*

(5) You must think value actually into your work, by concentrating thought of the *ideal best* upon every effort made;

(It is law that no good work can be accomplished unless the worker loves his work or loves the best completeness that work can be given.)

(6) You must carry yourself as a gentleman or lady, and, therefore, must be what the *ideal carriage* indicates.

By so much as these requirements are observed, by so much, infallibly, will the psychic values shown on the credit side of the account at the beginning of this section become more and more in evidence.

People laugh at the man who is "fussy" about his body in the desire to make it a fine thing, it may be to the limit of Adonis, until he *shows up the man:* then these very niceties count always in his favor. Too many business men treat the body infamously, breaking down, of course, or regard with indifference the delicacy and sacredness of this piece of divine machinery, and slouch through to mediocre success or to dollars that are dollars only. In every instance the account shows up at last the threat of physical insolvency. Many a man is "down" because he has ignored his best and finest instrument—that marvelous thing in which he lives.

The Factor of Dress.

§ 22. The Second Requirement—Dress. "Of course, clothes don't make the man, but they make all of him except his hands and face during business hours. It isn't enough to be all right in this world; you've got to look all right as well, because two-thirds of success is making people think you are all right." If a man is puddling iron in a rolling mill, shoes and trousers fit the case. Nevertheless, the sense of satisfaction induced by the right kind of clean clothes appropriate to the occasion is a psychic factor which reacts in better work with most people. Some men can do their best only when they are dressed as they think they ought to be dressed. Behind the counter, in the office, on the road, this psychic satisfaction and its consequent reaction in work are values to be looked after, and are multiplied in worth by the additional factor of the right representation of business. In detail, the account would stand about thus for psychic bookkeeping:

Dress.

DR.	CR.
To Expense Within Income.	By Financial Satisfaction.
To Attention to Correctness.	By Correct Feeling.
To Study of Personal Taste.	By Avoidance of Criticism.
To Effort for Non-obtrusiveness.	By Quietness of Tone.
To Adjustment to Time, Place, etc.	By Appropriateness.
To Adaptation to People Met.	By Freedom of Address.
To Representation of the Business.	By Credit of the Business.
To Readiness for Work.	By General Utility.
To Cultivated Sense of Right Looks.	By Satisfaction and Ease.
To Study of Naturalness.	By Habit of Fitness.

This account summarizes in five things:

(1) Your satisfaction and improved efficiency;

(2) The impression of others—favorable but unobtrusive;

(3) A good representation of your business;

(4) The magnetic personal atmosphere, which is impossible with a sense of dress out of harmony with the situation;

(5) And readiness for the work you have in hand, the dress not unfitting therefor in rough labor, and having inspirational influence upon your feelings in cleaner positions.

PERSONAL STYLE.

§ 23. THE THIRD REQUIREMENT—PERSONAL STYLE. It is here that the "golden mean" holds especially good. Many extremes in this matter are studies for avoidance, as, for example, the pert and "sassy" style, the over-confident style, the coarse, brutal style, the very humble style, the "down-on-my-luck" style. The golden mean is a style that is natural to the man who is thoroughly conscious of honesty, of a sense of ability held in hand by a reasonable knowledge of limitations, and of a courage-confidence which is born of a will to do good work and honorably to succeed. In psychic bookkeeping the account may be stated thus:

Style of Personality.

DR.	CR.
To Expense Items	By Psychic Income and Surplus.
To Aim at Best First Impressions.	By Agreeable Reception.
To Control of Embarrassment.	By Self-Control and Freedom.
To Cure of Fear and its Signs.	By Air of Controlled Courage.
To Ignoring Ridicule.	By Indifference to Annoyance.
To Ignoring Overbearing People.	By Personal Superiority.
To Keeping Cool—Always.	By Mastery of Situation.
To Maintaining Quietness.	By Vital Force Conserved.
To Cultivating Even Inner Temper.	By Psychic Mastery and Power.
To Use of Mask of Reticence.	By Air of Strength; Secrets Safe.
To Right Use of Frankness.	By Friendliness Established.
To Expression of Good-Will.	By Magnetism Developed.
To Maintaining Courtesy.	By Business Made Easy.
To Preserving Magnetic Atmosphere.	By Winning Personality.
To Charging Same with Energy.	By Self and Others Inspired.
To Judicious Laughter.	By Buoyant Influence.
To Sympathetic Adaptation.	By Magnetism Developed in Use.

To Care Against Overdoing Art.	By Sincerity and Genuine Art.
To Cultivation of Sincere Eye.	By Magnetism Developed.
To Training of Persuasive Voice.	By Magnetism Developed.
To Adoption of Attractive Touch.	By Magnetism Developed.
To Avoidance of False Motions.	By Force Conserved.
To the Bearing of Genuineness.	By Respect and Confidence Won.
To Self in Business for Business.	By Business Ability.
To Cultivation of Courage-Confidence.	By Success-Magnetism.
To Creation of Practical Manner.	By Reliability Suggested.
To Labor in Winning Confidence.	By The Reputation of Power.

The account shows plainly that any cost you may put down in the debit list exhibits larger values in the credit list, and the more the account is studied with reference to one's self, the more are the debit items seen to be *business commands* and the credit items *business assets* of the first order—qualities which the business world is always glad to reward. And the element of psychic satisfaction resulting from the discipline enforced on self discounts every other consideration.

The items speak for the most part in self-explanation. It would seem to be a perfectly plain matter, if only business people would be as strenuous in their efforts to secure qualifications insuring financial returns as they evidently are in the activities for the returns themselves. But such an account can no more be "made good" by a mere

reading than can the estimated earning power of a
manufacturing plant by a cursory examination of
its capital summation. "Making good" always
means effort intelligently directed toward *specific
goals*—and *unceasingly*.

"Life is not a bully who swaggers out into the
open universe, upsetting the laws of energy in all
directions, but rather a consummate strategist,
who, sitting in his secret chamber over his wires,
directs the movements of a great army." Personal
style is really such a strategist. And I hold that it
is just as feasible to put honesty into strategic
address as it is possible to buy and sell stocks
honorably and in the open. In either case, the
honor insisted upon costs a little more than mere
gutter care, but none the less is honest strategy
possible and imperative with the man of long-run
success.

BUSINESS LANGUAGE.

§ 24. THE FOURTH REQUIREMENT—LANGUAGE.
I have observed that the language of women is invariably superior to that of their equals among
men. Many reasons for this fact might be assigned
but one is evident. The work-world is forever in
a hurry, and it always studies economy of means to
ends. The business man's language is therefore
subject to great pressure in the matter of time and
swift conveyance of clear meaning. So long as he
knows that he is understood he is satisfied. Any
short-cut, any adopted lingo, any symbol for a
technical phrase, any bit of slang, if it speaks
quickly and clearly, has, then, the open door of
business English. Language, moreover, is the pro-

duct of human relations, and since in business these relations are born of efforts to adjust men and situations, there is always a pressure upon business expression to "get to" the other man's understanding and good feeling. Business language, therefore, has come to be somewhat marked by false grammar, cut words, strange symbolism, slang and profanity. Few of these things are real assets in the field, because they frequently represent deterioration and psychic debits, and are thus not at all necessary to successful business anywhere. The psychic income of discipline for improved style in language may, hence, be indicated as below:

The Speech of Business.

DR.	CR.
To Discipline in Items:	By Psychic and Business Gains.
To Correct but Natural.	By Right Expression.
To Adapted to Thought.	By Clear Understanding.
To Adjusted to Circumstances.	By Successful Use.
To Control of as Tool.	By Best Handling of Self.
To Slang as Salt Only.	By Vivacity without Coarseness.
To Profanity Eliminated.	By Respect of All Men and Women.
To Freedom from Impurity.	By Power.
To Loudness Controlled.	By Repulsions Avoided.
To Distinctness Acquired.	By Clear Hearing Assured.
To Slowness Quickened.	By Time and Irritation Saved
To Hesitation Cured.	By Attention Made Easy.
To Loquacity Curbed.	By Concentration Secured.
To Irrelevancy Checked.	By Distractions Avoided.
To Sarcasm Cut Out.	By Good Will Not Endangered
To Sharpness Smoothed or Suppressed.	By Good Will Not Endangered.

To Irritation Eliminated.	By Situations Controlled.
To Nervous Tones Avoided.	By Distrust Not Aroused.
To Oiliness Avoided.	By Suspicion Not Aroused.
To Confidence Expressed.	By Confidence Won.
To Confidence Inspired.	By Self-Confidence Increased.
To Self-Control Evinced.	By Mastery Suggested.
To Business Talk for Business.	By Business Faith Won.
To Words and Eye Joined.	By Conviction Assisted.

The enumeration, of course, is designed only for suggestiveness. Packed away in both the debit and the credit columns are matters of so great value that any one of the items might well be elaborated in a chapter. The account should carefully be studied, a comparison with self being constantly held in mind. *The business man is a part of his own capital, and the very best instrument of that capital in language should be sought both for psychic and financial profit.*

"A real salesman is one-part talk and nine-parts judgment; and he uses the nine-parts of judgment to tell when to use the one-part talk." This sagacious remark of old Gordon Graham is no truer of the salesman than of any other man in the business world. It is always a question between too much and too little, the right thing or the wrong thing, and so on, and the particular question in hand at any time must be settled invariably by the nine-parts of judgment. Nevertheless, Graham's rule is a good one: "Have something to say. Say it. Stop talking." Because it is not easy to determine what the "something" shall be, just how to say it, and exactly when to stop, business speech is a fine art, and such suggestions as are given in our psychic account should prove of

value to those who will absorb the items into
blood and soul.

Above all, I think, is the importance of optimistic tones and words in business speech, be the
latter hearty and bluff or polite and refined, economical with reticence or prodigal in effects. I have
written this chapter in the form of accounts in
order to show that the psychic income—and that
means the business income—is sure to the man
who energetically strives for the very best he can
see. Now this statement will be doubted by some
readers. They know many cases where the man
has tried earnestly and failed. *There was once a
man who tried earnestly to lift a huge rock out of a
mountain path, but because he had simple earnestness
only for his power, he failed. Then the man threw
himself down and died. But a second traveler came
that way and cut a lever and put his strength upon the
instrument and heaved the rock to destruction, passing on with a laugh.* The first had the reward of
the man who is willing to fail. But the man who
knows how disproves the failure's despair. Failures
have nothing to do with optimism. Optimism is
optimism because it is certain that the man who
wills to discover how to do things is sure of success. *This cheerful defiance of the devil and self
breeds power.* One of the greatest generators of
ability is the faith-feeling of a sane optimism.
Its symbol is its dynamo.

Orison Swett Marden has a pertinent word in
"*Every Man A King,*" as follows: "The great
business world of to-day is too serious, too dead in
earnest. Life in America is the most strenuous
ever experienced in the history of the world.

There is a perpetual need of relief from this great
tension, and a sunny, cheerful, gracious soul is like
an ocean breeze in sultry August, like the coming
of a vacation. We welcome it because it gives us
at least a temporary relief from the strenuous
strain.   Country store-keepers look forward for
months to the visits of jolly, breezy traveling men,
and their wholesale houses profit by their good
nature.   Cheerful-faced and pleasant-voiced clerks
sell more goods and attract more customers than
saucy, snappy, disagreeable ones.   Promoters, or-
ganizers of great enterprises, must make a business
of being agreeable, of harmonizing hostile interests, of winning men's good opinion.   Newspaper
men, likewise, depend on making friends to gain
entree, to get interviews, to discover facts, and to
find news. All doors fly open to the sunny man,
and he is invited to enter when the disagreeable,
sarcastic, gloomy man. has to break open the door
to force his way in. Many a business is founded on
courtesy, cheerfulness, and good humor." And the
way to become optimistic is—to assume, assert,
act—sure success.

CHARACTER.

§ 25.   THE FIFTH REQUIREMENT—CHARACTER.
The business world confronts the would-be business
man and demands of him unimpeachable financial
character.   Two things, therefore, emerge for consideration: He who desires a high position and
salary must demonstrate in character and practical
ability; and he who insists on character and ability
in the man employed must respect what he calls
for by confidence instead of the modern appliances

for checking (suggesting) dishonesty which surely
breed the counter craftiness, and he must pay for
what he gets on the basis of his exactions. *It is not
good business to expect a five-thousand dollar character on a thousand-dollar salary or vice versa.* A
little more of the co-operative idea in business
would represent a better valuation of character and
not reduce the world's net income by a penny. A
double maxim therefore appears: *If you want first-
class character in your employees, pay for it—for
just that; and if you want a first-class position, give
with your services first-class character—just that.*

The phychic account for business character
would become too complex for these pages. It has,
in fact, appeared more or less all along, but I must
now resort to a different method of presenting the
subject, and can only suggest general outlines at
that. We begin with some simple requirements of
the man who would succeed, and then indicate
certain indispensable qualifications apparent to all,
yet not practically realized by the majority of
people engaged in business efforts. You are invited
to make your own the following:

SUGGESTION-AFFIRMATIONS FOR CHARACTER.

I am an ambitious man.
I maintain a legitimate spirit of pride.
My character is the best value I possess.
I have strength of character for my needs.
I am bent on personal improvement.

I am self-reliant, but open to all experience.
I develop the powerful and symmetrical will.

I believe practically for myself in business promptness.

I train myself to absolute reliability.

My word is good for what I engage.

My reputation is perfect honesty.

I justly hold myself a man of honor.

I have no use whatever for immorality.

I regard the "square deal" as a business asset.

I have no questionable business methods.

I respect the laws of the land.

I want no wealth at public expense.

I cultivate the spirit of generosity.

I tolerate the right of differing opinions.

I cultivate largeness of nature.

I practically believe in humanity.

I am for the winning personality.

I am constantly bringing into action new areas of the brain.

I shall never reach the "dead line" in business.

I value the old for what it is worth.

I am open to every good thing.

I honor business as a world-builder.

I throw character into business for business ends.

§ 26. These affirmations are not, of course, complete or exhaustive, but are suggestive only, and in two senses. As they are studied, other important items will be suggested to the reader, and such additions should be listed for the purpose now to be indicated. What is it in the reader that offers such suggestions? It is what I call the deeper self. Now that deeper self not only offers, but re-

ceives, suggestion. That deeper self seems always
to be engaged, during all one's various conscious
activities, in a life of its own. Yet it is a part of
your self, and can be trained, as the self with
which you are familiar can be trained, to do your
exact bidding. Precisely at this point the value of
suggestion to self—from the conscious to the subconscious or deeper self—appears. *Our suggestion-
affirmations, purposely broad and inclusive, may be
given to the deeper self, incessantly, insistently, with
confidence, until that which they represent, character,
has been recognized and valued by the subconscious
self as the only thinkable and permissible thing in
life.* In time the whole personality will as surely
be elevated and safe-guarded against lapses, and
empowered for acknowledged commercial worth,
as any law of Nature will continue to operate.
This is my reason for giving the present chapter
the peculiar form of psychic accounts and inten-
tional suggestion throughout.

SELF MASTERY.

§ 27. THE SIXTH REQUIREMENT — SELF MAS-
TERY. The aim of self-mastery is two-fold. It
has to do with success in business, for one thing.
Man for man, he who is master of himself is
always the winner. At a meeting of a college
faculty, the President expressed a desire for certain extensive improvements by way of a new
building and equipments. The President of the
Medical Board of Trustees suggested methods by
which the Liberal Arts Trustees might be whee-
dled into line. Whereupon the College President
said:

"Mr. Blank, let it be distinctly understood that there will be no underhanded business in this matter. Whatever we do must be done entirely above board."

The President was right in his principle, but totally non-diplomatic in his manner. All present felt the threat of a clash. An angry gleam flashed from the eye of the President of the Medical Board, but for an instant only. Then he quietly replied: "Very well, Sir."

When I heard the incident, I said: "The President of the Medical Trustees will defeat the President of the College, for the man of self-control is either a great ally or a dangerous foe." *He is the man of power.*

But self-mastery is lord of the psychic income. "All objective income is entirely erased or negatived as soon as we apply our accounting to the body of the recipient (the man in business). The services of which that income consists empty out, as it were, their quota into the human body, but the ultimate result is not finally received until it emerges in the stream of consciousness. *We define subjective income, then, as the stream of consciousness of any human being.* All his conscious life, from his birth to his death, constitutes his subjective income. Sensations, thoughts, feelings, volitions, and all psychical events, in fact, are a part of this incoming stream. All these conscious experiences which are desirable are positive items of income, or services; all which are undesirable are negative items, or disservices." For the largest possible psychic income—and it is never to be forgotten that we have here innumerable human assets or instru-

ments in self-capitalization—self-mastery is really
the central determining factor. Its analysis reveals
the following:

§ 28. A. FIRST SIMPLE ELEMENTS. (For auto-
suggestion.)

I will to cultivate RESOLUTION;
I resolve to strengthen DECISION;
I decide resolutely for PERSISTENCE;
I persist in developing ENERGY;
I control energy for BEST USE OF SELF;
I MASTER SELF FOR BUSINESS.

The list of qualities constructs the following
sentence: *I will to cultivate Resolution, crystallizing
the resolution into Decision, and persisting with Energy in the Best Use of Self mastered for successful
business.* Here, again, we have the call for insistent and persistent suggestion until the whole personality becomes a dynamo of power.

§ 29. B. FIRST DOUBLE ELEMENTS. (For
auto-suggestion.)

I am my business master—

(Patience in)	DRUDGERY	(Use of)
(Meeting of)	OBSTACLES	(Overcoming)
(Worry over)	DIFFICULTIES	(Conquest of)
(Readiness for)	EMERGENCIES	(Solution of)
(Fear of)	DANGER	(Triumph over)
(Discouragement at)	DEFEATS	(Profiting by)
(Over-elation at)	SUCCESS	(Building better)

§ 30. C. SECOND DOUBLE ELEMENTS.

I resolve to control—

(Bad tendencies of)	BODY	(Right use of)
(Unnecessary)	GESTURES	(Improvement of)
(False, jerking)	MOVEMENTS	(Cultivate sure)
(Furtive, wavering)	EYE	(Develop frank)
(Objectionable)	APPETITES	(Train better)
(Needless, nervous)	HEARING	(Calm use of)

(Useless, unattractive)	WORDS	(Good selection)
(Lack; explosion of)	TEMPER	(Harness; handle)
(Foolish, defeating)	MOODS	(Build valuable)
(Undue, reasonless)	ENERGY FEEL-ING	(Master)
(Habit of)	INDOLENCE	(Use rest sanely)
(The bad)	HABITS	(The good)
(Myself in)	BUSINESS	(For business)

At the risk of undue repetition I must again remind the reader that the design of such lists of qualities and suggestions has in mind *constant affirmation until the deeper self has not only been impressed by directions given it, but has come to act spontaneously in accordance with the suggestions whenever occasion presents itself.*

"What determination could effect, that could Red Wull, (the dog, in '*Bob, Son of Battle*'); but achievement in inaction—supremest of all strategies —that was not for him. But in matters of the subtlest handling, where to act anything except indifference was to lose, with sheep restless, fearful forebodings hymned to them by the wind, panic hovering unseen above them, when an ill-time considered movement spelt catastrophy, then was Owd Bob o' Kenmuir incomparable." Owd Bob o' Kenmuir was perfect master. *The highest stage of mastery in self is that in which the one thing to do is to do nothing while the world swims and tumbles around you—and you stand still like unto an image of death.* That kind of man is very much alive.

THE FRONT OF BUSINESS.

§ 31. THE SEVENTH REQUIREMENT—THE FRONT OF BUSINESS. In the following suggestions we have in view any particular business transaction. It is not supposed, of course, that every affirmation given below will be used in every business contact with others. The idea is, rather, that some of the affirmations are always practically employed, and if the affirmations as a whole are studied and practically attempted from time to time, the subjective self will ultimately have absorbed them and will have developed a general attitude and alertness of response to the demands of any situation which will then prove a most valuable second nature. If we imagine a business situation in which a successful campaign is greatly desired—selling goods, handling men, etc.,—we shall see various opportunities for utilizing the following.

D. AFFIRMATIONS FOR THE FIRING LINE. (For auto-suggestion.)

I have a definite purpose in this transaction.

I have thought out the main campaign.

I see, now, the people, the scene, the outcome.

I propose to get right after this business.

I throw my entire personality into this work.

I intend to stay by until I win.

I shall sleuth-hound success-methods to a finish.

I am determined to prove attractive to all people.

I shall certainly win this particular man.

I wear with you the bearing of sincerity.

You can assuredly rely upon my word.

I am inspiring confidence in this person.

I am all alert to his moods and possibilities.

I am controlled energy.

I am laughter, gravity, sympathy, as he wishes.

I have entire confidence in myself.

I have perfect confidence in my goods.

I have exhaustless confidence in my business.

I have absolute confidence in the present transaction.

I have confidence in this man as a buyer.

This customer desires to buy, and he will.

I do not over-emphasize my desire to sell—or buy.

I take all rebuffs goodnaturedly.

I do not admit any failure to be permanent.

I follow this transaction until surely useless.

I am certain of immediate and ultimate success.

LEVEL-HEADED PERSONAL VALUATION.

§ 32.   THE EIGHTH REQUIREMENT — MEGALOP-SUKÍA.   This uncanny word is here employed because it covers important suggestions and is capable of good application.   Aristotle, in enumerating certain virtues exhibiting moderation,—which was this philosopher's ideal of morality,—mentioned Cowardice, Courage, Rashness, and, Humble-mindedness, High-mindedness, Vaingloriousness. *Megalopsukía* is the Greek word for "High-mindedness," and means a kind of ideal self-respect.

This virtue, highmindedness, is of sure importance in business. A man should take himself with reasonable seriousness and dignity. Nowhere is this more evident than among successful business men. Nevertheless, the business world is very quick to detect any cheap imitation of the virtue. Many men fail because of a lack in this respect, and many also fail because they have too much of the quality, or, rather, exhibit a spurious variety of the characteristic.

§ 33.   *In business one can never be too nice nor good for the doing of anything that ought to be done.*

My business friend obtained employment in an office, and the "head" found him the next morning scrubbing the floors. He had not been told to do this, but when asked why he had assumed the task, replied: "I did it because I couldn't stand so much dirt." A few days prior to the present writing, the "office boy," who later became master of steamship lines and builder of railways, and is now the head of the largest concern of its kind in the world, said to me, when I protested that he was not very economical with postage stamps: "Oh, I've got beyond any particularly small economy." This man has never been above doing anything which ought to be done.

One of the most successful lawyers in New England found it imperative once to get a small parcel immediately into the post office, and requested his stenographer to "run over to the office" with it. The lady demurred—and the lawyer, who had never from the first demurred to the doing of anything that ought to be done, secured a new stenographer before night.

There is a stupid prejudice on the part of some employees against carrying bundles, running errands, doing various things "not in my line," "not what I'm paid for." *A real man's "line" is anything that ought to be done which must be done by himself if done at all.* One is "hired" to serve the interests of the whole concern, anywhere, everywhere. Carrying bundles is "big business" when the business requires carrying bundles. The trouble with many people in the business or work world is the fact that their *Megalopsukia* is too large ("big head"); in common parlance, they are too big for the place they are supposed to fill. Any place is "filled" when its occupant can reach forth and take hold of things from the outside. One who knew this writing was in hand said, insistently and on several occasions: "Don't forget to warn your readers against the swell-head." When I see an exhibition of this weakness, I always think of Aristotle's *Megalopsukía*. A young man who had been put into the position of a branch-manager of a very large concern, lost his standing by going wrong financially. The "head" remarked: "He developed the big-head; knew too much; thought he was the establishment; then his money accounts went astray." It is the old, old story. Success turns the weak head, but merely steadies the man who is master of business and the situation.

Most Pilgrim Fathers had no cause for pride in blue blood. The great business man has truer reason therefor than the majority of the titled nobility. "I know that a man's will, and not a college of heralds, makes him what he is," said Ferne in *"Sir Mortimer."* "I have known churls in honorable houses and true knights in the common camp. And I submit not my destiny to that game-ster, Luck: as I deserve and as God wills, so run my race!"

§ 34. It will be remembered that in Section 20 of this chapter the "Ten Diamond Rules" and the "Ten Subjective Brilliants" were enumerated in connection with the First Personal Requirement. The study of Psychic Income may be furthered with "The Ten Rubies of Success," companion suggestions well taken with the "Rules" and "Brilliants."

The Ten Rubies of Success.

(1)   Cultivate the Magnetic Will. (See *"Power For Success."*)

(2)   Be Alert For Opportunities.

(3)   Study The Lessons of Experience.

(4)   Act With Deliberate Promptness.

(5)   Throw Best Self Into All Effort.

(6)   Preserve Undisturbed Poise.

(7)   Give Personal Judgment Confidence.

(8)   Make the Word Equal to Best Bond.

(9)   Keep the Risk Element Down to Bed Rock.

(10)   Sacrifice For the Long-run Goal.

INCREASE OF INCOME.

§ 35.   THE NINTH REQUIREMENT—INCREASE OF INCOME. We have seen that the business man's income—here meaning net profits from his business—is partly psychic. As a matter of fact, this psychic income is the last item in the final analysis of business—personal satisfaction and benefit to self and others. Even the monetary income ends ultimately in the same value.

A successful business career means capital employed and kept good, surplus carried over or added to original capital, and the important factor, "undivided profits," a surplus now gaining and not yet added to the bookkeeper's "carried over surplus." Precisely so should be stated the psychic elements of the man's self: Capital of the man, improvements established and "carried over" *because* established, and the undetermined but sure increments of present development — "undivided psychic profits."

We may easily enough represent the advantage
of "savings," any additions to original capitalization true of any individual.   Such increase may be
had (a) by increase of salary or wages, (b) by
increase of profits, (c) by decrease of expenses, or
(d) by maintaining expenses at a given level while
salary and profits are rising or remain the same.
*Ultimate success financially considered imperatively
demands one or the other of these methods.*   Multitudes of people fail to "get on" because they do
not attend to the "savings" item in the bookkeeper's account.   Money can earn money, but there
must be enough of it to do a day's work, and the
first thousand dollars is usually the hardest gotten
together.   Always, however, does good business
mean the credit item, "surplus."   That item is
especially a credit item psychically considered.   It
inspires a good deal of personal satisfaction, and it
is also a new business tool, signifying increased
efficiency in the old tool, capital. And in a business
sense, this item, "surplus," means that not only
has the credit side of the ordinary ledger risen in
value, but that the credit side of the psychic account must necessarily (as a general law) have
climbed with it.   The following diagram will illustrate the compounding value, so to speak, of earnings saved or of surplus held good.

Diagram of Compounding Earnings.

The diagram supposes that a man's salary for
the first year is $400, for the second year, $600, for
the third year, $800, and for the fourth and fifth
years, $1000 each.   His salary thus increases $200 a
year up to to the fourth year, when it remains sta-

tionary. The man's possible financial level from
year to year, that is, his ability to expend cash,
depends, then, altogether on the difference between

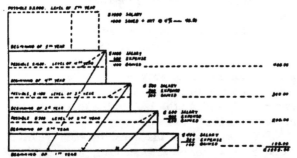

his expenses on the one hand and his income plus
his surplus savings, on the other hand. Thus—

If he always uses up his salary, he is financially
at the end of the fifth year exactly where he was
when he began, so far as surplus is concerned. He
still lives on the x-y-z line. (See diagram.)

If, at the end of the first year, he has saved
$100, he lives during the second year on the possi-
ble $700 level, for he has the salary of $600 plus the
$100 saved to expend as he will.

If, at the end of the second year, he has used
$400 for expenses and saved $200, he lives during
the third year on the possible $1100 level, for he
has $800 salary plus $300 saved—to expend as he
will.

If, at the end of the third year, he has used
$500 for expenses and saved $300, he lives during
the fourth year on the possible $1600 line, for he
has the salary of $1000 and the savings of $600—all
to expend as he will.

If, at the end of the fourth year, he has used
$700 for expenses and saved $300, he lives during
the fifth year on the possible $2000 level, for he has
salary, $1000, and savings, $1000—to expend as he
will.

In other words the supposititious man has a
total raise of salary during four years of $600 has
added $100 a year to his expenses, and has saved
$1000.   Attention to surplus has lifted the man
from the x-y-z line clean above his salary line at
any period, and at the last to the line just $1000
higher than his line of salary.

Had he lived up his earnings each year, he
would now be merely a $1000 man, not certain of
that, with never a penny of surplus on hand.

He began with $400 salary, and has had only
$600 increase, but during the fifth year he has the
possibility of living at the $2000 rate for one year—
or, of increasing his expenses and still adding to
previous savings.

Moreover, if this man has received interest at
4 per cent., his account will stand thus:

End of 1st year, (saves $100), $ 100.00
End of 2d year, $100+$4+($200, year's
     savings), $ 304.00
End of 3d year, $304+$12.16+($300, year's
     savings), $ 616.16
End of 4th year, $616.16+$24.64+($400,
     year's savings), $1040.80
And end of 5th year, $1040.86+$41.63+
     ($300, year's savings), $1382.43

During the sixth year he can live on the possible $2382.43 level.   And so on indefinitely.

§ 36. It is thus seen that the financial level rises rapidly during any rise of income if only the expense account is made to contribute to that end. Of course, so long as the expense account is controlled, the same result will follow any increase in the income.

§ 37. Now, precisely the *increase of right expense account* is required in the *psychic phase of income* if the end is to show any rapid rise of "capital" level. We have seen that the psychic credits will always offset the debit charges of labor, pains, weariness, discipline, so long as the individual earnestly strives for self-improvement. The "increase of salary" in the above case may now be taken for "business reputation"—using the phrase in a broad sense. Always has the man his psychic "surplus" in any event, some of which has been long established as habit, some of which, say during any present year, is more like "undivided profits" because not thoroughly settled. And as certain as natural law, though perhaps delayed, in such a case, the *salary rise* of the former case will be duplicated in a fairly regular *advance of reputation* for fidelity, reliability, practical ability and financial value in the public's books of psychic account. As in the former case, the level of the fifth year was $1600 higher than that of the first year, because of savings with increase of salary,—due very likely to the fact that the man was that kind of man who *would* secure a surplus,—so now the psychic level sooner or later will be vastly higher than at any given earlier period because of the inestimable "surplus" both of established improvement and earning reputation. *Once the world gets the idea that a man is growingly worthy of confidence, it multiplies its own faith by very great and rapid strides.*

And, as contributing to the "gain" element in the psychic account, the elimination of undesirable personal traits and bad business qualities is comparable to the factor "keeping expenses down." You live *within* your income in order to help the increase of salary to lift you to higher levels; so you assist gain in reputation not only by developing business traits, but also by "cutting out" the injurious elements of your personal and business character. The two processes carried on mean rapid psychic rise.

The sum and substance of all this chapter we have long ago discovered. It is all in the man. He it is alone who makes—or unmakes—himself and his fortune.

PART II.
ECONOMIC LAWS AND BUSINESS MAXIMS.

"'Suppose two men to be equal at night, and that one rises at six, while the other sleeps till nine next morning.what becomes of pour levelling'? And in so speaking he made himself the mouthpiece of Nature, which secures advance, not by the reduction of all to a common level, but by the encouragement and conservation of what is best."—TYNDALL in "Science and Man."

CHAPTER VII.

ECONOMIC LAWS AND BUSINESS AXIOMS.

PRACTICAL Experience writes dictionaries. Business has given the language innumerable words, the original meanings of which are almost lost to modern thought. *Trade* had the early significance of *tread*, and business is a beaten path, with new trails incessantly forming. *Barter* began with the idea of deceit or trickery, an element hard to be rid of even to-day. *Business* is busy-ness, regulated, however, and so conducted as to unfold great laws. And here we have *nomad*, from Sanskrit *nam*, "to count out, to share;" and *wick*, "a village," *vicinage*, "belonging to the same street," with the idea of sharing in some established way; and finally, *economy* (economics), from Greek *oíkos*, "a house," and *nemein*, "to deal out." So, *commercial* descends from Latin *merere*, "to receive as a share," and *market* is the place where or the conditions in which you receive your share. This is the significance of business: activity in established ways among men who are settled in places and have developed permanent conditions, to the end that all so engaged may receive a share of the

163

world's immense wealth—*if they can get it.* The
share (and any receiving) must depend on the *quality* of your *busy-ness*, and the highest, most deserv-
edly successful quality is *business power.*

§ 1. Economic laws and the laws of business
are, of course, very closely related. In some cases
it would be impossible to discriminate the one from
the other, or to say that a given law is that of business and not that of economics. Nevertheless, for
suggestive purposes, I shall distinguish between the
two sets of general laws, employing italics and the
letter (*E*) for economic laws, and black letter with
letter (**B**) for laws of business. Other italics show
general truths. It need scarcely be added that I
do not undertake an exhaustive analysis of the
laws in question, either of the one kind or of the
other.

INSTINCT AND KNOWLEDGE.

§ 2. Business power involves business instinct, which is, in part, a form of subjective
ability. But the objective business mind is indispensable leader. It is the activity of the latter that
suggests the facts of the business life to the other
and trains it in the development of instinct. *The
value of the instinct, then, is in proportion to the
degree in which it is so cultivated and guided as
to represent the largest possible amount of business knowledge.* Instinct, in fact, is a variety of
knowledge acting automatically from subjective
inspiration.

"Jadwin hesitated. In spite of himself he felt
a Chance had come. Again that strange sixth
sense of his, the inexplicable instinct, that only the

born speculator knows, warned him. Every now
and then during the course of his business career,
this intuition came to him, this flair, this intangible,
vague premonition, this presentiment that he must
seize Opportunity, or else Fortune, that so long had
stayed at his elbow, would desert him. In the air
about him he seemed to feel an influence, a sudden
new element, the presence of a new force. It was
Luck, the great power, the great goddess, and all
at once it had stooped from out the invisible, and
just over his head passed swiftly in a rush of glit-
tering wings."

§ 3. This quotation from *"The Pit,"* by Frank
Norris, is introduced as an illustration of a certain
phase of business instinct, which co-operates with
what we call "luck" only in the sense that it knows
how and when to act without carrying with it all
explanations. A little later Jadwin felt the same
influence. But he had studied crops, markets, financial movements, above all, wheat, as no other man
on 'Change had studied these factors. The real
secret of the value of Jadwin's instinct was his
accumulation of business knowledge. And the real
secret of the value of the latter was hidden in his
instinct. The greater the measure of practical
knowledge represented by instinct, the greater must
be the business man's efficiency. Inasmuch, too, as
business is a living thing moved by intelligence, it
necessarily presents various problems which mere
instinct cannot solve because they demand new
applications of the knowledge possessed and new
calls for knowledge not now in stock. Business
instinct is at its best when inspired and led by a form
of mental action that is not instinctive at all.

§ 4.   Hence, it may be said, first, that business
instinct should be accompanied by conscious knowledge of general business principles, and, secondly,
that business knowledge should constantly seek out
new forms of knowledge for the solution of new
problems.

REIGN OF LAW IN BUSINESS.

§ 5.   Gordon Graham said truly: "You can
resolve everything in the world, even a great fortune, into atoms.   And the fundamental principles
which govern the handling of postage stamps and
of millions are exactly the same.   They are the common laws of business, and the whole practice of
commerce is founded on them."

The book is not listed, I believe, in which these
fundamental principles are succinctly presented. It
is a difficult task to enumerate and state them, and
the attempt to do so will not in any complete form
be made in these pages. I shall content myself
with the more possible effort, a somewat exhaustive
treatment of such laws as seem to be most fundamental, and can only hope that, while the statements may appear to be a little technical, they will
be recognized as merely clean-cut propositions of
every-day business common sense.

§ 6.   Practical financial ability and business
progress are related somewhat as the hub and rim
of a wheel are connected by its spokes.   Let the
following diagram represent the wheel of business,
with practical ability as the hub, the spokes as
general principles or laws, and the rim as business
power running on the highway of business progress.
As a wheel may have many or a few spokes, but

must have some, enough to hold hub and rim
together, so business power in any enterprise may
not employ all nameable business laws, but must
employ some of them. As the hub in the wheel
must connect with the spokes if there is to be a
wheel, so practical ability surely becomes effective
through the fundamental laws of business. And
as the rim of a wheel is supported by the spokes
entering the hub, so business power is upheld by
business laws employed in the financial world. You
are invited, therefore, to master and use

THE WHEEL OF BUSINESS POWER.

Master	Follow These Laws
The Laws of Business.	In Your Business.

Business Power

The principles which constitute the spokes, so
to speak, of the wheel of business progress may be

said to resolve themselves into the full italicized
with letter (*E*) and black-letter statements with
letter (**B**) which are now to follow in this and the
next chapter.

§ 7. It should be understood, however, that
the principles so printed are not those of a purely
personal character, the latter being given elsewhere throughout the whole of this book, but are,
rather, the laws and axioms of the economic and
business worlds.   If we distinguish between human
and natural law, the former may be regarded as an
expression of the human will, the latter as an
expression of human nature.   In the sense that
law expresses nature, a law is a way a thing has of
being and doing.   The laws of human nature are
the ways human nature has of being and doing.
Hence—

§ 8. Business laws (not axioms) are the
established ways man has of being and doing in the
exchange of commodities and services which satisfy
human wants.   And of course such laws are the
ways the exchange activities have of being and
doing.   There are, be it observed, the *natural
activities of what we call economic effort*, and in addition, at least in the analysis of thought, there
are *certain principles which make for success in
the application of such laws and of human labor to
business life*.   The *former* activities follow *economic
law;* the *latter* application of principles exhibits
business axioms.   Oftentimes, as I have said, the
two phases of law overlap or blend together.

These ways or laws and axioms may be listed
in almost any convenient form.   Let us begin with
the main object of all business enterprise.

WEALTH.

§ 9. The aim of business is the development of wealth shared by society and the individuals who engage in business effort. Wealth is, of course, a relative thing. Definitions of the word differ among economic writers. In its simplest statement wealth may be regarded as "*material objects owned by human beings.*" But wealth in a concrete business sense is more accurately defined as (*E*) "*An accumulation of commodities with commanded service (a) possessing utility, (b) external to the individual owning or controlling them*—although it would seem reasonable that a man's self and abilities are a part of his wealth—*(c) limited in amount, and (d) exchangeable for other commodities or services capable of satisfying human wants.*

§ 10. This definition covers several other factors important in business. It involves (*E*) *Property*, the right to use wealth, the right to the uses of wealth; (*E*) *Capital*, a stock of wealth existing at an instant of time, and (*E*) *income*, which may be defined as a flow of service through a period of time. The word "service" here means "benefit accruing."

(*E*) *We may say that income is a periodic flow of exchangeable want-satisfying commodities which are capable of rendering demanded service, or of any agreed general medium to which exchanges are referred.*

When we fund income in its original or any transformed shape, we have capital.

All things thus exchangeable are the basis of property—though not exhaustively so. In one sense property is total income and capital. In a

derived sense property is "the exchange right of
ownership in any definite amount of wealth."
Some wealth is not exchangeable in a business
sense, as, for example, a public park. Should the
park " go into the market," it would continue to be
wealth, but now be also capital.

§ 11. The usual agreed general medium to
which exchanges are referred is money. Money is
merely a commodity, like horses or iron, but it
serves business as no other object not so devoted
could do. Certain propositions will illustrate:

(A) (*E*) *Money is an agreed medium of exchange*. Instead of bartering one thing for another,
we use money as a "go-between." Good money is
composed of a material which all civilized people
recognize as of about intrinsic value—or of a material so financially backed that it means precisely
the same thing—something in existence equal to
its declared or face value. Any representative
which may come to the same thing is good money.

§ 12. **(B) Business power insists on " good
money."**

(B) (*E*) *Money is a value-denominator*, a
standard of value to which exchanges of commodities and services are referred or by which they are
measured. It is then called "money of account."

(C) Money is also a standard of deferred payments, as for rents, debts, etc. And so, money is
a (*E*) *legal tender* for all debts. When it is not, it
is not real money.

§ 13. **(B) Business power insists on a legal
tender not depreciated.**

§ 14. (D) A man's financial worth is not represented merely by the amount of money which he

possesses, but by the amount of money which he can secure in exchange for his wealth, or by the amount of money possessed or securable and exchangeable for commodities or services capable of satisfying human wants.

In a story entitled "*Buried Treasure*," three men found a chest of gold coins. There was not a drop of water or a pound of food within hundreds of miles from the spot. One of the finders filled his pockets with coins, but the others dragged him away. The treasure could not be carried with the men, and they could not remain on the ground because of the threat of death from hunger and thirst. They traveled for days in search of "civilization," without meat and drink. In time, Schwartz, heavily loaded with "money," began to break down.

"Denton and I were navigating without any thought of giving up; but Schwartz was getting in bad shape. I'd hate to tote twenty pounds over that country with rest, food and water. He was toting it on nothing. We told him so; and he came to see it; but he never could persuade himself to get rid of the gold all at once. *Instead he threw away the pieces one by one*. Each sacrifice seemed to nerve him up to another heat. * * * It seemed all right, this new, strange purchasing power of gold—it *was* all right, and as real as buying bricks." Schwartz was buying, with each coin thrown away, a little more walk conducted by himself. He could not carry it all and live, but he thought he could carry some of it, and so from time to time gave up a portion, and the idea and the decrease of weight enabled him to go on a little

farther. That was the only value the gold possessed to him in his frenzied state of mind. In all
that country there was nothing desirable to be had
for his money. The treasure had no value whatever where it was, because it could not be exchanged. There were two ways in which this
money could have been made exchangeable: by
taking it away to civilization, or by bringing civilization to the place where the money was found.
Otherwise it was mere dump.

§ 15. **(B) Business power is never con-
tented until possible wealth is made wealth-
capital through exchangeability.**

(E) If cattle were agreed upon as a medium
of exchange, they would then be money. They
would prove an inconvenient medium, but the inconvenience would not affect their value as money
so long as all business men accepted them as such
a medium. As such a medium, they would be
desired by all because they could at any time be
exchanged for other articles or services capable of
satisfying human wants. And inasmuch as they
would be universally desired, the demand for them
would give them a certain superiority over all other
commodities.

(F) The secret of the value of money lies in
the fact that, because it is a medium of exchange,
a value-denominator, a standard of deferred payments and a legal tender, *it possesses earning power*.

(G) (E) *The earning power of money obtains
only when it becomes capital.* Mere income earns
nothing. Some portion of income must be capi-
talized, or funded, and used as capital, made to
render service, before it acquires earning power.

§ 16. (B) Business power always seeks to give money, as well as wealth, earning power.

An illustration will be found in Section 35 of Chapter VI.

§ 17. (E) *The funding of income represents the sacrifice necessary to bring it in*, using the word "sacrifice" as meaning any cost to the individual in order to secure the income, and abstinence, a refusal to consume the income in a non-productive way.

§ 18. (B) Business power makes all legitimate required sacrifice for the sake of income as such, and forces all legitimate abstinence for the sake of funding income as capital.

(H) But the earning power of money (or its equivalents, exchangeable commodities and service external to the individual—or, if you like, including the individual) depends also upon the skill with which it is handled in business.

§ 19. (B) In the financial world the demand for increased business skill is greater than the demand for increased capital.

§ 20. Sacrifice for income and abstinence for capital are the prices of wealth. (B) Business power accumulates. "One of the fundamental differences between savage and civilized man is the absence of thrift in the one and the presence of it in the other. When you begin to earn, always save some part of your earnings, like a civilized man, instead of spending all, like the poor savage." Follow this advice of Andrew Carnegie, and you will ultimately possess capital. Remember the earning power of funded income, and make it your partner.

The Foundation of Business: Wants.

§ 21.   Business secures its end, wealth or capital, through the satisfaction of human wants. The existence of wants is the occasion for business. Business thus signifies activity (busy-ness) in the exchange of commodities or services which satisfy the wants of man.

§ 22.   Human wants are animal, or *Existence Wants;* and *Culture Wants.* With man, progress in civilization leads to a very considerable increase of culture wants over existence wants. As incomes improve, the former develop more rapidly than the latter.

§ 23.   *Hence, the effort of any business should be, not merely to meet the demands of existence wants, but to create and satisfy a large variety of culture wants.*

If, for example, you are a bread-maker, you can give your loaves an extra touch of attractiveness by putting them up in decorated labels. You now appeal not only to existence wants but to culture wants increased or created.

§ 24.   **(B) Business power is always alert for the discovery of some new and higher avenue of appeal to desire;** higher, I say, no less than new, because the higher desires multiply other wants in a larger measure than do existence wants.

Wants and Utility.

§ 25.   (E) *Now, the ability of a thing to satisfy personal wants constitutes its utility.* The essence of wealth is utility. Such utility—ability to satisfy human wants—may inhere in material objects or in services.

§ 26. "Wealth is wealth only because of its services; and services are services only because of their desirability in the mind of man, and of the satisfaction which man expects them to render. Indeed, the desirability of services is implied in their definition as 'desirable events.' The mind of man supplies the mainsprings in the whole economic machinery. It is in his mind that desires originate, and in his mind that the train of events which he sets going in nature comes to an end in the expenditure of subjective satisfactions. It is only in the interim between the initial desire and the final satisfactions that wealth and its services have place as intermediaries."

So remarks Professor Fisher, and then goes on: (*E*) "*The desirability, then, of any particular goods* (wealth, property, services, constitute goods), *at any particular time, to any particular individual, under any particular conditions, is the strength or intensity of his desire for those goods at that time and under those conditions.* What is here called desirability is identical with what has usually been called in economic writings '*utility.*'"

§ 27. (*E*) *The business world is concerned only with those utilities that are limited.* A perfectly unlimited supply of a thing, say air, may have value, but it has no commercial utility. A natural universal object free to all may acquire utility if it becomes temporarily limited, or if a superior quality of the general stock can be discovered and controlled, or if some new use which can be limited is devised for it.

It is not to be confusedly understood, however, that an object which is itself limited in supply may not have value, and especial value, by reason of its ability to be unlimitedly useful. In such a case desirability would be enhanced because utility may continue indefinitely. But it remains true that the business world is interested financially in those objects the supply of which is more or less limited and which can be controlled.

§ 28. **(B) Business power never loses an opportunity for the discovery of new utilities or for the increase of the old utilities.**

Marginal Utility.

§ 29. In business life the important question concerns not so much utilities the objects under which are limited in supply, as utilities that are what is called marginal. (*E*) *Only limited utilities can be marginal. The commercial value of things depends upon the relation of total to marginal utilities.* The business man who handles a variety of goods, in the sense of merchandise, all desired by everybody, deals constantly with this principle. It makes a difference whether you are selling an article which will satisfy a want once for all (as, say, a dictionary), or one which will be used up but leave a similar want calling for a further purchase. And it makes a difference whether you have a stock of goods large enough in variety to satisfy wants after some wants have been satisfied —say, culture wants after existence wants.

§ 30. (*E*) *So soon as the ability to satisfy wants begins to be used, the utility (desirability) of any given supply of things—the things used, and, in some instances, related things—begins to decrease to the individual so using them.* Assuming a given supply of an article, by so much as some of it is used to satisfy an individual's wants, by so much will his effective desire for any part of the balance grow less; by so much will the utility to him of the balance diminish. The articles may still hold their full measure of utility—ability to satisfy wants—to *others*, but the given individual's wants are partially met, and hence any of the remaining articles possess less utility to him.

A man was heard to say: "I have three of the finest boys on earth. I wouldn't take millions for any one of them. But then I wouldn't give ten cents for another." This tells the story of marginal utility.

(*E*) *Marginal utility is utility of a supply of things remaining after satisfaction of wants for them has begun. As satisfaction increases, marginal utility decreases.*

§ 31. The thing is simple, but it has some important implications. Suppose a starving man who in ten hours, if he can keep up, will reach a place of plenty. If a wayfarer, possessed of ten loaves of bread for sale, meets the starving man, the ten loaves will have a total utility,—that of the available supply,—(a) to the hungry man by way of satisfaction of hunger, (b) to the salesman by way of satisfaction of desire for money. When the purchaser has eaten one loaf, any one of the remaining loaves will possess less, yet some, utility to him, the hungry man; that is, a marginal utility. After eating the second loaf, he will have less desire for any other loaf, and any other loaf will have less marginal utility in his mind. If his hunger is satisfied with the eating of the fourth loaf, the remaining six loaves may possess no utility for the present purpose, either marginal or total to the once hungry man. The marginal utility is measured at any time by the urgency of remaining unsatisfied want. But the purchase of any loaf after a partial satisfaction of want will depend on the strength of desire for more food as compared with the strength of desire for other articles to be had if self-denial is practised in regard to bread. (*E*) *This means that in estimating the power of marginal utility we must take into account the amount of exchange ability of money or other commodities left after purchase of immediately present desired articles has begun.*

§ 32. Business is always dealing with this comparison of marginal utilities by purchasers. All customers have a portion of many of the objects for sale: the kind of some objects not possessed may have to them only a partial marginal utility. What to purchase with remaining money is the question, for, of course, in a business sense, marginal utility is not only represented by unsatisfied desire, but also by ability to purchase articles in satisfaction; that is, utility is a practical affair, not a mere matter of abstract wish. *Customers measure wants against wants.* (**B**) **Business power decides the question by increasing the desire in various ways until it becomes practical.** This brings up another phase of utility.

SOCIAL MARGINAL UTILITY.

§ 33. If the bread eater can purchase the ten loaves, and if he can be satisfied with four, the total utility for the moment, before eating, will still be four to him, but the total utility at another time, or at this time for a different purpose, may go up to the ten loaves.

§ 34. To the same individual the total utility of ten loaves, satisfaction of hunger supposed at four, will still be ten before any are eaten if he can exchange the remaining six in procuring the satisfaction of other or future wants. The total utility of a stock of goods depends on the desire of some person to possess them. With every beginning to purchase, the marginal utility decreases in the case of each purchasing individual, at the time, but the remaining supply may still have marginal utility or even total utility to others as they have or have not been partially satisfied. (*E*) *In making purchases the individual finds that marginal utility— the ability of a thing to satisfy his wants after partial satisfaction—differs in one article and another, so that he compares the marginal utility of one thing with the marginal utility of a second or a third thing, and so on, and finally purchases that which has to him a surplus marginal utility over all.* This is social marginal utility—the shifting surplus marginal utility remaining for all sorts of people after partial satisfaction of wants and after comparison of any given desires with other desires.

§ 35. But individual utility is not the only factor in business. Business deals in utilities to all individuals. These utilities are constantly becoming marginal because individuals are constantly using portions of supplies, and do not immediately require the balance. Social marginal utility is just the whole of these individual marginal utilities bundled together.

§ 36. **(B) Business power manages to make the individual marginal utility as large as possible by manipulation of goods and methods, to increase economic marginal utility by manipulation of individual purchasers, and to appeal to social marginal utility by handling the greatest variety of goods and services.** An eraser on a pencil adds to marginal utility so far as pencils are concerned with one who has pencils without erasers. A frame on a picture may decide a purchaser to order the picture in preference to a needed chair. A larger variety of goods may concentrate a scattered trade.

§ 37. **(B) Business power is alert to detect and take advantage of all kinds of utilities.**

VALUE.

§ 38. "As is well known to all students of the modern theory of value, marginal desirability (utility) lies at the root of the determination of value and price."

§ 39. If the bread eater above referred to purchases the ten loaves at once, and satisfies his hunger with four, the six remaining loaves have for him no immediate marginal utility in the matter of present hunger, but they may possess total utility to other people who desire bread and have none, and marginal utility to those who have bread but not enough to satisfy existing wants. If these possess arrow heads desired by the owner of bread, the strength of surplus desire for bread over desire for arrow heads with them, or for arrow heads over bread with the bread owner, measures the play of economic utility. Business then begins. The quantity of goods possessed which either man is willing to exchange for goods desired indicates the value of the goods not possessed in terms of the goods possessed, or *vice versa.* When men adopt some standard by which all other goods shall be measured or valued, the standard becomes money, and the amount of this standard involved in any exchange is the money value of the other goods. On the other hand, the quantity of other goods which will be accepted for a given amount of the standard expresses the value of the money in terms of goods.

§ 40. Generally speaking, the value of a thing in business is its ability to purchase, or secure the exchange of, anything which can satisfy human wants.

§ 41. (*E*) *Value is the expression of the estimate of utility*, to begin with, and in business is the expression of the *prevailing estimate of social marginal utility*, exchangeable power to satisfy wants which in any given kind of supply have been met partially in the case of any given individual or number of individuals associated in community life.

§ 42. (B) **Business power is always endeavoring to keep this estimate of utility at a high level.**

Analysis of Values.

§ 43. We see that value depends upon utility. It is necessary to hold in mind that utility is not mere usefulness, but is some kind of usefulness actually desired by some individual. Now, utility is of several varieties, as: Elementary Utility,

Form Utility, Place Utility, and Time Utility, and may be increased through creation of new desires, and is likely to be unsettled in regard to some articles or services because human desires are more or less fickle. Hence, we may say that values are:

(1) *Intrinsic, or Elementary;* as, of raw material.

(2) *Determined by Place;* as, coal brought to markets.

(3) *Determined by Timeliness;* as, the loaves of bread to the starving man.

(4) *Determined by Form;* as, clay in the shape of bricks.

(5) And, we may say, *Artificial,* meaning not, caused by ordinary market fluctuations, but created by special extraordinary conditions, unforeseen or skillfully brought about.

(6) And, again, *Spasmodic;* as, stocks during a "flurry."

§ 44. **(B) Intrinsic value is the bed rock of business.** Yet the superstructure involves values that are far away from the intrinsic.

§ 45. **(B) Business power multiplies intrinsic value by giving raw material form, right locality, and timeliness, and seeks to create artificial values and to take advantage of promising spasmodic values.**

Elementary value—raw material—and form value—finished product—are the essentials in manufacturing, though, of course, time and place factors are altogether important.

The values of place and timeliness are essentials in commercial business, though artificial and spasmodic values call here for constant skill and foresight.

Values of time and place represent the circulation of commercial life. Good business, like health, demands a strong and ceaseless flow of exchange values.

§ 46. (B) **Business power makes raw material valuable, and puts goods where they are wanted and compels the public to buy.** Any one can sell goods to the man who knows he wants them and has the cash; good business creates desire and decides purchase.

§ 47. (B) **Business power has as much to do with the creation of demand value as it has with selling goods already in demand.**

§ 48. The ability to create new desires, and so, to develop new utilities, and to foster marginal utilities and cause them to hold over, represents the genius of progressive business power.

The man who builds a railway through a country where before was no usable wagon road increases desires, and hence utilities, with every inch of his track. No sooner is the first train scheduled than stoves give fireplaces the exit and beds take the room of corn-shacks. It is the law of life: intelligent action is creation.

Suppose one has a hundred pounds of peanuts and sells half the quantity to ordinary demand, but now proceeds to suggest peanuts as desirable pot-plants: immediately marginal utility revives for some part of the remaining fifty pounds, which may sell at a fancy price. If the final remainder, after this method has exhausted, can similarly be manipulated, the entire lot will be disposed of—

and with greater profit than from the ordinary handling of peanuts.

§ 49. **(B) Business power keeps a sharp look-out for diminishing marginal utility, and either "unloads" or turns the stock to new uses.** The latter would seem to be the preferable method. Inroads upon a stock of goods or services the marginal utility of which is rapidly diminishing, and the creation of new utilities in waste material, call for incessant alertness and skill on the part of progressive business.

Suggested Opportunities.

§ 50. **Business power, then, involves, among other things, the following forms of ability: (B)**
(A) To gauge existing marginal utilities ;
(B) To anticipate possible future marginal utilities ;
(C) To manipulate social marginal utilities ;
(D) To create desires and utilities ;
(E) To estimate comparative utilities ;
(F) To estimate possibilities of exchange values ;
(G) To change natural into artificial values;
(H) To change artificial into natural values;
(I) To anticipate the utilities of time and place ;
(J) To create the values of time and place ;
(K) To create form values ;
(L) To forefend against or to profit by popular fickleness.
&c.,   &c.,   &c.

You are invited to review your business with reference to all the above considerations.

VALUE RETURNS.

§ 51. Value has various forms additional to those above suggested. Remembering that, strictly speaking, the value of a thing is its *purchasing power*, at least in the business world, we may now note that it inheres in Service, Goods, Temporary Relations and Privileges in material objects, and Funded Capital.

§ 52. The (*E*) *value of service* is estimated in *wages or salaries; of goods, in prices; of relations and privileges, in rents; of funded capital, in interest.*

We hire service: pay for it in wage or salary; which is really a price. We hire money: pay interest for its use; which also is a price. We hire land or a building or an article—acquire certain relations and privileges with reference to them: and pay a rental price.

§ 53. Speaking largely, (*E*) *wages depend upon the supply and skill of service and the general run of prices for other desirable commodities.*

§ 54. **(B) Business power secure the cheapest and best service at the lowest price consistent with active and remunerative general business.** (*E*) *If you put wages too far down you decrease purchasing power and hurt business. If you put wages too high you more or less unsettle business balance or equilibrium, and hurt business*—unless other factors intervene to overcome the tendency noted.

§ 55. (*E*) *Rents depend upon condition and locality of their subjects and general business pros-*

perity. (B) **Business power guages the ability of prevailing prosperity to pay rents demanded and to continue or improve ; and it also gauges its own ability to pay such rents and share in the existing prosperity.** My friend the school-teacher business man cut down his ordinary expenses one thousand dollars a month and tumbled into a better locality by merely sacrificing a notion of place-pride.

If, in one instance, rental beyond the ability of present general conditions to pay is demanded, business is driven elsewhere. If, in a second instance, rental is paid beyond ability to share in existing prosperity, the *renter drives himself out of business*. It is an error to assume that general business is not injured by the financial death of some given individual. The man who overcharges and the man who overpays for rental privileges is equally an enemy to business life.

It is a curious thing that so many "business" people do not seem to know when they are putting a razor to their own throats.

It is a strange thing that some "business" men in our time are engaged with such consummate skill in repeating the practices which sent Rome and France to destruction.

§ 56. (B) **Business power represents all of self-interest and nothing of selfishness.** Self-interest in business builds business with reference to all business. Selfishness in business builds a mere enterprise in disregard of all business. There is some difference—the difference between a real man and a freebooter. Thorpe, the lumberman in White's "*Blazed Trail*," represents the man;

Thorpe, in Frederick's " *The Market Place*," represents the beast.

§ 57. Nevertheless, rental returns inadequate to business prosperity are equally wrong. (B) **Business power never forgets the mutuality of all legitimate business activities.** When a business does not sustain mutual relations with other businesses, it becomes piracy.

§ 58. (E) *Rent is price paid for the temporary use or control of a particular thing.* Rent is paid for the use of the thing itself. (E) *Interest is price for the substitution by a temporary use* by the borrower for other uses to which capital might be put by the lender, or by some lender. We hire money if we are willing to pay for its use an amount about equal (the matter of risk in investment and in loan play some part in determination of the price, generally speaking) to that which a proportionate part of the capital drawn on for the loan could earn if invested—not, of course, in an exceptional case, but in the present general run of business. (E) *If money could secure no investment return, it would have no interest value.* The interest value represents the general possible investment return.

§ 59. (B) **Business power seeks the best investment return consistent with general business, and so, seeks the highest interest similarly consistent, but pays the least interest equally so consistent.** Business power is not the power of some individual pirate; it is the power to make good business all round.

§ 60. (B) **Business power increases rental prices through business prosperity because the**

latter means flush times and ability to pay.
But of course, this principle is modified by supply
quality and availability of rent properties.

§ 61.   (B) Business power decreases interest through monetary prosperity because this
means the general increase of the supply of
money to be had in capitalistic enterprises.
As business prosperity declines, prices fall, money
flows elsewhere, and interest rises, depending on
demand in such a situation, for capital can earn
more elsewhere in business, and the law of interest,
a price paid for substitution of uses, must prevail.
As business activity advances, the supply of money
may not be adequate to the demand for enterprises
—business activity may run ahead of the monetary
inflow or circulation—and interest will rise because
capitalistic enterprises yield increased returns.   In
such a condition, a man may invest his money in
his own enterprises, and if he consents instead to
loan it, he must receive interest greater than would
be the case were business opportunities few and
slow.   If the supply of money keeps pace with
business activity, interest will stand accordingly.
When the supply of money happens to outrun
business activity, a good interest may prevail because of business confidence.   But a long-continued
overplus, other things being equal, must lower
interest.   As a general rule money and business
activity run together, so that what may be called a
normal rate holds on.   Too great a volume of
money and too small a volume are twin evils—like
congestion and anemic condition of the brain. *Business is the brain of prosperity, and money is the
blood of its health.*

§ 62. (*E*) *Business power always seeks to advance investment returns beyond ordinary interest rates because of the element of risk and personal service and the matter of greater gain.* But in doing so it seeks to keep money in free circulation in its own neighborhood, and to maintain interest at a normal rate because this is a factor in the general prosperity on which ability to pay for commodities and services must depend.

§ 63. (B) **Business power understands the law of depreciation.** Articles lose utility, utilities diminish with community changes, marginal utilities decrease as use continues, investment returns grow less under various conditions, rental and wages and salaries fall, property depreciates in itself and in its value. (*E*) *Many factors in business yield disservice as well as service.* Depreciation is a disservice. Questions thus arise, such as, How long will ability of service continue, utilities hold over, values remain, rentals bring surplus over cost of maintenance (a disservice), interest rates stand amid present fluctuations, and so on?

§ 64. (B) **Business power is prophetic of the future.** At times it discounts the future, and its success in doing so is important in relation to all utilities and values.

§ 65. Here appears the necessity of a sinking fund to offset various depreciations, and here emerges the value of the "compartment idea" in business, the "ship" floating if one compartment fills and becomes useless in supporting power.

§ 66. Business power understands also that however far its prophetic insight may penetrate the future (B) **there is a point which the business**

world in general may not see. At times this fact affords an individual some advantage, which he should be quick to seize. At other times assurance must be modified, at least make concessions, in order to induce other business enterprises to follow. The owner of a large tract of land on a river, so located that, by cutting a canal, extensive water-power privileges and riparian interests might be created, saw the far-distant possibilities of the property, but held his prices beyond the vision of others. The land stood idle twenty years—and so stood the owner's capital. Had he modified his demands in part, activity could have been started with his property by so much, and the returns would have been—prices paid together with increased perceived values of the remainder.

This incident is used only for illustration. The inability of others to see as far into the future as you are able to do is frequently your great opportunity. Land may be purchased on the outskirts of a city and held for prospective rise in recognized value. In such a case the purchaser is called a speculator and it is said that he keeps the land out of use. As a matter of fact, the land is in a certain kind of use, a use which merely defers a more evident use. "Wise land speculating means simply the discriminating choice, out of a number of uses, of that use or series of uses which affords to-day the greatest present value." And this statement is good with reference to any other article which may so be handled. **(B) Business power sees the superior future use, and plans accordingly.**

But on the other hand one may fancy a far vision, or even be sure of it, and because he cannot get the public to see with him, or because he does not discover conditions which the reality of his vision brings inevitably with it, be discounted in the practical world and perhaps ruined.

In "*The Pit*," the following scene illustrates the point in question:

"This market is going up to two dollars." (Jadwin.)

"Reports on the new crop will begin to come in in June (Gretry's warning was almost a cry). The price of wheat is so high now, that God knows how many farmers will plant it this spring. You may have to take care of a second harvest."

"I know better (Jadwin). I'm watching this thing. I've got it all figured out, your 'new crop.'"

"Well, then, you're the Lord Almighty himself."

"And for upwards of two hours Jadwin argued and figured, and showed to Gretry endless tables of statistics to prove that he was right. But at the end Gretry shook his head.

"If you run it up to two dollars, it will be that top-heavy that the littlest kick in the world will knock it over. Be satisfied now with what you got, J. It's common sense. Close out your long May, and then stop. Suppose the price does break a little, you'd still make your pile. But swing this deal over into July, and it's ruin, ruin!"

And it was—a frightful ruin.

On the other hand, again, all great cities stand on land that has been sold too soon by someone. It is just business power to know the right time—and no book in the world can instruct on that point. Business instinct knows; nothing else does know.

Business instinct is either born with a man or cultivated by the man himself.

§ 67. Now, (*E*) "*the fundamental law of value is the law of diminishing Utility.*" Marginal utility decreases as wants are satisfied. All things used in the production of other things which satisfy wants are subject to the law of diminishing returns. Returns increase up to a certain point, but they then may diminish. One man may handle one machine effectively, or two, or more, up to a given number, and beyond this point his effectiveness diminishes, and so the returns from his work. Similarly with the number of workmen engaged on a given task. So with the use of means of transportation, or of a piece of land, or of a business situation in a given place. There is, then, a *margin of utilization beyond which to go is poor business.*

§ 68. **(B) Business power perceives when the diminishing marginal utility of goods has reached the limit of appealing to desire, or when the cost in any sense of carrying a condition seriously threatens the prospective gain, and at that point it unloads at almost any price (or sacrifice) in order to a change of commodities, or conditions, and the holding of trade, or the "making good" out of a bad situation.** It is business ability to see when customers have had enough at old prices; when a situation (man or machine or condition) will not stand any further burden or pressure.

§ 69. A similar relation holds with reference to prices and the supply of money. (*E*) *Prices indicate value expressed in terms of money.* "Money acts upon prices in no other way than by being tendered in exchange for commodities. The demand which influences the prices of commodities consists of the money offered for them " (Mill). If commodity supply remains unchanged, but money supply increases, demand will quicken and prices will rise. But if the money supply decreases, demand will slacken and prices will fall. (*E*) *Increase of money supply means decrease in purchasing power of each piece of money* (reference, of course, is to the public supply, not the individual or private). (*E*) *Decrease of money supply means increase in each piece's purchasing power.* The money may be perfectly "good," but we demand more commodities for what money we have. If, now, the commodity supply increases while the money supply remains the same, more goods will be offered for each piece of money, competition will increase, and prices will fall. If the commodity supply be decreased while money supply remains unchanged, prices will rise, because we shall be willing to give more money for a part of a limited stock of commodities desired. When both supplies rise or fall together, the one change tends to offset the other.

§ 70. But most commodities pass through at least three hands: producer, wholesaler, retailer. The transactions involved call for more money than would the passing from maker directly to consumer. **(B) Business power gets the goods or services to the last purchaser as quickly and as cheaply as possible.** Money is then free to perform other and new functions. Yet a proportion of money ordinarily called for may serve all the people

mentioned.   Nevertheless, the demand for money is
still greater than would suffice to carry raw material to finished product placed in the hands of the
retail purchaser.   Speaking in a universal sense,
the (*E*) *supply of money is never equal to the volume
of business in a given time.*

§ 71.   (*E*)   *When prices fall, the value of money
has increased, and this fact tends to draw gold and
silver into circulation.   When prices rise, the volume
of increase of money supply tends to decrease because
mines cannot be operated so cheaply.*

§ 72.   Business power craves money, but it
remembers that beyond a given point, the money
supply may decrease the value of money units, by
decreasing their purchasing power, or by increasing
prices so greatly as to check business, and that below a given point the low supply may so increase
the value of money units as to check business by
decrease of prices.

A very successful business man, who had purchased "*Power for Success*" because it contains
some phases of the "new thought," which is really
hundreds of years old, for the most part, said to me:
"I found when I got into the book that it was
teaching many things I had practised all my life,
only I had never known them as you put them."
Precisely so in regard to the present and following
chapter, it may be, with some of my readers.   The
definite statements in italics and blackletter may
seem technical and somewhat foreign until they are
thoroughly understood ; and then they will appear
to be simply common sense.   *But always is it true
that a man is the better and stronger for knowing in
a definite way that he knows what he knows.*

§ 73. For, we acquire truth only through experience. It is experience that gives us the material with which thought is built up. Every vocation has its *body of thought*, and in each case—in business, in law, in medicine, in educational work—the body of thought is determined by the work demanded. Business experience furnishes the material which the business man builds into business thought. So of the professions. So of any department in business.

§ 74. Now, experience divides into—*external* and *internal*. There is outward experience of physical affairs. This provides the material of objective practical thought. There is inner experience of the mental life. This provides for the purely mental body of thought.

Observe, in passing: this is important. What a man's body of thought is, that is the man himself. The saying is familiar: "As a man thinketh in his heart, so is he." The truth may be put in this way:

Not, as a man thinks he is, is he; but as a man thinks, he is.

§ 75. The inner experience, again, divides, into, *experience of the self through mind*, and, *experience of the self in self*. Mind consists of certain ways the self has of being and doing. Self and mind, then, are not identical. We have mind-experience, and also self-experience below these ways of being and doing (mind).

§ 76. Therefore, the proposition that experience furnishes the material for every body of thought makes toward this deeper proposition:

By concentrated thinking instruction is comprehended, but *it is through the profounder experi-*

ence of the self working unconsciously, below the mere mind-operations, that a man's real body of thought is built up.

You are invited, then, to think the two present chapters (indeed, all of this book) with all your powers; to think them to the ordinary understanding of language, but—to think them in the light of, or in terms of, your own business experience. The invitation is of incalculable significance and value.

When you think the paragraphs in terms of your business experience, you force—or, better, lead—your subconscious self to experience their substance.   Then the finished materials of this "underground" process are turned over to the working of your business mind and built into your body of business thought.

CHAPTER VIII.

ECONOMIC LAWS AND BUSINESS AXIOMS: CONTINUED.

IN the preliminary of Chapter VII, I studied a few words which led to the notion of business as a share-getting. What water is to agriculture, money is to business. Without money, life is a desert, and business would be an elephantine swap. We may conceive of arid lands into which men have conducted from some distant river innumerable canals. The agriculturist here must dig his ditches and in one way or another get water to his acres. The process of doing so, among so many thousands of workers, will develop all sorts of laws or rules in the matter. The successful farmer will be the man who knows the laws, and knows the practical application thereof, and digs the best ditches, and controls the most water—according to the rules. As a business man you are merely digging canals for money to flow your way. You cannot create money; there is just so much in the world; your problem is simply this· to turn a portion of the total supply to your own uses. Business power "canals" money into its chosen territory.

§ 1. "Economics is the science which treats of those social phenomena due to the wealth-getting and wealth-using activity of man," says Ely in *"Outlines of Economics."* The field of activity may be divided into Public and Private. In the one we have, for example, "taxation in its various forms, the management of State property, the appropriation of State revenues, and the management of monopolies owned by the municipality or the State." In the other we have, Production, Distribution of goods (whatever has economic utility), Transfer of goods, and Consumption." When the wealth-getting and wealth-using activities of man as just indicated come together for mutuality of interest, we have in a broad sense—

MARKETS.

§ 2. (E) *The comparison of utilities and the play of values back and forth develop the market.* A market originally meant a place where desired commodities and services were exchanged. The market now signifies the existence of offers and demands for the same commodity or service affecting exchanges. There are thus as many markets as there are commodities and services bought and sold. In a more usual sense, markets are local, national, international.

§ 3. The world's great market, considered with reference to its total exchanges, may be compared to the circulatory system of the body. There is a constant circulation of things having utility, taking place from one town, city, county, state, nation, to another,—goods being exchanged for money and money for goods. This circulation requires great marts, banks for money accounts and clearing houses for the offsetting of financial transactions.

§ 4. (*E*) *The general market depends for its condition upon supply and demand, economic and social marginal utility, and volume and value of money and a general purchasing ability.* Actual purchasing ability is of course increased by credit. This broad statement might be reduced considerably, but its meanings will come out later.

§ 5. Incidentally it is the business man's function to assist in the circulation above referred to, goods-utilities or service-utilities passing to and from him, and money moving through his enterprise in various directions, but diverted in part to his own private uses.

§ 6. Every legitimate business serves the public and its owner, if it is successful, but only as both parties secure a proportionate benefit from its conduct. It is a popular error that a community is benefited by a losing business because of special prices. We need but to suppose such apparent advantage to be continued to the ruin of all businesses in order to see the end—a destroyed market.

§ 7. The factors of market are not only supply and demand, but also a kind of activity which is profitable to all engaged therein. Whatever really hurts a fair market, hurts the people. All market variations below a "normal" standard of price must sooner or later be equalized, and the people do the equalizing.

§ 8. Business power justifies only in a paying business, as well with regard to the public as with regard to the business man himself. The business man is a part of the public.

§ 9. The business man must know his own particular markets, for variations therein enable him to offset disadvantages in one market by advantages in others. One of these markets may give him a leader, while knowledge of another may suggest temporary withdrawal into more promising fields or conditions.

§ 10. **(B) Business power anticipates future markets.** It is alert and always considers such questions as: What will be the probable supply of a given commodity, probable demand, probable prices, local or national events capable of influencing markets and prices, probable offsets of custom and customary conditions, and so on.

§ 11. Not only are market contingencies to be foreseen, but *directions in which they tend and localities in which they are likely to spring up.* Most things in the world follow the line of least resistance, but markets often select the lines of greatest *apparent* resistance by sheer accident or because of remote offsetting advantages. It seems to be a general law that trade marks cannot successfully be built up at arbitrary will of man. The real-estate-agent's "town" sometimes proves disappointing. Business power often consists in an instinct to "get from under," or "to pull out" of doomed conditions, or to foresee new market localities. Some men are always too soon, while others are always too late. **(B) Business power "arrives" on time—a little ahead.** When the San Francisco disaster became known in the East, the head of one of the largest concerns for supply of

typewriting and office materials in the world, insisted upon immediately shipping to his agent in
the doomed city a large consignment to the Company
for its agent's use. The agent reported, "First
arrival of goods of the kind, and greatly needed."
This was business alertness and initiative in regard
to markets.

One of the writer's university classmates secured a position as land agent for a great railway
system. He soon discovered a considerable tract
of land on the railway's line out several miles from
a growing city. Accompanied by his wife, both
shabbily dressed, driving a wornout horse and
seated in a creaking buggy, the young man quietly
wandered through the neighborhood securing op-
tions on farms until he had gained control of the
entire tract. When the railway company got to its
necessary land purchase, it found my friend in
possession. A lecture followed on the college
man's methods of serving the system, which you
may or may not applaud; the land-agent's profits
secured independence. This also was alertness
and initiative in relation to market.

Supply, Demand, and Prices.

§ 12. Markets involve supply, demand and
prices. If we consider the total existing quantity
of a given commodity, we have in mind the whole
stock. A stock may or not constitute the supply.
(*E*) *Supply means "the quantity offered at given
price or prices in the market."* Thus, existing goods
are not always "in the market," and not, then, a
commercial supply. They may be "held back" by
operation of law, or for a rise in prices. (B) **Busi-**

ness power often withholds stock from supply
for better prices, or floods supply either for existing prices in anticipation of lower, or for the
purpose of securing lower and buying in for a
future rise, or manœuvres to get stock into
supply for the advantage of present or expected
prices.

§ 13. Demand indicates desire, but the (E)
desire-demand may differ from the market demand.
A market demand is a desire practically affecting
the market by offer of prices or taking at existing
prices. Demand is really an expression of estimate
of utility to the demander—signifying, How much
this article or lot is worth in usefulness of any sort
to me. This estimate differs as all of one's wants
or some of them are satisfied with reference to a
given article or lot. By so much as some of the
wants are supplied, by so much is marginal utility
diminished and demand made less. The man who
has a few needful things will demand less of any
other thing than the man who has nothing at all.
In other words, (E) *demand for any given needed
article is affected by possession of other different
needed articles in the measure of the limits of the
purchasing medium possessed.* Of course this is
also true of the same kind of articles. Generally
speaking, utility—"by and large," diminishes with
possession "by and large." A man who has just
dined off a boiled dinner does not now desire lobster salad, though the latter may be his favorite
dish, as he would have desired the salad had he not
already eaten. A merchant's feeling of "enough
goods" or "enough income" may have no room
for demand-desire for even the "choicest line.'

And if he has that line in sufficient quantity, your more or less has to him diminished utility. Business power is always dealing with this double form of diminished utility—utility diminished by possession of articles which temporarily "kill" other wants, and utility diminished by possession of articles immediately and specifically desired in sufficient present quantities.

§ 14. (*E*) *This sliding scale of utility affords the law of demand.* **(B) Business power meets the scale by manipulating goods, supply, or prices.** Of course, individual transactions are affected by personal qualities. Considered in its individual relations, business power consists in the ability to offset a diminished utility by demand-desire created through personal skill and address. At a satisfactory price any man can sell any other man what he immediately wants. Business power sometimes manifests in selling a man what he does not want. But that kind of *buying* is not business at all.

§ 15. A demand for commodities or services is a recognition of demand for money. The value of money expressed in terms of things desired depends commonly on supply and demand. "Money plenty, prices low; money scarce, prices high." And the more money a person possesses, the less the utility to him of any given piece of money—unless he is a miser. Hence, (*E*) *market demand is a kind of offset of the marginal utility of goods or services and the marginal utility of money.* A man buys when the first utility seems greater to him than the second, and never otherwise—except at an auction. **(B) Business power endeavors in some way to compel the marginal utility of**

goods to exceed the marginal utility of money —or the reverse, as the case may be.

§ 16.   Now, (*E*) *the marginal utility of money depends on its purchasing power*, or the degree in which individual wants are satisfied, and on the individual's income.   The statement is just as true in regard to the seller as it is in regard to the buyer. There is no business power without a keen appreciation of the marginal utility of money, not for its own sake, but for the sake of its value as an instrument.   The less the estimate of the marginal utility of money to the purchaser, the better for the business man, provided that estimate does not become universal among sellers, for then, since the latter will offer larger quantities for less money, high prices might more than offset all his advantages because he has to buy as well as sell.   Business power, therefore, desires that the general run of incomes be good, for while the estimate of the marginal utility of money will decrease somewhat with rise in income, the ability to spend money will also increase, and the satisfaction of further existence-wants and new culture-wants will counterbalance money's lesser personal valuation.   You cannot do a profitable business among slaves, either physical or industrial.

§ 17.   *The question of income is important in the study of demand.*   We may illustrate various factors indicated in this and the preceding chapters by means of a convenient outline given below.   Our basis for illustration will be the universal desire for objects deemed necessary to a reasonable existence.   Whatever the supply of such articles may be, income is always a factor when men decide among marginal utilities as to which shall determine demand. Statistics show that about nine-tenths of the incomes of very poor people are expended for the satisfaction of mere existence-wants,—for food, shelter, clothing, etc. Nearly half of the income of such a family will be expended for food alone. As the income of a family increases, its members prefer to expend a constantly increasing proportion of their means for the satisfaction of culture-wants. As the income increases, food expenses *relatively* decrease; clothing expenses and those of rent, fuel, light, remain about the same (at least for a time), and expenses for health, education, recreation, etc., increase.

VARIATIONS IN MARGINAL UTILITIES.

Living Wants Income Limited			Always the questions of comparative marginal utility and income ability obtain.	
	Food	Meats / Vegetables / Bread-Stuffs / Fruits		
	House	Rental Price / Owner's Expense		All these wants vary;
	Heat & Light	Wood / Coal / Oil / Gas / Electricity		Must be compared;
	Clothing	Men's / Women's / Children's / Necessary / Special		The greatest wants prevail
	Amusement	Recreation / Theatre / Vacation		Income *must* limit demand and prices
	Health	Medicine / Sanitation / Outing		
	Education	Common / College / Technical / Special		

Remembering, now, that effective demand depends not only on supply of goods in market, but also on the differing strength of differing desires, together with the question of ability to purchase, the suggestiveness of the illustration-table above becomes at once apparent. It indicates variations surely obtaining in marginal utilities, demands, and prices possible to consumers.

§ 18. Business power may adjust itself to the facts indicated in the table by putting prices within reach, by supplying the kind of goods that will satisfy demands possible to incomes, by catering to higher incomes. In other words, **(B) business power assists in making given incomes effective for demand, or creates demand by appealing to larger ability to purchase.** A grocer store in a tenement district does the one thing, a high-priced outfitter up town does the other thing.

§ 19. *(E) When price remains the same, demand for a commodity corresponds to its marginal utility. When the latter remains the same, demand corresponds with price. When income increases, demand advances for culture-wants for a time and then for existence-wants.* When income decreases, demand for culture-wants soon falls off and a margin of existence-wants will also decrease demand. **(B) Business power desires good wages and salaries** as a condition of its life.

MARKET PRICE AND VALUE.

§ 20. There is a certain price-point on either side of which the market-price fluctuates. This is the normal price. *The market value is the actual value or selling power in the market from day to day.*

of any given commodity. The *normal* price should not be confused with the *average* price. The latter can only be determined by averaging prices for a period, but the question is a question of business judgment. Business power cultivates such judgment. Average price may go above or below normal price,—for a time. Normal price, of course, may vary with long-run changing conditions. Normal prices during war are higher than during a time of peace, and differ in different localities. **(B) Business power senses normal values and prices and takes advantage of market fluctuations.** It studies the forces that produce such fluctuations and change the level of prices, and also all sources of supply.

§ 21. Business is the handling of comparative marginal utilities, as we have seen; hence, (*E*) *the law of exchange is just this law of comparative marginal utilities, or the law of reciprocal demand, under which a higher marginal utility of goods to one man than the marginal utility of money to him brings about an exchange of money for goods and of goods for money.* Business deals with comparative costs of articles purchased for a sale set over against comparative prices of articles purchased for consumption either in personal satisfaction or in manufacture. The successful business man is always studying these matters, although very likely he is not aware of the fact as above expressed.

COMPETITION AND PRICES.

§ 22. (*E*) *It is competition, speaking broadly, that sets a limit to market fluctuations and tends always to restore prices to normal.* But the state of

competition should be free and legitimate, that is,
uncontrolled by artificial means and consistent with
the doctrine, "live and let live." Under such
competition a single price will prevail for a given
commodity at a given time and place, as a general
rule. In competition the market price is that
at which the largest number of exchanges
can be made. When competition is absent or
one-sided, that is, when a monopoly prevails,
the highest price, so far as possible, will
ultimately obtain. Consolidation, reduction of
expenses, and so on, may for a time induce lower
prices, but in the end, if no other causes intervene, prices will follow the dictation of human
selfishness.

§ 23. **(B) Business power proves adequate
to competition.** This is really a vastly important
commonplace. Business power knows the field,
and the causes of all sorts of variations therein. It
seeks to regulate prices through regulation of intake or outgo of goods. It secures a monopoly
when able to do so through best service, or the
factors of form-value, place-value, timeliness, most
direct transportation, cheapest prices with superior
qualities,—through any legitimate exercise of business skill; but remembers that absolute control has
its responsibilities, and, therefore, its dangers.
The man who corners wheat must reckon with
wheat. He who builds a monopoly of what the
people need must at last face the popular monopoly
of power. Monopolies gained by fraud, secret
understandings not open to all, control of legislation of a discriminating nature, speaks for itself.
Criticism for such is due not so much to individuals

as to situations made or kept possible by the people who govern themselves.

§ 24. If a generally free activity of trade is the life of business, the annihilation of competition means financial death, and a wholly arbitrary manipulation of the market is really a threat against the manipulator, for it may kill demand, or compel new inventions or adjustments that will turn demand elsewhere.

§ 25. I have observed certain advertisements for and against "copper" interests. Vilification and what may be called "unbusinesslike play" by way of false rumors set afloat, secrets outside of legitimate use of business skill, and all that sort of thing, appear to be in evidence. Such "business" is based on none of the laws of economics and business maxims, but is purely a variety of grown-up boys' play, devoid of decent dignity and real commercial ability. Business is not trickery.

NATURE OF COMPETITION.

§ 26. (*E*) "*The existence of a market in which the same products exchange at a single price generally presupposes the existence of competition.* In its widest sense, competition denotes a struggle of conflicting interests, in which each person endeavors to accomplish his own ends, or to secure some advantage to himself, in the face of similar efforts on the part of his rivals." (B) **Business power is forever alert for these advantages.**

§ 27. (*E*) "*Competition is not simply a contest to divide an existing sum, but a struggle to share in an increasing stock.* The first requisite of securing an additional stock is to produce more. In this struggle to dispose of the increased product to the whole body of the consumers the victory will be with those that can create better or cheaper products. (*E*) *Thus competition as a business principle means a struggle to augment wealth through a lowering of cost.*"

§ 28. Hence, if the individual competitor incidentally amasses a fortune, he does so honestly so far as competition is concerned, but he also confers a benefit upon the public. **(B) True business power does not complain because some rival has achieved a greater success than another, but pays the greater heed to better business methods.** Jealousy of any man's success is a weakness altogether foreign to power in business.

§ 29. *Competition increases total capital —* when it is legitimate. Legitimate competition is competition in an open field and a fair fight conducted according to established economic laws and universally recognized business maxims. Such competition is the consumer's great protection against exorbitant prices. (It should be remembered that consumption in business does not necessarily mean destruction; it may mean uses for the furtherance of trade no less than for the satisfaction of final human wants. The business man is a consumer in that he transforms the shape or character of commodities in handling them for trade.) For competition is "the automatic force which reduces the gains of the inefficient and makes profits depend on law, rather than on high prices. It evokes in individuals the fundamental characteristics of energy, thrift and power; and it harmonizes to a large extent the interests of the individual and society, by making the success of one depend primarily on what he can accomplish for the other." True business power always benefits its own environment.

FORMS OF COMPETITION.

§ 30. Competition assumes various forms. *Commodity-competition* "is due to the existence of social choices. Every individual is continually debating with himself whether to purchase one commodity in preference to another. (*E*) *Where he is on the margin of doubt or of indifference the slightest alteration in the price will cause him to substitute something else.* The principle involved is called the *principle of substitution.*" **(B) Business power is alert to overcome this margin of doubt or indifference by personal skill while maintaining prices at the former level or up to profit.** But it knows that price is a heavy consideration which personal skill must reckon with.

§ 31. (B) "The vendor must constantly be on the watch lest any increase of price cause the disappearance of his sales."

§ 32. But the vendor should also be on the watch for any decrease or increase in the purchaser's ability to pay—meaning, of course, the purchaser in a general sense.

Competition among individuals denotes a rivalry, "not between the producers of different commodities or between the different factors of production, but between the producers of the same commodities or the same factors of production. Under normal conditions competition here puts every one on his mettle, and success is a measure of his contribution to the social fund. (*E*) *Competition between individuals is in its results a struggle to enhance efficiency, to increase faculty, to multiply productive power, to augment ingenuity, in short, to develop economic personality.*"

§ 33. (*E*) "*By market competition we mean, not the competition of individuals in the market, but the competition of markets with each other.*" "Every great city is constantly striving to develop as a centre of distribution and exchange, in the well-founded hope that the wealth thus amassed will lead to a productive efficiency in other lines. Here again market competition leads to reduced cost, and the struggle for market supremacy can be fought to a successful issue only through more effective service."

(B) Business power never regards its business as a side-show, but treats its own particular field as a centre of local conditions. The man who puts the "I-am-a-centre" thought into his business has surely a wider outlook and a keener alertness for that very fact. Leadership always insists on staying in the middle of the fight or on making itself a centre of activities.

§ 34. *Cross competition* is seen as between laborers and capitalists, or as between landowners and merchants or factory owners. **(B) Business power does not cross-compete when so doing will threaten its intake of commodities or services or its money income or its credit in any artificial sense.**

§ 35. (*E*) "*Whether the moneyed interest or the landed interest is more prosperous depends at bottom upon their success in making converts among the consumers, and the extent of conversion depends on what they (such interests) can offer in the way of better prices or better products."*

§ 36. (E) *Competition among nations is a struggle for foreign markets.* "The modern doctrine is that every nation is helped by the prosperity of its neighbor, on the principle that the more wealthy the consumer the greater will be his purchases." I do not see why the family should not be here substituted for the nation; nor why any reputable business should not be regarded as a nation in this matter—to the extent that each is benefited by the success of all, but not that any should be absorbed or driven out of existence by another. "The foreign markets can be retained only by underselling; the profits of one country can be secured only by conferring these advantages on the consumers of the others." The question is, On what underselling profits can a people thrive? for the underselling involves factors that come home to the people themselves. Precisely so in regard to the individual business; underselling not consistent with reasonable profit and general well-being is murder. And a nation has no more business right to murder another nation than an individual has to undersell a competitor out of business by surrendering his profits for the purpose.

§ 37. Competition of any form which goes to the extent of exhausting both competitors is, of course, suicidal. This human vice can never be a commercial virtue.

§ 38. Good business is actual mutualism. Under natural conditions, every kind of legitimate

business is benefited by the success of other kinds,
—even in straight competition if the successful
business develops in itself and its competitor
greater business ability,—and, to a degree, this law
holds good among different enterprises in related
lines. If one enterprise in a community does a
certain amount of business, it often *happens that
two enterprises of the same kind will do more than
the original amount, perhaps twice as much, perhaps
even more.* There is a limit, however, to the working of the law, and **(B) business power does not
crowd into a full field,** as a general rule, except
when positive leadership goes with it. It should
be remembered that where business is successful,
business conditions are constantly improving to the
limit indicated by population, and that business
itself is one important activity leading to such improvement. **(B) Business power senses the
possibilities of increasing population through
business activities.**

§ 39. **(B) "The greater the equality between the competitors, the more substantial
are the gains of consumers.** If the producer can
in some way be rendered more efficient, so that
the disparity will diminish, to that extent the
community will gain." **(B) Business power remembers that business of any kind is itself a
consumer and forms a part of the community.**
"The strengthening of a weak competitor may
redound to the advantage not only of the competitor himself, but to that of the whole group, and
ultimately to that of the community."

§ 40. "In ordinary private business, buyers
and sellers make their individual bargains with each

other; and while open competitive prizes tend to uniformity, there is nothing to prevent the more powerful or the more favored purchaser from secretly obtaining a lower price. **(B) Much of the profits of the business man, indeed, consists in this skill in purchasing on favorable terms**; the very essence of usual business practice is this system of different prices to different consumers." Business power secures these differences, but holds its own prices uniform for the sake of public confidence.

"Competition, therefore," as Edwin R. A. Seligman remarks in *"Principles of Economics,"* "is a force that must not be abused. It is applicable only in a slight degree to certain kinds of business, it works most beneficially in the presence of comparative equality, and its level of action (from 'fair' to 'unfair') stands in need of constant elevation. Within these limits, it is a vital and a salutary force."

Cost.

§ 41. (*E*) *"Just as the marginal utility of commodities determines the demand, so the cost of production is a force that governs the supply that producers will be willing to place on the market."* The word "cost" must not be confused with price, the first being sacrifice made by the seller in getting a commodity to sell, the latter being sacrifice by the buyer in making the purchase. (*E*) *"The normal supply price of commodities depends on the cost of production,"* or the cost of having in available stock, but this cost is "the cost of continuous production," not some exceptional cost; and it is

also not some individual cost, but cost in the larger
social sense.   This social cost of continuous reproduction has to be compared with the cost to individuals who might reproduce the article themselves.
If they can reproduce the article at a cost less than
the price asked, they will naturally do so.   **(B)
Business power is always asking, How can I
produce this article myself more cheaply than
those who sell to me?**   My friend the butter-case
man who had merely superintended a high school,
found here his opportunity, and began to feed his
city warehouse with his own products.   If the consumer cannot manufacture an article for less than
others can do, he will pay the price asked according
to the demand-desire possessed.   The producers
or sellers of commodities must keep cost to them
below possible cost to a group of individuals, or
they must go out of business because prices will
not be paid.   In a new country every man is more
or less an all-round possible producer, and one who
desires to sell an article which many can make
must produce below any other man, all things considered.   As individuals become occupied in specialization, cost may increase up to a certain limit,
when competition will force it back to lower levels.
**(B) Business power, therefore, constantly ad-
justs to the community change from simple
conditions up through complex business specialization.**   If it fails to make such adjustment,
it is simply buried out of sight.

§ 42.   (*E*) *"Normal value, then, depends upon
a balancing of marginal utility, the force that
governs demand, against the cost of production, the
force that controls supply."*   How much do the

people practically want your goods? and how much will it cost to supply satisfaction of that demand? This means cost-to-have brought to such a figure that you can induce greater desire for your goods than for other goods, selling price being considered.

§ 43. Every business man, "although his foresight may be imperfect, and his freedom of choice limited, is obliged to study most carefully and searchingly the probable demand for his products, while the closest attention must be paid to every circumstance that affects the cost of production."

§ 44. The normal price, independently more or less of cost, may be influenced by custom or by various personal relations, or by the money-character of patrons, and, as well, by failures of competition, by taxes, by unfortunate mistakes in production, by combinations, by the utilization of by-products in particular cases, by difficulty in determining expenses, and by monopolies of various kinds. To all these influences the business man must necessarily attend, or go to the wall.

PROFIT.

§ 45. The circulation of goods and money through a business enterprise must yield some return to its conductor. This return, net, is profit. "If you are not making, you are losing." Profit issues from dealing with labor (or service), land, or "capital," whether or no "goods" be involved. Profits are ordinary and differential. *Ordinary profits* are the differences between the cost of production or acquisition and the selling price, in regular business dealings, in a repetition of similar transactions, in competition with others. Certain important factors should here be noted. "If fifty employers are engaged in furnishing the needed supply of goods at a certain price, we know that the price will be high enough to cover the expense of producing the most expensive (to the producers) or marginal portion of the supply. Any employers who try to enter the business, but are unable to sell at this price, will have to fail. But the marginal producers, who furnish the most expensive (to them) portion of the supply, just manage to get a fair return on their investment—because their expenses are greater than those of others and they can only sell at the going prices. (*E*) *Prices must be high enough to allow marginal producers to secure a necessary or minimum profit.*" That is to say, the existence of people in business whose expenses are greater than the majority of other people indicates that the prices are higher than they otherwise would be under free competition.

§ 46. **(B) True business power is never a marginal producer,** because it discovers in some way a method for decreasing cost to make or possess, just as my friend the college-bred school superintendent who got into the butter-tub business, put his little country factory under the planer, so to speak, until he could more than meet his competitors' prices.

§ 47. "Other employers who produce goods at less cost than the marginal expense (beyond which no one could do business) will secure, not only necessary (ordinary) profits, but also a further *differential profit* that depends on the differences in their costs of production." **(B) Business power** is always engaged in seeking and securing the differential profit.

(B) In the long run the determining factor which gives a man the differential profit is superiority of ability.

§ 48. "The expenses of production (and, it may be added, of handling goods or services) are manifold," says Seligman, "but may in the most developed businesses be classified into wages, rent, interest, taxes and miscellaneous outlays like insurance, advertisements and transportation expenses. All of these obviously vary from individual to individual. Some will display more care in the selection and arrangement of their labor force (a young printer said: I have seen a number of my acquaintances go to the wall in my business because they hire help instead of working harder themselves when a little run of trade has come in); some will choose a more advantageous location, with a saving of both rent and transportation; some will accomplish better results with less capital and economize in interest as well as taxes; some will exercise more ingenuity in advertising or securing a market. At the bottom of the scale is the marginal producer (or business man), working under the least favorable circumstances, and who can nevertheless get no more for his goods. With him, price equals cost; with the others, price exceeds cost."

If you put lead shoes on the feet of *business power*, it will not remain at the "bottom of the scale," for it will sell the lead at the highest price and secure a further supply gratis.

§ 49. (E) "*In general it can be said that pure profits consist of wealth created by the power of given business men over and above what would have been produced by the same application of labor and capital under less efficient leadership or management.*" Such profits are doubly valuable: in themselves as extra profits, and in the fact that they do not affect prices, since these are indicated by the marginal expenses of production (or business) under the least efficient employers who are able to stay in business. **(B) Business power is in business, not to keep profits down by the fact that its prices allow it no leeway for the reduction of expenses, but to keep profits up by decrease of expenses so that it can always sell at an advantage.**

§ 50. Monopolistic profits may be differential (or superior) for the reasons above suggested, or because of control of "natural wealth." Those who secure control of such opportunity need to forefend against a point when the overplus of production decreases. At the same time, it may be said in regard to certain smaller opportunities that the question is decisive for real business power whether to dabble at a proposition forever or make a reasonable success within a reasonable time.

§ 51. (*E*) *Speculative profits result from "concentration and intensification of the forces which offset supply and demand."* What is regarded as legitimate speculative business is as subject to business law as any other enterprise. "The modern stock and produce exchanges have a definite economic function to perform."

§ 52. "Speculation occurs in securities or commodities. The qualities which render a commodity peculiarly fit for regular speculative dealings are three in number: (a) it must be a staple, with a large and regular production; (b) it must be homogeneous in quality, so that any unit will be as acceptable as another; (c) it must be capable of ready definition and measurement." This does not, of course, refer to "speculation in land," which is simply a buying and selling on an upward market, or deferring sale until conditions advance value, or manipulating environment for the purpose of enhancing value.

§ 53. The Exchange carries various risks which the ordinary business man must otherwise meet and for which he would not be equal. The Exchange keeps the markets open in a way, enables the business man to "hedge" against possible losses by buying and selling against himself, and tends to steady prices.

§ 54. In conclusion, certain rather familiar considerations may now be added by way of suggestion.

(1) The greater the long-run difference between cost and price, the greater the business success, and **(B) business power never forgets that long run.**

(2) It is better, therefore, to maintain profit by reduction of cost—quality remaining unchanged or improved—than by continuing an old price, for not only is competition a fact in business, but its usual results are demanded by consumers—that is, they are always in search of cheaper goods and services.

(3) Reduction of expenses, the stoppage of leaks, the utilization of waste, cheaper purchases, superior ability, economy and hard work, invention

of new methods for accomplishing old results, seizure of opportunity, and so on, are more valuable business items than increase or maintenance of prices, even when possible for the long run because such factors mean a closer and a larger business.

(4) An advantage slighted for the sake of patrons is often the straightest road to higher profits. In many cases of this kind business power builds solidly its best asset—public confidence.

CREDIT.

§ 55. (B) **Business power secures and maintains credit at its highest level.** If you wish a standing for "good credit," you must earn it. No man can earn such standing on a strict cash basis, for in that case, when inquiry is made as to his credit; nobody knows: "he always pays cash." Credit rating is purely commercial,—although the broad commercial sense by no means altogether excludes the element of character.

§ 56. Among the early Greeks credit meant the "art of prudent and systematic household management." This is one of the bed-rock factors of business power: *prudent and systematic management of financial enterprises.*

§ 57. If we look at the matter of credit from several standpoints, we shall obtain as many different ideas of the word and factor.

(A) One gets credit when another simply "trusts" him for an equivalent, agreed or otherwise, of commodities surrendered or services given. This transaction is merely an experiment so far as real credit is concerned. It really means nothing more than a "charge" made on a chance.

(B) One has credit when another surrenders goods or services with confidence that the equivalent will be forthcoming. The confidence may be tinctured with some doubt as to promptness, or as to full payment at once when due, or as to payment only after solicitation or compulsion. Or the confidence may be perfect and clear.

(C) One has credit when his reputation for business promptness and honor is established and well known.

(D) And one has credit when his property holdings are known or believed to be sufficient to cover his liabilities—when he is financially "good." A man's reputation for character may be "bad" while his commercial credit is nevertheless sound because his possessions furnish creditors ample resources.

(E) One has credit when his business honor and his financial holdings are known to co-operate.

§ 58. **(B) The credit of business power at its best is based on prompt and full meeting of all obligations, a high reputation for honor, and ample property back of all liabilities.**

§ 59. The above conceptions spring from the attitude assumed by one man toward another—say, lender toward borrower. From the view-point of *rights established*, (E) *"credit is the present right to a future payment, or credit is the right or property of demanding something from some one else.* It is the right to a future payment; it is the name of a certain species of right or property (Henry Dunning Macleod, in *'The Theory of Credit'*)—secured in one man by a transaction with another."

§ 60. Business power respects this right in a business and moral way, remembering that the right represents mutualism, and, in order to possess the right in full in regard to any, it also makes the right good in regard to all. You must accord what you ask.

§ 61. Viewed from the standpoint of the man who wishes to use credit, "*credit is a power to borrow*"—commodities or services to be returned in kind or in money or its equivalent, says M. G. Faucett, in "*Political Economy for Beginners.*" Thus, power to borrow depends, so far as the borrower is concerned, on reputation and supposed property. Doubt in these respects raises interest demanded and increases amount of security required.

§ 62. (B) **Business power maintains its credit at the highest, that is, the least expensive, level.** This least expensive level is maintained by personal integrity, business ability, and property backing.

§ 63. It is thus seen that credit "rests largely on confidence, trust, faith, and good opinion; that it is not moral character (*per se*), but business reputation, that establishes and maintains good credit; that it is a power inherently resting upon the qualities enumerated above to borrow money or any other class of property; that one of the principal elements entering into credit is that of futurity, or a deferred fulfillment of an obligation," says W. A. Prendergast "*Credit and its Uses.*"

§ 64. *Credit, therefore, is a business asset.* It is an asset in two ways:

First, (*E*) *its representatives* (notes, checks, drafts, accounts, etc.,) *may be used as assets because they stand for a legal right inhering in the lender to collect at maturity.*

"Every case of a 'loan' of money or a sale of goods 'on credit,' is an exchange, or an act of commerce. In exchange for the money or the goods a right of action is created; and is the price of the goods. The right of action is a saleable commodity; which may be bought and sold like any material chattel: and it has value because it will be paid in money. This right of action may circulate in commerce exactly like a piece of money, until it is paid off and extinguished; and then it ceases to exist."

Secondly, (E) *credit, in the sense of being a "power to borrow," is an asset because it may substitute for the actual use of other existing capital.*

§ 65. (B) **Business power keeps a close and constant watch on its credit rights,** for millions of capital are lost by failure in this respect; but in such watch it employs business tact, knows when to claim the right and when to forbear in the interest of its own future, and cultivates an instinct which determines its action in the matter.

Here, for example, is a foreign agent who manages to keep himself in debt to a manufacturing concern about $15,000, but who, nevertheless, turns into the concern something like $10,000 a year. The "head" says: "This man does so good a business with us that we can afford to carry over the $15,000 charge, and we *could afford* to cancel the debt for the sake of the *running business.* (B) **Business power knows how to offset an advantage against a sacrifice.**

§ 66. **(B) Business power maintains the
asset of credit at its highest level, does not
fear, then, to use this species of intangible
property, and studies how to employ it to the
greatest advantage.**

§ 67. You cannot construct the power called
credit; it must grow, and its growth requires the
three factors, personal integrity, business ability,
and property backing.   For such growth the chief
element would seem to be business ability—at least
in the commercial world, and taken by and large.
Your integrity may be undoubted, and your
material assets may be good, but without known
business ability your commercial credit, your
liberty to use the credit power as a business asset,
will be nil in the one case, and limited to the
credit-worth of such material assets in the latter
case.   If personal integrity is doubtful, the credit
asset will depend on the credit-worth of property
possessed.   But when business ability is believed
in, the use of credit-power as an asset may far outrun property basis and even leave personal integrity
untouched in the transaction because of assured
legal resources.   Nevertheless, an analysis of one's
credit-asset can never be altogether independent of
the element of integrity.   When business ability
and character combine in one man, his credit-asset
is often equivalent to millions of money.   Were
this asset not recognized in the business world
because of these two factors, its own activities
would be enormously curtailed.

§ 68. **(B) The credit-asset is kept good as
well as developed by strict business integrity,
by fulfillment of all guaranties, by prompt and**

full payment of all liabilities, by openly held property rights, and by demonstration of business ability.

§ 69. (B) The credit asset is depreciated by lapses in integrity, by looseness in dealings, by uncertainties and delays in payments, by putting property "out of sight," by business mistakes, and by other business methods not calculated to inspire confidence.

§ 70. In the last named factor we have two great threats against credit-asset: "speculation" and "overtrading."

Speculation tends to overload an otherwise essential and legitimate element in business—that of risk. There can be no business without some degree of risk. When a man goes into business with only his brains and body, he risks himself, his labor, his time and his future. Service rendered or goods sold on credit imply risk. (B) Business power is keen to detect risk to the full, alert to avoid its consequences, wise in accepting it under certain circumstances. Business power keeps risk down to the lowest level consistent with largest success. When business power shares another man's risk, it requires and secures corresponding compensation.

Business power may speculate in existing material property. Speculation which does not actually involve actual buying and selling of actual existing material assets of some kind, is apt to become mere gambling. Business power shuns gambling speculation.

§ 71. A legitimate form of speculation may overload. The speculation may itself become topheavy and so depreciate credit-asset. Or the credit-asset may be overloaded, with the same result. **(B) Business power will not impose on its credit-asset more than it can bear.** In building for wholesale storage, the "factor of safety" is about five. Business power looks out for the "factor of safety."

§ 72. Overloading does not imply a too rapid or extensive "turning over" of goods into money or money into goods—provided business ability corresponds with extensiveness of operation; but it may imply a stock of goods too large for the business, or a plant too extensive for the "prospects," or an undue use of credit.

§ 73. Credit is always threatened by indorsements not of a regular business nature, or an assumption of liability not belonging to the man or his business—at least to any great extent. Give away money; don't endorse outside of business rules.

§ 74. Business credit is also impaired by living "beyond" one's means, or by any factor of pronounced extravagance in the conduct of a business. Tools, machinery, and other equipments in excess of reasonable need, expensive or inappropriate stock, excessive employment, and so on, threaten collapse and depreciate credit. And if a business is merely keeping "its head above water," its credit-asset is likely to be low under ordinary circumstances.

§ 75. **(B) It is business power to live within one's means, to keep within the success-limits in the matter of time, place, instruments, stock, employment, running expenses, interest charges, and the like.**

§ 76. The nature and extent of the element of risk in any business venture, together with the venture's reasonable promise of returns, should determine the use of credit-power. Where the nature of public trusteeship obtains, risk should be reduced to a minimum, both to the public and to the institution. A general investor may take greater particular risks than one who invests permanently and in toto, since he spreads his investments, while the latter concentrates his on a single enterprise.

§ 77. He who overuses his credit with a bank threatens business in general. The bank that permits such overuse threatens its own credit and invites disaster. *A bank's risk element must be minimum, and its use of credit and assets must be highly conservative.* Above all is there no excuse for the power or liberty of bank employees and officers to wreck the institution. The man who has in his hands millions of trust-funds and does not insist that such possibility shall be absolutely precluded is really misusing credit-asset in his own case.

§ 78. The ordinary business man may tide over in various ways when obligations come due, but the bank must pay or go under. This is not always and absolutely true, although it is certainly a general rule. There are times when it is necessary for a bank to refuse payments in order to save itself and its patrons—and the public as well. The cashier of a western bank, when other institutions were going down, lived for days on milk and a little wine, took his place behind the screen every day dressed to a nicety, and with smiling countenance said to every depositor who appeared demanding his total cash,

"All the money you need for business, not a penny above that." He was threatened with the law, and only smiled: "All right, go ahead; but by the time the law gets around to us we'll be out of all trouble. I will not let a run on this bank start in to-day if I can prevent it." **(B) Business power refuses to allow its legitimate credit-asset to be destroyed by any unreasonable freak, or by any means whatever if a little skill and diplomacy can save the day.**

§ 79.   Business power is careful of its credit with banks, but is more careful, it may be, of its use of bank credit than of any other form of the asset.

§ 80.   The general and the special investor utilize the element of "capital credit." (*E*) "*Capital credit means the employment of capital in credit transactions in a different form from that in which capital is invested in a business enterprise by those who expect to make that business their occupation and realize substantial rewards in the shape of profits.*

"It may be asked why general investors should not expect to be the recipients of large profits to the same extent as any other type of investor. The difference is this: where a few men invest their funds in a business, those funds invariably represent their entire available means or wealth. They are working for themselves, and the profits of the business, whatever they may be, go to the owners alone. These owners, in order to reap this profit—which may be moderate or large, according to the nature of the business—have placed all they possess at the risk of the business. On the other hand the general investor, who is seeking merely a nominal or reasonable interest upon the funds invested, is careful to so place those funds that his investments will be very well distributed, and should any one or two of them prove to be losing ventures, he has others upon which to depend for an income." The credit asset rises or falls according to the character of the particular investment made by the general capitalist, and according to the nature and promise of the business into which one puts the whole of his fortune.

(B) Business power is conservative, takes risks, of course, but safeguards against outcomes.

§ 81. At this point, I want to quote from Prendergast's *"Credit and its Uses,"* because the words are so pertinent both to our particular study and to a prevailing tendency on the part of some people to loosen their hold on capital and earnings for some wild-cat venture presented to them in glowing terms. *"One of the important things in which the people should be educated is to understand the fallacy of a large earning capacity for money— that is, a capacity beyond the well-known earning rates on interest.* They should appreciate that where rates above those which have a recognized standing are promised or guaranteed, if paid in any case, it has been at the expense of the principle deposited, or by other dishonest means." The moral is evident: do not invest in schemes promising enormous and quick returns unless you have investigated them in a thoroughly business manner. An acquaintance called on the writer once with a brilliant mining venture on his mind. I said: "Why do you want my little pile ? If this mine is what you represent, men of extensive capital will be only too glad to take hold of it."

§ 82.   "*The elements of safety to be studied in capital credit are:* (1) the subjective nature of the enterprise; (2) its character for permanency of demand; (3) the actual value of its holdings; (4) the comparative value or merits of its franchises, patents, etc.; (5) its ability to earn a reasonable and steady interest on the investment; and (6) the character of its management."

§ 83.   But credit is not only an asset in business, it is also a risk considered on the part of him who grants it.   If a wise use of credit is important to business power, a wise giving of credit, or recognition of it as an asset in others, is equally important.   The risk of credit is a part of business, but business power keeps the risk down to lowest levels consistent with success.   In the strictly commercial world this matter has some degree of system, thanks to mercantile agencies and other factors. But in that immense field covered by "individual credit" no adequate system appears.   In all such instances business power must invent its own system and act upon its own judgment.   Nothing could be more essential than the study of best methods for forming such judgment.   In this matter instinct is indeed valuable, but accurate knowledge is far preferable.

One of my acquaintances had the "knack" for doing more "business" than any other man in his community, yet he achieved a failure: his credits were extensive and he fell short in his collections. A business man in the same community, referring to another, said: "He is the best collector among us—he never loses."   Yet the latter was above criticism, either in himself or in his business.

(B) Business power grants credit for the sake of to-morrow, and collects dues for the sake of to-day.

Business power, therefore, does not hesitate to go behind all occasions for extending credit. In ordinary business, credits are granted with great and unconsidered liberality. This is not "generosity." Generosity is personal, and never is and never can be a matter of business: a business man may be generous in business dealings, but that sort of thing is personal, not business.

"The failure to make proper investigations in individual credits may be traced to a few underlying causes," remarks Prendergast. "(1) The cupidity of dealers in extending credit indiscriminately in order to do a larger business than their competitors. (2) The fear of offending patrons by asking entirely legitimate questions in regard to their means and prospects, and thus driving trade away. (3) The absence of sound knowledge on the part of dealers in regard to the necessity of trusting goods to those only who are so circumstanced as to relatively insure payment being made to them. (4) The lack of facilities among the great masses of dealers for making such investigations as are necessary."

§ 84. **(B) Business power does not covet a larger business without a reasonably sure larger return.** To so covet indicates a false *Megalopsukia*, or, in common parlance, the "swell-head."

§ 85. **(B) Business power is magnetic enough to propound all questions needful in justifying credit given.** Some men will decline to give credit in such a way that the disappointed

applicant will return for cash purchases. Others
will grant credit in such a way as to repel even the
would-be debtor.

§ 86. **(B) Business power is always in
touch with regular instrumentalities for securing adequate knowledge as to character and
rating of others.**

§ 87. If the average of integrity were as low
as business power is compelled to assume, the
credits of a year would ruin a country.

§ 88. Inasmuch as the average of integrity is
no higher than it is, and the sum-total of credits
given during any year is enormous, some one must
pay for the risk, interest and losses. The people
always pay for any credit system that obtains.
Yet unquestionably a judicious use of credit is of
immense value to all, represents millions of capital
otherwise needful, and serves as a universal lever-
age against distress and in favor of success when
wisely treated.

§ 89. If, then, you wish to secure and
maintain good individual credit, you must establish a reputation for honorable character, be
cautious in promises, meet all obligations promptly
and in full, live within the income, make purchases appropriate to legitimate needs ($500 for
household furniture to start in life with is
one thing; $500 for dress goods in personal use
is quite another thing), and to business requirements and opportunities, protect all your paper,
invest soundly, and put business ability into your
enterprises.

§ 90. **(B) Business power does not advertise to give credit, and it does not found credit-**

confidence on directories of any local "four hundred."

§ 91. It would seem equally true that real business power must discountenance the mercantile practice of "dating"—making an obligation run from a future date, with cash and time-limit discounts added. "Dating" can never be a genuine right, and in successful business some one must pay for the use of the commodities from time of sale to time of date.

§ 92. (B) **Business power seldom pays undue interest rates for credit, for the very fact of doing so discounts credit.**

It would be impossible, of course, to treat the subject of credit exhaustively even within the limits of an entire chapter. The main thought here has been merely to cover in a general way the idea of credit as an asset and of credit as a risk, and to indicate only some of the fundamental axioms at that. Not specific methods for conducting any phase of business is the aim of the present book, but rather to suggest general principles involved in the development of business power.

LEADERSHIP.

§ 93. A factor which is being more and more emphasized in modern business publications is *system*. The intense stress of the financial effort to-day compels the utilization of system in continually finer and more comprehensive forms. Nevertheless, vital as is this factor to any great success, its value must be called for in actual financial results rather than in mere theory. System is after all a mere method—a means to an end. Business

power cares nothing for system in itself. And
business power is right. Time is often wasted
over details which do not signify increased inccme
or surplus carried over on the books. The real
success of system depends on personnel: each
"head" profiting by the detail work of all below him, doing his own work and demanding the
same from the others, the chief "head" acting as
chief only. *You can measure a man's system-success-
power by the fact that he induces in each man below
him full efficiency with the least expense of attention
on his own part to any one's duties but his own as
chief.* Of course this means co-operation and a
willingness on the part of every man to lend a
helping hand and to keep in his eye the success of
the whole concern, so far as reasonably possible,
but such co-operation really hinges on division of
labor and expectation that every one will exactly
fill his place. If each subordinate "head" is inspired to show a profit from his own work, system
has demonstrated. But system for its own sake
is a mere fetish. (B) **Business power subordi-
nates methods to dollars.** It is not a theory-
maker; it is a money-maker.

§ 94. The aim of a business "head" is control.
If one considers a single enterprise, this is entirely
evident. Has it occurred to you that (B) **every
other business with which you are favorably
related through your own enterprise may be a
servant just as truly as any man you employ?**
Why not regard all such business in this light—as
yours to direct in a measure for your own success?
Those who sell to you serve you, if you are a successful business man. Those who buy from you serve

you, provided you are successful. **(B) Business power does not forget what the other man is after, and refuses to do business for the sake of the other man's success alone.** You are the head of your own concern. Why not get to the headship, in one way or another, of those other businesses? In order to do this, you must lead. Business power declines to follow. As you control all employees below you, why not control business men on your level? When you are big enough, you can do exactly that thing. Then you will pay prices dictated in part by yourself, and set the selling prices because others cannot compete with you. And this is possible without violating a single law of Deity or man.

CONCLUSIONS.

It is understood, of course, that the foregoing analysis of economics and business is not an attempt at completeness. It is rather a suggestion for improvement in business power. The application to that end implies not only a reading of the chapters devoted to the subject, but a revised study many times repeated.

And now you are therefore invited to go over the analysis until you are able to answer in your own words this question: What are the accepted economic laws of the world and the fundamental maxims of the world's business? You are invited to classify such laws and maxims for your own practical use. You are invited to examine your own business habits and methods with the view to ascertaining whether or not your business life does actually embody such laws and maxims. You are invited to make a better study than the foregoing.

Above all, you are invited to remember that the chapters devoted to this study have aimed to give you a series of "pointers" by means of which you may intelligently set about multiplying your business power.   For again I say: Whatever the business man knows practically, he will be more efficient and derive greater satisfaction from his business if he possesses that knowledge consciously as knowledge and thought held in terms of itself. The practical farmer is preferable to the theoretical agriculturist, to be sure ; but if the two can be combined, the world and the man are the better by exactly as practical ability is associated with scientific knowledge.   **(B) Business power is not only power; it is also intelligent appreciation of the meaning and sources and methods of power.**

PART III.

PSYCHOLOGY IN BUSINESS.

The goal of mental effort is the uplift into consciousness and control of all personal powers. We grow from below and within. It is our task to raise the obscure possessions into the sphere of the practical life. In hypnotism, suggestion, magnetism, auto-development, auto-capitalization, auto-healing, and so on, we are doing precisely this and with increasing success because modern life constitutes a demand therefor. The medical profession threatened us yesterday: we grew out of its conditions chemical idolatry and drug chaos, until the very folly of it drew mind away from a purely objective search for health to the inner mind-force within. We now know that no drug ever heals or helps in disease save as it " suggests" the upspringing into action of that force, and that every human being healed in this world is self-healed. So, also, poverty and the lies of the poor man's Providence and Destiny threatened to dethrone selfhood among us until we discovered that, within limits which prevent the doctrine from becoming grotesque and defeating its own end in insanity or laziness, every soul may, by demand and action, draw to itself a sufficient measure of the benevolent well-meaning of the Universe, in food, clothing, home—all physical essentials—to realize perfect personal freedom, and to win success limited only by native endowment.

CHAPTER IX.

INITIATIVE.

"A man's mental powers," as remarked in Mencken's *"Philosophy of Friedrich Nietzsche,"* "are to be judged, not by his ability to accomplish things that are possible to every man foolish enough to attempt them, but by his capacity for doing things beyond the power of other men." The man who can thus surpass his associates has initiative. And it is for precisely this end that the human mind is capable of that master activity. Business is a fight against retrogression and for progress, and the heart of the fight is initiative.

§ 1. Every business man's life consists of two factors—*Being a business man, and Doing business things*. The doing business things can never exceed the being a business man. Moreover, the amount and quality of the being ought to decide the amount and quality of the doing, for the whole of a man ought to go into his action. But this is not always the case. In other words, a man's conduct cannot express more than he really is, while it frequently does express less than he is. Evidently,

the more being there is packed into a person's
nature, and the finer its quality, the greater and
more efficient ought to be his business activity.
The main thing is to be a business man; the next
indispensable thing is to do business. Here we
have the difference between failure with a peanut
stand and success in battle-ship building or gun-
making for nations. Now, being, of the highest
type, contains within itself—*initiative*.

A Ton of Coal and a Man.

§ 2.　A ton of coal is being. It is condensed
sunlight. Sunlight is etheric undulations. The
coal is just such undulations arrested and locked
together. Some one has called matter "frozen
force," an apt figure, for the greater the activity
going on in a given quantity of matter, the less
solid, liquid, gaseous, it is, until we have the material puzzle of the last analysis of science, the
ether itself, and perhaps still more attenuated
forms of existence. (I do not mean here to say
that the ether is matter; that question is not yet
settled.) When, in the case of the coal, the oxygen
of the air is caused to unite—or given freedom to
unite—with the carbon of the lump of coal, the
etheric undulations induced by the sun's activity,
and hitherto "frozen" and locked together, are set
free, and then "there's something doing": we have
what we call "fire" and heat—which is a mode of
etheric motion. But if the coal is "poor,"—mixed
with other material than carbon,—the material
having no affinity for oxygen—then, although there
may be "a ton of coal" in the dealer's mind, there
is not a ton of etheric undulations. Thus, it is

evident that, given any fixed quantity of so-called coal, its doing power depends on the purity of the mass of material—the exclusively carbon condensation—and *initiative*—some start to combustion, the liberation of energy.

§ 3. A man is precisely like a piece of coal, with one important difference. He is being that is capable of doing, and his power depends on the amount and quality of his being, *but his doing really depends on his own initiative.*

The Origin of Initiative.

§ 4. The all-important question, now, is this: who is to induce initiative in the man? himself or some one else? The ton of coal cannot initiate the extraction of oxygen from the air, nor can the oxygen cause the union of itself which is called combustion. In Nature inertia is king. In any given object there is a certain "store of energy," whether the object be moving or at rest, and it can never increase or decrease its store possessed at any given time, nor can it manifest more or less energy, except as some other and outside force may intervene—unless it contains the psychic factor, that wonderful existence which obtains within animal life. Radium does indeed appear to call the statement in question, but no one for a moment supposes that a better understanding of radium will not bring radio-activity within the great law. The correlation of force and the conservation of energy otherwise forbid any initiative *de novo* in the absolute sense anywhere outside of the psychic realm. Its presence in the psychic realm is the great puzzle with which the last named laws are confronted.

Any initiative in non-psychic Nature must be
merely an effect of a preceding cause ; and always
the effect is merely the cause in a consequent form,
as the cause is always the effect in a preceding
form.   *No one can point out strict initiative in
Nature without calling into view the psychic factor
in Nature, and when this factor comes into consideration, we have precisely the one and sole possible explanation of initiative in any realm.*

§ 5. *By the psychic factor I mean that something which builds a living organism in Nature,
adjusts the organism to environment through its
power of variation, develops instinct, mounts to
reason, acquires habits which it may more or less
control and direct, and in man climaxes in self-
consciousness and self-directive will of the highest
order.*   The psychic factor is *always possessed of a
measure of freedom.*

§ 6.   If we say that Nature is all material, we
slip the psychic factor in as material product.   It is
there, whatever our theories.   We might, indeed,
define "matter" as that which has no power of
originating activity within itself.   That which
exhibits such power is by so much not mere matter.
The field of the psychic factor, however, is very
wide, and must be made to include in our thought
the whole realm of animal life.   The lowest type
of animal existence is more or less psychic.   Any
phase of animal existence is a double somewhat,
one side of which is mere matter—that which in
itself can do nothing save react to external force—
and another side of which is increasingly psychic
in capacity, that is, capable not only of reaction,
but of original activity, from amœba to man.   A

psychic factor necessarily involves a measure of freedom—ability to act in one way or another, and so for or against self-interest. In man this psychic freedom-power reaches its highest form, so far as Nature is concerned. Living animals must possess some capacity for initiative, otherwise I do not see how progress—evolution—can be possible, since an "initiative" that is wholly "blind" and only free in appearance must be merely accidental, and is as likely to go in a direction which we are compelled to call backward as in one truly to be called forward. The highest evidence of such capacity is seen in man. The man-store of energy, speaking by the word of practical common sense, can do what neither coal nor air can do—*it can liberate itself.* Its power in this respect is enormous. *A man can manifest an amount of energy greater than the entire sum-total of "material" mechanics can account for. He can do more work than his whole body seems to justify, just as some heavenly bodies can move faster than the force of gravity requires. Man can draw on the unseen and universal store-house of energy, suck up into himself large "quantities" thereof by psychic compulsion, and manifest more power—more capacity to do work—than either physics or chemistry make lawful. If you could gather up and control the initiative energy of the human race during the world's history, you could sprinkle the heavens with stars.*

§ 7. Of this immense resource, there is a certain yet indefinite share for every living person. It needs but for the individual to set himself to a definite, steadfast, persistent, trained and patient seizure of a portion of the Universe of Initiative

Energy, to make himself a dynamic power in any field of effort into which he may be directed by native endowment. If he wearies himself with uncertainties and complaints, he can fail easily enough. If, also, he tries to bruise his way to success in some field arbitrarily chosen, he will, again, merely run to failure. *But if he takes the universal store of initiative energy as his banker, and honors the banking laws of the Institution, and permits a strenuous seeking for personal development to direct his life-work, he cannot fail.* In such a case, real failure is simply impossible.

§ 8. The thing that accomplishes the miracle of liberating stored energy by defiance of the law of inertia, is the will. Now, the will is not a something in the man which the man uses—unless power of will be regarded as precisely that connection between a body possessed of capacity for mind on the one hand, and the unseen storehouse of infinite energy on the other hand. I think that this is indeed the case. *Fundamentally speaking, the will is that in the man, or that phase of the man, which bridges over the chasm between inert matter and Infinite Initiative.* Every human roots into this Universal Energy. This it is that makes the Hindu right when he says, speaking to any individual in his relation to Brahma, "Thou art That"; which in the present interpretation, means that only will— not memory, not feeling, not thought,—can give a man connection with and control of the Universal Initiative.

§ 9. This seems to be true if we look from a man toward his Background, the Infinite. Observing the matter as it exhibits toward world-life, the will is merely a way—a tangled, complex way—or any given particular way—the man has of being and doing, just as remembering, thinking, and so on, are other ways he has of being and doing. The will is a phase of the sum-total manifestation of the man's being and yet a phase which is so inevitable *in all his manifestations* that we say, "the man is the will," "the will is the man." The more and better the being-state, then,—the static self,—the more and better the willed doing-state—the dynamic self.

§ 10. The action of the will gives us initiative in every man living—after a fashion. But in what fashion? When the action takes place, some one has spoken the command. That some one may have been another man. In such a case the will-action is a variety of initiative within the man (or doing could not have followed), but the initiative is the effect of an outside cause. *This is initiative in its common and commonplace form.* Or, the "some one" may be the man himself. In this case initiative is also within, but it is due to self-causing will-action. It is here of *a type superior to that of the first instance.*

§ 11. Initiative, again, may be due, not to intelligently apprehended outside commands, but to mere external influences of which one is unaware. You observe a cat watching a mouse. The feline body is a-quiver with muscular tension and hunger, the eyes burn like coals, the lips wrinkle and twitch. It is the cat that leaps, but the spring is a response to mouse-stimulation. Animal life is very much—not altogether, I think—a bundle or series of helpless (helpless in a large sense) responses to

external stimuli.   The initiative of a multitude of
people is little more, scarcely a grade higher.
Hence, we derive the analysis:

Groups of the Initiative.

*Group I.   There are those who perceive the thing
that ought to be done in any given situation for any
given improvement or venture, but who either do not
try, or never succeed in the effort, to get the thing
accomplished.*   These are the theorists, the dreamers—or less, the intelligent incompetents so far as
practical matters are concerned.   Other men see
the thing to be done, but not the how of its doing.
Still others see well enough in both respects, but
are unable practically to make good their precep-
tions.   (See the chapter on " Practical Ability "—
IV–section 8).

*Group II.   There are those who perceive the
things that ought to be done, without being informed
concerning them, and induce or compel others to do
the work.*   I am not speaking of tyrannical master-
ship, but refer to magnetic leadership.   *This is
initiative of the first degree.*   It is the Napoleonic
gift of government, war and commerce.   It is the
ability of the pioneers and the great constructive
builders of huge enterprises.

*Group III.   There are those who perceive the
things to be done, without being informed concerning
them, and themselves accomplish the work by personal
effort.   This is initiative of the second grade.*   It
has, generally considered, two levels: that on
which great things are perceived and done, and
that on which only small things are perceived and
done.   In some instances the man who is on the

upper level of this grade remains there because
he does things himself instead of inducing others
to do them; and in some instances the man
who is on the lower level of this grade simply
fails to trust himself to the undertaking of larger
affairs.

*Group IV. There are those who perceive the
things that ought to be done only when they are
informed concerning them (they never make independent discoveries), but they proceed to do these
without being told when so informed. This is initiative of the third grade.*

*Group V. There are those who perceive the
things to be done when informed, and only do them
when told. This is initiative obedience, or response-
initiative.*

Group VI. (Outside the field.) There are those
who see nothing without being informed, and do
nothing even when told. This is total lack of
initiative of any kind. Let us now add an

OUTLINE OF THE GROUPS WITH QUALITY.

§ 12. The above analysis may be condensed,
and at the same time elaborated with reference to
various qualities pertaining to the doing—and, for
that matter, the seeing, as follows:

(*The Will is the Man*)

(*in*)

(1) Initiative Vision. Non-Doing.
{ The how not seen.
{ Seen, but impractical.

(2) Initiative Vision. Inducing Doing.
Fair. Well. Best.

(3) Initiative Vision. Doing by Self { Large.
{ Small.
Fair. Well. Best.

(4) Non-Initiative Vision. Initiative Doing.

                                      Fair. Well. Best.

(5) Non-Initiative Vision. Non-Initiative Doing.

                                      Fair. Well. Best.

(6) No Vision.   No Doing.

You are invited to find your place in this analysis, and the reasons for your being there.

You are urged to remember that in human life all grades of being are improvable. Inertia is king in helpless matter, but a slave only in all the psychic realm—as individuals elect it to be so. *I define personality as that which contains the power to lift itself out of inertia by sheer assertion.*

§ 13. *Business power of the highest type is dynamic initiative inspiring others to do that which it wills for its own as well as their success.* Now this is the unseen power-house hidden away in the very centre of the commercial world. This made Rome Mistress, Napoleon Master, America free.

§ 14. When we add to the analysis the qualities indicated, it is seen that each class, from second to fifth inclusive, must, to be perfect, demonstrate the highest efficiency by getting the thing done, or by doing it, not fairly well, and not merely well, *but better than any one else can do it*, and better to such a degree that it is best possible. As you read up from class five to class two, you advance in the thought of financial value from poorly paid unskilled labor to the big salaried positions in great business enterprises and the high captaincies of finance at the top.

INITIATIVE AND THE QUALITY FACTOR.

§ 15. For there are numerous ways in which things may be done—fairly well, very well, better

than others can do them, and best from any point
of view. Initiative may exhibit in any of these
degrees. If you bring out the accomplishment of
your vision of improvement or venture, in yourself
or in your business, but only fairly well, or very
well, your initiative lacks in the highest value.
Your command over your people is weak by so
much.

§ 16. The goal of first-grade initiative is this:
*The thing caused to be by others accomplished better
than any one else can do it so far away that it is
really best possible*. You may say: "If I see what
should be brought about and induce others to accomplish my plans, I am not responsible for failures
on their part. I cannot guarantee perfection in
my helpers." But why not? *This is precisely the
task of first-grade initiative*. The man at the head
must make good his leadership. The inability to
to do this is failure. Explanations of failure are
mere theories, and nobody cares for them. What
the world demands is success, which means, not
only vision of a thing to be done, but of best practical methods therefor; not only selection of the
people who are to carry out the methods, but further, the ability to get them to do the thing in the
best possible manner with the best possible results.
Otherwise the initiative is not first-grade.

§ 17. The man of such high-class power, however, *must avoid two extremes*. He must not fall
into the error of fussy meddling with his lieutenants, or even of insistently dictating small details
of methods involved in the work. Some housewives, for example, are incapable of allowing their
maids to secure desired results in their own way,

but incessantly "show them how." Some otherwise great captains make the same mistake. The
leader must keep an eye on his entire enterprise,
but should find his men wisely, place responsibility
where it belongs, look after methods only in a
general way to see that they are consistent with
his whole campaign, and leave particular details
to the discretion of his men, reposing in them inspiring faith. On the other hand, *first-grade initiative never spares itself, is not easy-going in its
confidence, and backs up its entire enterprise by
omnipotence and omnipresence.* It demands and it
secures the best possible results.

In the conduct of the Universe the Infinite is
Initiative, and free responsibility is always with
the man or nation who can do things worth while.
Undeveloped man feels that imbeciles are under
the special care of the gods.

"Of these men Thorpe demanded one thing—
success ("*The Blazed Trail,*" Steward Edward
White). He tried never to ask of them anything
he did not believe to be thoroughly possible; but
he expected that always in some manner, by hook
or crook, they would carry the affair through. Ac-
cidents would happen, there as elsewhere; a way
to arrive in spite of them always exists, if only a
man is willing to use his wits, unflagging energy
and will. Bad luck is a reality; but much of
what is called bad luck is nothing but a want of
foresight."

And Thorpe never spared himself. "Impossi-
bilities were puffed aside like thistles. The man
went at them headlong. They gave way before the
rush. Thorpe always led. Not for a single in-

stant of the day, nor for many a night, was he at rest. He was like a man who has taken a deep breath to reach a definite goal, and who cannot exhale until the burst of speed is over."

All this captured the men inevitably. They adored him "because he represented to them their own ideal, what they would be if freed from the heavy gyves of vice and executive incapacity that weighed them down."

§ 18. *The ideal of quality holds also in the case of initiative of the second grade.* The man of power who does things himself is content only with the best final results, never with fair or very good results, nor even with results superior to those of other men's efforts—for the latter may be satisfied with very poor work.

§ 19. The vigorous man, however, is always tempted to do things himself rather than trouble to induce others to do them. He says: "If you want a thing done in the best way and at the least all-round expense, do it yourself." But this is often a mistake. The immediate and apparent expense may be less than would obtain were he to put the task on other shoulders, but the long-run cost is frequently greater. Inasmuch as we are dealing with initiative, and not with some other ability, this man misses two values: the development of initiative in his own people, and thus their greatest efficiency for general work and for special emergencies; and the unfoldment of first-grade initiative in himself, since this type of initiative consists not in doing things that others can do just as well, or may be taught to do just as well, but in inducing others to do them, reserving energies for the larger leadership. It is a higher type of mastery to handle men for execution of work than to execute that work oneself. It is not always true that "if you want a thing done right, you must do it yourself." The section-hand can probably lay a rail better than the road's president can do it. Take that as a representative fact. If you can use men profitably for best results, do so. Nevertheless, if you must do the thing yourself, the demand for quality emerges in such case also. And it makes no possible difference to this grade of initiative that the work accomplished will not be particularly before the public eye, or that other men will not know good from bad work. *The man who does a thing always has the thing he has done before his own eyes.* Some one said to me: "Why does it matter? Not one person in a thousand will see this work as you see it." I replied: "I will see it, and know that it is not the best I ought to do; and besides, that one man will be sure to run across the thing." Whatever the present writing may show of literary deficiency, that is the ideal. Make the goal of effort, then, nothing short of the nearest approach to perfection. *This is first-class second-grade initiative.*

In "*The Pharaoh and the Priest*," by Alexander Glovatski, are these significant words (the priest is speaking to the young Pharaoh):

"Draw on the earth, O lord, a square, and put on it six million unhewn stones; they will represent the people. On that foundation place sixty thousand hewn stones; they will be the lower officials. On them place six thousand polished stones; they will be the higher officials. On these put sixty covered with carvings; these will be thy most intimate counsellors and chief leaders, and on the summit place one monolith with its pedestal and the golden image of the sun; that will be thyself.

"The Pharaoh Snofru followed that advice. Thus rose the oldest pyramid, the step pyramid, a tangible image of our state; from that pyramid all others had their origin. Those are immovable buildings, from the summit of which the rim of the world is visible, and they will be a marvel to the remotest generations.

"In this system resides our superiority over all neighbors. The Ethiopians were as numerous as we, but their king himself took care of his own cattle, and beat his own subjects with a club; he knew not how many subjects he had, nor was he able to collect them when our troops invaded his country. There was not a united Ethiopia, but a great crowd of unorganized people. For that reason they are our vassals at present.

"The prince of Libya judges all disputes himself, especially among the wealthy, and gives so much time to them that he cannot attend to his own business. So at his side whole bands of robbers rise up; these we exterminate."

§ 20. The Egyptian government and that of Rome represented the initiative of the first grade: *delegated authority with responsibility, all associated workers being cemented by a common inspiration into one great unitary organization.*

§ 21. *The requirement of quality applies, again, to initiative of the third grade and to initiative-obedience as well.* The improvement-vision, the venture-vision, the methods and the results, are bound to run to perfection. "There is nothing perfect in this world" is false and a bad suggestion. The highest aim signifies higher results. The business world is crowded with people whose work is poor because they do not try to make it the very best possible. Business itself sometimes deliberately plans for inferior products, but it is excessively poor business policy. *Business power insists on the best things always and everywhere.* First-class men waste no time in hair-splitting discussions about the possibility of perfection; they simply "go after it" with might and main.

§ 22. *The best work demands keen and alert interest in the thing in hand, no matter what it may be.* The finest interest comes when a man loves his work, or loves the outcome of that work, or loves best work even though the labor involved may be irksome. It is simply impossible, as a general rule and in the long run, to do good work unless the man is interested in his effort in one of these three ways. The secret of much inferiority in results obtained lies in the fact that men put no love, and so, no interest, into the matters in hand. When a man takes no pride in the outcome of what he is paid for, he cannot expect to "get on" in any line of business. *The highest grade of initiative obedience requires demonstration in at least relative perfection.*

INITIATIVE AND THE TIME FACTOR.

§ 23. *The question of amount of time* involved in initiating or doing a thing is always important. There are various ways of doing things with reference to the time factor.

(1) Some men have the initiative vision, but while they are getting ready to act, others make the same discovery and leap to capture results.

(2) Some men, when informed of things to be done, delay attempting them, or dawdle about the doing, until it is too late. A clergyman was called to attend a dying parishioner. In his prayer he embodied nearly the whole of "divinity" before coming down to the sick man's needs. And in due time some one touched him on the shoulder with the remark: "You're too late, sir; the man's dead.'

(3) Some men, when told to do a thing, destroy the value of their doing by consuming too much time in the matter.

Most people are blind to their own faults, and it is a singular fact that one may read all about such faults without making the least discovery of a personal nature. During twenty years one misspelled certain words because it never occurred to him that he did not know how to spell them. You are therefore invited to investigate yourself with regard to the three deficiencies just indicated.

§ 24. If we combine these time factors and quality-faults, we shall have exactly what every field of effort exhibits. You are urged to examine the following analysis for the purpose of self-discovery.

Things may be done

(1)	Slowly, and not in time.	Very low value.
(2)	Slowly, but just in time.	Fair value.
(3)	Slowly, and poorly.	No value.
(4)	Slowly, and very well.	Fair value.
(5)	Slowly, and better or best.	Good value.
(6)	Quickly, but not well.	Low value.
(7)	Quickly, and well.	Good value.
(8)	Quickly, and better or best.	Highest value.

Items 1 and 3 explain failures in life. If your money paid for them, what would be the wages? Item 5 explains several grades of ordinary living, from ditch-digger's to business proprietor's. Item 6 explains failures. Item 7 explains common success. Item 8 represents highest efficiency, results depending on bigness or smallness of matters involved, and at the top signifies kingship in business, the greatness of which is invariably determined by the grade of initiative in which it appears. How does the analysis characterize your work?

Climbing by Initiative.

§ **25.** *To see the thing to be done when informed and to do it quickly, better or best, when ordered—this is to maintain yourself in employment, and possibly to win promotion.* It is for the will to mount higher. And the will is the man. If the employer will not recognize such a value, discharge him. Don't be tied to any living man. Were the alternative presented to some people to submit as others submit to another man's orders or "go on the road" as tramps, they would instantly choose the hoboe's life.

§ 26. *To see the thing to be done when informed and to do it quickly, better or best, without being ordered—if the doing makes no mistakes—is probably to win promotion;* provided, employers know enough to appreciate a good value. If they do not, discharge them. If you fear to do that, you confess weakness. What has fear to do with an honest real man?

§ 27. *But the element of mistake in doing a thing without orders must be avoided.* Business does not pardon errors, although the business man may do so. The thing done without orders must be needed, must be important, and must work out happily. Business does not see errors in the presence of success.

§ 28. *To see the thing to be done without being informed and to do it without being told—blunders not permissible—quickly and better or best, is to earn the valuation, "indispensable," to make promotion almost certain, and to prepare for initiative of the first grade.*

§ 29. You are urged to "be alive and be alert" (see "*Power for Success,*" sixth lesson) for the initiative vision and action in *your own business.* A great business man will not follow others; he insists on leading. Any one can do the successful thing others are doing, *perhaps;* but your leader only can set the success-pace for the crowd.

§ 30. You are urged to "be alive and be alert" for the initiative vision and doing made possible in the *business in which you are employed.* Study the situation for suggested improvements. When such appear, set about bringing them to pass, or indicate them to the attention of those to whom they may properly belong. Make a note of all such matters in a book prepared for the purpose. If you delay this, you are likely to forget the ideas suggested. Do not be balked by the indifference of superiors, but employ tact and the unostentatious spirit of helpfulness and interest in the business. Avoid, of course, fussiness and meddling. But above all, do not say: "It's none of my business; not what I'm paid for; would only induce a 'call down.'" No one is "called down" for the

right presentation of a "good thing." The man
who is willing to do what he isn't paid for in the
interest of the business, is sooner or later paid for
precisely that practical willingness. If you have
the wrong kind of employer, discharge him.

§ 31. You are urged to "be alive and be
alert" *toward any new ideas your employees may
discover in connection with your business—and to
reward them accordingly*. You are preoccupied
with the whole, and are accustomed to its ordinary
operation; they perceive many details where improvement is possible simply because they are not
occupied with the whole—are, so to speak, "outside the game." Only a false *Megalopsukia—*
"swell-head"—can be above suggestions from any
human on earth. The great lawyer is glad to get
at O'Sullivan's, the Ditch-digger's, point of view;
the real railway president is eager to know what
improvement in the system the agent at a four-
house station in Montana has discovered in the
leisure of his loneliness. Little business people
wish their employees to "attend to their work,"
but *business power feels that a man is "attending to
his work" if he can offer anything for "the good of
the house."*

"It is the duty of every employee," remarked
W. Graydon Stetson, "to bring forward for discussion, and for rejection possibly, but for accept-
ance, perhaps, any new idea which may occur to
him. It should be borne in mind that the most
revolutionary idea that was ever suggested, had a
value, and a big value, at that, in the negative
sense of pointing out the right way, in, perhaps, a
diametrically opposite direction. The fact that an

idea appears revolutionary at first sight does not prove that it is valueless. Remember that the man who presents the new idea may have spent a lot more of time on its development and on the proper method of using it than has the man who first hears of it from the originator. His mind is unprepared, is, perhaps, fitted into a groove, from which his mental eyesight finds difficulty in looking clearly over the rut into the open field suggested by the other's new idea."

§ 32. *The "rut" in business makes millions of men mere "tail-enders." Initiative is the born enemy of ruts.*

§ 33. *To see the thing to be done without being informed, and to bring about its accomplishment without being told—this is to stand first in any field of effort.*

INITIATIVE AND SUCCESS.

§ 34. The highest success, then, calls for work like the following:

First. Men on the sixth level (see section 18) *must climb up to the fifth.* Until they can succeed in doing so, they are helpless puppets of chaotic fortune. The chances that they can rise to the fourth grade except by passing through the fifth— to the doing of things when informed but without orders except by learning to do things under orders—are about as one to millions. Good initiative obedience is a first-rate schoolmaster for independent initiative doing.

Secondly. Men of the fifth level—of initiative obedience—must climb to the fourth level: doing things discovered to them without orders. The method for accomplishing this advance may be long, and heavy, and tedious, and exacting, but its observance pays.   It consists of (but see also sections 43 and 45 of this chapter)—

(1) Immensely *magnified interest* in the business in all its details;

(2) Self-inspired, *imaginative-inventive thought* in regard to all possible improvements (see chapter XI);

(3) A persistent and practical *determination to improve* all doing from fairly well to better and best;

(4) *Promptness and decision* in all doing and in immediate realization of suggested improvements:

(5) A lively and alert *endeavor to see the things* that ought to be done without being informed, and to do the same (within the rules of the business— see sections 43 and 45) without being told.

§ 35. I am acquainted with few people who are not possessed of more ability than they use. The English essayist, Hazlett, well said—and the quotation has a wide application in business:

"If a man had all sorts of instruments in his shop, and wanted one, he would rather have that one than be supplied with a double set of all the others.   If he had them twice over, he could only do what he can do as it is, whereas without that one he perhaps cannot finish any work he has in hand.   So if a man can do one thing better than anybody else, the being able to do a hundred other things merely as well as anybody else would not alter the sentence or add to his respectability; on the contrary, his being able to do so many other things well would probably interfere with and encumber him in the execution of the only thing that others cannot do as well as he, and so far be a drawback and a disadvantage. *More people, in fact, fail from a multiplicity of talents and pretensions than from any absolute poverty of resources.*"

Nevertheless, if this man, possessed of so many tools, and needing a tool not possessed, has initiative talent and inventive skill, he will *put some one of the instruments in his shop to the use required—* that is, a new use.

§ 36. It is the task and privilege of initiative, in business as elsewhere, to *find uses for all talents possessed. If initiative misses out of its endowments one needed talent, it puts some old talent to the required purpose—or finds a way to dispense with its necessity. If it cannot do as indicated, it simply finds some other man who will supply the requirements demanded.*

§ 37. Now, initiative is practical original thinking, and, as one has said: "The principal obstacle in the way of original thinking (and business initiative) *is the habit of living in fixed channels, and must be removed at once,* because we shall never become any more than we are, so long as we live, think and act according to prescribed rules and preconceived ideas. No growth, no development and no advancement can possibly take place while we live and move in grooves."

§ 38. Another obstacle to originality (and initiative) is "*the habit of seeing things through the eyes of others* (the manager's, the business neighbor's, and so on); or accepting the conclusions of those in whom we have confidence, without giving the matter the least individual thought."

§ 39. To the above may be added: *content-ment in seeing things in old, familiar conditions,* as we have been accustomed to seeing them, with-out effort to see them differently and in a new light. Your tools, your shop, your counter, your department, your store, your plant, your methods—these you see as they are, as they have been, as others have made them, giving no thought to vari-ous original lines or striking departures—and you become a follower.

§ 40. *"To be a follower is to prevent further growth;* to become a mere machine in the hands of your favorite 'system'; and to take the path to mental, moral and spiritual atrophy. No mere follower can ever become great, because he is daily becoming smaller."

§ 41. *Thirdly. Men on the fourth level must climb up to the third—with an eye on the second,* avoiding doing things themselves which they can induce others to do, not for shirking, but in the interest of first grade initiative success. From perceiving things to be done only when informed, they must rise to the ability to see things for them-selves. The method for such advance is seen—

(A) *When the man multiplies the whole of himself into his work*

With the most alert and intense interest in the business and all its details,

And bends all his powers to discover all possible ways for improving it,

And determines to get out of ruts, do original thinking, and dare to venture into new paths,

Refusing to be a follower, bent on leadership of the first grade.

(B) If, now, this man manages, in some way, to develop the ability to handle other men in the realization of large plans, he will rise to general superintendency or independent lordship in finance.

All this is for the man. Books may instruct; they cannot do the things suggested. Inasmuch as most people possess more ability than they use, he who throws himself into the tasks here set forth, or carries out the ideas involved, with determination and persistence, may cherish in his soul the inspiring assurance that the matter of advancement is already practically accomplished. There may intervene interruptions, temporary discouragements, many obstacles of an external nature, but the long-run outcome is about as certain as natural law.

INITIATION DEFINED.

§ 42. And now it is time this great quality essential to highest success should be defined. Either the discovery or the practical use of every new thing in the world exploits *initiative*. The best thing of its kind always means *initiative*. The man who sees a thing to be done and inspires others to find out for him how it can be done, has *initiative*. The man who is given a bare order to accomplish certain results and pushes through till they are secured, has *initiative*. The leader has *initiative*. Life is brilliant with flashes of initiative thought and enterprise. But the mere follower is just initiat*ed:* he is either a tool or an imitator. The tool and the imitator are out of the same box—with this difference: the tool knows himself, while the imitator knows not even his own business.

§ 43. *Initiative, then, may be defined as the self-originated perception of any kind of possible and practical improvement in existing conditions, any new and reasonably promising venture, together with necessary practical ways and means thereto, and the ability and movement required to secure such improvement or bring to a successful issue such venture: either through the controlled services of others* (first grade), *or through one's own personal labor in necessary details* (second grade).

In every known phase this splendid value is everywhere in high demand. Its best use, and methods for its development, additional to preceding incidental suggestions, may be indicated as follows:

USE OF INITIATIVE.

We begin with the *use* because development is necessarily involved in suggestions under the present head.

§ 44. Whether you are an independent business man or an employee of others, it is vastly important that you make definitely sure that your initiative is not a mere dream and will not turn out to be a bad blunder. Success is forgiven any sin, but failure may not even plead its own virtues. When audacity pays, it is courage; when it discounts dollars, it is foolhardiness. Achievement is often the sole difference between an idiot and a Napoleon. The shadow of the Emperor cannot swallow up Waterloo: the defeat looms darker than the shade. *Hence, the man who initiates must know what he is about.* In so knowing, he must not haggle with courage, for fear destroys original thinking, but he must know—see or feel—that he is right. Therefore—

(1) *Make sure*—as sure as first-grade initiative can—that the improvement or the new undertaking is *real and worth what it will cost.*

(2) *Make sure* of the *ways and means thereto;* do not guess; do not begin to act in a hazy state of hope or expectation; do not run your engine until the rails are laid, nor lay rails until the road-bed is decently ready, nor build that until you know reasonably well where you are coming out. The difference between the dreamer and the practical man is this: both have initiative vision, but the latter's vision includes ways and means.

(3) *Get the thing done!* Be not over scientific and fussy about the conduct of methods; go steadily and persistently for results. The way of winning a battle or selling a bill of goods is important; still, the real thing is the battle won and the goods sold. And it is infinitely pleasanter telling how you got a thing done than explaining why you failed—at least to men with money in the venture. After success, one may multiply "ifs" indefinitely—"*if* I had done so and so—but I didn't, and I got there." After failure, these "ifs" are "a drug on the market."

(4) *Make sure* of the *right amount and quality of results.* When you are fishing for big salmon, a one-pounder is salmon, of course, and bass are fish —but they are not satisfactory. If your initiative does not bring better results than old methods have secured, its only value is practice. Nobody is in business for practice.

(5) *Make sure* of the *men you handle* for the prosecution of your plans and any others who may

interfere with them.   First-grade initiative knows
men.   How often you hear, on the failure of a
plan, words like these: "If it hadn't been for A."
But A, or some one in his place, was a part of your
problem.   Know your man first; afterward is too
late.   Any one can acquire that sort of knowledge,
because it is the most expensive.   It is a singular
thing that the most expensive experience is the
kind the poor man and the weak man always acquire. *Business power has an instinct for the right
men in the right place.*

(6) *Make sure* about yourself, in regard not
only to *initiative vision*, but *initiative doing*, as well.
This is, of course, absolutely indispensable if you
are an independent business man, but proportionately important in any initiative effort.   You may
be strictly under orders: it is a delicate matter to
depart therefrom, and success is the only permissible justification.   Nevertheless, when chances look
a little less than even against independent action,
initiative is often the thing that pulls a man
out of the disfavor of defeat: the effort wins ad-
miration.   Where one has some general latitude
of action, the main thing is success.   In other
words, if you are under strict orders, and failure
is inevitable *with* obedience, if your disobe-
dience is daring and in the interest evidently of
the business, you at least get the credit of the
venture, even if you do *not* succeed.   But if you
have some latitude of conduct, and fail while misusing it, you get only credit for failure, for your
latitude was given for success alone.   Make sure
therefore, that you are equal to the initiative
responsibilities.

(7) If you discover possible improvement in the business or undertaking in which you are employed, *make sure* of the *right opportunity* for broaching the subject to superiors. If this is done at the wrong time, or in the wrong manner, you are snuffed out. When another person seizes the "psychological moment" for unfolding the same thing, it is of no consequence that the idea was yours. Argument on that point is now as water to an ash heap—it will not absorb. You have missed the real power of initiative.

(8) *Be always on the alert for the betterment of business*, for means of bringing that betterment to pass, and for just the "nick o' time" for suggesting the same.

(9) *Study the comparative value of direct and indirect ways of getting a thing done and of broaching ideas to superiors*—especially to highest superiors. The road to success is not a mathematical line; sometimes it is fairly straight, sometimes it is so crooked that you can only see "two looks and a yell," as they say in the Blue Ridge mountains. The fact is, no man surely knows that road until he has traveled its length—although the tried maxims and great principles ought to be evident to all. It is precisely so in regard to methods of dealing with men and conditions. The direct approach often means failure. This is equally true of the indirect. Initiative must decide, and it can acquire the necessary ability to decide correctly only through study, observation and experience.

(10) *Study the value of delay in timely initiative.* The adage, "strike when the iron is hot," calls for the *hot iron* no less than for the stroke. Premature initiative is often a burial.

§ 45. In these advices, however, it is immensely important to *guard against excessive caution*. Some men are so cautious that they are always behind opportunity. Between rashness and timidity initiative makes its own characteristic choice because of its nature. The ideal of initiative is a balance of caution and courage, "make-sure" and confidence, hardheadedness and "nerve." "Be not too bold," sang Longfellow in *"Morituri Salutamus;"* he meant, "Be just bold enough." This balance can only be suggested; it comes of intuition, and intuition is the stir of experience in a man's "great within,"—and as well the product of a solid resolution to compel self to acquire it through thought-aspiration and cultivated alertness.

DEVELOPMENT OF INITIATIVE.

§ 46. The development of initiative can only be ordered as a bunch of muscles should be ordered. It will not "grow" in a barren nature. Yet it is possible to develop the ability, or it would not exist. What some men have acquired, any man may strive to acquire. I believe the power is largely subject to the will; that is, to persistent determination proceeding in the right way. That right way, in part, at least, may be indicated as follows:

FIRST METHOD FOR DEVELOPMENT OF INITIATIVE: ACQUIRING COMPREHENSIVE KNOWLEDGE. The man who would have initiative must *study the business in which he is engaged until he knows it*, inside and outside and all around. This involves, (a) the particular part of that business in which he is immediately at work; but, (b) all related parts in his neighborhood; and, (c) the whole of the business as a unit.

SECOND METHOD FOR DEVELOPING INITIATIVE: ACQUIRING EXTENSIVE KNOWLEDGE. He must *get a birdseye view of the business as a unit* in its connections with other related kinds of business.

THIRD METHOD FOR DEVELOPMENT OF INITIATIVE: ACQUIRING INTENSIVE KNOWLEDGE. He must exhaustively *know particulars and details within these fields.* If you have read Kipling's "*How the Ship Found Herself,*" you have observed exhaustive knowledge of details. *It is by knowledge of particulars that initiative secures its inspiration, and the habit of attention to parts and relations is formed.* Ignorance suggests nothing. Knowledge in *general* suggests vague dreams. Practical detail information in a live brain "bristles" with initiative possibilities.

FOURTH METHOD FOR DEVELOPMENT OF INITIATIVE: ACQUIRING KNOWLEDGE OF MEN. He must *study himself, the men around him, those remote in the same business, and the kind of men who succeed best therein,* or, are best adapted to the places filled and the work carried on (see Sections 48-54, Chapter XI). Few people take the trouble intelligently to "size up" others on the debit and credit side of their capacity and peculiarities, but this work is indispensable to initiative. And with this should go the great study of adjustment to all sorts and conditions of people in the business world. You are referred for further details to the chapter on "Personal Requirements" and to the author's previous volume, "*Power for Success.*"

FIFTH METHOD FOR DEVELOPMENT OF INITIATIVE: ACQUIRING KNOWLEDGE OF BUSINESS CONDITIONS. He must *study and know the conditions of the business in which he is engaged,* and of *business in general*, together with such factors as raw material, finished products, cost, demand, competition, machinery, methods, and so on, and so on.

SIXTH METHOD FOR DEVELOPMENT OF INITIATIVE: ACQUIRING PROPHETIC KNOWLEDGE. He must *cultivate commercial imagination* (see chapter on that subject). He must acquire the ability to see, not only situations that now are, but those that may be and ought to be; and he must forepicture plans, means, methods in operation for realizing improvements and ventures. All previous items lead up to this. But they do not necessarily secure the outlook indicated. That demands effort to imagine as just above suggested, constant, patient, studious and tireless. In other words, *the man who would have initiative must try for the initiative vision— and continue trying, with relentless, but intelligent determination, to gain it.* He is, let us say, tying bundles in a paper warehouse: how can tying be done better and more rapidly, with less strength, time, paper and twine? Or, he is handling customers: how can they be best and more quickly satisfied with the largest sales at right profit? Or, he is superintendent of a railway line: how can other competing lines be "systemized" and a bigger territory be covered by one office? The question is always: How? How? How? That question is the nurse of initiative, for the reiterant query, How? drives brain-cells to build the eyes of initiative vision, just as sunlight, beating for ages on the epithelium of a lowest organism, at last compelled the inner cells to construct that window of the psychic factor, the organ of sight.

SEVENTH METHOD FOR DEVELOPMENT OF INITIA-
TIVE: ACQUIRING VITAL INTEREST. He must *cultivate immense interest in his work,* his "line," his
department, the whole business. (See Sections
37-40, Chapter X) The man who is only interested in "his job" bids successfully *against* a
better job. The world that serves for wage or
salary alone has a bad disease—half-heartedness.
The cure consists in huge doses of interest accompanied by electric alertness.

EIGHTH METHOD FOR DEVELOPMENT OF INITIA-
TIVE: ACQUIRING PSYCHIC POWER. This may be
called the *psychic method* by way of special distinction. *It consists, first, of the enlargement of consciousness, and, secondly, instructing the subjective
self to discover and reveal to the objective self initiative visions and methods.* The work now before us
may be divided as follows:

(A) *The sense of consciousness may be expanded*
by a persistent effort to lift the awareness-feeling
up, out of the body, so to speak, to the spaces of
astronomy. Ignorance may smile here, but I know
that one may seemingly lift off the bony cover of
the mind and become aware of the whole heavens
above. You say that this is all imagination. Of
course; and that is exactly what we are after: the
expansion of the self-feeling in imagination beyond
the petty details and the mere routine of every-day
life. The effort to do this should be varied by passing
the thought-consciousness out in all directions away
from the limits of the body. To accomplish either
result, concentrate attention upon the brain. You
have a sense of awareness in the brain; now, in
imagination, remove the covering and expand the

awareness-sense to embrace the sky, the starry heavens; then throw the sense, as it were, out from the body all around, to embrace your village, town, country, the world of tumultuous human life. Do not picture anything; *simply enlarge the scope of being aware of more than the limits of your body seems to encompass.*

(B) The initiative vision and spirit may be developed *by commands given to the subjective phase of the self*, in addition to the preceding methods. Initiative involves an enlarging personal consciousness, as just above indicated — but, of course, through all experience and education as well; and the deeper self may be trained to alertness and suggestiveness by being frequently ordered, with confident expectation, to outlook for new ideas and to report its discoveries. If you doubt this, where did you get your last discovery? That which you may appear to do by accident, as it were, you certainly may train yourself to do by design. Concentration of thought (and that subject will be treated in the next chapter) compels the deeper mind to bring forth what it filches from the Infinite Vision. We are manifests of, and we background in, the Infinite. There is an Infinite Universal Mind, and there seems to be something like a Universal Human Mind; the individual human drawing from this and the larger Infinite, so that the Universal Human Mind seems to draw on the Infinite Universal Mind. When the individual gets large control of his mind, subjective and objective, he deliberately draws on the Universal Human Mind, or, if you prefer, on the minds of other individuals, but certainly on the Infinite Universal Mind, because he is a human being and a manifest of that Infinite Mind. Wandering of mind frequently flashes forth things new as well as old. Whence came these new things? Partly from the native initiative of any human mind; partly by telepathic methods from other minds. But what *is* the *native* initiative of the human mind? The result of the action of the Infinite Universal Mind up into the individual human mind. If such considerations are true we may train the subjective mind, that which connects the individual mind with the Infinite, to use its telepathic ability and to draw on the larger Infinite Reservoir, for new ideas and greater intuitional knowledge of even practical affairs. So, by insisting to yourself, say, at stated times—morning or night—"I, IN MY DYNAMIC POWER AS A THINKER, COMMAND THAT PHASE OF MYSELF WHICH RESTS ON AND NEAREST THE INFINITE, AS THE LOTUS RESTS ON THE SURFACE OF THE NILE, TO DRAW FORTH FROM THE DEPTH AND THE VASTNESS OF LIFE, NEW POWER, NEW THOUGHT, NEW PLANS AND METHODS FOR MY BUSINESS AND MY SUCCESS." Sooner or later the subjective self will hear, obey, and report.

If, now, you merely read the above suggestions, you miss the intention behind them. The intention calls for practical effort to realize more and more each specific goal indicated. This will require time and patient work. Not by mere ideals do we come to better things; labor must follow the ideals. I find abroad a foolish notion that the waving of a wand—by a medical lecturer, by a college professor, by a business man in a "talk," by a book on a practical subject—has some mysterious power to lift one out of mediocrity into ability. There are no miracles of this kind. The present work is simply a book; the reader must put himself into the labor indicated, for long, and patiently, and believingly, if he expects results of value.

The suggestions given in this chapter, if acted upon by persistent effort, will infallibly develop in any man or woman, according to individual make-up, some degree of initiative. What degree may turn out to be yours, can never be known until you have given the directions a thorough trial. If you actually resolve to build the essential factors of the chapter into your character and life, and set about the work now, and "stick to it,"—that will be initiative of good value. Thereafter the outcome is simply a matter of hard climbing.

§ 47. Could you have the best things in this world *without* effort, or *with* effort, what would be your choice?

Your answer is vastly important to you. If you answer one way, this book is now closed. If you answer another way, what are you now going to do about it?

Initiate!

CHAPTER X.

BUSINESS MENTALITY.

SAID Friedrich Nietzsche, in a manner that well might arouse the dead, "I wish to preach, not the doctrine of ignoble ease, but the doctrine of the strenuous life, the life of toil and effort, of labor and strife: to preach the highest form of success which comes, not to the man who desires mere easy peace, but to the man who does not shrink from danger, from hardship, or from bitter toil, and who, out of these, wins the splendid ultimate triumph." With such a spirit must the business man's mentality be saturated. The very feeling will stimulate every power of mind, direct every activity of life.

§ 1. *Our minds develop in differences by reason of occupation.* The very highly trained business brain performs functions fully as complex as those involved in the scholar's work. For this reason our study in the present chapter must be elementary and comparatively brief, the aim being merely to adduce enough mental science to furnish a basis for practical suggestions in the conduct of business.

§ 2. A human person may be regarded as a kind of corporation having two great departments of activity: those of physiological processes, and those of conscious mentality.

The Human Corporation.

§ 3. "All those internal motions of animal bodies," said Erasmus Darwin, more than a hundred years ago, "which contribute to digest their aliment, produce their secretions, repair their injuries, or increase their growth, are performed without our attention or consciousness."

§ 4. The physical processes, in distinction from the physiological, yet relating to the same department of the personal corporation, involve the furnishing of nutrition, the care of the body, and the activity of the external organs under direction of the mental powers.

All this constitutes the organized business of physical being.

§ 5. The word mentality is defined as "the sum of the mental functions, as distinguished from the physical." Self-conscious mentality is that in which the I-notion is capable of appearing. At this point we vaguely approach the controlling "head of the institution."

§ 6. The sum of the mental functions exhibits on two levels: the *subconscious and the conscious.*

§ 7. The subconscious mental functions conduct the purely physiological processes, and, at times, more or less, in varying degrees, the physical functions concerned with the external organs, together with certain habituated and "unaware" mental activities. In other words, the business of the corporation is so systematically organized that much of it is carried on without specific attention or direction from the level of the conscious mentality.

§ 8. In conscious mentality there are three departments, which, however, have frequent connections with the subconscious. These departments are devoted to willing, feeling, thinking.

Willing involves an idea of action which is carried out. Feeling is an active state, physical or mental, that reports in self-consciousness, of agreeableness, or disagreeableness, or indifference. Thought involves various activities, as, perception, conception, memory, imagination, judgment, and so on.

§ 9. In the three activities above named—willing, feeling, thinking—we see the real business of the corporation. All other activities are preparatory for or subservient to this prime business end: the personal life in its deepest, widest, highest and richest sense—richest, too, in the quantity and quality of its contents. Within and behind all these activities operates, as it is said, the will. Here we have the real head of the concern—if the corporation transactions are conducted according to the evident design of the whole institution.

§ 10. But the will—what is that? The will, precisely speaking, seems to be the idea of action carried out, and must obtain, I think, in both the subconscious and the conscious levels of mentality. Confining our attention to the latter, we may say that when the idea of action obtains and is carried out, the mentality exhibits initiative, control, direction, in relation to physical and mental activities. The will, then, is not a power to be regarded

as separate from the person. It is the personal
capacity for initiative, control and direction. It is
all-in the person. It is in every activity in which
the idea of action obtains and is practically realized.
The headship of our corporation reduces to precisely that: an idea of doing which is made good as
the idea suggests.

§ 11. The kind of activity which the corporation office initiates, controls and directs, it is evident,
depends on the amount and quality of mentality in
the office itself. The amount and quality of mentality are determined by heredity, environment, and
training, and they influence and are influenced by
the active pursuits of life. The artist, the statesman, the business man, owe something to their
ancestors and something to their environment,
although they are capable of modifying the same,
more or less, and the "bent" or "set" of mentality
exerts an influence on the choice of pursuits; yet
nevertheless, as environment varies mentality, so
the business in which we are engaged modifies
and moulds the character of mental life. *Any man
who has been long engaged in a pursuit, makes and is
made by the pursuit.* We may say, then, that mentality differs in degree according to its long-time
work. There are thus the innumerable types of
mentality which we observe, as, that of the judge,
the artist, the statesman, the scholar, the
teacher, the business man. In all such cases,
differences in character of mentality are largely
differences in the matters handled by the corporation — legal decisions, political situations, classified knowledge, methods of instruction, material
wealth.

Business mentality is the work of the main office in the personal corporation conducted in the pursuit of material wealth.

§ 12. You are invited to make this notion of yourself as a *personal corporation* a working principle in your life, to proceed to a better and more comprehensive understanding of its entirety, and more perfectly to organize all its departments and its unity for greater efficiency.

§ 13. Now, in the work of the main office there is a general activity which is associated with that of the subconscious and the physical departments. If we consider all the mental activities taking place at any time, we have what is called "mind." *"Mind" is the sum-total of mental activities* so far as psychology is concerned. And now, if one were to catch an instantaneous photograph of a busy manufactory's interior in operation, he would illustrate for mind what we call consciousness. All mental activities carry with them some part of awareness. *Consciousness is a complex of awareness taking place now.* When you become aware of a mental process and have the *I-notion in the awareness-feeling, self-consciousness emerges.* And when various *mental activities are ignored by the awareness-feeling, so that, for the most part, only one activity seems actually engaged*, we have that shifting somewhat called *attention.*

§ 14. The personal corporation thus involves —body—physiological processes—physical activity of external organs — mentality — mind — including willing, feeling, thinking—consciousness on the two levels, self-consciousness, and attention. It is with the latter that we are now to deal.

§ 15. *Since attention is not a separate mental faculty, because it obtains in the action of all the faculties, it is simply a characteristic of the activity of any of them.* With this distinction in view, we proceed to an analysis of attention.

THE ELEMENTS OF ATTENTION.

§ 16. *First—The Element of Ideas.* In order to see, mentally or visually, there must be in the mind, so far as attention is to be secured, (a) the *attention-idea* or impulse, (b) the idea of the *thing in mind,* or (c) the idea of *searching for something* not yet definitely made out. When you feel the *impulse* of attention, the mind has the *idea* of *attention.* When you *attend* to an object, there is in mind the *idea* of the *object.* When you attend to *thought,* the *latter* is the *idea* in mind. When you are mentally *searching,* say, for an illustration, a conclusion, a truth, you have the *idea of search.* The ideas referred to need not necessarily be consciously held in the ordinary sense, but the mind must have them, or it will not yield the characteristic of attention.

§ 17. *Second—Intensity of the Ideas.* Intense attention means

(a) The *fixed,* almost unwavering *attention-idea,* held to

(b) The *idea in mind*—mental thought—external object;

(c) Or held *for the sake of something* sought and to be definitely made out.

The *intensity of attention* is measured by the degree in which at least two of these ideas are exclusively present—either (a) and (b) or (a) and (c).

§ 18. *Comprehensive attention* involves the number of such ideas going together in mind: attention-idea (one) and mental idea or object-idea (one or more).   The number of ideas or objects to which we can attend at once is comparatively small. We carry many things in mind in a more or less closely associated grouping, but at-once attention to them seems to be a case of "lightning change" from one to another.

§ 19. The word attention originally meant "to stretch," with a physical application which has been transferred to the mental region.   If we think of "mind" as the sum-total of mental processes going on now, and of consciousness as the sum-total of awarenesses in those processes going on now, *attentiou must be a "stretcking" of some one or all of the processes toward an object without or an idea within*—toward a self as being or doing, a state of the self, a feeling, a series of acts, a line of conduct, a whole bundle of activities, a goal or a purpose.   Thus, attention may be involved in any activity of the self which has the power of reporting in self-consciousness: in the sensations of seeing, hearing, smelling, tasting, touching, and in emotion, memory, reasoning, and so on.

§ 20. A general rule for attention, then, may be stated as follows: *Intensely will intensely to attend, carrying exclusively in mind a vivid idea of (b) the object or thought considered, or (c) the search for a something which will be recognised and satisfactory when it " comes up," and hold steadily to the effort.*

§ 21. Now, intense attention to a specific thing for long is very difficult, but a *certain continuousness of attention to a search* or a purpose may obtain according to the presence or absence of the next element.

§ 22.   *Third — Power of Will.*   Having (a) the idea of attention, and (b) the idea or thought in mind, or (c) the idea of search, the self may will itself to hold to the (a) attention-idea and the (b) object-idea or thought-idea, or the (c) search-idea, for a varying length of time.   The greater is the self-control or will-power, the longer will be the continuousness of attention—within limits.   The limit is an individual matter, in no two persons being, perhaps, just equal.   But naked will-power is usually quite soon a helpless thing.   A further element is commonly required for "good" attention, that is,

§ 23.   *Fourth — The Motor Interest.*   In an absolute sense, sheer will-power in attention is backed by interest in the mere ability to will attention, in ascertaining what one can do and for how long one can do exactly that.   For the most part, however, all sorts of interests obtain, inciting attention now to one thing, now to another, and it is the function of will

Simply to let the interest run its course
Until some interest becomes stronger,
Or, for the sake of a purpose.
Or of a selected object of attention,
To compel attention to a given thing or in a given direction.

§ 24.   *The secret of attention*, thus, seems (1) to lie either with will, considered from the point of view of self-control, or (2) to lie with interest considered from the point of view of reason for self-control in the matter, or from the point of view of external influence; or to lie with a combination of the two factors difficult to separate.

§ 25. When an interest is allowed to run, will is in operation in the sense (x) that the self uses its powers of perception or thought, as in gazing at an attractive landscape or indulging in a pleasing train of reveries; or (y) that the self may interfere in any process going on and stop it for the sake of some selected object of attention. This general fact just adduced brings us to a further element:

§ 26. *Fifth—Inhibition.* Where all sorts of ideas are appearing and fading, if there is to be attention to one, (a mental "stretching" toward that one), *a process of prohibition may take place.* There is, at any instant, attention to something, whatever that may be. If this something has then the most interest, or if it seems to be actually or possibly connected with the interest of some prevailing purpose, or with the interest of something sought for, the self may pause, give additional or exclusive attention thereto, and "push away," "shut out," disregard or ignore, all other ideas and objects that clamor for consideration. We have here *inhibition.* There is now attention to one thing. This one-thing attention may be due to immediate predominating interest, or it may be due to will, in which case, as we have seen, a remoter interest prevails—perhaps the mere interest of knowing self and its mental ability, perhaps some larger interest in life.

ATTENTION AND ITS INSTRUMENTS.

§ 27. Now, attention may be—of the *senses,* of the senses with *conscious mental action,* and of the *"mind" solely.* It is important to note this further analysis of attention, because it represents facts in our life, and because the cultivation of attention or concentration must employ the results of the analysis. We may say that attention is

(1) *Organic: employing some one or more of the sense-organs.* The attention of the sense-organs is always more or less with us during waking hours. Sensations arise from bodily conditions within or from the action of external objects upon the sense-organs. The sensations themselves are reported in consciousness, but some of them are apparently "lost" in the subconscious field, while others enter the field of the awareness-feeling. Sensations are characterized by quality, intensity, extent and duration, terms which are self-explanatory. If any one of these characteristics are absent, all are absent. Sense-attention, therefore, turns toward any of the factors or all of them. You are invited experimentally to test this statement. The ability correctly to observe—use the senses—is of the greatest importance in business life, and the lack of it is a universal complaint. For instruction in development of sense-attention you are referred to the author's previous work, "*Power of Will*," third edition. We can here give only a general rule or two, which, however, should be carefully studied.

Be as attentive as possible to any object without or process within which gives rise to a sensation, and when the object is removed, or you have turned from it, or the process is completed, recall the sensation by an act of memory as vividly and completely as you can. This rule is taken from Titchener's "*Outline of Psychology*" and is precisely the method involved in the detail work of "*Power of Will*," though not there suggested by that author.

§ 28. (2) *Organo-Mental: employing conscious mental action or effort with awareness of sensation.* The directions just given merge into this form of attention. The differences between the two phases are these: sense-attention, where there is no particular accompaniment of thought, may be general only, or vague and confused, and much of it may be "lost" in the unconscious, because the mind is occupied with thought not related to internal bodily conditions or external objects. The attention is then organic. But when thought becomes engaged with the sensations, or, better, with whatever occasions them, attention is organo-mental and it brings to mind information of all appropriate kinds. By as much as the factors of attention in such case—the use of the senses—become habituated, by so much does voluntary effort in attention become less requisite. The goal of attention, indeed, is right habituated attention acquired and made easy, so that there may be an increasingly larger facility of intense attention for new discoveries.

Your power of attention, so far as the above analysis goes, depends on (1), your ability to put the whole of the awareness-feeling into any sensation and the knowing process involved in that sensation, and, (2), your ability wholly to exclude from the awareness-feeling any other sensation and the knowing process connected therewith. The kind of attention indicated is of the greatest importance in business. The merchant who knows men and goods often perceives what others are unable to

detect. Some people see, hear, observe very little
going on around them. Of others it seems to be
true that they see in the dark, hear flies walking
on the ceiling, and feel your brain-cells in thought.
Many men are unsuccessful simply because their
sense-organs are such non-conductors of interest
and fact.

Business power demands that the organs of
sense—and the mind behind them—be alive and
alert. It is the complaint of the business world
that employees do not engage active observation and thought in what they are doing. You are
urged to cultivate the habit of investigating
attention and thoughtfulness in all your business
details.

§ 29. (3) *Mental Attention Exclusively.* The
senses give the mind the "raw material" of the
mental life, but *purely mental attention,* in the
meaning here employed, *concerns only the processes
and results of the same in the inner world of the self.*
There are in the general field of the consciousness
all sorts of "goings-on." Attention, which is always passing from one thing to another, may be
held to some one thing for a time, but only for a
brief time so far as unbroken continuousness is
concerned. *The ideal of mental attention, then, is
this: to bring attention back, again and again, to the
desired object, and to hold it hard, when brought
back, and to hold it hard for long.* The ability to do
this kind of work is immensely in demand in the
business world. You are therefore urged to cultivate deliberative and continuous attention to all the
details and their connections in your work or business. For elaborate instruction in the matter,

reference may be had to "*Power of Will*," but it should be remembered that there is no magic method by which the ability can be secured, for the only conceivable general rule for the development of intense and continuous attention in the field of thought is the rule of persistent practice in thoughtful attention and attention to connected thinking—which is here made a suggestive régime for actual use by the reader.

ATTENTION IN CONSCIOUSNESS.

§ 30. All attention involves consciousness, of course, since consciousness is the "now sum-total of awarenesses in mental processes," and attention is one of the processes or a direction of any of the processes. But we are not to assume that attention is a sort of additional process, an extra introduced into consciousness under certain conditions. *Attention is rather a peculiar characteristic of any of the awareness-processes consisting of permission of one and inhibition of others*. The inhibition may be regarded as acting in a way to "focus" consciousness because it reduces the awareness-feeling to a single process, either simple or complex—as, in scrutiny of an object or absorption in a train of thought. Using the idea of focusing in this sense, we concentrate consciousness as a lense concentrates light. If the one ray of light be passed through a prism and its elements thrown upon a screen, a spectrum is formed composed of the seven primary colors. In a similar way we may imagine consciousness passed through the focusing "lense" of attention, and if we carry out the imaginary action of the original elements to a screen of analysis, we shall have what may be called a mental "prism," as follows:

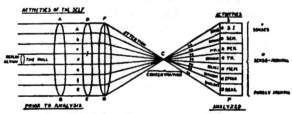

When attention is merely a reflex action, as when one notices a fly on the ceiling, we may have involuntary (passive) attention. Voluntary attention implies the will in effort. The lines, a, b, c, d, e, f, g, represent the elements of the sum-total processes going on in your mind. The circle, AB, indicates those processes at any now-moment—giving consciousness. The circle, DE, indicates the same with the idea of self (I) included. The circle, FG, represents the sum of the processes capable of coming to attention. As the whole awareness-feeling, or the most of it, that is, if I may so express it, conscious consciousness, goes into a, or b, or c, or d, or e, or f, or g, and through the corresponding points in the circle FG, then a, or b, or c, etc., converge at C (standing for either attention or concentration), and attention occurs of the kind indicated in the mental spectrum analysis, as in mere unaware Sense-Impression (SI), or sensation (SEN.), and so on.

The "spectrum" SP is merely an analysis of the mental processes after attention has enabled us to separate them. The illustration of attention as a passing of consciousness into a condition, as light may be passed through a concentrating lense, stops, of course, at C. The rest of the figure simply analyzes the elements involved in mind and capable of attention, as the prism analyzes light into the colors — the etheric waves — red, orange, yellow, green, blue, indigo, violet.

CONCENTRATION.

§ 31. *Attention means the self centrally devoted to perceiving or studying an object or a thought* (focusing), other states (processes) of consciousness obtaining more or less ostensibly. *Concentration means that all or nearly all such states are arrested or ignored to permit the one state to continue.* Attention, then, is a phase of concentration, and at times shades into the latter, as the self more and more arrests or ignores all mental processes (states) for one. Concentration, therefore, may weaken, so to speak, into casual attention, as various other mental processes than the one just engaged are permitted to claim consideration one after the other. The difference between attention and concentration is measured, we may say, by the scope and power of the act of inhibition, concentration being more "perfect" in (a) intensity, or (b) exclusiveness, or (c) comprehensiveness, or (d) continuousness, at least practically considered.

§ 32. When some definite purpose-interest (see section 23)—either (a) a temporary purpose-interest, as, the solution of a problem for its own sake or for discipline, or (b) a long-run purpose-interest, as, the accomplishment of a prolonged business task or the building of a great financial enterprise—when such *purpose-interest obtains, and*

the self, for that reason, wills definite and ex-
clusive attention to the matter raising interest, we
have an illustration of continuous concentration.
The focusing of consciousness may be intermittent,
but it recurs repeatedly for a long period.

§ 33. *Concentration is exclusion of various*
other-interests for the one-interest. The one-interest may be one out of a thousand other-interests,
in a subordinate sense · or a primary sense—of a
temporary duration or of a considerable period.
There are many subordinate interests (mental)
in your business, and now one of them becomes
the one-interest for a time and you shut out all the
other-interests; but again, that one-interest—the
one thing in hand or being accomplished—becomes
a mere other-interest because a second previous
other-interest has taken its place as the one-interest.   In every such case you give a degree of attention to the matter in hand (or in mind).   In
some cases, you give your whole "mind" to the
matter in hand.   Here you become absorbed; you
really concentrate.

§ 34. *There is thus a constant change of posi-*
tion going on among all the other-interests, some one
always being a one-interest, but only for a time, each
of the other-interests always being thrust aside for
another one-interest.   Ever, in the career of success,
there is some great one-interest which steadily holds
its place and power as THE *one-interest.   It never*
becomes a mere other-interest, but remains first, the
interest of prime importance and influence—just the
one-interest of life.   This is the ruling passion.

§ 35.   If the one-interest continues first for a
period, we say the man has a definite purpose: he

concentrates on this one-interest through all the jostling play and constant supplanting of ten thousand coming and going other-interests, until his object is gained. If this interest continues to be the ruling one-interest of life, he similarly concentrates all his life forces on the realization of the idea or object involved in that interest.

Business concentration is of this character. The supreme one-interest is inspired by the idea of financial success; to this may be subordinated, now one interest of a period, now another of a further period, but all interests, coming and going, jostling and changing places temporarily, are perfectly subordinated to the period-interest of a period and the ruling passion of life — the life-long one-interest, master and supreme.

Mind-Wandering and Cure.

§ 36. There is very little purely mental concentration among average people. The larger proportion of our attention is organo-mental, and vague and confused, at that. In the mental realm we are all familiar enough with mind-wandering, and may attribute a degree of that condition to the fact that we are so largely occupied with the world of sense. But some mind-wandering is due to inability mentally to attend in any concentrated way. How shall such mind-wandering be cured? The methods that follow are general and brief, but they will bring to you infallible results if you will persist for long in observing them in the details of your work or business.

Observe: the methods are all applicable to organo-mental concentration no less than to the purely mental. You are urged to adopt them as working principles. We may call them the Ten Golden Rules of Long-Run Concentration.

THE TEN GOLDEN RULES OF LONG-RUN CONCENTRATION.

(1) There must be a very *great desire to conquer*.

(2) There must be a *tremendous determination to conquer*.

(3) One must remember that *determination is not doing*. There must be *action in the line of the determination*, and persisted in day after day, for long.

(4) The will must *force the mind to attend now*. Will hard, look, listen, think, hard—on this particular matter; that is, on all matters.

(5) The "mind" must be given occasional *opportunity for rest* and reaction, for it simply will not, with the most of us, hold hard to one thing for long without a break. You will get better results by "easing up" now and then, returning, however, to the purpose and action that mean ultimate victory. The work meanwhile will be carried on by the subconscious self.

(6) *The act of attending now must be repeated*, and again repeated, day after day, week after week, until concentration becomes comparatively easy and its habit is established.

(7) *Attention must be kept up for a long period on some particular train of thought or practical pursuit.*

(8) One must never *become discouraged* and must *admit no defeat* as possible.

(9) One must *never permit thought to dwell on weariness*, difficulty, the cost to be paid for the power; but must always *hold in view* the idea of the *ability* and its *utility* in all the affairs of life.

(10) One should *practise on an object* or in a *line of effort* that is *really worth while*. This brings into play the great factors of interest. Interest moves the world.

§ 37. At this point appears an important law, as follows: *The acquisition of the power of concentration, and its best use in life, depends on whether or no it has behind it a great passion.* The highest type of concentration probably always is thus backgrounded, but any practical concentration certainly is related to some pronounced interest.

§ 38. A second law now emerges: *Whether or no mind-wandering is an evil or a benefit depends on the man's ability to concentrate in the interest of a great passion.* If there be no mental mastery of concentration, mind-wandering not only is, but indicates, an evil—a mind unstable as water. If there be no great passion—as, for a bank account, for promotion, for personal improvement, and so on—concentration may be a mere accident of one's native endowment, and its achievements may fall short of any special value, or they may be criminal. For it is the will that acquires or directs concentration, but it is the great passion that leads the will.

§ 39. If the self is master in concentration, and is urged on by a great passion, *mind-wandering may more than likely prove a benefit.* We all know, for example, that trying to recall a thing often fails until we cease trying. Then the thing "drifts

up" to the surface of consciousness like magic.
Some of our best thoughts come when we are
thinking of matters foreign to them. But these
best things are best because the habit of concentration has been acquired—the self is master of
mind after all and notwithstanding the wandering
thoughts. The fact seems to be, in such cases,
that the subconscious self is really occupied with
the main thing, while the objective mind is turning
now here, now there, and so, when a less intense
conscious condition comes about, just the fact of
the mind-wandering gives subjective operations
opportunity for the "casting up on the beach," so
to speak, of the subconscious conclusions or its
stray suggestions.

INTEREST AND BUSINESS POWER.

§ 40. The passion for success will furnish
sufficient general interest for the inspiration of
concentrated attention to long-run and all related
purposes. But, as a steam engine requires particular pounds of steam, which must be constantly
supplied, so the "mind" needs, in addition to a
general passion, specific interests connected therewith, which must unceasingly be renewed. An
interest, indeed, is never entirely a fixed thing;
it is ever a varying thing. The mental activities
must keep it going, by giving it incessantly different details of form. Otherwise it palls. A realized
interest fails as an interest since it tends to crys-
tallize or to petrify. Hence, interest must be per-
petually nourished. One of the problems of
prolonged concentration to business is exactly this:
how to maintain the feeding of interest so that

effectiveness and power may be continued at a high
level? The solution of the problem can only be
found in effort to secure interest when the general
run of life fails, and that effort must be put forth
either by the person himself or by some one else
for him. *If, then, you are an employee, you should
remember that one of the keys to success is a vital
and ever-renewing interest in the work and business
in which you are engaged. If you are an independent employer, you must have a care for the best results in your business by inspiring your employees
with fresh interests and by devising new channels
for your own activity for the sake of vital detail-
interests and every-day interests in your own case.*

You are invited to review your work or business
with reference to this important matter of renewing interest as a financial asset.

A great public journal purchased an entirely
new outfit of type, involving thousands of dollars
of expense. Many agents for type foundries strove
to secure the order. One young man, on a small
salary, made his proposition to the right person,
at the right time, in the right way, and captured
the sale. The foundry people gave him no commission—the usual commission, had he been employed on that basis, would have amounted to a
couple of thousand dollars—and did not increase
his salary. They would, of course, affirm that the
sale was this young man's duty if he could effect it.
Here we have a false attitude which some business
men assume; it is likely as not a cloak for selfishness. The obvious reply is: *if you put your people
solely on the level of duty, do not complain when
they take care not to exceed their duty.* I conversed

with the general manager of a Western railway
system.   It is a rule, he said, among railroad officers, not to commend their men for special services,
since absolute devotion to the road is supposed to
be every employee's duty.   The rule is crude.
Management of large concerns may be conducted
on the iron-clad plan, and secure good results by
reason of discipline.   But there certainly is a better
plan, involving no less of discipline but more of
sensible psychology. You invariably get the best
out of a man when you appeal to his self-interest.
The general method of such appeal consists in incitement, rewards, commendations, and ingenuity
in devising the fresh play of the man's best forces.

You place, for example, a clerk behind a
counter, and make of his life a monotonous routine,
expecting him to possess something similar to *your*
renewing interest in *your* business, but you put
him where old interests run out, necessarily and
naturally, and you do nothing to renew his interest,
making him a mere "piece" in your own "game."
You pay wages or salary to precisely what you
create—an automatic "dead man."   Real modern
business power is an electric charger to every soul
"on the place," for its own interest incessantly appealing to the self-interest of all engaged in the
undertaking.   If you say that the man need not
take the "job," you forget that the question is not
one of any particular individual, but concerns *all
who might take the place.*   Moreover, it is not a
moral matter, nor even a social matter; it is purely
a business affair.   By exactly so much as you reduce your people to automata, by so much,
inevitably and invariably, you miss their best ser-

vice, and you rob yourself of the greatest business success.

But the subject has its reverse side. You work for another, day after day, in the same old "dead-man's" way, and you expect that your employer shall be eager to pay your wage or salary, present you with gifts, promote you and take an interest in you without stint. You have lost your interest in the business—and ten thousand men are ready to take your place with equal ability. *No man can rise in the world who suffers his interest in the thing he is doing to fail.* Interest is mortal. The law of it is, an early grave, with one monument: Died of Misplaced Confidence.

§ 41. *It is especially important that people who have arrived at the middle period of life should man-age in some way to maintain a high degree of interest in their work and of capacity for renewal of interest continually.* Many persons at that age lose position simply because, while abilities remain unimpaired, together with capacity for service, otherwise con-sidered, they have suffered a diminution of active interest and enthusiasm in whatever they under-take or do. The remedy consists in a wholesale arousing of the personality, by use of will and by all sorts of ingenious devices, so that interest may be kept up to required standard.

§ 42. This value of new interest may be se-cured by an effort of will in attention with the idea of discovering new, unknown things in surround-ings and the matters dealt with, and of applying such new ideas or aspects in work or business for the sake of greater efficiency and success. Agassiz used to keep his students for days engaged in the

study of the externals of a common fish, requiring
them to report all that they saw, using the eyes
merely.   Two or three weeks of such effort were
bound to test the student's scientific interest and
to bring to light an astonishing amount of information.   There is nothing you handle about which
you may not make new discoveries beyond what
you believe you already know.   But it should always be borne in mind that the effort is put forth
for the sake of new interests, for the sake of
greater concentration to business, for the sake of
larger personal efficiency and success.   As a suggestion, then, let us assume a card printed as
follows, and placed where it may be frequently
observed, or kept forever in the mind's eye:

NEW INTERESTS TO-DAY!

For   Greater   Concentration

And, Therefore,

Larger Life!   Larger Success!

---

§ 43.   The details of the process are simple—
but about as difficult.   The will must hold to the
purpose—The mind must persistently and enquir-
ingly scrutinize surroundings and business—goods
—people—ways of adjustment—and faults—and
"best points" of self.   It would require pages to
elaborate on this phase of the process by which
concentration may be acquired (see section 24).   In

order to brevity, and practical stimulation, therefore, the entire matter may be graphically presented in the pyramid outlined below:

THE PYRAMID OF BUSINESS CONCENTRATION.

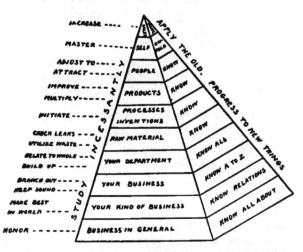

§ 44. The practical pyramid is not complete
unless you make *profits* in your business, or *sales* in
your employment, or some kind of *improvement* in
your work, and incessantly and increasingly.—The
study of self goes to discovery of faults, old failures,
and new ways of improvement.—*People* present new
faces, manners, peculiarities, and so on, and always
the problem is: just how to please this particular
man or woman.—By "*products*" is meant the goods
you handle, and, no less, those handled by your
competitor.—If you *invent* better ways for handling
or making goods, you are in demand.—How can
you do any of these things unless you *know* existing

processes and methods?—In your department you may be employee or "boss." In either case, *know the whole matter*—so far as opportunity permits—and create opportunity. Many a man has climbed higher, been promoted, simply because he knew some important things which he had not necessarily been called upon to know.—*The success of your business depends on the excess of your marginal knowledge over that of other people in your own kind of business.*—Finally, since you are in business, know business in general.

CONCENTRATION AND TEMPERAMENT.

§ 45. The kind and degree of concentration which one is able to put into his work depends more or less upon personal make-up or temperament. Some people exhibit what is called the *motor temperament;* they are excessively and variously active in all sorts of matters and plans. Their attention is not necessarily weak; it is, indeed, often of a very good ability; but it is really born of the active habit, and just because it is so largely a thing of habit and of this temperament, it is apt to be light or transitory, quickly coming and quickly going, and thus is seldom concentrated attention at all. *In such a case the will must restrain the running touch-and-go habit and compel the mind to fasten on matters attended to, and hold there, and try to get the whole subject as it is, and to impress it deeply in memory.* For example, a boy runs past a picket fence and draws his fingers across every picket. That is the motor attention. Now the boy walks slowly and feels of each picket, getting a distinct impression from each as he proceeds.

Concentrated attention to a succession of things is like that. There is no objection to motor attention if it be taken well in hand. *Business power, indeed, appreciates the man who can give his "mind" deeply to many subjects one after the other in rapid succession—if he can successfully get hold of and master each item as it comes along.* But he must be able to do this latter, or his value depreciates.

§ 46. Some people, again, are *attentive through one or another of the senses.* Let us assume that the sense is that of sight. This fact indicates their temperament, so to speak, so far as attention is concerned. Unconsciously they have formed the habit of getting things through the eye. If they secure a position requiring this talent, they do well. But just because seeing things is with them a habit, their attention, unless that is their especial work, is almost sure to be light and changeful— and oftentimes even when such talent is the kind required of them. Such people, therefore, *should force new or additional attention to other senses, and compel the mind to concentrate on ideas, thought, conduct, methods, improvement, for a larger personal efficiency and success.*

§ 47. Then there are those whose attention is *"fluid."* It *flows,* to and fro, quickly, everywhere; it is like running water, never "continuing in one stay." It gets all things easily, after a fashion, and this "fashion" is precisely the trouble. Because attention flows so easily from one thing to another, concentration does not occur. Because it "gets" after a fashion, it is its fashion to *forget.* The secret of not forgetting is merely good foregetting. *The remedy for fluid attention consists in*

fixing it. You say: "Pay attention!" He *is* paying attention—his kind. He must pull himself
together, make an effort, "freeze to" the thing in
hand. He must hold his mind stopped on the
matter in hand until it takes the mold of the
matter. Then, after attention breaks up, he has
the cast in his "consciousness," and he will not
forget.

§ 48. Since this kind of attention is what it
is, the method for bringing about the above directions consists in *putting the mind to difficult tasks,
so that understanding cannot be had, or success
achieved, unless the attention is fully and sufficiently
given to the subject under consideration.* People
with this sort of attention do ordinary things just
about as sea gulls dip to the water surface; and
they attend scarcely longer. Their minds must be
harnessed, so to speak, to hard things; thus attention becomes indispensable. It is not easy to
harness the sea gull, but that is what you must do
with that kind of "mind." If it is your kind of
"mind," that is the demand on you if you care to
achieve any great success.

§ 49. There is another type of "mind" that
remembers best in the form of *mental pictures.* If
this variety of memory is required in business, *the
labor of getting the pictures must, in many cases, be
gone over again and again until the details are correct and connected in thought, and the wholes are
deeply "stamped in."* Such people find abstract
concentration difficult, if not quite impossible.
This difficulty may prove their salvation. If they
will force profound concentration to the work in
which they are engaged, the fact that it is hard

doing so will immensely deepen the power of concentration and strengthen the memory as well. If you are employing men, you should put this kind of "mind" where its efficiency will prove of the greatest long-run benefit to yourself. That means that you either take immediate advantage of the man's bent, or that you place him where the development of concentration will bring you larger results.

Business and Types of Attention.

The proprietor of a printers' supply establishment said to me: "One of my men has just left my employ, and the concern to which he has gone may be disappointed. A casual on-looker would think him a "terrible" worker, and so he is, in his way; but if you were to follow him long you would discover that he never sticks to one thing for more than a few minutes. He works hard and is all over the place, yet he simply has to keep going incessantly, engaged in about a dozen tasks at once —like a circus rider dancing over the backs of as many horses."

§ 50. The illustration presents a two-sided suggestion. The man who is blessed with such a scatter-brain attention should *take himself in hand*, for unquestionably he misses some of his own power. And the employer who would get the most out of such a man must *adjust him to work* that permits the up-going of new interests from a variety of effort. You can't saw boards with a plane, and you can't make such a "mind" pay you if you hold it rigidly and long to one thing—unless you can successfully employ the method suggested in section 48 just above. Even then, you are in danger

of losing your man: he is apt to be a great
"quitter."

§ 51.   If, on the other hand, you have in your
employ a man who always concentrates and sticks
to one thing, *give him one "horse to ride" until he
knows that animal from ear to fetlock.* At that
point you must bring to such a person a fresh
interest, or you will lose some of his value.   Put
him into another long-time task.

§ 52.   These illustrations suggest the law:
*Business power knows its human instruments and
adapts them to the work required, but keeps those instruments sharpened and in the best condition by shifting the point of interest and in some way incessantly
intensifying the interest itself.*

§ 53.   If you desire promotion in business,
concentrate on your work, and dig out of it unceasingly new interests, if necessary forcing such
interest either by search for new discoveries or
through the mere determination to test your ability
in this respect.

§ 54.   If you desire success in your business,
concentrate the whole of you (with resolution in
plenty) on that business and every least detail
thereof.

"Let a man work at a thing till it looks right to
him," says John Jay Chapman in "*Causes and Consequences.*" "Let him adjust and refine it till, as he
looks at it, it passes straight into him, and he grows
for a moment unconscious again, that the forces
which produced it may be satisfied. As it stands then,
it is the best he can do." When that paragraph is
completely understood, its principle will have become one of the working factors of your life.

§ 55. If you wish to get the best results from your employees, adapt types of "mind" in the matter of their ability for attention to the most appropriate kinds of effort, and maintain in them, in some way, a lively interest in yourself and your business and in the work they are doing. When an employer puts men and women on the level of the horse, he has no one to blame if he gets out of them just the work of a horse—and of an ordinary kind of horse, at that. And when a man or woman gives to the employer merely perfunctory work, without real interest or zeal, only self can be blamed if the wage or salary is doled out according to "dead work," measure for measure.

§ 56. For always do self-interest and other-interest revolve together in the successful life, and concentrated attention to mutualism is the one abiding force that binds them in dual success.

Well said a successful business man in this connection: "Business requires the best that is in a man. Often men put into it their worst. If they always devoted to business their best energies, intelligence and foresight, there would be comparatively few failures. Beyond doubt, most of the business failures are due to conditions lying entirely within the business men themselves. I believe that almost any business will succeed if it has the concentration and effort that go to make success. Concentration is the quality I would emphasize, because it is one that embodies all other qualities.

"Concentration means a fixed resolve. It means thorough study of the business and of conditions governing it. It means effort applied intelligently, with due regard for cause and effect. *Concentration*

means never-say-die. If truthful history could be
written of many successful business men of to-day,
the world would be astonished at the seemingly
narrow escape they have had from business failure.
Men often come perilously near giving up the
struggle, yet fight on, and overcome. It is because
so many men give way at such a crisis that business
records are strewn with failures."

Thus it appears that business concentration
signifies not only the power to bore into a matter
and to hold the mind steadfastly thereto, but al:o
the ability to glue to a purpose of the long-run
type and to go on when going on seems hopeless,
and to double twist and renew all efforts before
obstacles of whatever occasion or character.

A very successful business man complained
that he could not "concentrate" his mind for fifteen minutes on a single subject; yet almost in the
same breath remarked that during the years of his
life difficulty and opposition had only rendered him
the more determined to overcome and to win out.
No one can hold the mind without a break to any
subject for fifteen minutes; the mind will flit and
return, only to flit again. It is enough to compel
the return incessantly until the matter is disposed
of. But all may hold to the life-long purpose, and
this variety of concentration, as suggested in the
last quotation, is absolutely indispensable to business success—indeed, to success in any field of
human effort that is worth while.

CHAPTER XI.

COMMERCIAL MEMORY.

EVERYONE understands the importance of a good memory, especially the business man. But the memory is not a thing apart by itself. It is, rather, a power which goes with every so-called "faculty" of the mind, as is true of attention and consciousness. Sir William Hamilton calls the memory "the faculty possessed by the mind of preserving what has once been present to consciousness, so that it may again be recalled and represented in consciousness." But the truth is that nothing is "preserved" in the mind; we have merely the power to re-enact various experiences of the inner and outer life and to know then that we have already had such experiences. This *knowing-I-have-had* is memory. In the business world the vital importance of being able at will to re-think what we have once thought, to do again what we have once done, and to train the self to the re-thinking and re-doing of needed things when they are needed or when we know they will be needed, is recognized by all practical ability. This chapter deals with the power as defined and its training as required in business effort.

§ 1. The only difference between the business man's memory and that of any other person consists in the contents of his experience and thought and the individual habits of his mind.

§ 2. If, in the preliminary sections of this chapter, we seem to have entered at least the edge of a jungle in psychology, it should be remembered that our effort at memory improvement ought to proceed more intelligently and to bring about better results when we have revived for use our general knowledge of the power and its action than would probably follow a less thoughtful method. Our work, therefore, will begin with a brief presentation of the mind's background facts in memory, and will then go on to practical suggestions for the use and improvement of the faculty itself.

Preliminary.

§ 3. The word "memory" is here employed in a very general sense, standing for (1) Retention or Conservation, (2) Reproduction or Recall, (association) and (3) Recognition or Identification, omitting Representation or Imagination, except as incidentally involved, because Imagination in its common meaning is reserved for another chapter.

§ 4. Of Retention we have no rational explanation (Hyslop). We seem to "retain" past experiences, but nobody knows how we do it.

§ 5. "*Reproduction is the process by which the past is recalled to consciousness*, and it acts according to certain definite laws"—the laws of Association, such as Redintegration (see section 8), similarity, etc.

§ 6. "*Recognition is the consciousness that the recalled incident belongs to the past and so sets the*

phenomena off from a present sensation. How it
occurs and what its conditions are we do not know.
It is an unique act of mind, quite as unanalyzable
as any other consciousness, and is the crowning act
of memory."

§ 7. "In order to reach the act of recognition," says Hyslop, quoted above, "the mind has to
have the preceding steps of retention, reproduction,
and representation or imagination. Recognition
is the one function by which we appropriate
consciously the past experience."

§ 8. "All the importance of conscious regulation of life depends on the extent to which the
recognition of the past is accurate and relevant,
and that accuracy and relevancy will depend upon
the quality and quantity of redintegration,"—"the
reproductive tendency of the mind to restore the
past collective experience in its totality "—the tendency of the mind in memory to restore the whole
of a section of past mental experience to which
the thing reproduced belongs. If you recall a tree
in a certain landscape viewed months since, the
tendency of the mind is to restore the whole, not
of the landscape, but of that section of it, or that
group of its objects, or that phase of its entirety,
which you really observed in the first place. "Interest and attention are more or less necessary to
the quality of what is recalled, and the development of complexity of association is necessary to
its quantity." If, with great interest, you concentrated on the landscape, the qualities first obtained
recur in mind clearly and distinctly, more or less.
If the scene, with various parts, was associated
with other experiences, this fact assists in bringing

up various details of the view. "The co-operation of these influences produces the maximum of conscious appropriation of experience and the healthy action of the mind and will."

§ 9. It is said that Napoleon "pigeon-holed" the things he wished to remember, so that, when he desired to recall a matter he simply looked into the proper "compartment" of his "memory." How did he know, first and last, that proper compartment? The notion that we mentally "pigeon-hole" anything belongs to the "bulgine" stage of psychology. "There is no such thing as mental retention," says Titchener in "*An Outline of Psychology*," "the persistence of an idea from month to month or year to year in some mental pigeon-hole from which it can be drawn when wanted. *What persists is the tendency to connection" among mental activities*, and rather, among physiological processes in the brain.

§ 10. The brain-processes which originally corresponded to those of a memory occurring now, or which took place when the matter remembered now first got into the mental field, *are never the same as the brain-processes taking place in remembering*, for in that case we should suppose, not that we are remembering, but that we are having the original experience which occurred when the thing originally got into consciousness. The process of remembering must differ from the process of the original experience which is remembered, or the two will be simply identical. This identification would be a state of consciousness, but it would not be a memory, because it would not have connected with it a feeling of a past experience.

MEMORY AND CONSCIOUSNESS.

§ 11. Consciousness has been defined as a bundle of present mental states. It may be called a bundle for two reasons:

First, consciousness is marked by a certain *unity;*

Secondly, consciousness is marked by an appreciable *variety.*

§ 12. "By the phrase '*unity of consciousness*' *we mean the fact that, at any time, whatever is present tends to form an always incomplete but still, in some respects, single conscious condition.*" Several things seem to be at-once present. "The facts present to mind are not merely various; they occur together. In what way they occur together, in what sense we are 'at once' aware of them, every person must observe for himself." And the unity is indicated by the fact that they are observable in himself. They are *his* facts of consciousness. The consciousness is his own.

§ 13. "On the other hand, the fact of the variety present to consciousness at any moment is equally obvious. *The one conscious state of the moment is always a unity consisting of a multiplicity.*"

§ 14. All this would seem sufficiently plain if we recall that consciousness is the sum-total of our now-mental-awareness activities. "Many things are going on in the mind at any instant: that constitutes the variety. The unity consists of the totality, either of all the mental activities, or of all activities in this or that group as determined, let us say, by some predominating idea, by interest, by concentration, by purpose, and so on.

§ 15. *If there were no variety we could not be conscious in the ordinary human sense. If there were no unity we could not be conscious as of the self.*

§ 16. Now, this *variety obtains because of differences.* When we say there is variety in consciousness, we say there are differences among our mental states or activities. And yet, we could not clearly make out these differences unless there were some sort of similarity among the states. How do you detect differences in objects? By comparing certain features with others resembling one another. And how do you detect resemblances? By comparing certain features with others that differ. "Thus, sameness and difference are inseparable characters." We could not have the idea of similarity unless we had the idea of difference, and *vice versa;* and the ideas could not arise without the facts.

§ 17. *Consciousness, then, is a unity of mental states or awareness processes which are nevertheless various and possess differences as well as resemblances.* When the differences stand, so to speak, on a background of the resemblances, and the resemblances stand, so to speak, on a background of the differences, consciousness is clear. But when certain features have scant background of resemblances, it is difficult to state what the differences (and so the mental processes) are; and when certain features have scant background of differences, it is hard to say what the resemblances are. There may be present a vague feeling of resemblances and differences, but consciousness is confused, not clear.

§ 18. One important principle of memory, then, consists in having *clear consciousness of the matter to be remembered.* It is largely because we fail in this respect that we so easily forget, become absent-minded, use the wrong word, do the wrong thing with the right idea in mind, and so on.

You are urged to cultivate the habit of observing resemblances and differences as reported in sensation and as given in mental images and thoughts, for in this way you will acquire the ability of clear perception and thought which will prove of the greatest value in the business consideration of unfamiliar details and ventures.

§ 19. *We remember, it would seem, because, in part, we are restless;* because our mental life, having its unity, consists, nevertheless, of a number and variety of mental activities or processes which differ.

§ 20. If we had but one mental process, instantaneous or continuous, we might possess consciousness, but it would necessarily be excessively simple. But we could not know that we were conscious. In its derivation, the word "consciousness" is a "knowing-with"—*scio*, "I know," and *con*, "with." The one process could not know for the one process must be either the "know" or the "thing-with;" it could not be both the "know" and the "thing-with," and still be the one process. *Consciousness involves mental activities re-acting against one another.* When you fall asleep, the aware-activities gradually "fall out," cease to react, and the last you know is some sort of simple fading unitary mental process.

Let us suppose a person who has never heard of books or human beings, yet who all his life is studiously interested in plants and animals. What ever such a person may know about himself, he cannot possibly know that he is a *naturalist*, because he has no means of comparing himself with any other person. So, were our life one single process, there could be within the mind no unity of variety, no differences, no relation of difference to similarity, no relation of mental process to mental process, no comparison of process with process. Without some such "reaction," we could not be conscious in the human sense, we could not remember in the sense with which we are familiar.

§ 21. The mental processes are constantly changing, and so, in *some difference between a process that has taken place and that which substitutes for it as a memory, resides one of the elements of the feeling of the past.* As existing at-once, the mental process constitute consciousness. Consciousness is always now. This "now" is not a mere instant: it has some length of time; and meanwhile it contains a little series of successive various states or processes. "Every consciousness of change depends upon our power thus to observe 'at once' a considerable, though also, from a larger point of view, brief sequence of mental states. Now it is in following such a sequence of states that we tend to become especially aware of the differences which are there present." It is this sequence of processes that enables us to perceive differences, and to remember. If there were no differences, we could not be conscious of remembering, for there could be no comparison of processes in a series,—of any smaller group, or the entire self,—and hence, no idea of past.

ASSIMILATION.

§ 22. The incessant changes going on in consciousness—among mental activities—involve more or less repetition of acts, but also involve new acts. There is, moreover, a tendency to repeat these new acts, or processes, otherwise we should never "get on" in mental development, never accumulate, as the saying is, new facts and ideas. This process may be called assimilation. *Our mental processes vary from old, set ways, and "work over" into new processes.* Such repetitions and such variations form the central factors of experience. It is thus that we are able to acquire new things by memory. The tendency to repeat is associated or connected with other things, and when any of these other things "come up" in mind, the latter, so to speak, tends to get around to the things most repeated. But the incessant activity of mind induces processes that are more or less new, and then the tendency to repeat influences the new activities, as before stated. *Whether we shall remember clearly and easily depends upon whether our differences and resemblances of mental acts support one another—stand to one another—so that the new activities "make round" to the older processes, and also upon the conditions attending the repetitions, such as amount of effort, comfort or discomfort of the same, associations, and so on.*

§ 23. When the mental processes *come to repeat in a certain way, without covering new activities of any great extent, a mental habit has been formed.* This does not mean that there is a rigid, mechanical "set" of activity, but that a general tendency of repetition, on occasion, becomes established. Habituated acts, that is, mental acts that are of habit.

tend to drop out of conscious memory unless accompanied by some "sign" associating them with acts that "revive" them. Such acts belong largely to the subconscious control, which is an advantage. *One secret of remembering to do a thing, consists in getting into the habit of doing it.* But we cannot act along the channels of habit alone. *One secret of remembering to do a thing, then, consists in associating with it a "sign," another mental act, to which any present act will naturally run.*

You are invited to form the habit of associating "signs" which will probably and practically serve you with matters of the past which you may wish to recall, and matters of the future which you desire shall "come up" to mind in the future. If these "signs" can be connected with present knowledge, or with any habit that will likely be in operation at the future time, such association will prove of great value.

BASIS OF MEMORY.

§ 24. The essential *basis of memory* consists of

(A)—*Unity of consciousness,*

(B)—With *varieties* (giving mental initiative) and *repetitions* (establishing habits) of *mental states*

(C)—*Compared* through the *differences* and *similarities,*

(D)—The latter being *associated,* differences with differences or similarities, and similarities with similarities or differences,

(E)—And *recognized and referred to a past* of the consciousness as of the self.

§ 25. We have thus, of mental processes, unity, variety, differences, resemblances or similarities, associations, repetitions, assimilations, recognitions, the idea of past and the idea of self.

§ 26. The idea of past is of your own past, but what that past has contained has depended in part upon the then present time of other people in the line of your ancestry. *Your "mental make-up" is more or less the outcome of their mental make-up, and theirs was more or less the outcome of the make-up of still others in the ancestral line.* Heredity, the tendency of Nature to repeat herself—a kind of huge and age-long habit—has been at work during years and centuries to give you the mind you possess. We say that one inherits a strong or a weak memory, or a memory of some peculiar character.

§ 27. But just as truly has another tendency been all along at work. The ancestral line has held certain general mental characters in the main, more or less, for how long one cannot say, but for some time back of your existence. Meanwhile, *every person in the line has been restless, responding to circumstances in all sorts of ways and striking new, independent ways for himself.* Add to these facts the additional fact that every person is the offspring of two persons more or less differing, each standing for heredity and each representing the tendency to vary from his ancestors and from himself at any previous time, and we perceive somewhat the power of heredity to hold you down or up to what we may call the level of endowment, and the utility of the tendency to vary to give you control over your own mental life, so that, with the one as foundation you can build, and with the other as instrument you can improve.

You are invited to remember that what your
ancestors have done for you, your mental endowment, can never be fully known, so that no man
knows to a nicety his own mental limits. Only a
lifetime of effort can demonstrate that limit—and
a lifetime of effort must leave undemonstrated a
large mental ability developed through that effort.
*You are, therefore, urged to utilise the power to vary
from ancestral tendencies for personal betterment.*
Whatever your peculiarities or weaknesses of
memory as a matter of endowment may be, you
still possess the power of variation in some degree,
since you are a human being, and can build,
reasonably speaking, any sort of memory you
thoroughly determine upon—if you remember that
the test of determination is always persistent
doing.

Control of Mental Processes.

§ 28. Now, mental states or processes do not
originate themselves, strictly speaking, although
they sometime appear to do so. *You have no direct
control over an act of mind.* You cannot immediately will to think a given thought, or have a
feeling, or recall a fact, or imagine a scene, for
when you will, the thing is already in mind. Try
it. "I will think——sales!" The idea slips in
itself. It is always so, as concerns direct control.
The actual control is secured by indirection, for example, by saying, "I will attend to one certain thing,
and refuse to attend to anything else." This looks
like direct control, for the will is to attend to this
particular thing, but the thing itself has, again,
slipped in. Often the mind says "no" to several

things that slip in, one after the other, but when it settles on some one thing, the thing is already there. About the only act we can directly control is the act of refusing. Yet it is a nice problem not settled whether we refuse the matter or the matter refuses itself, or gets out on its own motion.

Erasmus Darwin said, as early as 1794: "In respect to freewill, it is certain that we cannot will to think of a new train of ideas, without previously thinking of the first link of it; as I cannot will to think of a black swan without previously thinking of a black swan. But if I now think of a tail, I can voluntarily recollect all animals which have tails, my will is so far free that I can pursue the ideas linked to this idea of tails, so far as my knowledge of the subject extends."

§ 29. One outcome of the above analysis is the fact that our mental processes do not altogether originate themselves. They are induced. The ways in which they are induced, or the things that induce them, determine the differing forms of consciousness with which we are familiar. Thus we have

(1) *Sense-consciousness*, induced by the outside world (outside even in the body), through vision, hearing, touch, smell, taste, inner physical states;

(2) *"Faculty"-consciousness*, as, of memory, thought, imagination, will, reasoning, and so on;

(3) *Feeling-consciousness*, as, of any emotion or passion;

(4) *Appetite-consciousness*, as, of hunger, thirst, other cravings, and the like. (The last form is a phase of the third, but is given for the sake of suggestion.)

DEPTH OF CONSCIOUSNESS.

§ 30. It is evident that these forms of consciousness differ among different people, so far as
minor phases and characteristics are concerned.
Take a case of sense-consciousness. With one person this is keen and at-once inclusive of a considerable number of things or elements. With another
it is comparatively dull and simple. Thus with all
the familiar forms. If we analyze, say, the consciousness of music, we find that, while any one
can indeed detect several elements in a single
moment of harmony, the trained musical genius
gets "at once," tones, notes, qualities, ideas, feelings, to which the untrained hearer is a perfect
stranger. The more completely one can be conscious "at-once" of all there is in music's power
to affect the mind, the more surely can he remember
the whole, provided he attends to the composition
and secures the suggesting "signs" as the music
proceeds. So, it would seem, in regard to any
other form of consciousness and any particular
phase of that form. Education consists, for one
thing, in developing ability to get at the detail
elements of which a phase of consciousness might
possibly be made up. Consciousness is what it is,
contains what it contains, and, taken as a complex
whole, is one thing, but if, in the psychic moment,
it has come to detect more successive details, more
blending phases of mental activities, it is by so
much the richer in content. There is more in the
consciousness of the educated mind (not necessarily
the collegiate) than in the uneducated, notwithstanding the fact that the things inducing the state
of the consciousness may be the same in both cases.

Objectively considered, the external things are the same in both cases, but subjectively the activities induced thereby are vastly different, and the difference depends on the ability of mind to come to a superior, that is, a richer, state of consciousness with the same objective inducement. The business "head" of a great manufacturing plant "senses" more in the establishment than the errand boy can recognize. This "depth" or "content" of consciousness, whether secured at Harvard or "Brush College," is one of the accomplishments of a "good" memory. And the chief power employed in acquiring this desirable "wealth" is attention for the sake of discovery.

You are therefore urged to cultivate the habit of securing a larger number of details and associations in all the various forms of consciousness— that of sense, that of emotion or feeling, that of the intellectual mentality. *If you will maintain the attitude of attention, receptivity, and discovery in your place of business and during business hours, you will find depth and content of the mental life appreciably enriching.*

Consciousness, Memory and Brain Cells.

§ 31. Within the brain structure are vast numbers of nerve cells or fibers, which may be compared to minute branching rootlets proceeding from seed-like swellings. It is not determined whether these fibers actually touch each other or merely "neighbor." A writer has said that a model of the brain sufficiently large for a convenient counting of the fibers would equal in size a great cathedral, and that to enumerate them counting fifty a minute, twelve hours a day, would require over two hundred years. If, in this forest-like mass of fibers, the latter do not touch one another, then "what a cell does to its neighbor with which its fibers bring it into reaction must be something analogous to 'induction' as known in the case of electrical phenomena." In some way, the fibers in a state of excitement, do influence each other. Of course the whole nervous system of the body makes into the brain substance, so that there are two sets of highways for nerve action—from various portions of the body to the brain, and from the brain to all the organs of the body. The sole function of nerve matter is irritability; that is, to undergo some sort of change in its substance under stimulation, now discharging energy, therefore, now storing energy. All our mental activities are accompanied by nerve excitement; or, all nerve change tends to "go with" some mental process. Without saying, then that all activities in nerve fibers are accompanied by mental activity *realized in consciousness*, we may say that all mental processes *in consciousness* are preceded by activity in nerve fibres.

§ 32. The immense number of the nerve fibres in the brain, and their vastly tangled intricacy, make the sum-total of activities going on enormously complex. Nevertheless, a wonderful orderliness obtains amid all this complexity, for the nerve fibres have a way of tending to do that which they have already done, but have also capability for doing new things (see sections 22 and 23), or for doing things a little differently from what they have already done. Moreover, it is now well known that there are *certain brain centers which tend to do certain kinds of things,* or to act in certain ways that are, broadly speaking, of the same general kind, so that "each of the numerous habits of the brain means, tendencies to the excitement of localized tracts and paths under given physical conditions."

§ 33. But the brain is also a product of heredity: other brains in the line of ancestry having come to be so and so through this tendency to habit. And equally true is it that such other brains have possessed the power to vary, to act in new ways, and to establish in habit those other ways, and thus to develop, it may be, beyond the limits of preceding brains in the same line. "But what is still more significant for our mental life is, that general forms or types of activity, however subtle their nature, when once they have resulted from a given exchange of induced activities, may tend thereby to become more easily re-excited, so that the habits of our brains may come to be fixed," not merely as to the mere routine which tends to this or that special act, but as to the general ways in which acts are done. Thus, one brain has the habits of business, another of scholarship, another of the lawyer, and so on. *And a man's memory takes the general form of these general habits of brain activity.*

Here, then, we have *several interesting facts:*

(1) We thus have the brain containing a vast number of nerve fibres in a state of general and constant activity. It is one person's brain; the activities go on within that brain. Thus there comes *unity of mental processes.*

(2) The nerve fibres act in more or less typical ways. Thus there come *typical mental forms*.

(3) The nerve-actions in any typical mental
form present individual differences. Thus there
come *differences* in any sort of mental process.

(4) The activity in any given case may also
tend to vary from former ways. Thus *variation in
mental action* occurs.

(5) Still, there is a tendency toward repetition
of nerve-action. Thus *mental habits* appear.

(6) But, inasmuch as the tendency to new
forms of activity goes on with that to repetition, or,
vice versa, the new activities come to be established,
and we have *assimilation*.

(7) Inasmuch as repetitions and variations are
related, as the nerve fibres mutually influence one
another under the action of the tendencies to repetition and variation, *association of ideas* appears.

(8) Such association induces the general mental process called *comparison* of differences and
similarities.

(9) The probable fact that not every nerve-
action tends to a mental action in the field of
awareness, but that all may so tend, lies at the
basis of *analysis of mental activities;* for when the
non-reporting nerve-actions come to be at last accompanied by mental actions in that field, the
hitherto non-reporting activities are, so to speak,
added to the sum-total previously occurring. The
air-waves caused by a Sousa band are all present,
whoever may hear them, and all fall upon the ear,
and all may cause nerve-action in any brain present,
reporting in the field of awareness, although in
some brains not all of these nerve-actions may be

accompanied by mental action recognized—sensation, enjoyment, appreciation. But Sousa's brain responds more completely to all the stimulation of the music than any other brain present, his nerve-fibres are more fully active, and so correspondingly completer mental processes accompany such action.

It is so in other respects. More and more the nerve-fibres may come to action, more and more this action, growing, so to speak, minuter and more complex, may accompany such increased nerve excitement. That growing process represents in part brain education. It is, as we shall see, one of the important factors in the development of memory. The commercial life is precisely such a field of education constantly engaged.

INHIBITION.

§ 34. Among all these complex actions of the nerve-fibres another immensely important power, that of *arrest of process*, should be noted. (See Chapter X, Section 26.) At no time is the arrest total—at least during waking hours. You cannot wholly empty your brain of its activities. You cannot altogether stop your mental processes. Try it. Strive as you will, something is going on within the brain, some form of activity continues. Even in sleep, the brain seems to act. Yet the power of arrest is always present in a degree. Some of the nerve-actions may be quieted; or, some of the accompanying mental processes may be ignored, which amounts to their suppression below the field of awareness, at any rate. Mental processes are constant in the mind, but if you attend to one rather than another, you suppress the latter. This ability, as we have seen, exhibits inhibition. We may inhibit all sorts of mental actions. Yet we may never inhibit all nerve-actions in the brain at once. It is because the mental activities are incessant, and have formed habits, and have come to be associated in the unity of consciousness, that things "come up" and are recalled without effort. *It is because you can arrest some mental activities, or suppress them out of the awareness field, and can attend to others in the passing association of all, that you remember as the result of effort to do so.* In such a case, you "find your way," so to speak, through a tangle of matters soliciting attention, refusing now this, now that, until you reach your goal.

THREE LAWS OF MEMORY.

§ 35. Three laws, then, lie under the fact of memory: (1) The law of *habit;* (2) The law of *association;* (3) The law of *arrest.*

The law of attention is only another side of the law of arrest, for, when you wish to recall, you simply repress the mental processes you do not care for until what you want appears under the law of association. You "look" at the panoramic succession of processes, suppressing one after the other, till the right one "comes along."

Out of all this tangle emerge some important conclusions with regard to memory; and so we have

CERTAIN TYPES OF MEMORY.

§ 36. *First: There is what may be called the haphazard memory of things, experiences, events.* The law of association is here at work. All sorts of remembered things "come up" in consciousness, without effort on your part, when you are not "looking for them." Sometimes they are important, and again they are individually unimportant. When they are important, you say: "There, I came near forgetting that!" The "train" of your mental processes has brought the thing around into the field of attention. For such cases, no injunction has more value than "Do it now!" Here we have one of the prime habits of business. We have then—

RÉGIME ONE: "DO IT NOW!" *You are urged to remember that the present doing of things should be gauged by their importance, and that the time for doing an important thing which is not set aside for a more important thing, is not "presently," nor "when it will serve just as well," but NOW.* If you fail in this respect, very likely the thing will not again occur to you, or, if it does, the time may be too late. *Your subconscious mind will serve you faithfully if you treat it with respect, but if you ignore its suggestions, it will conclude that you do not care for its warnings, or for the matter brought up, and cease to serve in the case involved.* But if you are not able to perform the act now, attend to it, shut out other thoughts and actions, *and will instantly to remember at the right time,* but above all, fix some "sign" upon it and connect it with matters you surely will be engaged in at the right moment, so that association may serve you when such matters call for action. If the thing to be remembered occurs to you prior to the time when you can attend to it practically, repeat the process just indicated.

§ 37. *These memory "signs" are important.* Let us observe some of them.

(a)   *Anything* may serve as a memory sign.

(b)   Sometimes the signs attach to a *mental process* as if by accident.

(c)   At other times they result from *your own effort.*

(d)   The sense *needing to recall* at a future time may act as a sign.

(e)   Or the mere *influence of will.*

(f)   Beyond these services as signs, *association* by thought with any *object or idea* or act raises the latter to the office of a sign.

(g)   In some instances the *connections* between sign and thing to be remembered, *disappear*, leaving the latter only.

(h)   Or the *sign may drop out*, so that the connections become the signs. You see a face; it is somewhat familiar, but you do not quite recognize the person. In a moment, some idea or scene comes up in thought, and now you definitely recall. You come to know a person by means of some sign, but in time forget the latter, while the connection— some event in which the sign first appeared—is with you.

Sometimes everything disappears but the thing *to be* remembered or the thing that *is* recalled. How do you know it is so and so? You cannot tell, but you know. In this case the habit, so to speak, of a particular memory has become established. In a general way this may be called the *memory of recognition.*

You are urged to cultivate habit and facility in observing the signs which make up in part your memory machinery, and to attach to matters to be recalled in mind and performed in practice such signs as will

*co-operate with your mental life, its peculiar ways, in
bringing to use your store of knowledge and in suggesting matters to be taken care of as they may be
required in business.*

§ 38. *Second: There is the memory of habit.*
The preacher knows when Sunday arrives without
being told the fact. The physician falls into the
habit of making his round of calls in a certain
general order. The business man remembers the
usual routine of each day with no particular effort.
This kind of memory holds up the world. Hence,

RÉGIME TWO: GET THE HABIT. *If there are
certain things which must always be done, every day,
you are urged to acquire the habit of doing them when
they ought to be done and as they ought to be done.*
This habit is another great factor in business power.
So far as externals are concerned, the best method
for insuring obedience to such an injunction is that
of system in business, because system saves the
mind a vast deal of willed attention in the way of
memory, its operation serving as a constant reminder and an immense economizer of time. *In
developing the habit, associate some sign with the
thing to be done* (in a system, the automatic working
of things constantly brings such signs to the fore),
say, "trouble if not done," or, "some benefit if
done," *meanwhile keeping the idea of attending to
the matter in mind*, as we say. In the formation of
a desired and willed habit, associations are, it may
be said, "paths" along which the mind "moves"
until the highway of habit is worn broad and deep.
Business means hundreds of such habits: such as,
of energy, of promptness, of accuracy, of attention,
of courtesy, of fair-dealing, of self-control, of

reticence when required, of quick perception, and so on and so on.

§ 39.   Third: *There is the memory of mind-recollection, voluntary effort being involved.*   This kind of memory brings into action the laws of association and arrest—with attention (a part of the latter). In recalling by effort a date, a face, an experience, a resolution, an appointment, an event, etc., you attend to the " passing show " of the mind with the idea of recalling something (the idea of search noted in Section 16 of Chapter X), and suppress or ignore all the associated things that pass in review until the right thing comes up.   Of course you are not conscious of this process in any extended way, but such is indeed the process involved.

§ 40.   In this third sense, *the act of remembering or trying to recall consists of the fixation of attention on a mental succession of activities which are ignored as the details take place until a final act of recognition occurs involving the matter sought as having been in the past our own experience*, either mental within, or concerning some act of the person in a larger sense.

§ 41.   And memory as a result of such a process is *the fixation of recognizing attention upon a mental process thus secured*, the power of arrest ceasing to act at exactly that point.

§ 42.   *In some cases, the memory-result appears immediately* because association cross-cuts, so to speak, to the thing desired.   The corresponding memory-process is equally direct.

§ 43.   In some cases, the *result occurs only after intermediate processes have occurred.*   The corresponding memory-process is, then, indirect.

§ 44. In other words, the process of getting at the thing desired may be very round-about through all sorts of associations, or it may be very brief and direct, the associations being abbreviated to one or two only. I am here speaking of recollection with effort.

§ 45. The general process above indicated may be roughly illustrated as follows:

DIAGRAM OF MEMORY PROCESS.

§ 46. The spaces between the lines may represent the senses, and the wide space between the two sets, the brain, wherein the mental processes take place. The twisting line A to B may represent the "passing show" of mental activities, while the points of crossing in that line indicate processes that are associated together, the association being indicated by the extent of line between any two points of crossing. The idea A is connected with the idea B by various associations. The idea A is present when the effort begins to recall some idea or thing yet to be recognized as B. Of course the mind does not move along the twisted line. The

ideas, or mental activities, simply continue to
"come up," as indicated by the small letters and
figures, and are ignored until B finally appears,
the notion of search being kept up and present always in the meantime. It will be seen that the
crossing points are numerous, and that there are
many associations in the train, some of differences,
some of similarities, (not indicated). Beginning
with A, then, the passing of mental states may be
illustrated as, A to b, through c back to b and on
to d; or, A to b (ignoring associations b, c, b) A to
d and through e f g h i, h, j, g, f, e, to m; or (ignoring everything), A to b, d to m, and (ignoring
l, k) from m to o, p. And so on. Taking up o, the
process may run through all points of crossing, or
it may ignore some and attend to some; or, by a
lucky chance, it may proceed through the least
number of crossings points, that is, associations, as
directly as possible, to B. When B appears, it is
recognized by some sign.

In these tangled processes, A suggests a, a
suggests b, or c, c suggests d, d suggests e, etc.;
or m, etc.; or n suggests o, and so on. The main
thing here is attention, passing from one matter to
another, and ignoring various items as not wanted,
until B is reached and recognized.

RÉGIME THREE: PUSH THE SEARCH. *You are invited to persevere in any recollective search, never
giving up when once you have begun, to practice holding the "mind" to definite lines of thought or topics
inhibiting every picture or idea not pertinent thereto,
and frequently to review a day or a longer
period, trying to recall as many details as possible.*
This régime will assist in correcting mind wan-

dering and greatly develop the power of voluntary recall.

§ 47. In some such way, speaking by means of the illustration, your mind works in the effort to recall. *Recollection by effort is attention putting things aside but holding on until the desired thing is discovered.* It is a state of attention held while other possible states are suppressed until a final state is reached in which recognition occurs. Then the thing desired is remembered.

§ 48. *Fourth: There are types of memory which depend upon the individual mental character or general tendency.* We may, for convenience, divide minds into those "living" in the outer world and those "living" (chiefly interested) in the inner world. Thus we have the *sense-memory* type, and the *thought-memory type.* If your business depends greatly on the use of the senses, the sense-memory should be cultivated—but you may make the mistake, as most people do, of neglecting the thought-realm and so the thought-memory. If your business depends largely upon thought-power, the thought-memory should be cultivated—but many people of this mental type neglect the sense-life and thus neglect the sense-memory, which looks like a mistake again.

RÉGIME FOUR: CULTIVATE NEGLECTED POWERS. *The first class may well do more intelligent thinking; the last more intelligent observing.* If you are habitually *forgetting outside matters,* herein lies your remedy: *the cultivation of the sense-observing habit.* If you habitually *forget dates, ideas, principles,* etc., your remedy is equally apparent: the *cultivation of attention and recollective associations.*

MEMORY CHARACTERISTICS.

§ 49. (Continuation of Régime Four.) In a very general way the mental characteristics in the matter of memory may be indicated by the following analysis:

(1) Mind and memory especially occupied with *objectively induced sensations.*

(2) Mind and memory especially given to *emotions* of pleasures and pains.

(3) Mind and memory especially running to *mental pictures.*

(4) Mind and memory especially good in the matter of *dates and numbers.*

(5) Mind and memory especially attentive to *abstract ideas.*

(6) Mind and memory especially interested in *principles.*

(7) Mind and memory especially *elaborative of laws.*

(8) Mind and memory especially given to *details.*

(9) Mind and memory especially given to *construction of wholes.*

§ 50. *Now, all minds and memories of average intelligence possess all the characteristics indicated in some degree, but none of us possess them in an all-round equal degree.* The type of mind is determined by the prevailing characteristic. Thus also with memories. If your type of memory is shown above, and if you require improvement in some one or more of the particular types portrayed, *the method consists in persistent attention and the formation of habits in the desired direction by constant practice and the constant use of associations.* You are urged especially to observe that the words: Resolution—Attention—Persistence—Repetition—Associations—Habit, represent the amount and kind of effort demanded.

Take, for example, the *memory for details.* Are you lacking in ability to recall in that respect? You are urged to resolve on improvement, to attend to all details with all your mind, to persist in such labor, to repeat the attention, to associate the details with recollective signs of any sort that you may invent, to form the habit of doing all this in regard to details.

§ 51. The trouble with people who forget is in part the fact that they fail to fore-get. In some cases, the fore-getting is actual, but it is too easy and quick, for one thing, so that a good rule in such cases is this: *"My work really begins when I think it is finished."* With most of us it is there that we close the work. In other words, when you are sure that you have a thing, proceed to hammer it into mind, so to speak, for safe-keeping. But always should the fore-getting in some way be assimilated by association with something already possessed in the mind. In the process of fore-getting, repetition is also required because this habituates the mind or the brain-elements in certain ways so that accompanying mental actions or associations are developed which assist in memory.

MIND AND MEMORY IN BUSINESS.

§ 52. In a more particular way the mental characteristics in the matter of memory may be shown in the analysis to follow:

Mind and memory prone to *sounds and harmonies.*

Mind and memory tending to *observe colors.*

Mind and memory running to *forms and outlines.*

Mind and memory appreciative of *textures and surfaces.*

Mind and memory grasping *scenes.*

Mind and memory perceiving *details.*

Mind and memory taking in *relations and proportions.*

Mind and memory photographing *faces.*

Mind and memory recording *names.*

Mind and memory recognizing *individuals.*

Mind and memory observant of *crowds and masses.*

Mind and memory occupied with *events and experiences.*

RÉGIME FIVE: SELF DISCOVERY. *You are invited to discover in the above analysis your own peculiarities of memory and the mental life, and carefully to note your weakness in any particular mentioned.*

You are urged to—*resolve on improvement,*—to attend to the matters indicated above,—to persist in such labor,—to repeat the attention in any given case,—to associate the subject of memory, as suggested above, with recollective signs of any sort which you may invent,—to form the habit of doing these things in reference to the items in the list. This involves an immense amount of work to be sure, yet work which you can in time teach the subjective mind to carry without your objective supervision, and which will prove of almost incalculable value in your business life.

For example: you recognize faces, but do not readily recall names. The fact probably is that you give the names no particular attention. If intense attention is habitually given to names associated with faces, and if the habit of putting the two things together is formed, and if the required attention is mentally repeated, in each case, for a reasonable length of running time, the so-called forgetfulness may be overcome. That is an illustration of the method which may be adopted for all the particulars given in the last analysis. Business power requires all the items, and the man who is bent on acquiring business power will not haggle about the labor involved, especially as that labor is of such a nature that it may be taken right into business itself, and will make business all the more easy and successful.

Conclusion: General Principles.

§ 53. In support of these general principles we may quote from James: "Memory proper is the knowledge of a former state of mind after it has already once dropped from consciousness; or rather it is the knowledge of an event, or fact, of which meantime we have not been thinking, with the additional consciousness that we have thought or experienced it before.

§ 54. "*A general feeling of the past direction* of time, then, *a particular date* conceived as *lying along that direction*, and, *defined* by its *name* or *phenomenal contents*, an *event imagined as located therein*, and *owned as part* of *my* experience—such are the elements of every object of memory."

§ 55. Analysis seems to give us retention and recall. But, as Titchener says, "there is no such thing as mental retention, the persistence of an idea from month to month, or year to year, in some mental pigeon-hole from which it can be drawn when wanted. What persists is the tendency to connection." "The cause both of retention and recollection is the law of habit in the nervous system, working as it does in the association of ideas." (James)

§ 56. "In short, we make search in our memory for a forgotten idea, just as we rummage our house for a lost object. In both cases we visit what seems to us the probable neighborhood of that which we miss. We turn over the things under which, or within which, or alongside of which, it may possibly be; and if it lies near them, it soon comes to view. But these matters, in the case of a mental object sought, are nothing but its associates. The mental machinery of recall is thus the same as the machinery of association, and the machinery of association, as we know, is nothing but the elementary law of habit in the nerve-centres. The condition which makes the recall possible at all (or, in other words, the 'retention' of the experience or whatever the thing be) is neither more nor less than the brain-paths which associate the experience with the occasion and cue of the recall. When slumbering, these paths are the condition of *retention;* when active, they are the condition of *recall.*" (James)

§ 57. "Memory being thus altogether conditioned on brain-paths, its excellence in a given individual will depend partly on the number and partly on the persistence of these paths."

§ 58. "*The improvement of the memory lies in the line of elaborating the associations of each of the several things to be remembered.*" "All improvement of memory consists, then, in the *improvement of one's habitual methods of recording facts.*" "The mechanical methods consist in the intensification, prolongation and repetition of the impression to be remembered." "Judicious methods of remembering things are nothing but logical ways of conceiving them and working them into rational systems, classifying them, analyzing them into parts, etc., etc." Ingenious methods are seen in various artificial devices the mastery and use of which involve greater labor than the original difficulties of the weak memory.

§ 59. The essentials of commercial memory are business habits and systematized associations of ideas that represent to the mind the ten thousand objects, relations, laws, principles, events and experiences of the business world. Success in business requires nearly all types of memory as here indicated. Any one of these, within the limits of a man's native endowments may be developed if only the *backbone activities: resolution—attention—persistence—repetition—association — habit*—are put into every-day business life and kept at work until victory is accomplished.

§ 60. You are especially urged to train and rely upon the unconscious mind in the matter of memory. We remember the statement that memory is due to reproduced action of brain cells, which action is recognized as referring to our past. Subconscious psychic activities do not preserve in existence any previous activities, but it is prob-

able that previous activities have affected the
brain cells in two general ways: In those which
involve consciousness, and in those which induce
states of deeper self of which the superficial objective (every-day) self is not distinctly aware. By
willed effort that these things *shall* occur, we may
train both conscious and unconscious minds to
remember.

It is as if, during your life, you had erected a
huge building filled with intricate machinery. Of
this building you are master, but a mysterious
other-self has, under you, come in charge of the
mechanisms,—your subconscious mind. What this
other-self is and shall be, depends on you—conscious will. You may order the other-self to set
various mechanisms in various ways, to do various
things, to repeat various activities. You will be
obeyed if the other-self finds you in earnest.

Thus may you train the deeper mind to remember—recall—recognize. As a matter of fact,
that is exactly what you have done all your life.
The purpose of this chapter is to help you to do
such work understandingly and more effectively.

For additional suggestions in the way of memory improvement. you are referred to Chapter XXI
of *"Power of Will,"* second edition, revised.

CHAPTER XII.

THE PRACTICAL MAN'S IMAGINATION.

MULTIPLY nought by nine and add one; one by nine and add two; twelve by nine and add three; and so on, until you have reached 1, 2, 3, 4, 5, 6, 7, 8, 9 + 10. All the multipliers, except the second, will repeat the next preceding with a next higher figure annexed, as, 1 x 9, 12 x 9, 123 x 9, and so to the end. Moreover, the numbers added after the multiplications have been made will make a series from 1 to 9 (and 10), and these figures will give you your last multiplier. Finally, every product of multiplication and addition will be composed of the figure 1. If, again, the multiplicand is 8, and you multiply and add as before (omitting 0 x 8), the products will be 9, 98, 987, 9876, a next lower figure being the last in each new product, until the final multiplier and last product are (left to right and right to left) two sets of the same figures in reverse order. "A man who knows only the externality of these results will naturally be inclined to occultism. The world of numbers as much as the actual universe is full of regularities which can be reduced to definite rules and laws giving us a key that will unlock their mysteries and enable us to predict certain results under definite conditions. Mathematics is a purely mental construction, but its composition is not arbitrary. On the contrary it is tracing the results of our own doings and taking the consequences of the conditions we have created. Though the scope of our imagination with all its possibilities be infinite, the results of our construction are definitely determined as soon as we have laid the foundation, and the actual world is simply one realization of the infinite potentialities of being." These remarks of the editor of " *The Monist* " are applicable to the world of business. Here, also, we have a realm of regularities confused by apparent irregularities. It is the successful business man's task to discover the regularities—the definite rules and laws—and to use and control them for his enterprise. A large part of this work must be done by the imagination, and the imagination itself must be taken in hand and trained both for power and for clear headed effectiveness.

§ 1. It may be thought that the imagination has only to do with artistic or poetical conceptions. The entire literature of science corrects this view, and the world of business exhibits mental activity of the imaginative order on every hand. The following illustrations mingle consecutive thinking and the play of imagination in about equal proportions:

"Various writers have called our attention to the fact that man may be rightly regarded as an engine. The food consumed is analogous to the fuel put under the boiler of the steam engine, and serves similar purposes. As fuel produces heat and performs work in the steam engine, so the food partaken, by its gradual oxidization, keeps up the temperature of the body, and is also used as a source of energy on which to draw for the performance of work," remarks Balfour Stewart in "*The Conservation of Energy.*"

And in "*The World To Come*," by J. W. Reynolds, occur these words: "Lines finer than a spider's web, the nervous filaments of the senses, are our avenues of communication between the world without and the world within. Spread over a little space at the roots of the tongue, they make the savours of nature tributary to our pleasure. Unfolded and ramified over tiny spaces in the olfactory organs, and the hollow of the ear, they enable us to catch the perfumes of every fragrance, and to attend to the many voices of nature. The insect and the song-bird, the roar of the thunder, the murmur of the ocean, are the earth's orchestral service in the cathedral of the universe. Within a small spot, on the eye's interior, is a chamber of representation where are gathered the glitterings of constellations, very remote, even on the verge of space; and there the beauties of every fair landscape are painted quick as thought, and with a flash of light. By a series of pre-established harmonies, our outer man makes our inner man to know the things in heaven and the things on earth. Millions of lines, more wonderful than any telegraphy of man, converge in focus for our organs; and are inlets of light and knowledge from the past, the present, and what we know the future will be."

The theory of pre-established harmony is itself a good illustration of the philosophical imagination, but it does not explain the relation of man's self to the outer world. It would seem better to say that all is mental in this universe of ours, and that man, when he knows the outer world correctly, is simply and freely thinking the Thoughs of that Infinite Somewhat whose Mind-action constitutes creation and preservation of worlds and life.

DEFINITION AND DIVISIONS.

§ 2. *The imagination may be defined as restoration in mental activity of experiences one has had, and the recombination of the elements of such experiences in forms hitherto not experienced.* The process may involve any mental experience recurring, whether originally induced by sensation, or embracing sensation, or representative of other mental activities. Thus, the imagination should be discriminated as *Reproductive* and *Productive*. *Mental reproduction of experience when referred to the past is imagination in the form of memory. Productive imagination also reproduces past experience, but it combines the elements into new forms.*

§ 3. It should be remembered that when we speak of the mind, or of mental activity, we are employing the language of convenience. There is no mental activity in the sense that an entity, the mind, is doing something, for the mind is no such entity, unless we choose to make mind and self synonymous. This can hardly be done, since an actor and its action are not the same. *The real mind is a complex of activities of the self conducted in certain ways and for certain purposes.* The thinking self has ability to do various things in various manners. Thus we have feeling, recalling, picturing, recombining, willing, reasoning, and so on. Our idea of all this in sum-total gives us the notion of "mind." But it is always the self that is really active. It is, thus, the *self in mental action which attends*, not a *power of attention;* that *remembers*, not a "*faculty*" of memory; that *imagines*, not an *ability* to recombine past experiences. As a matter of fact, we are coming to-day to enlarge our former conceptions of "mind," because we are discovering new powers of the self, so that, while yesterday consciousness was always regarded as a condition of "mind," what is called the "unconscious mind" is by many spoken of as a very distinctive feature of the active self.

§ 4. Productive imagination is more than memory, although it must, of course, involve the memory form. *Productive imagination recombines any sort of so-called mental "material": sensations, ideas, pictures, emotions, and so on—both in parts and in wholes*. All this "material" "exists in mind," as it is said, in numberless varieties of certain definite relations (associations). That is to say, all the past activities of self in mind may again recur as imaginative "material"; they do not, however, really exist in the sense of imagination until they thus recur. This is the meaning of "material existing in the mind." Nothing mental exists save in the sense of present action.

§ 5. Observing, then, that the "material" need not necessarily be "present," but that the subjects of imagination must be composed of "material" which has, in its various parts, been in the mind at some former time, and so, may "come into mind" now, we discover that *such "present material" exists in certain relations.* Strictly speaking, the past experiences of the self within the field of mind recur and are recombined in the relations to be given. If the "material," the activity, recurs, the recurring is in and with the relations. These relations are called *associations:* mental activities occur together and are thus *associated according to certain laws—that is to say, in certain established ways:* those of *resemblances or differences,* those of *nearness or distance* in point either of *space or of time,* and, it may be added for the sake of apparent completeness, *those of logical thinking.* So, the recombined past mental experiences occur and recur in one or more established associative ways.

§ 6. Now, imagination, like any other mental activity, is determined by the laws of the mind, but no particular act of the self in imagination is predetermined by the laws of logical thinking except when logical thinking is the main thing. If I think: "All men are mortal; I am a man; therefore, I am mortal"—I employ the laws of logical thinking, but may or may not have in mind a picture of a man or crowds of men. The picture is merely incidental. *In imagination, the "mind's material," the mental activity, present or possible, is recombined into free, not predetermined relations which are new as compared with formerly experienced relations.*

§ 7. Some authors speak of the imagination as mathematical, artistic, philosophical, inventive, and so on; but *true imagination is all one,* and the division springs merely from difference in the sub-

jects of mental action. It is curious that I nowhere find a reference to commercial or business
imagination, yet surely this variety should be classed
in the above list, for no form of imagination plays
a more important or a more real part in the world's
affairs. *The business man can no more succeed without imagination than a bird can fly without wings.*

VALUE OF IMAGINATION.

§ 8. The reader may ask, however, "What
has the psychology of the imagination to do with
my bank account?" *In reply it may be said that what
such mental activity has to do with anything in business is exactly measured by the difference between the
business man as a human and the squirrel as a business animal.* The squirrel takes instinct ("purposive action without consciousness of the purpose "),
but no thought (checking, limiting, regulation, of
the constructive mental activities), for the morrow,
and is usually "hard up" in winter. The business
man's "to-morrow" is a marvel of constructive
imagination. He must think, plan, foresee, and
carry out, and all this requires recombining the
things he knows in the form of things as he desires
them.

§ 9. Here, for example, are two illustrations
taken from Tyndall's lecture, "*Science and Man*":

"You have probably heard the story of the
German peasant, who, in early railway days, was
taken to see the performance of a locomotive. He
had never known carriages to be moved except by
animal power. Every explanation outside of this
conception lay beyond his experience, and could
not be invoked. After long reflection, therefore,

and seeing no possible escape from the conclusion,
he exclaimed confidently to his companion, '*Es
mussen doch Pferde darin sein*'—There must be
horses inside.   Explanation is conditioned by
knowledge." But prevision—imagination—is conditioned by knowledge, and hence, the greater one's
experience and knowledge, the larger and richer
one's imagination.   Let not the business man be
indifferent to knowledge of anything under the
heavens.   But particularly is it to be understood
that the man who cannot imagine at the heart of a
situation something different from what seems to
be there or evidently is there, cannot possibly
succeed in business.   The inventors of the modern
locomotive saw wagons drawn by horses, and
imagined horses of a superior kind placed inside
the vehicles, that is, wagons moving without real
horses at all.   Therefore, locomotives, trolley-cars,
automobiles.   If you interpret the incident in
terms of business life, you begin to see something
of the value of the psychology of imagination.

The second illustration is found in the same
lecture by Tyndall, but given as borrowed from
another writer.   "A merchant sits complacently
in his easy chair, not knowing whether smoking,
sleeping or newspaper-reading, or the digestion of
food, occupies the largest portion of his personality.
A servant enters the room with the telegram bearing the words, 'Antwerp, etc., * * * Jones & Co.
have failed.' 'Tell James to harness the horses!'
The servant flies.   Up starts the merchant, wide
awake; makes a dozen paces through the room,
descends to the counting-house, dictates letters,
and forwards dispatches. He jumps into his carriage,

the horses snort, and their driver is immediately at
the bank, on the Bourse, and among his commercial
friends. Before an hour has elapsed, he is again
at home, where he throws himself once more into
his easy chair with a deep-drawn sigh, 'Thank God
I am protected against the worst, and now for
further reflection.'" In all this scene, from start
to finish, the man's power of imagination has been
at work, darting from one thing to another and
shifting possibilities and situations with lightning
rapidity; and when he says, "Now for further reflection," imagination will still serve him, with all
the powers of logical thinking at the fore. Had he
possessed none of this ability, he could never have
built a business of any kind. *Wealth may be defined as the crystallization of the world's financial
imagination.* The first primitive man did not see
our present civilization, but he saw some of it, and
every successful man since has contributed to the
final outcome by his imaginative thought.

IMAGINATION AS MEMORY.

§ 10. It will be recalled that imagination has
been divided into reproductive and productive, and
that reproductive imagination is simply a phase of
memory which reproduces that which has already
been "in the mind," and, as nearly as may be, as
it then "existed" therein. *If that which has previously "been in the mind" is recognized as one's own
past experience, it is then remembered.* The ability
thus to remember is called imagination (but not very
fittingly, since one word is used for two different
functions) because the mind's previous objects are
imaged, so to speak, in present consciousness. It

would be better to say that present mental activities duplicate, with more or less exactness, previous mental experiences recognized as of one's past.

§ 11. The "images" which are reproduced from past experience are not to be understood as pictorial merely. *They seem to be re-presentations of previous experiences in all the senses.* Thus, one may have a mental picture of a scene once observed, or an "image"-reproduction, fainter than the original, of the sense of hearing, taking various forms, so to speak; and thus with smell, taste, touch, weight, pressure, energy, muscle-sense, and so on. The imitation of the sensation had is what is meant by "image." There is no real image; there is merely reproductive mental activity.

§ 12. "Our ideas or images of past sensible experiences may be either distinct and adequate or dim, blurred, and incomplete. By some people certain sense-experiences cannot be reproduced at all. They know, in some way, that they have had them, but they cannot actually call them up as reproductions."

§ 13. In the following quotation a double illustration may be found: one of productive imagination, another of the kind of reproductive imagination, or memory, now being discussed. "A mass of beeswax that had been employed again and again, melted and re-melted, in an electrotype foundry; which was all blackened with graphite, and had, apparently, lost forever the cell-structure of the honey-comb, was found to present on its surface, with great distinctness the outlines of the polygonal cells." (This is stated as a fact, but it is here used as an illustration only.) Can you form a mental picture of that mass of black beeswax, with the cell-shapes visible? If so, you possess a degree of productive imagination, because you have combined form, mass, color, material and the particular outlines of cells. Can you recall a piece of filled honey-comb as once observed? If so, you possess reproductive imagination.

TESTS OF REPRODUCTIVE IMAGINATION.

§ 14. You are now invited to test your reproductive imagination or sense-memory (in these cases) by noting the following questions. Please observe: The idea here is not what you *know* in any given instance, but what you *recall and see in the field of mind*.

RÉGIME ONE: DISCOVERY OF YOUR MEMORY-IMAGINATION. Absent therefrom, can you recall the appearance of your dining-room, with table set, furniture, pictures, etc., all in customary places?

Can you now see the chair which you commonly use?

Can you see distances separating objects as recalled?

Can you see objects as flat, or solid—as recalled, of course?

Can you get a mental picture of a surface having various peculiarities—color, shining, smooth, rough?

Can you see a moving tongue of fire? A bird in flight?

Can you hear a musical selection? A ringing bell? A groan? A squeak? Thunder? All as recalled?

Can you smell a rose as recalled?   Thus with other perfumes?

Can you in mental action re-experience a past physical pain? A handshake? A chill? A weight? Exhaustion? Buoyancy?

Can you mentally taste an orange which you ate yesterday? An onion? Pepper? Salt? Butter?

Can you recall the look of the printed letters of a book you read recently?

Can you revive the sound of voices heard some time since?

If you have never gone into this matter, you will likely make some surprising discoveries. People differ immensely in respect to these phases of memory, and oftentimes one's deficiencies or possessions are largely unknown to self in the field indicated.   Whether or not any total defect in the regards suggested may be obviated would seem doubtful, but that any defect in mere degree may be removed is altogether probable. Such improvement must be sought through directed and attentive practice. The author's previous work, " *Power of Will,*" contains exercises looking to such improvement.

§ 15. "A person whose visual imagination is strong (it is difficult to say whether here is meant reproductive or productive imagination: let the meaning be both), finds it hard to understand how those who are without the faculty can think at all. *Some people undoubtedly have no visual images at all worthy of the name,* and instead of *seeing* their breakfast table, they tell you that they *remember* it or *know* what was on it.   The ' mind-stuff' of which this 'knowing' is made seems to be verbal images exclusively."

§ 16. "Those who think in auditory images are called audites." "This type appears to be rarer than the visual. *Persons of this type imagine what they think of in the language of sound.* In order to remember a lesson they impress upon their mind, not the look of a page, but the sound of the words" (as spoken in their own minds). (Do you enjoy having others read to you? Some persons detest the experience. They attend better through sight than through hearing.)

§ 17. *There are what may be called "motile" memories.* "His recollections both of his own movements and of those of other things are accompanied invariably by distinct muscular feelings in those parts of his body which would naturally be used in effecting or in following the movement." This person was a scientist, and in describing an experiment, used only words which he had already associated with the details of his observations.

§ 18. "Most persons, on being asked in what sort of terms they imagine words, will say, 'In terms of hearing.' But some have a faint sensation of pronouncing the words." Can you say Hulla-gaboloo with the mouth open—mentally, of course? The writer can do this, but he has the sensations of pronouncing the word in the lips and tongue, but not in the throat. (See Professor James' *"Psychology,"* briefer course.)

§ 19. Thus we see that great *differences obtain in respect to the various forms of reproductive imagination, or sense-memory mentally conceived.* Possibly, defects or possessions in this regard account for differences in the power of productive imagination. The latter merely involves activities (or "material") made possible by former experiences. If sensations can be recalled only dimly, the corresponding imagination proper must also be dim. Or the reverse. *The extent and richness of the imagination, moreover, depends on the extent and richness of one's knowledge.* Hence, we readily see that if a person is what may be called normal,— has ability to recall sensations all-round, and vividly, —he will have an advantage in the matter of imagination over persons of less ability. The importance, therefore, of knowing your own type of sense-memory in order to correction and improvement for the sake of a rich and strong imagination, together with the importance of a mind well stored with all other thought-material, becomes evident when we see the immense function which the imagination serves in all the business world.

TESTS OF PRODUCTIVE IMAGINATION.

§ 20. We now indicate various tests for your personal power in productive imagination similar to those given for the reproductive form. You are invited to make the study practical by persistent self-examination and patient exercise of the ability in the ways suggested.

RÉGIME TWO: DISCOVERY OF YOUR IMAGINATION PROPER. Can you call up in mind any or all of the following objects, not from memory, but in a purely imaginary way, as though experienced through the appropriate sense in action now? and with what degree of vividness—of detail?

A South African forest, or a North Polar ice view.

Various geometrical figures, plane and solid.

Curious combinations of parts of animals.

A warehouse full of particular kinds of goods.

Various types of men and women; faces especially.

All sorts of fruits; natural colors.

Situations: yourself, others, and objects involved.

Sounds: screams, shouts, commands, songs, instrumental music.

Perfumes; odors; of many different kinds.

Pains; pleasures; bodily, mental.

Touch-feelings: muscular sense; weights; pressures; motions.

Printed words in many different styles and sizes of type.

The voices of persons speaking.

Your place of business as improved. Sanitary conditions; conveniences.

The characters, scenes, situations, in a work of fiction.

The probable outcome of any situation in a work of fiction.

You are invited to invent additional tests and exercises.

§ 21. Observe: "*In order to attain the highest form of memory, we must cultivate the faculty of imagination, or the power of holding up to mind past sensations or impressions, as if they were actually present to us. We can retain the impression of an object for some time after the object itself has passed away by allowing the mind to dwell upon it, and we can afterwards readily recall it.*" (I am compelled to leave the old style language, as "mind," "impressions," and so on, as I find it, since it is

everywhere in the books; but do so with the suggestion that we remember always that there is only
a complex of activities of the self which is called
"mind" and that the so-called "impressions" are
nothing whatever but mental activities having a liability to repeat). "In this way one may soon learn
to remember all the cards that have been played in a
game of whist, which mere playing for a lifetime
may not teach him.   That mere playing may never
teach a man this, is owing to the attention being
taken up with the play and not sufficiently directed
to this operation—that of instantly noting a card
when thrown down, then two, then three, and so
on, until the ability to remember a large number is
acquired.

Practical Imagination.

§ 22.   *The ability mentally to work over your
business in general, or in any particular phase, into
new and improved conditions, by planning prior to
action, depends upon your power of imagination in
the productive and the reproductive senses here indicated.*   In testing your power by attempting to
carry out the above suggestions, you discover your
talents and defects.   Practice in improving a poor
imagination in any respect should in the long run
increase your business efficiency.   All the factors
in business situations, materials and people constantly change.   The business man who does not
keep in advance of such changes must fall behind.
But keeping in advance as indicated means great
and incessant activity of the imagination.   This
foreseeing, foreknowing, anticipating ability is absolutely indispensable to any large success.   It

follows the form, of course, of the memory type, but involves the creative or productive type in planning for all sorts of new elements in the business life. If you have discovered your variety of memory—visual, auditory, motile, etc.,—you then know the form of imagination with which you best can work, and this is probably the form to be employed and cultivated for your particular business.

§ 23. Coming, now, to the general run of commercial activity, yourself supposedly engaged in some special line, and, therefore, constituting, as one may say, a personal and business centre, you are invited to *observe that your outlook on the financial world involves for success certain altogether essential factors in which imagination plays an important part.*

We may summarize these factors as: *Judgment —Discernment—Anticipation. Imagination* without *judgment* is merely a useless action of mental life; without *discrimination*, cannot be operated in a practical way; without *anticipation*, is lacking in that purpose-vision which gives it finished value. *Judgment regulates, discernment furnishes practical material, and anticipation pioneers action successfully into the future*—"looks around three corners," as one has very suggestively said.

§ 24. When we submit to analysis the idea of business, any variety being covered, these factors naturally refer themselves to *four classes of other common factors in all-round financial effort:* Business Men, Employees, the Business Individual, and his Occupation. Proceeding therefrom, a further analysis yields the following:

§ 25. RÉGIME THREE OF THE UNIVERSAL SCHEME OF THE PRACTICAL MAN'S IMAGINATION.

FIRST DIVISION.—GENERAL BUSINESS:

(1) Discernment of Natural Resources. Judgment. Anticipation of future value.

(2) Discernment of Natural Forces. Judgment. Anticipation of future working.

(3) Discernment of Human Movements. Judgment. Anticipation of opportunities.

(4) Discernment of Drift of Trade. Judgment. Anticipation of best localities.

(5) Discernment of Transportation. Judgment. Anticipation of future Centres.

(6) Discernment of Markets. Judgment. Anticipation of Various Futures.

(7) Discernment of Legislation. Judgment. Anticipation of Attitudes Toward.

§ 26. SECOND DIVISION.—BUSINESS MEN:

(8) Discernment of Monetary Conditions. Judgment. Anticipation of present Adjustments.

(9) Discernment of Competition. Judgment. Anticipation of Adjustments.

(10) Discernment of Credits. Judgment. Anticipation of future needed Action.

(11) Discernment of Abilities. Judgment. Anticipation of Means to Success.

(12) Discernment of Schemes Presented. Judgment. Anticipation of Outcomes.

(13) Discernment of Motives. Judgment. Anticipation of Personal Action.

§ 27. THIRD DIVISION.—EMPLOYEES:

(14) Discernment of Kinds of Men. Judgment. Anticipation of Various Cases.

(15) Discernment of Adaptability. Judgment. Anticipation of Increased Values.

(16) Discernment of Your Attitudes Toward Men. Judgment. Anticipation of Outcomes.

(17) Invention of New Uses for Men. Judgment. Anticipation of Probable Results.

(18) Discernment of Possible Contingencies. Judgment. Anticipation of Adjustments.

(19) Discernment of Possible Failures. Judgment. Prevision for Same.

§ 28. FOURTH DIVISION.—SELF AND BUSINESS:

(20) Knowledge of Self. Judgment. Anticipation of Improvement.

(21) Knowledge of Past Errors. Judgment. Anticipation of Remedies.

(22) Knowledge of Successes. Judgment. Anticipation of Wise Use of Same.

(23) Various Imagined Methods for More Effective Self-Handling.

(24) Discernment of Business Possibilities. Judgment concerning the same. Anticipation of Actual Facts.

§ 29. *Observe: The value of the above scheme depends on yourself.* You are invited to improve the analysis above given, so concentrating upon the work that the scheme may be taken wholly to pieces in your thought. It is designed to be suggestive only, but with the presumption, permitted perhaps, that if you will think your way through it in a persistent effort to realize in an imaginary manner the factors indicated, three results will follow: Self-discovery, Improved Imagination, and Increased Business Efficiency.

SPECIAL USES OF IMAGINATION.

§ 30. We now come to the use of imagination in endeavoring to discover some particular line of action by which one's business prospects may be improved, and that especial line finally decided on may successfully be carried out. It is understood, of course, that this study is ideal and general, that it cannot suggest how to manufacture ability, and cannot in any way substitute the living man himself. The lesson does not even "touch the button" —that the student must do—and all "the rest." Meanwhile, let us observe:

First, the imagination, always accompanied by Discernment and Judgment, *is preceded by the purpose of some kind of improvement in life, and proceeds to "cast about" for a best possible and available plan of action, as yet undecided, but persistently sought among all suggestions which are brought forward in your thought.*

Secondly, the imagination, accompanied as before by Discernment and Judgment, and preceded by the definite purpose of success in the plan decided upon, *steadfastly outlooks and forecasts the end of final success in the largest possible degree.*

§ 31. The magic words are now, therefore, *Concentration—Memory — Imagination—Initiative— Tireless Energy.* This introduces

§ 32. RÉGIME FOUR: APPLICATION OF IMAGINATION IN GENERAL. In the problems presented by the scheme, you are invited to

(1)—Concentrate all the mind's power of attention;

(2)—Bring forth all the mind's possessions;

(3)—Foresee and forecast all possible situations;

(4)—Strike out anew into old paths or enter entirely new fields.

With these suggestions in mind, we are ready for the scheme promised.

RÉGIME FIVE: APPLICATION OF IMAGINATION TO YOUR CASE.

§ 33. IMAGINATION IN PLAY FOR SOME PLAN OF IMPROVEMENT AS YET UNDECIDED BUT PERSISTENTLY SOUGHT.		IMAGINATION IN PLAY FOR THE SPECIFIC PLAN DECIDED IN ESSENTIAL DETAIL AND CARRIED OUT.
Below is a Framework	24	I WILL
For Your Personal Imagination	23	FORELOOK
Making Its Way	22	NEW ADJUSTMENTS
Through the Problems	21	ACTION PERSISTENCE
How Can I Improve	20	PEOPLE SELECTED
My Present Condition?	19	INVESTMENTS MATERIALS
(Read from below up to 14)	18	METHODS ADOPTED
	17	PLACE SETTLED UPON
	16	TIME LIMIT SUGGESTED
	15	VALUES AT DISPOSAL ASSISTANCE
SCHEME SELECTED	14	SPECIAL SCHEME DECIDED
DECISION	13	(Read up from 14)
JUDGMENT	12	
WEIGHING OF POSSIBILITIES	11	*Carry out the*
COMPARISON	10	*How Can I Best*
SUGGESTIONS FOR VARIOUS PLANS	9	*Through the Problems*
CONSTANT THOUGHT	8	*Making its Way*
MENTAL EFFORT CONCENTRATION	7	*For Your Imagination*
I WILL FIND SOME PLAN	6	*Above is a Framework*
PURPOSE	5	
DIFFICULTIES	4	
UNCERTAINTY	3	
VALUES AT DISPOSAL ASSISTANCE	2	(Read up)
FUTURE BETTERMENT	1	

§ 34. The preceding framework may be used in various ways. For example, let us suppose as follows:

1. You wish to decide as between business and a profession. The effort to come to a definite choice then runs somewhat as suggested on next page:

The idea of the *future and of betterment* is before you. (1) (See dotted lines previous page.)

Consideration of *values at disposal* occurs: energy, abilities, special talents, friends, money, opportunities, and possible or assured *assistance* from others. (2)

All these matters pass in review before the mind, and induce your best judgment.

The question of business or a profession indicates *uncertainty*, (3) and *difficulties* (4) which involve years appear, but *purpose* (5) to make the most of life holds good and grows stronger, so that you affirm "I will succeed, whatever line of effort I may adopt." "*I will find some plan.*" (6)

More and more are *mental effort* and *concentration* (7) brought to bear on the question before you, whatever it be; *thought is constantly engaged* (8) in examining the entire subject, various *plans are suggested* (9) from time to time for carrying out your decision, one way or the other, and these are carefully *compared* (10) and *possibilities weighed*, (11) so that *judgment* (12) finally begins to trend in a certain direction, and at last a *decision* (13) is made—business—profession—and the particular kind of lifework is *selected.* (14)

During all this complicated process, you are employing *practical imagination.*

2. Or, having decided to enter the business field, and having chosen the variety in which you observe the greatest advantages, you now pass to *item 14*, and proceed to enumerate *values at your disposal* (15) and to anticipate their best use, together with such *assistance* (15) as may seem possible, to set up a certain *time limit* (16) in which

you think of yourself as achieving definite success, to revolve in mind the possibilities of *various localities*, (17) to imagine *methods* (18) of various sorts for building up the business, to cast about in thought for the best *investments* (19) of your resources, to see already your *materials* (19) (buildings, furniture, stock, *employees*, (20) etc., in place, to enact a mental drama of *action*, (21) to fortify the feeling of personal energy, to call up all kinds of contingencies and *new adjustments*, (22) to *forelook* (23) as far beyond as possible, and to conceive one unalterable determination, "I will!" (24)

It should be noted here that in both of the above cases, the items enumerated are suggestive only in the author's design. In both cases the imaginative work will be conducted differently by different individuals, and will vary constantly from time to time. Nevertheless, something like the above goes into the experience of every practical man in actual business. The fact that the reader may not recognize such processes as here given has no bearing on the value of the scheme. Hard-headed business men are forever doing things which only other thinkers observe and which they alone must analyze. An immensely successful business man remarked to the writer, after a thorough reading of "*Power For Success*," "I constantly found in that book the explicit statement of principles and rules which I had followed all my life without knowing that I was doing so."

3. Or, you are now, let us say, in actual business, yet desire to improve your line and bring your entire "place" to greater efficiency. Reading up in the scheme as given, we come to *item five*,

and here resolve takes shape with the sense of the
future strongly felt; then follow the remaining
items until imagination and judgment have decided
on some definite plan of action, in which items
fourteen to twenty-four are involved.

SUGGESTED APPLICATIONS OF IMAGINATION.

§ 35.   The complicated movements of imagination are evident during every hour of the business
day, from selection of business to change in a show-
window or choice of an advertising medium—often
greatly condensed from the outline of the scheme,
but employing, nevertheless, the essential factors
therein indicated from start to finish.

RÉGIME SIX: SUGGESTIONS FOR APPLICATION.
There is no phase of business which does not make
heavy drafts on imaginative ability.   As suggestive
illustrations, take the following factors (*Thus you
have to study, and imagine, and anticipate*):

Your *employer:* What is his probable future
conduct?

Your *employees:* What is their foreseen conduct?

Place of *business:* Its probable future.

Kind of business: Its relation to coming changes.

Goods in stock: Probable demand; popular tastes.

Arrangement of store: Possible improvements.

External displays: Something new, yet precisely right.

Advertisements: Appearance; selling qualities.

Customers: As satisfied; as inspired to purchase.

Creditors: As handled on their own suggestions
for your interests.

Debtors: As induced to settle, yet to remain
"with you."

Investments: As safeguarded and shifted to better.

Some *particular transaction:* As planned; plans changed, yet effective.

And ten thousand other items which practical imagination must care for as surely as a dinner requires wiser preparation than throwing food at a hot stove.

§ 36. A college professor of physics once stopped in a factory where an electric engineer was employed. The professor could talk *ohm, amperes,* and *volts* smoothly, and he used some of the technical words in his conversation with the engineer. The latter looked at the college man with a blank countenance, and then said: "You can't prove it by me. I don't know what you're talking about. All I do know is to turn on the 'juice' and let her buzz!" How much "juice" is wasted in this cut-and-dried world of ours, and how much might be saved if only all who use our own powers and the forces of Nature were a trifle more intelligent regarding the laws of business. This engineer's imagination was the like of that which holds many a man down and sends many a business to bankruptcy. "All I know is to turn on the 'juice'!" When the human brain comes in contact with the fact of electricity (or any other proposition of fact), it becomes the moral duty of that brain to run the fact to cover and drag into daylight its secrets of value and operation. The man who permits himself to say, "All I know is to turn on the 'juice'" is guilty of an immorality.

§ 37. Imagination is related to business somewhat as the "keeper" is related to a magnet. A

horseshoe magnet will hold its magnetism for long
if given something to do. Without the "keeper" the
magnetism will in time dissipate.   With the
"keeper" the magnetism "balances," so to speak,
and will not attract other bodies. When the
"keeper" is removed, attraction takes place.

§ 38.   Imagination alone builds no business,
accomplishes nothing practical. Business without
imagination gradually dissipates energy and fails.
Yet the play of imagination must, in proper time
and measure, yield to practical activity. If the two
abilities combine, seasonably, and in right proportions, the word, "business," ought to be
synonymous with the word, "success." Nevertheless, it is here, as elsewhere—"the man behind the
throne" who makes imagination and common sense
the great co-operatives of financial power.

CHAPTER XIII.

THE ENERGY OF SUCCESS.

I SAW a man at work in a quarry. He thrust the end of a crowbar under a huge rock and threw into the effort to move the obstacle his utmost strength. He had enthusiasm for fierce endeavor. Energy leaped up within him and rushed to the strain of a Hercules.

My friend, the railway builder, said to me that the greater the obstacles that confronted him, the more determined he became to overcome them.

The one instance illustrates physical energy, the other shows us psychic energy. The energy of success consists of both phases, together with an unyielding mood of confidence in self, one's effort, and the outcome. It is not merely physical, for Sampson was no great success. It is not mental alone, for that may be passive. It is not simply a sense of ability, for that may exhibit in a mild and negative form. *But when a man has in him the day-after-day and year-in-and-year-out mood, " I can and I will," controlled, restrained, used, exactly as he will, yet never surrendering, then he has it—the energy of success.*

369

§ 1. The energy of success is a compound of two general factors: *a continuance-feeling of great confidence and a sense of driving and practical ability.*

§ 2. It is not only for every one to possess this quality, but as well to *know that he has it*. All persons are endowed with a measure of the quality, at least among average classes, but comparatively few seem to be conscious of its possession. One who flames out in a rage may be aware of his passion yet totally unconscious of the central energy which has thus become manifest. His consciousness in the case might be called objective. A person may be aware of intense determination to achieve some difficult task, yet give no thought to the focusing energy of his mind. He is aware of a particular fact in experience, but his self-knowledge does not necessarily embrace the inner psychic state. A measure of success worth trying for demands not only that one should possess some energy, but that one should recognize the quality within himself, and intelligently control and use it with reference to a goal that is capable of engaging his utmost interest. These considerations suggest the present chapter.

FORCE AND ENERGY.

§ 3. Force and energy do not represent the same thing. Modern chemistry and physics make a distinction between the facts and define differently the corresponding words. "*Force is any agency which can cause a motion, arrest a motion, or change the direction of a motion, while energy expresses in motion or the capacity to become motion.*"

§ 4. "There are two kinds of energy—*kinetic* or moving energy, and *potential* or energy of position." (Like the dynamic self and the static.)

Let us suppose a cannon, loaded and ready for discharge. The explosive behind the ball contains molecular energy—capacity for motion, for work. When the charge is fired, the explosive generates gases which are confined but seek to expand and in that effort start the ball and the cause of that start is the force of the explosion, while the moving ball represents energy capable of performing work the moment it is stopped. If the ball is projected perpendicularly into the air, it has the energy of motion—kinetic—until it ceases to mount higher, when, for a theoretical instant, it has no kinetic energy (as it will in a moment on its descent), but does at that instant of mid-air "rest" possess potential energy, the energy of position, because it may now fall to the ground from its present height and regain all the energy of motion which it had when it left the gun.

MAN A FUND OF ENERGY.

§ 5. Now, man is a store-house of various forces capable of causing the energy of motion. Inasmuch as the forces are, broadly speaking, always discharging and inducing all sorts of motions, we may say that *man is himself a great unit system of stored energy*. Not only does he incessantly release energy, but he also constantly stores up force essential to the required energy of life and action. Taking man as an animal alone, he is more wonderful as a force-storing and an energy-releasing machine than any mechanism his inventive genius can produce. He is exceedingly complex and he is exceedingly economical in the transformation of his fuel into energy. Ho "may be regarded as a self-contained 'prime mover,' including its furnace, its mechanism of work and energy-development, and possessing mechanism of transformation of power peculiarly and exactly adapted to its purpose."

§ 6.　Referring a moment to the teachings of science, it is to be observed that the attractive force which the earth exerts on a body at its surface is called the force of gravity, while that which is exerted between two or more molecules of matter is termed chemical affinity.　In both cases, we have, as Tyndall remarks, "working power. That power may exist in the form of motion, or it may exist in the form of force, with distance to act through." "The former is dynamic energy (the energy of motion), the latter is potential energy (the energy of position)." So, then, the cannon ball at rest an instant in air, and the molecule of matter yielding to the pull of some other molecule, and thus capable of exerting that pull because of position, but only capable, as the ball at the highest point of its ascent is only capable, possess potential energy— that of position.

§ 7.　Thus, in the animal machine also the two forms of energy obtain.　And as potential energy is capable of becoming dynamic (in motion or action), and as this is simply capacity for work, the body is seen to be capable of working very economically and to an enormous degree.　Huxley, speaking of a certain amount of food being turned into energy, has said: "The energy available by the oxidation in the body of this particular diet is more than sufficient to balance the total amount which we saw was expended "—1,152,473 kilogramme-metres (the energy available) against 150,-ooo kilogramme-metres (the energy used in a good day's work). The work done in lifting 2.2 lbs. through a height of 39.37 inches is a unit of work, or a kilogramme-metre. That is to say, a certain amount of a certain kind of food was found to be more than sufficient in energy secured for a given amount of work actually employed: *the work could have been done with less food-energy than the food taken obtained.*

§ 8. Having in mind the idea of such a machine as was characterized in section 6, together with differences of mental characteristics, it is evident that "*for every sort of task there is to be found a kind of man specifically and peculiarly adapted to its successful accomplishment.*"

§ 9. One of the most important general laws of business energy, then, demands the *adjustment of the right kind of man to the right kind of work.* In practical application of this law of common sense, the man who works under others should try to put himself where he can do the most work of the highest value; and the man who works over others should see to it that every man under him is placed in a corresponding position of greatest utility. This is the rule for machines; why not for men? The use of the law is a maker of values.

ENERGY AND HEALTH.

§ 10. In the operation of the human machine considered as a transformer and user of energy, it is *indispensable that the intake should be more than equal, at any given time, speaking loosely, to the outgo.* This is because the man must conduct the preservative and developing operations of body and self in addition to those of his work, and the former operations require energy-supplies for their own needs. If you constantly release all the normally available energy you possess, you leave for the maintenance of your personal well being no supply, and the end, sooner or later, is bankruptcy. Business energy demands health. With some men, and for a time, health seems to take care of itself. But health really does not take care of itself. Right financial returns mean right physical returns in advance. A surplus bank account is never so valuable as a surplus energy account. "Business suicide" would be a correct characterization of many activities in business and out of it. "Can't help it" is only another phrasing of "Don't care." Many a man says, "Let her go!" meaning himself, when he would better mean "the job." It is difficult to understand why business should make one perversely obstinate or obstinately foolish. The science of business is founded on some one's health —that marvelous hard-pan of compacted energy. This is not the place for descriptions of health-giving régimes, which are everywhere available, and certain suggestion in which may be found in the author's other works, especially in "*The Culture of Courage*," but the consideration of "business energy" emphatically calls for the conservation of the business man's health as the very basis and source of his ability and power. It ought in modern life to be perfectly understood that every physical

requirement of common sense means actual financial values. The ethics of business at bottom is the
two sides, say, of a fifty-dollar gold piece thus in-
scribed: "Do thyself no harm" and "Be good to
yourself." It may be suggested that you cause
these advices to be engraved on the opposite faces
of any coin to be carried as a permanent pocket
piece and reminder wherever you go. It would
give some men a start if they could look attentively
at such a "talisman" when they find themselves in
some places or engaged in various injurious
practices.

§ 11. For an instructive treatment of the
"*Culture of Body Character*" you are referred to
"*Power For Success*," the twenty-fifth lesson. In
that chapter the author seeks to rise above the mere
level of health-régimes to suggestions for the development of the finest instrument of the business man's work—a body pervaded by the keen-
est psychic feeling and brought to the most
efficient condition. It will serve our present purpose to quote from the lesson mentioned the
following:

"The majority of people seem to be indifferent
to the nobility and dignity of the physical life. The
present régime does not necessarily imply knowledge of the body's structure, forces, materials,
laws and operations. It does call for a larger, a
more elevated, thought concerning that wonderful
'temple,' your own body. You are urged to think
of its greatness, its usefulness, its divinity,—even
if not ideal in your case,—and to make this thought
a permanent factor in consciousness. The purpose
will demonstrate itself in interior conditions which

must inevitably react beneficially upon your physical nature."

"Environment exercises incessant, and oftentimes an unconscious, influence. If it is dirty, disorderly, depressing, unattractive, uninspiring, the effects will first appear in the physical life. Your body responds, not only to internal psychic nobility, but also to external uplifting conditions. You should, therefore, put into your surroundings, as far as possible, the elements, cleanliness, order, thrift, beauty—all things that appeal attractively to the senses and the white soul. In thus environing yourself, however, you should not lose sight of the psychic influence sought, but should maintain the consciousness, "*I, the upright self, appreciative of the nobility and usefulness of the physical nature, maintain these surroundings that my life may come to its best and my body may acquire a corresponding character.*"

ENERGY AND THE BRAIN.

§ 12. Business energy is not confined to the general structure of the body. The nervous system centres in the brain, and the latter organ is a perfectly marvelous engine for the storing and releasing of energy of many varieties. Energy is, of course, energy, but the energy of the brain exhibits in almost innumerable activities. The structure of the brain, therefore, must be immensely complex, with its general protoplasmic substance, its lobes, its convolutions, its nerve fibres, and so on. The complexity of the organ it is that makes possible the enormous accumulations of the mental life. Such accumulations indicate that peculiar grade of

energy which we call personal. Small brain capacity means a comparatively small number of brain
cells. Some brains, however, are not developed to
anything like their limit. In any brain at birth
there is a given number of cells never exceeded in
that brain. Personal development means development of the given brain cells (and other nervous
matter situated elsewhere—see below) given at
birth. Such cells are never created after birth,
and they are never repaired when injured. A life
may signify a limited development of a very limited
number of the cells of the brain. Every individual
has his limit of power in this respect, but few ever
approximate that limit. Or a life may signify a
limited or a vast development of a considerable
number of brain cells. It is the fact that you do
not know your limit, either in number or in capacity for development of the cells, that raises for
you the privilege—it would seem, the obligation—
to put forth unceasing effort toward greater mental
improvement. But whether or no, we have in the
average man's brain a marvelous structure adapted
to the storage and the release of energy. Other
things being equal, the more abundant and the
purer and richer your blood, the greater your brain
power, for the brain is like a great sponge loaded
with blood. Hence the importance of health and
all the laws that conduce to the best physical tone.

§ 13. In regard to the unknowability of brain-
limits, "It is estimated that there are from 600,-
000,000 to 1,200,000,000 of nerve cells in the brain
for the generation of nerve force (but some hold
that the cells merely receive and pass on the force),
and the moulding, fashioning, and storing up of

our ideas, each having a separate existence, but all
acting in subordination to the requirements of the
organs.   They are connected together by probably
from 4,000,000,000 to 5,000,000,000 of fibres which
convey impressions from one to another and bring
them into combined action." Observe, however:
that the nerve-cell fibres are, as units, connected together is not altogether clear, indeed, is questioned;
nerve action in the brain seeming to be carried on
through the surrounding material acting as a conductor between one system of cell and fibre and another system, in a way analogous to the conduction
of electric currents.   But, whether or not this be
the case, there seems to be in any man's brain all
the physical material the utmost diligence for a
lifetime might require.   If one's mental life is
measured by the growth of the greatest number of
cells possessed, and if the number that may be developed is so enormous as above indicated, the
proposition that no one can know his personal limit
becomes evident.   It is not because men are not
sufficiently endowed that many fail to exhibit great
power, but this fact is rather due to the negligence
of brain material possessed by all normal people.   I
do not forget *psychic* endowment, but still hold that
this has no *known* limit.

MENTAL ENERGY.

§ 14.   The releasing of brain energy is accompanied by mental activities.   As the brain stores
nerve energy, and as nerve energy accompanies
mental activity, we may well speak of the store of
mental energy which a person possesses.   It is
always to be understood, of course, that by "stor-

ing energy," we mean simply securing conditions in which energy may manifest, for we have seen at the beginning of this chapter that energy expresses in motion or the capacity to become motion, and it is evident that motion or the capacity to become motion cannot be stored in any ordinary sense of the word. The conditions making motion possible may be secured in the brain, and these conditions, together with psychic conditions, may be enlarged in scope; in that sense one may store mental energy. The phrases, "He has no mental life," "He is a person of great energy of mind," show the common recognition of the fact. The meaning is, of course, that one has scanty or large mental ability. Such power exhibits in various ways, as, in a "strong will," "a keen insight," "ability for intense concentration," "an iron faculty," "a powerful memory," "a great imagination." *Power of mind means conditions favorable within the brain and self to intense and varied mental activities habituated but with a considerable action of mental initiative. The only way in which such power can be acquired is through incessant, varied and initiative exercise of the self in large thoughts and affairs.* The great business man is one who through the making of a great business has developed his own mental resources and thus secured constant conditions in which mental power may exhibit.

§ 15. When a man hypnotizes himself into believing that he is bound by narrow mental limits, it is even so, for he makes it so. When a man cultivates a healthy, large-sized idea of himself and backs up the notion with intelligent and persistent effort, it then may *not* be "even so" to the fullest

extent of his idea, but it *will* be more truly or
extensively "even so " than on any other plan.

§ 16.   The amount and quality of your mental
power, within the unknown limits of some millions
of brain cells, depends on the amount and quality
of mental accumulation, that is to say, the habituated and initiatory conditions favorable to ideas and
psychic activity which you make possible by personal development and intelligent reaction with the
world in which you live.   And it will be of immense
inspirational and other assistance to you if, along
with all your mental activity, you will carry the
thought from day to day, asserted throughout your
entire personality, from brain to toe and finger-tip,
"*I am bent on the largest and richest mental life,
and even now the physical instrument is yielding to
this determination.*"   Thus you suggest to the brain
within the skull and the nervous system which the
self pervades in all nerve regions everywhere in
the body, and so to the subconscious self which resides, God knows where, in the human being, that
growth has become the law and must be realized.

USE OF ENERGY.

§ 17.   The outcome of employed energy also
depends on the method of its use.   Pyschic energy
develops through pyschic activity.   But you are
not interested in mere power, however great; you
desire power for business purposes.   Your psychic
energy must come, then, through the right business
use of body and mind.   To refer to one phase of
the matter of use, in any mechanism into and
through which energy is passing, the less the friction
of the parts involved, and the more easily the

forms which energy takes are changed from one into another, the more effectively does that energy perform its work. All this requires skill of adjustment. *In adjustment we have the first law of the use of the energy of success.*

§ 18. *Skill is demanded in the control, direction and employment of business power.* Some men have the energy of Niagara—and the skill of a goat: they can only batter. The result is, a jarring conduct of business. I heard a section foreman torturing the air, his nerves and the bystanders with marvelous profanity; but he did not disturb his Italian workmen in the least, nor secure more efficient labor. Good business is not a battering-ram. Skilled energy is nice adjustment of mechanism, whether human or material, to achievement. An illustration may be seen in differences between two kinds of memory. One man remembers things in pictures, another by means of sounds, as we have seen in a previous chapter. Should either try to memorize in the other's way, this would be unskilled use of energy. Or, one man must do all things himself, driving those associated with him in the work he simply cannot perform, while another man gets things done by inducing those with him to do every thing to the limit and the best without friction. The former has push, the latter skill. Both men may possess equal energy.

§ 19. The difference in value between the two methods is evident. Men who are driven will not, as a general rule, accomplish the greatest amount of the best quality of work. Men that are induced, may accomplish that sort of work, depending on the skill employed with the inducement. Skill of use conserves energy and secures best results. *Energy is capital; skill is its investor. Energy is power; put skill into its direction and it is more and better power.* Ignited gun powder yields force which develops energy in the moving ball. Skill is the inventor, and maker of the gun, *and* the gun's mechanism, *but*—"the man behind the gun." You can be a mere bullet, or, a mere gun, or—a man. If you want to be a mere day laborer, be a bullet. If you want to be a *somewhat* skilled controller of energy, be a gun. If you want to control energy in the highest manner possible, get behind the gun. This means that you can be a mere implement wielded by some other man; or you can be a trained machine, still used by some other person; or —*you can be the director of tool and mechanism: all depends on your skill in handling yourself and others.*

The development of such skill requires persistent thought, alertness for opportunity, seizure of the same, the forcing of confidence in yourself, culture of magnetism for control or winning of others, determination to attain the goal, and the study of mental invention and initiative—in other words, the qualities set forth in this book.

The skill demanded in the development and use of personal energy must be sought, of course, in actual experience. For experience there is no substitute, because it is the application of any teaching to practical affairs that demonstrates the instruction's value and works its principle into the personal life. But every man is a human being to start with, and is endowed with more or less of what we call the instinct of human progress. That is to say, we start with the advantages gained by the experiences of our ancestors to a considerable degree, and begin life with the ability to do many things without experience in its fullest sense and possess an impulse associated with a measure of power to get on in the world.

§ 20. The man who depends wholly on his own experience and refuses to profit by the experience of others, puts himself inevitably in the rear in any undertaking. Why not start with the results of the common experience, relying upon your own as a utilizer and modifier? You are then so much ahead at the beginning of your effort. The age of fifty is always wondering why the age of twenty is so excessively fond of hard knocks. Of course the age of twenty does not "see it that way," but why should not the young man *assume* that the older person may *really know something worth while*—take the matter for granted, in a way, or on trial, at least? The curious quality which I have called *megalopsukia* in the chapter on "Personal Qualifications," is in evidence when experience which is already established and has learned some important matters remarks, "Oh, you can't teach him anything, he knows it all," and the shrug of the shoulders indicates the despair of the older man. The cause of many a bankruptcy in business is nothing more nor less than the "big head." You must, of course, stand by your own experience, but it would seem to be common sense to give the other man's experience reasonable consideration. The finest of practical instructors is just the compound experience of all other men in business and the man in any particular line of business—yourself.

§ 21. But the development and use of business energy may also come to involve valuable skill in the study and practical absorption of suggestions outlined in the Hand of Power as seen in Section 19 of Chapter IV. You are invited to turn to the diagram on page 69 and to observe that the cultivation of the qualities there indicated cannot fail to result in larger personal skill. The definitions, for example, now become doubly significant, because the question of skill is before us.

Energy—"Inherent power." *How* will you acquire it, how use it, in gun or machine or man? The question applies to *your* body and mind. Answer: By entertaining the idea of energy, by trying to feel it, by assuming that you have it; by acting intelligently on that assumption.

Force—"Power in action." *How* is again the question. Sell goods, for example, with a club or by magnetic diplomacy? *How?* Answer: By development of practical ability and magnetic power, by economic use for highest results, by taking yourself in hand, refusing "fuss and feathers," unnecessary activity and waste and all nervous excitement, but employing self-possession, nicely adjusting your machine and the energy behind it to the work to be accomplished.

Firmness—"Power of grip." The manner in which the grip is taken is important. Grip a man wrongly, you irritate him; rightly, a personal feeling secures your end. To the question, *How?* may briefly be answered: By cultivating the self-possessed consciousness of a strong yet non-nervous and non-irritating grasp on self, on others, on the situation, holding smoothly but resistlessly to the matter before you.

Self-reliance—"Assurance of power." Shall the assurance be blazoned forth in gesture and feature, or felt yet masked behind suggestion of the other man's interest? Here, again, the word *how* confronts us. One should assume possession of assurance and confidence, and forever try to feel and think, quietly, not obtrusively, that one is equal to the occasion and can surely accomplish the thing in hand.

And thus with other digits in the Hand of Power. The highest type of power consists of energy employed with skill. Indeed, business energy lacking in skill is never actual power at all. You will find this important topic of the right handling of self elaborately and practically treated in the volume, "*Power For Success.*"

THE MAN AND THE BUSINESS.

§ 22. The best use of personal energy involves the *individual* and the *business*. Let us consider both factors simply as individuals. Each is a field of energy. Energy is in each constantly storing and releasing. In each energy is, so to speak, flowing from one place to another, there being not one "stream" but all sorts of "streams," moving back and forth every instant of the day. Now, all this activity within a certain "field" demands a kind of balance, so that always energy is available at any one place for any given requirement. "Balance rules the world," says the author of "*Balance.*" "Balance is the key that unlocks them, the word that explains them, the principle that unifies them."

The author, Mr. Smith, employs an illustration
which always applies everywhere in the business
world. "A deficiency in crops is balanced by an
excess in prices; an excess in crops is balanced by
a deficiency in prices. Other balances, corrective
in their nature, rise up also. A deficiency in crops,
with the corresponding high prices, stimulates
efforts, such as better cultivation and increased
planting to overcome the deficiency, while an
excess of crops sets forces at work to repress over-
production." *The financial world is one vast exhibition of balance, and every detail individual business
is an equal illustration.* We have, let us say, proprietor, manager, clerks, laborers, errand boys,
and so on. *Every man, every "field" of energy, must
connect, in some way, with every other man. The
sum-total of activities must be an equilibrium and
a forward movement.* That is to say, a good day's
work all round means constant give and take, with
the least possible friction, on the part of all concerned. This double requirement may be expressed
in two words—*Rigidity—Yielding.*

§ 23. Mind-body-man, on the sea of business,
is very much like Kipling's steamship, *Dumbula*,
during her first voyage ("*The Ship That Found
Herself*"). *The Dumbula* came into a huge storm
on her way to New York, and every part of the
craft was put to terrific strain. Then ensued a
long-continued and lively conversation of complaint, advice and vituperation, conducted by bolts,
plates, uprights, timbers, and so on, to the end of
the voyage.

" 'Come back!' said the deck-beams savagely,
as the upward heave of the sea made the frames

try to open. 'Come back to your bearings, you slack-jawed irons!'

"'Rigidity! Rigidity! Rigidity!' thumped the engines. 'Absolute, unvarying rigidity—rigidity!'

"'You see!' whined the rivets, in chorus. 'No two of you will ever pull alike, and—and you blame it all on us. We only know how to go through a plate and bite down on both sides so that it can't and mustn't and shan't move.'

"'I've got one fraction of an inch play, at any rate,' said the garboard strake triumphantly. So he had, and all the bottom of the ship felt the easier for it.

"'Then we're no good,' sobbed the bottom rivets. 'We were ordered—we were ordered— never to give, and we've given!'

"'Don't say I told you,' whispered the steam consolingly, 'but you *had* to give a fraction, and you've given without knowing it. Now, hold on, as before.'"

So, in every kind of business, *rigidity, rigidity*, is the law of energy, but only part of the whole law, which also embraces, *give, give*, just enough to save friction and hold together. No set of people can work successfully in company without the law in its entirety. In a new business force the need is apparent; in an old business, if successful, its working is evident.

§ 24. It is precisely so as regards the individual. There are more parts in body-mind-man than in the best steamer afloat, for the brain alone contains millions of cells, and all the parts are forever doing things, forever taking up energy and releasing it, under the immense strain of forces with-

out and forces within, and so, always, so to speak,
are complaining, advising, standing out, combining,
soliciting, refusing, vituperating (in disease), while
the long "game" of "give and take" goes on.

"Look out!" shouts heart to the legs. "You're
going too fast, and I'll break something."

"We should say!" respond the lungs; already
there's a pain here with its warning."

"Have a care! Have a care!" the brain tele-
graphs down to the heart; "I'm nearly drowned.
Too much blood."

"You're loading me up with too many foolish
things," cries the memory.

"Stand fast, there!" shouts attention; "don't
give!"

"Ease up! Ease up!" the eyes moan to the
will; "you'll hurt the optic nerve!"

"Keep at it! Keep at it!" the will urges
mind. "But I've got to give a little," replies
mind; "everything is a mere blur now."

"Rigidity! Rigidity! Rigidity!" thump the
compound engines, Determined-Persistence. You
must all hold on and never let up an instant, or
everything goes to ruin."

"Give away a trifle!" insists the unconscious
self; "I want more time for the making of energy,
and all you parts are throwing it away!"

Only in such a play of powers by give and take
may right balance and adjustment essential to any
life success be secured.

Energy and Success.

§ 25. A business man, because he is living
and a human animal, is a complex system of force,

energy, power, of a certain running amount, exerted in certain generally established directions, and always bent on the work that means success. The success depends on the *amount* and *control* of all sorts of energies, in the first place his own, and in the second place those of others. The control must be managed by effort: power must handle power—if success is to be sure and large.

§ 26. Success may be defined as the *crystallization of a certain quality of energy*. Business success constantly calls for force, energy, power, effort, in immense amounts, and of precisely the right character. Definitions of these factors tie up into one bundle—*Efficiency*.

DIAGRAM OF IDEAL AND IMPERFECT USE OF ENERGY.

Use of Self   Use of Others

The above lines analyze as follows:

The Ideal.	The Imperfect.
Energy Controlled and Trained	Diffuse
Economical	Wasteful
Concentrated	Scant Attention
Steady	Fitful
Best Use	Poor Use
Great Thoughtfulness	Unintelligent
Use of Others	Used by Others
One Aim	Conflicting Aims

One who expects success from the second line

of procedure must believe in hit-or-miss miracles. One who looks for failure from the first line of procedure has no faith in law.

§ 27. *The test of success is the amount and kind of effort which a man can voluntarily hold good during a lifetime.* The idea may be represented by a line always extending and always straight and of such breadth as to indicate room for energy. The heavy straight line of business energy, however, is ideal, and observed in the lives of few men. The real line varies, all the way from heavy to light, from straight to uneven, from constantly extending to some definite limit. Thus we may place side by side the ideal line of lifelong skilled success-energy, and the curious, telltale line of unskilled, broken and unsuccessful energy.

EXAMINATION OF THE DIAGRAMS.

§ 28. Let us examine the foregoing illustrations.

(A) Business education, if really practical, means, for one thing, *trained*, which is or ought to be, *controlled* energy. It is at this point, frequently, that men fail. "It is characteristic of all untrained activity that it is diffusive." "The boy, when first learning to write, is unable to prevent the simultaneous motions of tongue and legs, which are ludicrously irrelevant to the purpose of writing." So, some business men can never keep their business to its own kind, but are forever putting effort and time into irrelevant channels; or they themselves are forever doing unnecessary things within the business in hand. "The effect of training and attention is more and more to confine the activity to special channels, so that the actions themselves are better performed, and can be kept up longer without producing fatigue." Whatever amount and kind of energy one possesses, then, we have the following exhortations:

EXHORTATION ONE—ELIMINATE FROM YOUR LIFE DIFFUSIVE EXPENDITURE OF ENERGY.

EXHORTATION TWO — MAINTAIN CONTROLLED ENERGY AND PUT INTELLIGENCE INTO ALL USE OF IT AT ALL TIMES.

The fault of diffusive energy, however, appears not merely in its spreading around, but as well in its failure to "pan out" anywhere. An inventor may carry on a dozen schemes during a period, yet succeed in some of his efforts because he transfers concentrated energy now to one, now to another. One clerk may be first-class for the reason that he is "all over the place," but doing things of value meanwhile. Another may be equally omnipresent, yet fail because he is never precisely *where* he is wanted *when* he is wanted, and is seldom, if ever, ready to do the one thing needful without being hunted up and told to do it. Your great business man may have "many irons in the fire," yet he concentrates tremendously on each of them in turn. Robert Houdin, the famous prestidigitator, acquired the ability to keep four balls in the air while reading. Thirty years after, during which period the trick had been neglected, he was able to read while keeping three balls going. His attention, fastened, released, fastened, with lightning rapidity passing from one thing to another, not consciously, of course, but instinctively, perhaps we should say in the subconscious

self, and it thus managed to take precise care of
every ball and the printed page.   Diffusive energy
cannot concentrate.   What we may call differential
attention has the power to do exactly that—concentrate because it can instantaneously specialize
in a running series of effort.   Diffusive energy
never heats the iron.   Some business men succeed
because of many investments, but others fail for
precisely that reason—they lack the differential
concentration of energy.   The difference is largely
a matter of energy uncontrolled by trained intelligence.   A good corrective rule is this: *All attention to all one thing at a time, and to all things in
due time.*   The rule has its value for the best
handling of a business, but also for the individual
himself.   In the first place, one must have energetic control of the entire bundle of his personal
energies.   In the second place, and meanwhile, one
must mass his personal energy, when required and
as required, for the best results.   It is simply a
case of keeping all the balls going while taking
full care of each.

A man's life is very much like that of a variety
of *amoeba*, a microscopic bit of living protoplasm,
looking now like a star, now like an oak leaf, always
changing its form, always putting forth arms, or
"feet," pseudopodia, or "processes," and withdrawing them.   As one observes it under the lense,
fine particles are noticed which stream into an
arm (or foot) or process from the whole extent of
the tiny animal, the process lengthening, and then
withdrawing into the body entirely, while another
process begins to extend into which the former
streaming of the particles now goes on.   Our

energy must diffuse somewhat, perhaps, but in successful business it is controlled, thrown now into one channel, now into another, but forever handled for success.

(B) *A fault allied to that of diffusiveness is seen in wasted energies.* Observe a person who constantly performs unnecessary actions—fingers drumming, face twitching, arms jerking, head turning, and so on. Here is a type of wasted energy occurring in the mental lives of many, and no less obtaining in the business world. The waste means wild ventures, poor investments, unsalable goods—activities and facts of all sorts ending in nothing of value. It also may mean too much energy—quantity beyond the demand—in the physical, or the business life. Some men are all "fuss and feathers." Other men are all "slam-bang." These people can never nicely gauge requirements. If they drive a nail, they must dent the board. They lift a one-pound weight with five-pound effort. Their intensity is consuming. They assault a matter of no importance with enormous fierceness. When they criticise, they slaughter. They rush at a task with destructive power. Without knowing the fact, they are headlong spendthrifts of value.

REMEDIES FOR UNSKILLED USE OF ENERGY.

§ 29. The false application of energy found in poor use is common everywhere. *It can be remedied only by patient, persistent attention, experience, and the determination to acquire that skill which makes every effort count.* Observe one compositor in a printing office. Every move tells; every type is seized as desired, adjusted between the fingers

while moving toward the stick, and placed precisely
in the right way. Ten or twelve thousand ems a
day are to this man not impossible. His neighbor
labors furiously eight hours and is content with six
thousand ems for his day. He makes three or four
motions for every type placed. This difference
puts an Atlantic ocean between millions of neighbors in the business world.

§ 30. Poor use of one's powers is often due to
scanty attention and fitful concentration. Effort
may be adequate when applied, but it is intermittent, and is often just short of the required degree
of concentration. A blacksmith may heat an iron
with a given number of blows of given force; but
a blow at long and irregular intervals never heats
bar iron greatly, though the force when applied be
that of the whole man. *It is a curious law of things
that they refuse to change in condition unless mind
charges into them with continuous intensity of energy.*

§ 31. Nevertheless, *intelligence is required
with the most unrelenting attention.* Illustrations
are seen in the injunctions: Don't try to sell goods
to an angry man; Don't waylay a lawyer when he
is rushing to court if you really desire a place in
his office; Don't purchase a big stock of silks for a
country store; and so on. No sort of human effort
demands more downright power of intelligent mind
than business. The larger the amount and the
finer the quality of actual thought put into any
venture in the general run of business, the surer
and better the resultant success. All this is commonplace, perhaps, but justified by the fact that
business intelligence consists in a mass of truths
vitalized by interest and the action of an acute

mind. It would be difficult to decide whether thoughtlessness in place or thoughtfulness out of place can be worse for success. It really seems evident that thousands of energetic people are unsuccessful because their efforts are not intelligently controlled and directed. How often it is heard: " Why, he's active enough, and means well, but he doesn't seem to know anything." The world forgives the born fool because he had to be born, but for no other cause of lack of brains has it the slightest tolerance. Your energy is merely the output of yourself in mind, always to be directed by every ounce of intelligence possessed.

§ 32. By contrast, then, is indicated the ideal energy that is surely prophetic of some satisfactory degree of business success. *It is energy concentrated as required by reason of training and mastery, and therefore economical of outlay and seldom running to direct waste, meanwhile steadily pushing on with the utmost skill of brains through the best use of self and others toward the one, all-absorbing, never-forgotten goal—honorable financial success.*

Training the Subconscious Self.

§ 33. The personal sphere in which such ideal energy may be developed is the subconscious, or, as some writers call it, the unconscious, self. (See Sections 15-26, Chapter 1.) This mysterious self we can only know by inference, and of course understand by it merely a phase of the whole individual, yet here is a region which alone seems to explain many actual facts in mental life. *The subconscious self is the real creator of the human person and all his energies.* Lack of space forbids any

extended discussion of this wonderful matter, but
the reader who may be interested is referred for
further suggestion on the subject to the author's
"Practical Psychology." That we may forefend,
however, against the charge of mere "occultism,"
a few quotations follow which have the authority
of acknowledged thinkers.

Thus, Kant remarks: "We may become aware
indirectly that we have an idea, although we be
not directly cognizant of the same." And Schel-
ling declares: "In all, even the commonest and
most everyday production, there co-operates with
the conscious an unconscious activity." So, also,
Richter held, in poetical language that "our measurements of the rich territory of the Me are far too
small or narrow when we omit the immense realm
of the Unconscious, this real interior Africa in
every sense. In every second only a few illumin-
ated mountain-tops of the whole wide globe of
memory are turned toward the mind, and all the
rest of the world remains in shadow." To the same
effect Wundt states that "our mind is so happily
designed that it prepares for us the most important
foundations of cognition, whilst we have not the
slightest apprehension of the *modus operandi*. This
unconscious soul, like a benevolent stranger, works
and makes provision for our benefit, pouring only
the mature fruits in our laps." Bastion even believes more than this: "That it is *not we* who think,
but that *it* thinks *in us*, is clear to him who is wont
to pay attention to the internal processes." Ros-
mani makes the astonishing statement: "A close
attention to our internal operations, along with induction, gives us this result, that we even exercise

ratiocination of which we have no consciousness, and generally it furnishes us with this marvelous law, that *every operation whatsoever of our minds is unknown to itself until a second operation reveals it to us.*"

The practical bearing of the subject may be hinted at in the following propositions from Professor Holman: "All percepts are practical judgments, and are intuitive judgments. The mental processes involved constitute what is called practical reason (that which is in evidence in practical ability). Its most striking form is seen in those inventions which are so often made by artisans. There is no explicit thinking out of matters by, say, a bricklayer; but a kind of almost instinctive realizing that such materials will lead to given practical results. The individual himself regards the whole matter as one of doing and not of thinking."

§ 34. *The suggestion issuing from this general conclusion, then, is that the development of personal energy, among ten thousand other matters, may be confidently given over to the subconscious self, the conscious, meanwhile, of course, co-operating by aware feelings of assurance and expectation and action corresponding to the ideal sought.* If you want energy, think and feel and act energy until you have it, as you surely will,—may be given as a working method.

§ 35. Here, then, is the real engine room of personal power. You are continually engaged in bringing about these conditions of the personal life in which energy is generated, force exhibited and power used. But the processes involved go on

in a more or less haphazard way, accompanied by
much waste, and lacking, of course, the most efficient directing.   I hold that such processes may be
made more intelligent, and that personal energy
may be generated, or brought into the conscious
field from without and the subconscious within and
used in ways more surely contributory to personal
success.   Methods for realizing such results will
now be given, it being understood that our purpose
is suggestive only, in order that the reader may
receive impulse toward the ideal of self-help and
the masterful use of his own unconscious powers.
" Be ye not faithless; only believe": here is a perfectly inexhaustible storehouse from which you
may draw at will and during life.

FIRST METHOD: PREVENTION OF WASTE.   This
method demands, (A) deliberate, persistent watchfulness repressing all *unnecessary physical action* or
movements.   The rule is now, patient and confident practice in detecting such movements and in
repressing them whenever discovered.   The goal
is not merely the elimination of those spontaneous
actions listed as undue winking, twitching, jerking,
swinging, snuffing, shrugging, kicking, and so on
(which wastes, however, *are* distinctly to be suppressed), but also the most economical use of
muscles and organs—eyes, ears, vocal organs,
hands, feet, for any given purpose.   If you learn
to maintain in conscious thought for a time these
talismanic ideas,—" *Economy of Action* "— " *Precision* "—" *Effectiveness*,"—your subconsciousness will
ultimately act habitually on the suggestions given.

The method also demands, (B) *economy in the
mental life*.   We all find ourselves frequently

working mentally in a perfectly useless way. When this discovery is made, we should bring the processes "up standing" with the question, "Of what possible value can this mental activity be to me or others?" and we should then direct the "current of thought" into some channel worth while, or, it may be, tone down all mental activity for rest. Patient action of the will-power will accomplish the desired end. Since the self is forever mentally active, the question of energy is one of conservation and direction promising some value to your life. In mental as well as in physical spheres, the words, "*Economy of Action*"—"*Precision*"—"*Effectiveness*,"—are suggestive talismans which will finally educate the subconscious self to maintain rather than waste, and to use rightly rather than at haphazard, the personal energies possessed.

SECOND METHOD: DEVELOPMENT OF THE ENERGY-SENSE. We may indicate this method by quoting from "*Power for Success*":

"Disregarding all that may be going on around you, stand erect, breathe deeply and slowly a few times, and summon a sense of great internal energy. This feeling may be described as follows: Suppose yourself about to undertake some great physical feat. You are ready; you are intensely alert; all your powers are subject to instant command; your feeling of will-power is wrought up to the highest pitch; your entire attitude says, 'I can and I will accomplish this one thing.' In such a case your muscles are probably tensed, but the exercise requires that there be no muscle-tension whatever. So far as the body is concerned, you are inwardly calm and outwardly motionless, but your whole being is charged with the feeling of mental and physical energy. Observing the conditions, repeat a few times mentally, with a sense of intense energy all through the body, the words: 'I can and I will accomplish whatever I undertake.' This method should be practiced now and then daily for a long period."

THIRD METHOD: UNFOLDMENT OF WILL-CONFIDENCE. We have here as it were, the core, the pulsing heart, of physical and mental energy urging economical and directed use to the greatest success made possible by personal endowments. Every man is possessed of will, but the energetic *sense* of will is not, in all, consciously present. One may secure the feeling by asserting in regard to self, "*I will! I am will-power!*" and in regard to any task, "*I am equal to this work! I will myself squarely into it! The thing in hand shall be done, and well done!*" *The assertion should not be left merely to mental areas in the brain, but should be made with intensity until the whole personality seems to be involved and the feeling of willed energy and energetic willing pervades every part of the body.* In time the subconscious self will permanently assume the attitude indicated. Of course the value of relaxation and rest must always be regarded.

Along with the cultivation of such energy-will-sense should go *effort toward the feeling of confidence.* The confidence here suggested is not a merely intellectual belief; it is a profound feeling saturating the entire being. The cultivation of this feeling involves the persistent elimination of doubt and fear, timidity and hesitation, by resolute banishment whenever such enemies "come up in mind," until not a shred remains. The writer knows that this is no light task, but he also knows after a ten years' fight that the thing can be accomplished. This result, however, is only part of the goal. The more important thing is the will-confidence-feeling. You are requested to recall how you felt in some experience when you knew you surely could accomplish a task which you did successfully perform. The Count of Monte Cristo, in the work of fiction of that title, when he had escaped from his island prison, and stood up, drenched and alone on the shore which he had gained by a long swim, lifted his hands to heaven and cried, "The world is mine!" That was the will-confidence-feeling. Such a compound may be acquired. The process of development demands time, and it may not be altogether easy, but if you will act on the suggestions given, you cannot fail to acquire the value.

You should throw into the will-energy thought and feeling—into these—the idea and feeling of confidence—in yourself, in Nature, in people with whom you deal—that whatever you really undertake is bound to go successfully through. In order to this general mood of confidence, you are invited to affirm, frequently every day, for months, "*I have perfect confidence in myself. I am confidence!*" In time the subconscious self will have no contrary thought; it will have acquired what the psychologists call "the set," or the bent—the prevailing mood and way of acting—essential to success.

Thus you educate the deeper self by means of detailed suggestions. This education may now be broadened and at the same time given a particular-general or long-run character by frequently *inform-ing* the subconscious self, "*I am sure to succeed in life! I am even now succeeding! I am success! I am! I am power!*"

§ 36.   The above methods refer especially and ostensibly to the individual within himself.   The final results would be eminently worth the while if they concerned this only—a happier and stronger personality in a business sense.   But the results embrace as well the attitudes and activities of others in relation to yourself and your business. *You cannot acquire the traits and powers indicated without favorably affecting and influencing people all about you.*   Your energy inspires their energy. Your will-power stirs their will-power.   Your confidence begets confidence in them.   You "in-fect" the whole place with the visible evidences of your development.   If an employee, you influence your associates and compel the employer to take notice.   He will.   If an employer, you dynamically *charge* all your people with an all-round success-feeling.

These results come about in ways that are on the surface, so to speak.   But your endeavor to develop will-energy-confidence exerts an "occult" influence as well.   You are a power among men. *Your personal atmosphere* (the sphere of your per-sonality which extends beyond the body and involves surrounding etheric conditions to a varying distance) *reveals psychic force which has the character of move-ments that others will interpret, consciously or uncon-sciously felt, as meaning will, energy, confidence. Your attitude of assured success will induce attractive currents unseen which will* (if you are active, intelligent and persistent) *draw men to you, draw trade your way, influence events through natural laws, and bring to you financial resources which would otherwise go elsewhere.*

§ 37. FOURTH METHOD: PSYCHIC INSPIRATION OF OTHERS. Some people are not susceptible to inspiration to any purpose. When you discover this fact, further effort in their behalf only wastes your own forces. Not often, however, is this discovery made. The majority of those with whom you come in contact can be influenced to energetic activity if you employ the right methods. You must, of course, set the example, for energy cannot make inertia captain. And interest is the inspirer, the director and the maintainer of life. You must awaken the feeling in others that activity and achievement are worth their while. In the meantime, you can carry the thought, about people whom you wish to inspire, that they are charged with energy and are to be practically active in the business. You are yourself poised, controlled, always putting achieved things behind you—without fuss or flurry. They are to do the same. You are confident that they will do likewise—are now doing likewise. (Never mind the facts; stand for the goal. You are employing a method.) You do not merely think the matter, however, as it were, in the upper chambers of your mind; you really *feel* the thought, are *assured* that it is even as you wish, *realize for them* energy as moving in every part of their being. It is not simply a mental thought that you are to carry; it is a psychic inspiration that you are to convey to these people, projecting it to them by

your steady thought and your perfect assurance.
A formula for the process might be as follows:

" *You are charged* (this to the people whom you
wish to inspire) *with energy which you control and
use in the interest of our business.*"

The affirmation should be repeated and felt
wherever you are. If you say no man has time for
all this, you miss the method. I am instructing in
the building of acquired power, which means a
cultivated, habituated *attitude* of your deeper self
in the things in hand, and the present is but a part
of the entire system. You can repeat and feel the
thought just given in italics until you have developed
a psychic habit of feeling precisely that way. When
you have so *affirmed and felt* for a time,—a few days
—the method being referred to thereafter now and
then, you acquire a psychic attitude of such affirmation, such feeling, and you develop an inspirational
expectancy that those whom you wish to influence
will surely respond to the treatment. Kindly observe, too, that many men have been sceptical about
steamers, railways, telephones, wireless telegraphy.
You do not *know* that anything can *not* be done
until you have thoroughly tried that thing in the
right way.

PART IV.
BUSINESS IN FACT.

The machinery of any well-ordered business runs smoothly and true when its proprietor is temporarily absent, but—and here appears the psychic factor—the master mind is not now (during absence of the man) in the concern's atmosphere, and the subconscious movements of the employee mind are instantly diverted. Then the business goes wrong, no matter what the system, until the employee mind catches the master spirit. This is the secret. The master mind's confidence and psychic compulsion, moving from him like a Niagara, drawing toward him like gravitation, coerce those conditions which insure success. I have a case in point. A kingly business man wishes to put aside the burden of his manufacturing plant. The business is perfectly systematized, as I know. Whatever he would do his associates and employees would do were he wholly away. He is compelled to remain, however, until he can train their minds (no less than their hands) into the currents and dynamic action of his own. Then he can go, and the business will not suffer. The supreme factor of success is the psychic compulsion of the confident man—who has practical ability.

CHAPTER XIV.

BUSINESS UNDER DIRECTION.

THE design of the preceding pages has been similar, in a very limited way, to that of a school of direct personal culture for growth of the self and its most effective handling in any department of the business world. Such a school, which I have long desired to see in actual operation, would embrace all ordinary grammar, high school and collegiate work, but would hold steadily in view, from entrance in the grammar school to graduation from college, one fundamental principle:

The human person should be trained to direct or immediate discovery and development of all his organizing powers, by concentrating consciousness, not upon objective tasks alone,—almost the entire methods in present systems,—but as well, and very emphatically, upon the self as possessor of such powers and upon the self-entering use thereof in daily practice, whatever the work in hand; following which discovery and development by consciously purposed use, it should be systematically trained in the most economical and effective handling of self as determined by the life-career to be taken up.

407

The design of Parts I and II and III has merely suggested this broad educational work. If a book can be a school, the present will be so only as the student may succeed in transforming its chapters into as many teachers. The volume has sought to serve such a suggestive purpose, first in its instructions bearing on the general personality of the business man, employed or employer, and secondly, in its brief treatment of the psychic processes involved in business efforts. This instruction has all along been applicable to any line of commercial endeavor. We now enter upon the study of business power as required in the general departments of the business world.

THE WORLD'S BUSINESS DEPARTMENTS.

§ 1. The world of business may roughly be divided as follows:

A. Business Under Direction—
  I. Permanent Employees:
    (1) Common Laborers;
    (2) Skilled Craftsmen;
    (3) Clerks and Office Help;
    (4) Representatives, such as Private Secretaries, Correspondents, Credit Men, Cashiers, Traveling Salesmen, Agents, Managers, Superintendents, Presidents, etc.
  II. Temporary Employees:
    (1) Brokers; professional people, etc.;
    (2) Unskilled Odds-and-Ends People.
B. Independently Conducted Business—
    (1) Canvassers;
    (2) Commission Men;

(3) Agents;
(4) Jobbers;
(5) Brokers;
(6) Real Estate Men;
(7) Advertisers;
(8) Mercantile Agencies;
(9) Merchants;
(10) Publishers;
(11) Manufacturers;
(12) Bankers;
(13) Financial Promoters;
(14) Syndicate Managers.

The foregoing analysis will now be discussed, omitting some phases indicated as sufficiently covered by the general treatment. Always be it understood that we keep within the field of the present book, which concerns only the elements of psychic power in business operation.

(A) Business Under Direction.

This general division, we have seen, is subject to analysis, giving us Permanent Employees, such as common laborers, skilled craftsmen, clerks, office help, secretaries, credit men, cashiers, traveling salesmen, correspondents, solicitors, agents, managers, superintendents, presidents, etc., and various sorts of representatives. The significance of this analysis is covered by the words *discretion* and *personal scope*. As you examine the list from the top to the bottom, you observe that the individual sphere and element of power widen more and more, from the common laborer, who is extremely limited in these respects, to the general manager and superintendent and president, who may almost be regarded as independent business generals. Representatives may also exhibit a similar gradation from immediate control of superiors to very great freedom.

§ 2. *Here, then, is one phase of your goal in the business world—constant enlargement of discretionary powers and personal scope.* The goal should be definitely sought by every one engaged in business enterprises, and should never be thought of as beyond one's personal powers or the possibilities of one's life. *Don't set your limit where you can see it.*

§ 3. There is one only perfect law by which that goal may be reached: *demonstration of greater business value in your present service than is now being realized where you are.* That demonstration involves actual business value as shown in your business hours, but also unimpeachable personal cleanness, integrity and safety outside the business hour or field. Promotions in certain towering financial institutions were made of recent men over those of longer service because the private lives of the fortunate ones endured detective scrutiny, while those of the older service were found engaged in questionable conduct. People in authority who themselves may not be superior to investigation frequently insist, inconsistently, it is to be granted, yet none the less effectively, that those under authority shall be altogether blameless, and the fact certainly reveals business wisdom. They promote, not their own kind, but their betters.

I. PERMANENT EMPLOYEES.

§ 4. *Lifelong employees are comparatively few in number.* Their permanency *may be due to their own lack of ambition and power*, and it is always a factor for consideration that one may rest content in an inferior position when a little daring, with confidence and courage, might break the strengthening bonds of fear and habit, and greatly improve personal conditions. You are therefore urged to adopt for life this simple maxim:

Indispensability to my employer, who is not indispensable to me!

The realization of that maxim means the multiplication of the best self into all your work, together with the preservation by the consciousness that such is indeed the character of your service, of the conviction persistently asserted: "I am not dependent because my value is demonstrable to any man I meet!"

The state of things indicated is exactly true with regard to those whose tenure of position is extendedly *permanent by reason of their established worth.* In such a case business power simply requires that a man should guard against contentment with "a good thing" when, on cautious action, he might secure the better thing and hold it as firmly as he now holds the lesser position. The general rule, hence, for permanent employees is this:

Assume, first, last, and middle, that you are to serve your own highest self-interest as freely and surely as your employer seeks to serve his own interest.

These suggestions may now be applied to the various classes of employees which were enumerated in the first section of this chapter.

(1) THE COMMON LABORER.

§ 5. Where there are no legal or business laws to "keep a man down," one who continues long as a common laborer has only himself to blame—*as a theory.* If such an one chances to read this page, he is urged to think over the following suggestions:

(1) *Intoxicating drink only and always hurts the workman and never does him the least nameable good.* Poor food badly prepared and sloppy table-drinks, with lack of personal grooming, unhealthy conditions of sleeping and recreation, and reckless squandering of the sex-power, these things keep the nervous system in a state of constant craving which drink only satisfies to increase. The remedy is home betterment and physical kingship, suggestions for which may be found in "*Power Of Will*" and "*Power For Success.*" Business power condemns liquor.

(2) *Haste in marriage* has put multitudes of people at the foot of the ladder, insuring the using up of all income from the start, promising debts, and prophesying hapless bondage for life. This paragraph does not question a man's rights; it simply suggests a matter of best policy for the long run. Business power advises: *Get your trade and a bank account first.* Yet—many successful men have married early. It's the will that wins.

(3) *The common laborer should awaken to the fact that he is a human being.* Many a man who is now handling a pick would soon drop the tool if he could make that discovery. It is one thing to class yourself by *name* as a "man," and a most astonishingly better thing to feel, *clean to the centre of the*

soul, that you are actually a MAN. In this case
there is a marvelous *body* to be brought to its best,
there is a human *self* to assert sovereign independence, there is an *emotional nature* to be enlarged
and enriched, there is a wonderful *mind* to be
aroused, stimulated, elevated and trained and used
for betterment. Nobody is a man merely because
he looks like one. You are, therefore, urged highly
to resolve that sooner or later the "pick" shall go
forever out of your life. To the objection, such as
an English author has actually made, that this
advice would deprive the world of its common
laborers, the reply is in order: Let all work be
done by machinery, if needs be; in any event the
world would be all the better for the fact that not
a human being could be *compelled by his need of
food, drink and shelter to engage for hire in common
labor,* provided every soul were developed to a
degree which should make him independent of the
necessity of some particular form of labor in order
to the support of himself and family. *It is not
labor that keeps men down; it is the compulsion of
engaging in labor determined by others which a man
should seek to put out of his life.*

(4) The mere awakening of a common laborer
to such a consciousness of his human selfhood as
will drive him to effort for betterment, should be
followed, however, by exactly three things:

(a) The aroused "man with the hoe" must
multiply himself into his work to his utmost best. I
do not mean that he should work harder or longer,
although an honest day's work is an honor to any
man, but I do mean precisely that all the thought-
power the workman has must go, with *awareness*

*of the fact and of the thing doing, into every task
assigned him.* Everywhere I observe common
laborers who work exactly as horses work—dully,
with no thought, no consciousness of trying to make
the matter in hand fine and true and perfected once
for all. Few seem to "care a rap" whether such
results follow their efforts or not. Many employers
are fools; but many laborers are dead with indifference. The present situation looks like an
equation—fool-heads : indifferent heads.

Let us suppose that the "pick-man" is a lover
and is making a garden for his sweetheart. He
will *do the work finely and truly and to last.* He
will think himself into garden. He will sow that
ground with fidelity and pride. That is the idea.
Its realization need not be sought for the employer's sake, which is not in the least important
in this connection.

The ideal should be sought by the workman
for the workman's own sake, which is a matter of
the greatest importance. For then the employer's
interests are bound to be served, and the laborer
will demonstrate value for greater things, and at
last come to confidence and power to drop the tool
and take charge of the work, and to rise from this
position to still larger scope and utility. I do not
care for power in the employer as such; I care for
power in the *man* whatever his position.

(b) With all this must go that almost greatest of
our human traits, *alertness.* Alertness has extended
treatment in "*Power For Success,*" and can at this
point only be indicated. The quality involves the
open eye for better employment, but that is really
subordinate to the further factor, a live mind intent

on being serviceable in every way and on finding improvements in present methods and ordinary results. It is treason against self for a man who sees better methods and results in ditch-digging or ploughing to dully acquiese and say: "It's none of my business." *It is the business of any man, doing anything, to do it, or suggest its doing, better than it is now being done,* if possible.

(c) If now, the common laborer shall put behind multiplication of best self into every piece of work, and alertness for improvement not only in work, but also in opportunity to get on, *persistent will-power and faith in self and destiny,* asserting in his soul daily, "*I can and I will rise above my present position,*" he will have acquired inevitable power sooner or later to realize his ambition. Here is a treatment from deepest chambers of our nature. A purposeful soul says: "*I resolve to win success! I am power! I am the king!*" In time that declaration is in the air, blows with the wind, shines in star and sun, sings with rivers and seas, whispers in dreams of sleep and trumpets through all the hurlyburly of day. Eventually the thought becomes a feeling of success saturating consciousness. The man now *knows* the outcome, because all the prophesies of his life have one reading. He has begotten the instinct of victory.

It seems true that the above suggestions may loom rather high as regards the ordinary common laborer. You are invited to observe that the wages you pay your people do not exhaust your opportunities in relation to them. The business man who does not seek to induce self-help in all his employees for better things than they are now receiving

misses his greatest success.   If you fancy that
money is the gauge of achievement, you are behind
even Protagorus who said more than twenty-five
hundred years ago, "Man is the measure of all
things."

(2) THE SKILLED CRAFTSMAN.

§ 5.   Skilled labor of all varieties is a very
marked exhibition of one phase of natural evolution.
The world of Nature acts like a living person.   In
the great play of its laws we have the deeper action
of what may be called the Subconscious Mind of
the Universe, and in the play of the forces of
crystallization among minerals, indicating powers
of repair and readjustment, and of the life-forces
or bio-chemistry of the lowest plant and animal
organisms, together with general animal instinct,
we have the *primary evident movements of Nature's
subconscious mentality*.   The vast apparent operations of her organisms are also comparable to the
human objective or directly conscious mind in
man.   In the long history of these huge phases of
the living world's mentality, two perennial factors
have appeared: *the tendency to habit, or fixation of
operations and methods, and the tendency to variation
in operations and methods.*

§ 6.   *Now, man, as a product of evolution, has
exhibited precisely the same tendencies—toward habit
and toward initiative.*   In him also we see the
settlements of habit in the subconscious mind
backgrounded by the action of the great laws of
his being, and we see the working of free or varying initiative to use habit, to break up habit, and
forever to acquire new habits.   As in Nature the

more apparent Objective Universal Mind emerges from the deeper realm of crystallization, biochemistry, primary life, and instinct, so in man the whole objective existence comes up from and out of the very deeps of his conscious self.

§ 7. *Nature is everlastingly restless*, and this restlessness, always persisting until a habit of some kind is formed, and often increasingly active in breaking up that habit and establishing new operations,—this it is that has brought the world of Nature from slime-ooze to man. How many skilled trades the living earth has learned, and unlearned, and forgotten!

§ 8. We have in this long law the further backlying law of skilled craftsmanship among men! Man is the most restless thing in the world. As Professor Josiah Royce has written: "Certainly a general view of the place which beings with minds occupy in the physical world strongly suggests that their organisms may especially have significance as places for the initiation of more or less novel types of activity." *Every variety of skilled work had its origin in this restless initiative for new and better ways of doing things.* Every variety is also a demonstration that life's surroundings need not necessarily determine its unfoldings. "The most important consequence of this vague struggle for something more will be that opportunities will be given to the organism to acquire adaptations which it never could acquire unless this predisposition to endless experiment and to the trying of various relations with the environment were present."

The "endless experiment" is tireless perseverance, and our "power to learn decidedly new variations of our habits will usually depend upon the presence of this perseverance.''

§ 9. ''What a man can do, depends upon what he can observe, upon what he can feel, and upon what he can learn as his instincts are trained. And when thus regarded a man seems to be the creature of his environment. *But there is one thing that his environment cannot determine. That one thing is the power of the organism to persist in seeking new adjustments, whether the environment at first suggests them or not, to persist in struggling toward its wholly unknown goal, whether there is any opportunity for reaching such a goal or not.* Such persistence is the one initiative that the organism can offer to the world.''

§ 10. From this little study emerge *two facts in the skilled laborer's life*—himself being, as all skilled workmen are, an exhibition of human nature's restless initiative and the fixation of acquired habits, both in the conscious and in the unconscious phases of mind, together with an incessant tendency toward variation in new acquirements. The two facts are as follows:

(*a*) *His success depends upon the intelligent direction, by himself, of his native restlessness into new, because better, achievements, and the* (*b*) *settlement, in the unconscious mind particularly which originates such restlessness, of skilled habits and skilled powers.*

§ 11. As a skilled workman, therefore, you are urged to *maintain the free action of your entire self* by thought, invention and initiative, *never settling down* to contentment in the mere routine of even skilled labor, and you are so urged because the *latter is your deadliest enemy*, while the *former is your greatest guaranty of success.* "The restless men may prove to be failures, but the most successful of human beings are the men who are in some respects prodigiously restless."

§ 12. But it should be remembered that the restlessness here referred to and commended is not that which drives one from place to place, rendering the man incapable of concentration upon any given thing, but is a spirit which, holding steadily to the thing in hand, yet turns incessantly in anticipative thought to something different and better than that which is now in vogue.

§ 13. On this idea of the subconscious restlessness of human nature may now be based certain practical suggestions, as follows:

(1) We are not to suppose that the restless efforts toward new things pertain even largely to the outward man alone. *It is the inner self that ever seeks the new and the improved*, and particularly is it that phase of self of which we are altogether unconscious—at least directly. *This unconscious restlessness needs, now, repeated suggestions from the conscious self to give it direction and purpose.* The outcome will be a certain habituated tendency of the restlessness making for some definite goal: improvement in general in one's life, or in one's manner of working, or in tools and machinery, or in opportunities for advancement, and so on. A suggestive talismanic sentence would be, say, *"Alert for the new and the better in (self)—(place)—(work)—(implements)—(relations)—(products)—(personal uplift)—I am surely coming to a greater working value and a larger financial recognition."* This sentence may be divided into as many régimes as

there are words in the parenthesis, each being inserted, the others omitted, and each sentence,
containing the chosen word only, being held in
mind for a number of days, the sentence with a
different word being then employed for a second
period, and so on until each word has been inserted.
The purpose is simply the education of the subconscious self.

(2) If we remember that the skill of the
artisan is greatly due to the acquired or developed
power and the action of the subconscious self, we
shall see the value of cultivating and maintaining
a *feeling* of *nice* and *confident* skill while engaged in
work. The idea is a *sense in consciousness* of *nicety*,
delicacy, *perfection*, in every member of the body
used at any time. This gives harmony between
the conscious and the unconscious elements which
is needful to the best work. One man is the "bull
in the china closet:" another is deftness itself. As
a matter of fact, the most skilful persons possess
this consciousness without being particularly aware
of it. It is nevertheless a part of the soul's feeling.

(3) The objective thought, however, is not
wanting in the work of trades and crafts. The
best results demand a man's best conscious powers
on the matter in hand. You are urged to multiply
yourself into what you do. But in doing a thing
skilfully, having the skilled *feeling* developed, you
really depend on the acquired habits and ability
which previous thought has "bedded down" in the
subconscious self. You should, therefore, *remember that the trained subconscious self may be trusted.*
Oftentimes, when your objective thinking becomes
overanxious or "flurried," you confuse your own

skill. Some things which we do perfectly without conscious effort, we immediately "muss up" if we try carefully to attend to all details of them. When you think about your "four-in-hand" tie, you very likely go wrong with it. If the foreman stands over you and you are especially careful to do a piece of work particularly well, your conscious efforts interfere with the free action of subconscious skill. "The skill that depends upon knack," as Jastrow remarks in "*The Subconscious,*" "that enables us to do but not to tell how we do,—the billiard player depending upon his general impressions and feelings rather than upon calculation in striking the ball,—these in turn represent the greater reliance upon subconscious training."

(4) It is well, therefore, *now and then to take attention away from the matter in hand, and to give the subconscious and conscious "minds" opportunity for readjustment.* I recently remarked to a department manager in a large factory in which I had set up a printing outfit, as I had just composed a title-page and wished his criticism, "Sometimes I look at a thing so much that I fail rightly to see it." He said: "We have machines for distributing carbon on tissue paper for typewriter duplicating, and the man who 'tends' the operation comes gradually at times to allow too much carbon to distribute over the paper. The moment our inspector puts his eyes on the work, he perceives the excess." In the first case, the conscious self of the operator slowly deceives the subconscious self— or is not sufficiently alert to catch the warnings of the subconscious mentality—and the carbon is allowed gradually to increase. In the latter case,

the subconscious, having been engaged in other
matters, is under no impressions given it by the
conscious, and the excess is instantly detected.
The skilled workman should, therefore, occasionally
turn the objective consciousness elsewhere for a
brief time, that harmony with the subconscious
may be established. He then will return to his
work fresh and true.

(5) *A skilled workman should seldom push himself beyond his normal "pace," and should never work
in a "flurried" or excited condition*, since in either
case he is disturbing subconscious poise and is thus
throwing both "minds" out of adjustment. When
hurry and flurry emerge, you are advised to drop
the work for a little time, attend to other matters,
get yourself "in hand." On return of the normal
skilled feeling, your work will move skilfully and
smoothly.

§ 14. The above paragraphs have in view the
workman's value. If the elements of rapidity and
certainty of best results, pride in the work, and
loyalty to the concern, with magnetic adjustment
to every man in the place, are added, business
power will surely, in the long run, estimate the
man rightly. I know very well that selfishness
makes exceptions to this statement. That ruthless,
brutal disregard for others which characterizes
some would-be business men, however, by its own
nature is rendered hopeless so far as these suggestions are concerned, and must be dismissed with
the remark that it is not business at all. Such
people are thugs; they are not business men. And
it must be remembered that in the business world
the question always and necessarily is: "How

much is the man worth as a workman?" That
question can only be answered by controlled, effective skill itself.

§ 15. The design of these pages is not to
instruct skilled workmen in their own trades; it is
rather to suggest some of the laws of the psychic
self which are involved in development and use of
the craftsman's abilities. If a man knows his skill
and value, he needs merely ambition to suggest independent work for himself. Such knowledge and
ambition should be backed by courage and determination to quit the ranks of employees and join
those of men who by the same abilities have left
the shop for superintendency or proprietorship in
the office.

§ 16. The preceding considerations ought to
prove suggestive to the *employer*. If he employs
skilled workmen, he should place his people under
the very best psychic conditions. There is, perhaps, not a shop or factory in the world where the
subconscious self of skilled laborers might not be
made more effective by greater cleanness, system,
attractiveness and a general "atmosphere" conducive to the skilled feeling indicated in section
thirteen above. The suggestion has a monetary
value.

(3) OFFICE HELP AND CLERKS.

§ 17. If you stand behind a counter or sit at
an office desk, all the essential factors referred to
under the preceding heading are immensely important in your business life, and should be studied,
absorbed and observed, especially the suggestions
relating to the unconscious self.

§ 18. The positions now considered demand
nerve-poise and inner peace and self-control. Such
conditions may be secured by entering upon a course
of self-instruction by means of auto-suggestions,
like the following:

"*All quiet within!   All good influences of the
world are flowing into my soul!   I am master and
serene, friendly and tactful, with every human.   I
am sure power!   I am success!*"

You are urged to cultivate the spirit and assumption thus indicated and, in order thereto, to repeat
the substance of the above formula while engaged
at breakfast, just before going to sleep at night, and
now and then during the work of the day.

§ 19.   You are invited to take up the study of
"*Power For Success*" for the cultivation of the magnetic will, alertness, fidelity, the tone-power of
honor, hopefulness, courage, confidence, brain-
power, and intelligent faith, which is a resistless
demand on the magnetism of the nature of things.
The reader undoubtedly will assume that references
in this book are attempts to sell the former.   That
is true.   Nevertheless, you are absolutely assured
that the study of "*Power For Success*," if resolutely
carried on, will prove of more value in the development of practical success-qualities than the study
of any other work known to the author except the
present, and, of course, technical text-books—and
not excepting these within the exact lines of direct
culture in handling self for down-on-the-ground
affairs.   The qualities named in the above reference are indispensable to the greatest efficiency
in your position.   It is your work to sell goods or
to conduct office details.   These qualities will ac-

complish the matters in hand in your business places.

§ 20. The positions before us, especially the position of the clerk, are more or less in touch with the public. You are, therefore, invited to multiply yourself for an indefinite period into the following régimes:

(1) RÉGIME OF THE HAND OF POWER. You should study, and master, and apply the suggestions of the Hand of Power, given in Section 18, Chapter IV.

(2) RÉGIME OF THE SYMMETRICAL WILL. You should embrace every opportunity for developing a great and symmetrical will (see Chapter IV, Sections 12 to 18).

(3) RÉGIME OF MAGNETIC PERSONALITY. You should make a part of your character the elements of the attractive personality (see Chaper III, heading, "Magnetic Characteristics," and Chapter VI, heading, "Personal Requirements in Detail ").

(4) RÉGIME OF OPPOSING TRAITS. You are invited to examine the traits given below and to compare yourself therewith.

(On which side of the line will you stand?)

Clerks out of Favor.	*Clerks in Demand.*
Indifferent.	Eager.
Careless.	Thoughtful.
Unbending.	Gracious.
Cold in manner.	Agreeable.
Inattentive.	Observant.
Slovenly (work or dress).	Punctillious.
Slow.	Alert.
Indolent.	Industrious.

Sarcastic.	Respectful.
Impertinent.	Courteous.
Forgetful.	Recollective.
Blundering.	Careful.
Inaccurate.	Accurate.
Procrastinating.	Punctual.
Wrangling.	Harmonious.
Critical.	Fair-minded.
Crafty.	Straightforward
Unreliable.	Trustworthy.
Impatient.	Self-controlled.
Weak-willed.	Persistent.
Dishonest.	Honest.
Truthful.	Veracious.
Moody.	Even-tempered.
Morose.	Sunny.
Pessimistic.	Hopeful.
Slighting.	Thorough.

(5) RÉGIME OF THE LONG-RUN GOAL. In pursuing the qualities of the clerk in demand, remember: to permit no present gratification to jeopardize the long-run goal—goods sold, promotion secured. A single fault tells compounding against many virtues.

"A vain woman may be very anxious to win A., the magnificent, as a partner for life ("*The Parisians*," Lytton), and yet feel a certain triumph when a glance of her eye has made an evening's conquest of the pitiful B., although by that achievement she incurs the imminent hazard of losing A. altogether."

(6) RÉGIME OF LIVING ILLUSTRATIONS. You are invited to reverse, both in imagination and in conduct, the following illustrations, taken from actual observation:

Illustration Number One (Reverse): Diner: "I wish broiled mackerel, green peas, baked potatoes, hot biscuits, and coffee." Waitress, expressionless, voiceless, doughy, starts away. "And bring a dish of sliced cucumbers, please." No response. Part of the order is served; no cucumbers. Diner waits. Catches eye of waitress, now busy elsewhere, who finally approaches with a dead stare. "I will have cucumbers, please." Waitress, utterly indifferent, a little impertinent: "*I* am waiting for them."

Illustration Number Two (Reverse): Customer enters shoe-store. Two clerks conversing with friends; topic personal. Customer stands waiting, in plain sight. Neither clerk approaches. A long minute passes, in which one might decide on securities for the loan of a million. Customer turns toward the door. Both clerks hasten to his side. "What, so soon?" "But we were busy—engaged." "*Both* of you? Good morning." Within a block there are a dozen shoe-shops.

Illustration Number Three (Reverse): Man with poor eyes to oculist: "Why, I can't see so well with the new glasses as without any. I should have to look over the rims in order to see clearly." Oculist: "Can't very well make a glass-front for your face." Customer: "You may omit that, Sir; weather's too hot." Oculist indignant. But why?

Illustration Number Four (Reverse): Book-buyer: "Have you any work on salesmanship? Or business conduct? Anything of that general character?" Clerk, without stirring, coldly: "No." "But yours is a large stock; won't you look about?" Clerk: "Nothing of the kind," turning his back.

Customer edges away and begins a furtive search.
"Ah, 'Elements of Financial Success!' That's
something like." Calls clerk: "Here, perhaps, is
just the thing." Clerk, glaring: "You said,
'salesmanship.'" "Ah, well; I presume your
neighbor has it." Clerk frowns, then yawns.

Illustration Number Five (Reverse): Lady, in
apartment store, to "floorwalker:" "Where is
your stationery, please?" "Second floor." Manager hurries away. Lady, to clerk: "Let me see
that paper, please," pointing toward sample in
case. Clerk: "That is very expensive." "Yes;
but I will look at it, if you don't mind. What is
the price?" "Two dollars a box," coldly. "Oh!
It *is* expensive. Let me look at this," indicating.
Clerk: "I thought so; that is twenty-five cents."
Lady bites her lips and departs to another store.
Clerk sneers, turning to associates: "Wonder what
she did want!" Clerk's salary is six dollars a week.
The customer edits a magazine.

The life of a clerk or an office help is a trial, to
be sure, but the reverse of the above illustrations indicates the *easiest way through difficulties and the
surest method for securing promotion.* The public is
not without faults; nevertheless, you have to deal
with it precisely as it is. If you drive it away,
your wages go with it.

7. RÉGIME OF THE GOLDEN DYNAMICS. In
opposition to the conduct illustrated in the preceding paragraphs, you are now invited to commit to
memory and to carry out in practical affairs the
Golden Dynamics of successful employment:

"*Intent on the interests of my employer, and so,
on my own, I here and now, by every external act,*

win this customer to my personal liking for myself, and thus for the establishment; and I am resolutely willing, from my personality to him or her, an over-powering desire immediately to purchase these goods, because the goods and the prices are right."

§ 21. But now, *your work means much to your-self.* These pages have in mind the success of the employee; and, therefore, if you have achieved a measure of business power, which gives you value to your employer, stand resolutely, but with a wisdom that knows where it is coming out, for your own interests. Other people rise: why not you? Only, a clerk or office help who would get on in the world must base his courage on absolute worth, and must control his ambition by the possi-bilities of the situation. These factors, worth and understanding of conditions, being assumed, *you are urged to ask for what in clear reason you ought to have.*

"Ask, my dear sir! Look! There is young Hexarchy with six years' service and half your talents. He asked for what he wanted, and he got it. There's McArthurson who has come to his present position by asking—sheer, downright ask-ing. Call it cheek, call it insolence, call it anything you like, but ask! A weak man doesn't say: 'Give me this or that.' He whines: 'Why haven't I been given this or that?' Do something. You have thrice the wit and three times the presence of the men up there, and—and in any way you look at it, you ought to."

(4) THE CORRESPONDENT.

The correspondent may be a special business

representative, in which case his functions are sufficiently treated under other heads to follow. But any representative must share in the correspondent's duties and personal scope, and for that reason specific suggestions are in order under the caption given.

"'Practical fermin!' Certie, he shall hae that, or my name 's no' James Gregg! ("*The Stickit Minister*"). Whereupon, in five minutes, the delicate-handed Peter found himself on the top of a cart with a fork in his hand, taking his first lesson in practical farming by learning how to apply to the soil natural fertilizers necessary for next year's crop. He had two days of that, when he resigned and went home, having decided that after all scientific farming was more in his line."

§ 22. Nevertheless, *the business world knows the value of the scientific and the theoretical.* The correspondent may be manager, broker, agent, solicitor, yet profit by scientific power in practical affairs. As the instrument of trade manipulation he may well grant large attention to the following factors:

A. THE DETAILS OF WRITING. (1) The correspondent must *know precisely what he has to say.* The method for acquiring this value consists in thinking the matter through in actual words until you *know you know* the thing in hand.

(2) The matter set forth should be *clear*— separated from non-essentials—and *definite*—all its details distinctly indicated. Only persistent practice can accomplish these results.

(3) *Words and phrases exactly to the point* are imperatively demanded in business writing. The

study of one's dictionary and the best business language is therefore indicated as your method.

(4) Business correspondence *excuses no errors, misunderstandings, misconstructions, or false applications.* The goal of good correspondence is not what any person of ordinary sense should understand, but what *any average mind is simply bound to take correctly.* This value requires constant and careful attention to precisely the one way in which to make a proposition.

(5) The general statement should be *boiled down to the limit* set by all other requirements, yet it should clearly and precisely state the thing in hand, and be given considerable scope for magnetic handling where the aim is to influence the reader. If you practice maintaining the attitude of face to face magnetism and the inner psychic feeling, as you write, that your man is surely to come round your way, you will find that the exercise and the subconscious operations of mind are giving your correspondence the quality desired.

(6) The *particular statements should be precise, yet compel understanding.* This requirement looks to details, which may be overlooked in the feeling that the general matter is clear and magnetic.

(7) Correspondence *conveys information, or argument, or both. The first should be complete; the second, convincing.* The acquiring method consists in doing the thing sought, but in doing it with the idea always present, now of giving information which would satisfy an inquiring person entirely ignorant of the subject, now of convincing the other man through his own way of looking at things and his own interest.

(8)   But the *main object is often inspiration*, so
that the person to whom you are writing will decide your way or for your principal's interests, yet
suppose that his decision runs to his own welfare
especially.   You are then bound to impel the other
man to do as you desire. *To this end you have to
adapt your style and matter to his capacity and make-
up*.   Your inclinations, preferences, beliefs, impulses, and so on, are all "beside the point," and of
no consequence if they interfere with the goal.   You
should "put yourself in his shoes;" think inside
his skull; see with his eyes; talk to his level; fit in
with his moods;—without disclosure of the effort,
and for your own profit, not merely for his pleasure.
If honesty interferes with this method, sacrifice
the method.

(9)   *Observe:* There is a true distinction in
business between the attitudes—"I wish to sell
or influence," and, "He wants to buy or yield."
The "I wish to sell" may be taken for granted,
and should not be emphasized. The "He wants
to buy—to do my will" must be incessantly suggested without revealing the fact that you are
deliberately inspiring such inclinations.   Aside
from the necessary externals of correspondence
looking to that end, this suggestion may be given
by concentrating your whole thought-will-power
upon his deepening desire, which may be assisted
by the mental affirmation, "*The man surely desires
the thing I will.*"   And in the externals—the writing—appeal must always be made to the other
man's evident advantage.

(10)   As a magnetic element in inspirational
writing, the correspondent should study the

qualities of and the proper occasions for *pure diplomacy*. Honorable courtesy is not hostile to certain pleasing "personalities" to which even business men are open—if tactfully, naturally, masterfully, but unostentatiously, applied. The method for this procedure consists in acquiring the habit of pleasing address and using agreeable personal references.

"What do they say of me in the Departments through which you have passed?" asked Napoleon. "Sire," replied M. de Narbonne, "some say you are a god, others say you are a devil; but all are agreed that you are more than a man."

That was diplomatic. Napoleon knew that he was called a god and a devil, but "more than a man" smothered impossibility and drew the sting.

(11) Of course the correspondent must write *legibly*, *correctly* (in form and in language), and his *printing and materials* should be always *first-class*. This requirement is imperative. Fine tools inspire fine work—in the kind of people these pages have in mind—and they indicate a reputable prosperity.

(12) In business correspondence, *business only* should appear.

(13) Above all, the correspondent must reasonably *know himself* and his limitations, and maintain unvarying courtesy and self-control. *Never give any man in writing a handle for ill-will or business advantage over you.* Speech passes; but ink holds over till doomsday.

§ 23. B. THE PRINCIPAL. The correspondent's business again illustrates the matter of personal relations. He has to do with his principal, and his skill pushes the latter's interests to the utmost,—as in the following:

(1) For the most part the essentials of business writing apply in correspondence with the home office, but they are modified by the relation of employee and employer, and largely limit to explicit business information.

(2) This correspondence, moreover, should *avoid prolixity* and undue frequency.

(3) The successful correspondent *reserves no secrets* from his principal.

(4) He *obeys orders* absolutely and undeviatingly, except where utter common sense declares that the principal would order otherwise if clearly informed—and the matter is then a taking chances with good fortune. If the correspondent demonstrates reliability, his scope of emergency-freedom will naturally be conceded as larger than that of a day laborer.   ·

(5) He *reveals no secrets* to clients or patrons which would jeopardize the principal's interests.

(6) *When he is in doubt* as to orders or interests, *he does nothing*, unless certain that his judgment will be approved, whatever the outcome.

(7) In all his attitude toward the principal he is *master of himself*, invariably courteous and respectful, yet agreeable in all sincerity with the man whose values he handles.

(8) And *with the interest* of that man he is *perfectly identified.*

§ 24. C. THE BUSINESS TRANSACTION. In the practical transaction as between principal and correspondent, certain demands are imperious:

(1) The correspondent must *thoroughly under-*

stand his own business, and every other line intimately connected therewith.

(2) His *principal* should be to him an *open book*.

(3) He must *know human nature* in order to commercial adaptation and adjustment.

(4) The double task of *adjustment to principal and clients* or patrons he must certainly master.

(5) And he must, in some way, *bring clients and principal together* on a business basis and in harmony with exchange of values.

(6) It is evident that he therefore needs great will-power, sleuth-hound persistence, energy, alertness, resourcefulness, courage, decision, promptness, bull-dog determination, confidence, and sometimes magnetic daring, and that he must slay all fears, worry, moodiness, regret, and acquire the ability to profit by experience, laugh at rebuffs and defeats, and build wisely on mistakes.

These factors can be secured by experience studied with watchful thoughtfulness.

(7) Perhaps nothing is more important in business correspondence than *system*. This is suggested in various material contrivances, but the greatest values spring from a systematic mind schooled in regulated thought and activity.

(8) In many forms of correspondence, the *persistent follow-up* is an absolute necessity. The chief difficulty here is the phrasing and timing of the follow-up itself. Back of brains in the matter should go the psychic "pulsation" of the idea of "advantage to the other man if he yields."

"My success is due chiefly to my system," said one. "I simply work hard and systematically. I keep right on writing, whether I get any answers

or not.   I never let up as long as there is a possibility of closing a deal."

§ 25.   These suggestions invite much more
than a cursory reading.   They may be approved,
to be sure, but they call also for resolute work on
the part of the true student.   *The will that sets itself to the mastery of each detail will embed them all
solidly in the subconscious mind as perpetual moni-
tors.*   In the end the driving power of your life
will become surprisingly great.   You are, therefore,
invited to make the present pages permanent
régimes, first for study and review daily, and,
secondly, for practical application to your business
as a correspondent.

§ 26.   The preceding sections may seem to
involve labor for a life-time.   Yes, and no.   The
instructions ought to be used throughout your
entire business career, but this does not signify
that you are to become a slave to any book.   *If
you will utilize the time spent on trolleys and
trains, and the like, in absorbing present values, you
will within a year be able to make them all practically your own outfit.*   Said one business man to the
writer: "I have taken up the study of Spanish on
trains and I read no Spanish anywhere else.   Two
weeks were enough for the Grammar,—essential
principles,—and now I have started in to read '*Dona
Perfecta,*' by Galdos, the greatest and the most
difficult of Spain's fiction-writers."   I said to him:
"Why do you tackle the most difficult work first?"
"That's just it," he replied.   "I get at once a large
vocabulary and the living idioms."

This is an example of the quality that succeeds.
By the use of your traveling time, perhaps, you

can surcharge your subconscious mind with the suggestions of this book and make its principles second nature.

The sections which follow under the next heading are now referred to as parts of the present study for correspondents.

(5) ALL REPRESENTATIVES.

The student of the paragraphs given below is invited to incorporate the preceding suggestions as involved in the work immediately before us.

§ 27. The class of positions here treated embraces *all permanent representatives in business*, such as managers, superintendents, presidents, department heads, correspondents, agents, and so on, the scope of the business being in general that of management of an entire business, a branch, an agency or a section.

§ 28. Speaking generally, representatives may be divided into *two classes:* those having *full discretionary power* and standing practically "in the shoes of the head" or owners; those whose conduct of the business is considerably *limited by a policy of general and special orders*. The first class are frequently in positions where the arts of diplomacy are indispensable as regards the public with which they deal, a diplomacy sometimes great and astute enough to resemble that obtaining in national affairs. They therefore require the qualities of broadmindedness, self-mastery, large outlook, magnetism, insight, financial and prophetic vision, reticence, courage, prompt decision, persistent but unobtrusive energy, firmness and ability to inspire confidence, together with every characteristic

named below. The list looks formidable; yet there
are thousands of men who manifest all of it in their
business cónduct.   Men are simply compelled to
the possessions.   As an aspirant for such responsibility, you are urged to enter upon a long régime
for the development of these essential factors.   It
would require a volume to furnish detail suggestions in so large a field, but it is believed that the
following will be found helpful:

§ 29. *Assumption! Assertion! Practice!* "*I
assume . . .* (say, broadmindedness, and, again,
. . . each trait inserted, one for one day, a
second for the next, and so on) *to be a real and
growing characteristic of my own personality!*"

§ 30. *Assumption! Assertion! Practice!* "*In
all my feelings and mental attitudes I assert this
quality* (following the above order) *for all my business life: quietly, without airs, but with unfaltering
determination and the utmost confidence.*"

§ 31. *Assumption! Assertion! Practice!* The
assumption and assertion should always be *accompanied by corresponding practical conduct* in every
possible way.   You have thus entered an educational method which is infallible for large results,
depending, of course, upon native endowments.

§ 32.   Both widely discretionary representatives and those of more limited powers must be
*constantly alert in three directions: toward their
superiors, toward those whose business action or labor
they must control, and toward the public*—often in a
fourth direction, *toward their associates.*   This fact
of three or four relationships demands that representatives shall cultivate ability in various very
definite and important ways.   As one striving for

such possible position, you are therefore invited to study and practise in your business life for the purpose of "making good" in each of the following factors:

CERTAIN GENERAL LAWS FOR REPRESENTATIVES:

(1) The representative's success, whether he be "floor-walker" or branch-manager, simply must be personally attractive to his "head" or the controllers of the business and every person above and in contact with him. The surest method for becoming so consists in the utter extinction of every contrary thought and feeling, and the cultivation of the art and power of personal magnetism. *This is the Law of First Magnetic Adjustment.*

(2) The representative must scrupulously carry out the policy of the concern, or the department or branch of which he is head. *This is the Law of Self-Interest Fidelity.*

(3) The representative must make himself equally attractive to all associates, which is *the Law of Second Magnetic Adjustment,* and to all persons below him, *the Law of Third Magnetic Adjustment.*

(4) The representative must win the public to the business and himself personally—unless the policy of the concern forbids the latter. *This is the Two-Fold Universal Law of Magnetic Adjustment.*

(5) The representative must be possessed of executive ability and hard-headed practicality, for he must secure increasingly large results. *This is the Law of Initiative Power.*

(6) The representative must be able to push his business and his people by sheer inspiration (not

mere driving) of energy, confidence and magnetic
power, without endangering the business or alienat-
ing or overcrowding the employees. *This is the
Law of Inspirational Driving Power*.

(7) The representative must reduce his business to such running order that he can inventory
the establishment, the branch, the department,
within thirty minutes, and may know that all
departments are working like a great machine with
the least possible friction and the smallest degree
of immediate personal supervision. *This is the
Law of Subjective Business Automatics*.

(8) The representative must be in direct or
indirect contact with every person, machine and
department of the business, from top to bottom—
not personally, but by system and through sub-
ordinates. *This is the Law of Organized Omnipresence*.

(9) The representative must be able daily to
offset reports against reports in order to detect
errors, malfeasance, or deception. *This is the Law
of Counter-Revelation*. The failure of a bank or a
trust company through the criminality of any of its
superior officers is a perfectly needless crime, in
itself, against business power.

(10) The representative must eliminate business leakage, prevent unnecessary waste and
utilize unavoidable waste, so far as possible, reduce
expenses when consistent with business progress,
increase the scope of the enterprise and multiply
financial returns. *This is the Law of Developing
Management*.

(11) The representative must know the business completely, its relations with other businesses

needful to it, and he must seek to make it first among its kind. *This is the Law of Financial Comprehension.*

(12) The representative, therefore, must know markets, materials, supply and demand, prices, money, competitors, outputs, future probabilities. *This is the Law of Large Financial Detail.*

(13) The representative must embody the great psychic qualities indicated in the chapters devoted to Initiative, Business Mentality, Commercial Memory, Practical Imagination, the Energy of Success, Practical Ability and the Hand of Power. *This is the Law of Psychic Mastery.*

It is believed that the persistent study and practice of the suggestions of this book will actually develop, according to original endowments, the qualities indicated by these great laws. .

What principals, representatives and employees may accomplish when working in harmony and under inspiration, is illustrated by Alexander Dumas' remarkable piece of fiction, "*The Three Guardsmen*," in the unity and the feats of Athos, Porthos, Aramis and D'Artagnan: "In fact, four such men as they—so devoted to each other, with their purses or their lives; so ready to support each other without surrendering an inch; executing, either singly or together, the resolution they had formed in concert; menacing the four cardinal points at one time, or concentrating their united efforts on one common focus—ought inevitably, either secretly or openly, either by mine or by trench, by stratagem or force, to find a way to what they had in view, however well-defended or however distant it might be. The only thing that

surprised D'Artagnan was, that this capacity had
never yet occurred to his companions.   He himself
had thought of it seriously, racking his brain to
find a direction for his individual power four
times multiplied, with which he felt assured that
he might, as with the lever which Archimedes
sought, succeed in moving the world."   When you
think of it, that is exactly the power of "high
finance."

In the financial world the dream of D'Artagnan
was realized when the Carnegie Steel Company
went into the United States Steel Corporation.
"Mr. Carnegie," said "*The Iron Age*," "has
carried the American iron trade with him.   He has
been the unswerving advocate and his plants the
most shining examples of the policy of running to
full capacity.   He has been the man above all
others who created and fostered the ambition of
record-breaking.   He has more than any other
producer spent money lavishly in equipping his
plants with the very latest appliances, who has
invested money most promptly in enlargements.
He has set a pace in the iron trade of this country
which all have been forced to follow."   And so, as
Edward Sherwood Meade remarks in "*Trust
Finance*," "The management of the Carnegie
Company represented the acme of productive efficiency.   Every officer had risen from the ranks by
dint of compelling merit.   Every head of a department had an interest in the business apart from
his salary.   The workmen had been spurred on by
high wages and the promise of advancement.   No
visitor to the Carnegie Mills could fail to be impressed with the intensity of the effort and the

strained attention evident in every department. Not only was money lavishly spent on salaries and wages, but large sums were paid for information." In the Carnegie-Frick controversy it was claimed that the total profits of the company for 1898-'99 exceeded $70,000,000. When the right hour appeared, the steel trusts did what D'Artagnan desired for his companions in arms—they combined with the Carnegie Company. "The United States Steel Corporation was backed by the strongest financial houses in the United States. It included the Carnegie Company, the strongest steel company in the world, it completely realized the ideal of independence for which all the merging companies had been striving; it exorcised the forbidding spector of competition."

Here, then, we see, right or wrong, the law of harmony, in which all the laws above given are exemplified. Such huge affairs instruct us.

(14) D'Artagnan and his companions represented a quality which Carnegie inspired in his partners—Loyalty. The French soldiers exhibited not only fidelity in its ordinary meaning, but loyalty in its highest sense, which is the intended significance of "fidelity" in this book and in "*Power For Success*," in which this dynamic power is fully discussed. It may seem that fidelity is merely cold devotion to duty; loyalty (fidelity in the highest meaning) is whole-hearted devotion to person, business or cause. It is not enough to serve your principal up to the limit as legally defined. Success demands love for the work, the concern's interest—blooded interest in the onward march of the enterprise in which you are engaged.

And it is *your* success that so demands. This is true personal loyalty.

Some representatives fail because they think only of dollars. Dollars have never yet called forth the best in any man. D'Artagnan was loyal to his sovereign, and the three guardsmen were loyal to one another. The great steel corporation was built up on this quality in its partners and lieutenants. It is so with all co-operative business effort.

Co-workers in *The Power-Book Library* who have succeeded have invariably learned to love the Library—while the mere dollar-lovers have found their reward and dropped out.

Only reading that *bites* you, *serves* you. A man said: "I took a drink, and as it didn't bite enough, I took another." This book holds that the business representative cannot afford to drink, but the remark is illustrative of a law in life: The thing that takes hold of your vital interest is the thing that makes you—for good or ill. So, *The Power-Book Library* seeks to stir and inspire your best mental and business effort. So, as a business representative, you are urged to see to it that your work, your concern, your principal's interest stimulates in you splendid loyalty, blood-interest loyalty of co-operation. There lies *your* way to success.

CHAPTER XV.

INDEPENDENTLY CONDUCTED BUSINESS.

YOU are invited to discover why success in the following incident occurred so easily. It is taken from Winston Churchill's "*The Crossing.*"

" 'Xavier,' said Nick, gently taking the tiller out of his hand, 'I will teach you how to steer a keel boat.'

" '*Mon Dieu*,' said Xavier, 'and who is to pay Michié Gratiot for his fur? The river, she is full of things.'

" 'Yes, I know, Xavier, but you will teach me to steer.'

" '*Volontiers*, Michié, as we go now. But there come a time when I, even I, who am twenty year on her, do not know whether it is right or left. Ze rock—he vair' hard. Ze snag, he grip you like dat,' and Xavier twined his strong arms around Nick until he was helpless. 'Ze bar—he hol' you by ze leg. An' who is to tell you how far he run under ze yellow water, Michié? I, who speak to you, know. But I know not how I know. Ze water, sometime she tell, sometime she say not'ing.'

445

"'*A bas*, Xavier!' said Nick, pushing him away, 'I will teach you the river.'

"Xavier laughed, and sat down on the edge of the cabin. Nick took easily to accomplishments, and he handled the clumsy tiller with a certainty and distinction that made the boatmen swear in two languages and a patois. A great water-logged giant of the Northern forests loomed ahead of us. Xavier sprang to his feet, but Nick had swung his boat swiftly, smoothly, into the deeper water on the outer side.

"'*Saint Jacques*, Michié,' cried Xavier, 'you mek him better zan I thought.'"

§ 1. There are times when a man's sheer confidence given to his subconscious self will enable him to accomplish what otherwise would require years of training.

§ 2. Nevertheless, the amateur must sooner or later have come to grief on the mighty flood. One may delineate a good riverman, but one cannot make him, offhand; the skill, the daring, the caution, the practical ability,—these come only from experience. And it is experience that develops business power.

§ 3. It should now especially be remembered that the purpose of these pages is suggestion for unfoldment of personal qualifications only. The aim here, as in all preceding chapters, falls, as we may say, this side of the actual conduct of business affairs. It will be necessary to bear this in mind as the subject of the present chapter comes up for discussion, since otherwise the business reader may feel that the treatment is inadequate.

§ 4. *Observe!* It will be recalled that in the preceding chapter general business was divided into two great departments: Business Under Direction, and Independently Conducted Business, the minor subdivisions being outlined in part in section 1 of that chapter. With the first subdivision, Permanent Employees, we have already dealt. The second subdivision, Temporary Employees, remains, but needs no special discussion since it is covered either by the preceding or the present chapters. In the work that follows you are invited to observe that many of the suggestions to be given are wholly pertinent to all employee representatives, such as correspondents, solicitors, cashiers, managers, and so on, and that some of the classes considered below should look to the sections of the preceding chapter devoted to representatives. One may canvass or solicit for another, and in practice be substantially independent as an agent, jobber, broker, advertising man, or promoter; or, on the other hand, one may act almost entirely under at least general orders. Because the business functions now before us blend in the two respects, representing sometimes one man or concern, sometimes another, and often being in part under orders, and in part independent, but in a way self-directing, the classes below are taken up in the present rather than in the previous chapter. This section is important as avoiding the appearance of confusion.

BLENDING OF BUSINESS FUNCTIONS.

§ 5. *Observe!* *Business specialization is an absorbent of various traits.* An analysis of the independent business functions will exhibit a further blending tendency in practical life, in that every successful business man is to-day a specialist—that is, a single-department man, more or less—for the greater his success and field, the larger the number of specific departments which his "one line" absorbs and represents. Business Power has, indeed, this among other measurements: the greater its real exhibition, the greater its all-round ability. The financial world gauges a man by the question, How much does his hand successfully cover? and the question is an estimate of power, not a judgment in morals. Yet no matter how big the business hand is, it is made in outline not very differently from any other man's "executive member"—it has wrist to turn, push, pull; palm to cover, grasp, uphold; thumb and fingers to clutch, press, loosen, "give and take." It is merely a human hand, at a peanut stand, or at a "private bank," which sometimes means a world-builder or a nation-slayer. Thus with our personal qualifications: they are human and common (for the most part); embracing almost exclusively those elements which you may discover in any country town,—yet emphasizing one or two factors in a very special manner, and now and then disclosing a *phase* of a trait which is really unique. It is just that special phase in the whole combination of traits which is important, but always in its relation to its other backing.

THE RULE OF SPECIALIZATION.

§ 6. Now, it is merely because a man possesses some emphasized quality, or a group of qualities unusually compacted and harmonious, and, rarely the *unique phase* of a trait, that he specializes in his work. He *specializes because he is driven thereto.* This fact gives us a rule of business conduct.

§ 7.   *You are invited experimentally to specialize on one and another thing in business, but neither miscellaneously nor like a gambler, and when the drive of your nature is felt, to specialize definitely and for life on " one big thing," seeing to it that business power in your case represents, absorbs, as fully as possible, all the qualifications required by every business function inferior to your own.*

§ 8.   Examining the analysis of independently conducted business given in section 1, of the preceding chapter, we shall see that canvassers, agents, jobbers, brokers, and all representatives previously named, together with traveling salesmen, commission merchants, credit men, and real-estate men, require certain characteristics which will be indicated later? The analysis is designed to show the qualifications demanded of the different business classes and to suggest the fact that the first-class business man possesses traits and abilities which make him " good," in a broad sense, in any department below him at least, but that certain kinds of business require, in addition, other peculiar qualities which exhibit the specialization of the named occupations.

§ 9.   *Observe!*   The analysis may be examined with three questions in mind: (1)—What personal qualifications are required in my present occupation? (2)—What abilities do I require in preliminary planning? (3)—What traits and qualities do I require in *my* business action?

You can read the lists and questions once and

drop the matter, or you can resolutely put yourself
into the examination as a piece of actual work.   In
the latter case you will infallibly unfold a larger
measure of business power.

Success in business imperiously demands *right
personal qualities, right preliminary planning, and
achieving action.*

It is here assumed that the first phase of our
study will be taken up by the reader in a determined and prolonged manner.   No person or
book can create the required factors; the man must
himself read, resolve, build up.

THE WORK OF PLANNING.

§ 10. *Planning, whether it concern a single
enterprise or transaction, an achievement involving
considerable time and effort, or a prolonged campaign,
is indispensable to business success.*   Such planning
demands more or less mental labor, bringing into
action memory, imagination, initiative and foresight.   You should possess a good memory in order
to carry the plan forward; you should be able to
see in mind scenes, situations, people, contingencies; and these things both in detail and in outline.
This outlook should be a familiar vision.   You
should possess foresight for possible emergencies
and for variations in your plan and new adaptations
and adjustments as exigencies may arise.

§ 11.   The methods essential to the above
work are three:

(1) *Mental practice in actual thought-planning,*
both with regard to possible efforts and ventures
and to those in fact constantly coming up in business life.

(2) The endeavor in practical business to *carry out plans* previously made.

(3) *The education of the subjective self.* The more you follow suggestions 1 and 2, the more surely will the subjective self acquire wisdom, intuition, planning facility, and ability in making plans rapidly and smoothly, varying practical details and methods for assured success.

In the meantime, the subjective self should be educated to confidence in your executive and planning ability—or, perhaps, in its own ability in these respects. The methods here are, again: *thought-assumption of power*, *thought-assertion of power*, or vigorous insistence on its possession, and *practical "make-good"* in conduct determined to realize assumption and assertion. In this one section is suggested a great deal of patient labor, which, however, will prove of indescribable value.

BUSINESS ACTION.

§ 12. One of the chief values of business fore-planning consists in the fact that the work familiarizes both the subjective self and the objective with the idea and feeling of *action in some definite form*. You are invited to estimate the value to business capacity of this advance idea and feeling of practical action.

§ 13. Because of such advance familiarity with details, contingencies and activities, *the plan should be adhered to, with judgment, with confidence, and with courage.* You are urged to look well to the preservation of the integrity of your feeling of ability to plan and carry out. The man who plans should stand by his pre-determination if reasonably possible. One who plans, then wavers for slight reasons or obstacles, then shifts his line of action, surely abdicates control of self and situation. You are urged to employ judgment, but especially persistence in "hanging on" to your selected course. When completely convinced that a different course will bring larger results, throw the first plan overboard. It is not wisdom to stick merely for the sake of sticking.

§ 14. A good plan is not a stereotype plate which cannot be varied. Indeed, *one element of such is a forecasting of contingencies and a foreseeing of variations induced thereby*. It is here especially that the subjective activities come into play. Your subjective self often perceives in advance of your objective senses, as is the case in the animal world, the necessity for change in physical action, in both that which is automatic and that which is volitional. Leaping to one side, throwing up an arm, stooping, closing the eyes, and so on, are examples. Precisely such advance subjective action is frequent in business. One becomes uneasy, intuitive, apprehensive, suspicious, is aware of a vague feeling that a change of front is required: the undercurrents of business education are seeking to serve you. These deeper stirrings are, of course, not to become freakish or moody; yet, on the other hand, they should be given sympathy and due attention. When variation of a plan becomes necessary in action, it will be all the more successful if the plan has been forethought with reference to contingencies—provided, you do not make the matter of possible changes the main thing, as did that general during the southern war when he fortified the rear of Washington.

§ 15. *Always must action be timely.* Timeliness is, of course, a matter of experience, good thinking and common sense; but it is also a matter of intuition and feeling. You *feel*—that "now is the time," "the situation is ripe," "the conditions are favorable," "the person is in a propitious mood," "the hour of success has arrived." These signals from the "head office" of the subjective self are, in the long run, reliable evidences that your action will indeed prove timely.

§ 16. Both in the variation of plan and in all human relations, *successful action involves concession.* Some people are mere rigidity, and little else. If life is adjustment, a degree of elasticity is imperative. It never hurts a business man to acknowledge fallibility, concede the possible value of other opinions, and yield somewhat to the interest of the man whom he seeks to influence. Business power does not plow through men and things; it pushes, pulls, yields, adjusts, slips around, goes under or over for the sake of its final purpose, making details and immediate ends secondary, creating as little friction as possible, leaving in its own path as much satisfaction and friendliness as may be, and perennially conceding one thing and another in order to reach the long-run goal, success. An ounce of concession is worth a ton of business activity under some circumstances. If the concession of any intermediate end will make for your ultimate purpose, business power pauses not on the choice.

THE OTHER MAN.

§ 17. *In business action, conviction of the other man which shall lead to conduct on his part that you desire, is the main thing.* Business is a condition, whatever its theories. You wish to sell, to buy, to borrow, to invest, to secure investment, to enlist co-operation, to "get out," or to "get on." Always must you convince the *other man* that your propositions are for *his* interest. He knows that to you they signify *your* interest; but in business he does not act on that basis. He may see that both interests are consistent, or at least he may think he sees better than you in regard to the transaction, or he may really be the more sagacious man of the two. But always it is *his* interest which impels him to action. You must in some way convince the other man so that he will do what you desire. Business power holds that such conviction should be honestly brought about. Dishonesty is robbery, not business. The business code of honor is just plain business *life.* The highwayman in a "business suit" of clothing is simply Dick Turpin: none the less, be he little or big. The principles and the morals that govern business in railroading, mining, insurance, stock-broking, or "high finance," are precisely those which legitimately obtain in running a corner grocer-store. The magnitude of an operation and the impersonal character of its combinations can never make a bad financial principle good nor an immoral dealing ethical.

BUSINESS FEELING.

§ 18. As underlying and feeding these essentials in business action, *the presence in the underground or subconscious man of the true business feeling and attitude are of prime importance.*

The *feeling* referred to is, first, a *business* feeling

as distinguished from a professional, an artistic, or the like. It is a product of business life, and reacts upon business itself. The method for securing it is activity of body and mind in commercial pursuits, but that method may be given increased effectiveness by repeatedly thinking the idea of the feeling, by calling the feeling up in consciousness, and by asserting its actual possession as a permanent factor in life.

The business *feeling* is, secondly, *a prevailing and deep-seated mood of success.* Of course the best tonic for the mood of success is actual success. You are therefore urged to magnify your thought of the business feeling and every practical success which you have achieved in your life. Think highly of these factors and place great value upon them. *The success-feeling is another of the many essential elements which a man may cultivate by the already-suggested régime of assumption, assertion and corresponding conduct.* In psychotherapy this régime is all-important. You *assume* that you are not ill and that you are in health (no matter what you know you are dealing, not with known physical conditions alone, but with the unknown exhaustless resources of the subconscious self); you *assert* that you are well and shall of course be precisely that—all right. In the meantime, you *act accordingly*, adopting every known means which will assist the "make-good" of assumption and assertion, such as a first-class physician and all obedience to the laws of bodily well-being. "If you only care enough for a result," says James, "you will almost certainly attain it. If you wish to be rich, you will be rich; if you wish to be learned, you will be learned; if you wish to be good, you will be good. Only you must, then, really wish these things, and wish them with exclusiveness, and not wish at the same time a hundred other incompatible things just as strongly." That is exactly what I mean by "acting accordingly." *Corresponding action feeds belief and draws upon the deeper sources of energy and ability.*

§ 19.   This is all of a piece with the prevailing conceptions of the subconscious "mind." "Mind can do its work unconsciously," says one. "This unconscious mind is constantly springing up to sustain the conscious life," another remarks. "This unconscious soul, like a benevolent stranger, works and makes provision for our benefit, pouring only the mature fruit into our laps," a third declares. These testimonials are the words of writers whose text-books are acknowledged in the educational world. Only, it is for the conscious self to educate the unconscious in the feelings referred to, and the methods for such education are seen in the dynamic words—*assume possession, assert possession, act on the basis of possession of the quality and power desired.* Business power incarnates this threefold method.

The Business Attitude.

§ 20.   *Business attitudes are determined by business feelings.* The attitudes spring from the feelings. Nevertheless, the two things are not identical. The *feeling* is purely *internal,* while the *attitude* cannot appear until the feeling *begins* to take outward expression. The *attitude* does not *consist* in outward expression, but it is a *position of the self depending* for one thing on the *feeling within* and for another thing on the *inception* of some form of external action.

"The captain's attitude on board ship is quite different from that of a passenger (Jastrow, in "*The Subconscious*"): nor is this difference confined to the hours of his watch, nor to the moment of his giving orders; the entire background of his occupation, night and day, is tinged by the underlying currents of responsibility,—tensions of duty, that hold him ever ready for the crisis of action." This officer has the *feeling* of being captain; he assumes, therefore, an inner *attitude of captaincy* which, whether he be acting bodily or no, is an expression within of that feeling.

Business power roots in a general or some specific business feeling, but the *business attitude is practical expression beginning within and continuing outward.*

Now, this general attitude involves certain factors which are of prime importance in every successful life, as follows:

FACTORS OF ATTITUDE.

§ 21. FIRST FACTOR: INTEREST. The business attitude centers in interest. Interest is the zest of work. It secures and holds attention. It concentrates mind-power by magnetising every personal function. It immensely stimulates and so, engages, the subconscious self. Perfunctory work is never good work. If you desire to do anything in the best possible manner, you must possess and unfold, or coerce and maintain, in an increasing degree, a vital interest in the details and the department in which you are engaged. *The psychic and infallible method is seen, again, in assumption, assertion, corresponding action.* You assume that you have interest; you assert your interest; you act on the basis of possessing interest.

§ 22. SECOND FACTOR: ALERTNESS. Vital interest is always alert in some direction; but the alertness of the business attitude not only covers the most interesting point of a field of action, but also keeps an eye out all round. This one qualification, alertness, is enormously demanded in the business world. *The psychic method consists in cultivating a general feeling of aliveness and watchfulness and throwing the same into practical action.* (See "*Power For Success.*")

§ 23. THIRD FACTOR: PROMPTNESS. This factor includes the common meaning of the word, but, more, embraces the habit of attacking any problem or piece of work when one's inner feeling is that "*now is the time!* I am myself in exactly the mood and condition for achievement." You are, however, invited to observe that the present factor never involves waiting for such a mood, since it *consists in part of the habit of decision and promptness in all things, but that it adds to such habit an included habit of throwing the self, when it especially feels ready, then and there into the work or undertaking urged.* This double habit swings the whole force of the subconscious self into best possible action.

§ 24. FOURTH FACTOR: COMPLETING ADEQUACY. The normal mind is always discontented with an unfinished piece of business, especially if it hang over for long. The mood of achievement-to-the-finish is natural. We wish to get through and be done with things, and it is distressing to feel inadequate to the completion of a task or article which ought to be now finished. *Business power has a great capacity for completing what it undertakes.* The achieving personality always carries with it in its work the active attitude of accomplishing and closing out matters, thus always being ready for others as they may appear. The value of this attitude is in only comparatively small degree the mere completion of work or undertakings; it is, above all, that of the mental condition which the attitude maintains. After you have caught the swing of action which finishes up what you have gone into, one matter succeeding another, you have acquired great mental momentum and facility of mind and body, your interest is stimulated incessantly, alertness becomes sharpened and becomes a habit, promptness marks every act, and the whole self of you comes to the fore, the unconscious no less than the conscious. Then *you* drive *work*, which is vastly superior to driving yourself. Then a sense of fineness or excellence is apt to prevail in your use of your powers. Then the mood of real success spreads throughout your entire person, and you actually become hungry for other conquests.

§ 25. FIFTH FACTOR: THE WILL-SPIRIT. The above attitude merges into the will-attitude, which is the aggressive posture of the will-spirit. This is really the success-attitude, for the will-spirit is not brute force, but is rather determination, confidence, courage—one dynamic compound.

"Every leader or captain among men is thus an embodiment of will: his domain may be great

or small, spiritual or physical, civil or literary; he
may be king or shoemaker, archbishop or machinist,
inventor or novelist; whatever his position, * * *
he stands to them (others) in the relation of imperious, domineering, willing self."

A patient had been advised by his physician to
take a long walk. The day after the first attempt,
the sick man reported as follows: "Yesterday, according to your advice, I went to town, and for the
first hour all went very well; but when I had to
pass over a bridge, I was taken with dizziness, a
sort of undefinable discomfort, and it took a good
deal of courage to continue. This was still worse
when I entered the historical museum. I was
seized with all the troubles of which I complained
before my treatment (suggestion). Şuddenly I
felt myself bored and sad and ready to weep; I felt
a sense of pressure on my head; the dizziness became unbearable, and I was going to go out without having visited the museum, when my eyes fell
on a flag which bore on the arms of a white cross
these words in letters of gold: '*Honor to courage,
to weakness, shame!*' 'Ah, yes; to weakness shame!'
I cried, and as if by enchantment all my discom-
forts disappeared. I was able to visit the rest of
the museum and to take that long walk home in
very good condition and proud of my success." *Here
we have an example of the cultivated complex—will-
courage-assurance—which exhibits in all successful
business, especially in times of stress.* Business
power itself never gets nervous or grows tired, but
business men under load sometimes do fall into
such conditions. Then it is that the will-attitude
enables them to draw on what Professor James

would call a further reservoir of energy of which they had been unconscious, and oftentimes the one thing that suggests such a "run on the bank" is the idea: "Honor to courage, to weakness, shame!"

Specific Business Department.

§ 26. With these considerations in mind, we are now ready for the specific phases of independently conducted business enterprise. The field, even when divided in a rather simple manner, is vaster than any which has hitherto confronted us, and only a very brief treatment can be given it. But if preceding pages have been assimilated by the student, any very elaborate discussion will have been obviated.

Even within such a limited scope, the purpose is of course immense, but it may console us to know that whatever your specialization in business may be, your work is based more or less upon maxims, methods and principles which must govern all commercial enterprise, and that you share in those personal qualifications which all business men must possess. In the present chapter the author had thought of listing in a general way such personal elements, and then of indicating special requirements for the several business occupations taken up, but it soon became apparent that many specific requirements were peculiar to a number of occupations, so that it seemed impossible to state just what trait or ability must be regarded as prime in any one, as, say, that of the jobber, and not of the broker, or that of the manufacturer, and not of the merchant, and so on. Hence, the present pages, though divided in treatment, apply more or

less to each of the business functions below
considered.

The Canvassing Agent.

§ 27. The canvasser solicits for himself; the
solicitor, for others.   In Milton's line, "That fruit
solicited her longing eye," we have the very gist of
this line of effort.   Your fruit will never "solicit"
unless the other man's eye is "longing."   In the
hands of the successful canvasser his values *seem*
to create desire and *seem* to sell themselves.   But
to accomplish the ends indicated, the canvasser
requires a number of prime qualifications.

For the acquisition of such qualifications,
reference is made to all the sections of this volume.
If they are faithfully studied and carried out, large
practical results are absolutely certain.

§ 28. For the particular work in hand, the
following condensed essentials invite your attention.
They are designed, it should be remembered, not
for cursory reading, but for concentrated thought
and downright practice:

(1) The great principles of successful canvass-
ing are covered by six words: *Health* * * *
Morals * * * *Address* * * * *Will-Power*
* * * *Magnetism* * * * *Values.*

(2) The *values* may be merchandise, publications, shares, stocks, bonds, investments, social,
political or religious interests, and so on. *They
must be actual, desirable, adapted to purchasers,
right-priced, strongly appealing to increased self-
interest.*   Here we have the First Iron Principle, requiring the best preliminary thought
of which you are capable: Canvassing with poor

OR ILL-ADAPTED VALUES IS A FAILURE TO START WITH.

(3) The canvasser's values naturally suggest *territory*, which may be determined by geography, education, class-distinctions, prejudice or preference, availability, financial resources, and so on, but *the territory, however determined, must be* RIGHT if success is to follow effort. This fact gives us our SECOND IRON PRINCIPLE, which demands the utmost thought-will possessed: MISPLACED CANVASSING IS A SURE BID FOR FAILURE.

(4) The territory and the canvass are problems calling for solution in advance. *The work should be planned, with every faculty concentrated to the limit, and then given a persistent fair trial.* In most cases, if brains and will-power are in action, the plan can be pushed through without essential variation. Thus we educe the THIRD IRON PRINCIPLE: HAPHAZARD CANVASSING IS DOOMED BEFORE IT BEGINS.

(5) Canvassing which is properly planned is preceded by some sort of thought-willed heralding. The minds of the people are already pre-occupied; the proposition finds surprise, dullness, indifference, prejudice, irritation. Against such conditions *local advertising, or attractive and weighty pre-announcements from principals or third persons should be sought.* THE FOURTH IRON PRINCIPLE has thus appeared: UNHERALDED CANVASSING IS BADLY BEGUN.

(6) *Close planning has a wary eye on times and conditions.* Seizure of those that are favorable, together with good nature in the act of doing so, is now indispensable. These requirements call for alertness, patience, shrewdness, promptness, in

the canvasser as a matter of course. But they
demand active and acute thinking as an element of
the applied plan. Hence the FIFTH IRON PRINCI-
PLE EMERGES: MAL-ADJUSTED CANVASSING WINS
MERELY THE SUCCESS OF CHANCE. Mere chance success can never content real business power.

(7) *First impressions are vastly important in
any personal contact.* In addition to apathy among
the people which one must meet, there is, perhaps, psychological antipathy to overcome, and
an agreeable feeling to establish, in many instances positive personal attraction to arouse, and
all such conditions should be sought at the outset.
Here, then, we come to our SIXTH IRON PRINCIPLE:
CANVASSING WHICH BEGINS WITH MAGNETISM IS AS-
SURED OF THE LONG-RUN SUCCESS.

(8) Nevertheless, sales may still hang on the
manipulation of human nature. *The canvasser
must know men as men, women as women, children
as children, and be able to adapt himself to the curious varieties on the spur of the moment.* The problem of address now confronts him. Shall he be
direct, straightforward, frank—or indirect, circuit-
ous, feeling his way, coming around at opportunity?
Shall he be friendly, or merely businesslike? Shall
he be grave, or gay? Shall he give the prospective
customer large liberty, say, in handling his goods,
or restrict him by unperceived personal control?
All these questions and the above requirements
involve very much genuine thinking and alert and
prompt resourcefulness. So, we have the SEVENTH
IRON PRINCIPLE: CANVASSING REQUIRES THE ADAPT-
IVE ADDRESS.

(9) *And every personality has somewhere in its*

make-up a central principle or key which opens the way exactly to what you want. The lock may vary with moods or times, but the key thereto hangs near-by, and he who properly uses it may have his wish—within reason, of course. This key is, perhaps, a weakness, a foible, a prejudice, a penchant, an affection, a pride, an egotism, a hobby, a social, political or religious peculiarity. It may be anything. It must be found by the canvasser and deftly used. That is the EIGHTH IRON PRINCIPLE: SUCCESSFUL CANVASSING UNDERSTANDS THE KEY OF PERSONALITY.

(10) The canvasser's health—that is, his physical and mental harmony—is an important factor of success. *"Body and mind sound and attractive,"* ought to be aims with all who make canvassing a business. The motto for a perpetual régime might well be: *"Every unattractive feature eliminated, every pleasing characteristic cultivated."* This becomes our NINTH IRON PRINCIPLE: ATTRACTIVE HEALTH-TONE MAGNETIZES CANVASSING.

(11) *The business of canvassing has its eye frequently on permanency.* One essential pre-requisite here is character. These pages regard reputable business power, not morals as such; but it is important to know that immorality undermines health, thrusts betraying signs on the outside, and destroys personal magnetism. The TENTH IRON PRINCIPLE is now evident: PERSONAL MORALITY GIVES CANVASSING STANDING AND PERMANENCY.

(12) The externals of personal magnetism have already been indicated. Yet there are certain additional factors which every canvasser should cultivate: *the inner and quenchless feeling of hope-*

fulness, courage and confidence, and the outer appear-
ance of cheerfulness, buoyancy and prosperity.   Within these qualities resides a vibrant physical and
psychic force-combination which some individuals
naturally possess and most may develop by proper
exercises persistently followed.   The combination
exhibits in the clear, frank, intelligent, sympa-
thetic eye, in the full, pleasing, appealing, per-
sausive, compelling voice, in the firm, warm, tactful, nerveful touch.   But it also extends itself
through channels that are not open to any sense
(See "*Power For Success*").   It is one of the great
gifts of business power.   This, then, is our ELEV-
ENTH IRON PRINCIPLE: SUCCESSFUL CANVASSING UTI-
LIZES TO THE FULL PERSONAL MAGNETISM.

(13)   It would be difficult to name the all-important thing in the canvasser's business.   Nevertheless, a prime requisite is seen in what we may
term thought-will-power.   *Here we have energy-*
resource-determination-decision- firmness- patience- en-
durance-self-control-self-reliance-push.   This is, as
one might say, about as complex as the chemical
make-up of protoplasm, and—as capable of great
things.   The power now conveys to the whole
system.   The man is enthusiastically and always at
it.   He plans a street or a state, and doggedly
proceeds with his work, slighting, turning aside for
—nothing! It is business he is doing.   Reasons
against continuous activity become reasons for.
Night finds him, or Christmas overtakes him, able
to say: "I never failed to do my level best!"   This
is the TWELFTH IRON PRINCIPLE: PERSISTENT MULTI-
PLICATION OF SELF INTO CANVASSING RUNS INFALLIBLY
TO SUCCESS.

THE JOBBER.

§ 28. The abilities which insure success in this line of business are acquired, of course, through actual experience. As our work here concerns the psychology of personal business power, the principles and maxims which jobbing has built up within and for itself are not before us, except in so far as they involve psychic factors. Since, however, experience has to do with those processes that have created such principles and maxims, we may here take a moment to explain what we mean by experience as an instructor and guide. (See first italics of Section 16, Chapter V; a good definition of psychic experience.)

To begin with, we mean by the word "experience" a noun and a verb. We experience (verb) various experiences (noun). The experiences (noun) we have, and each of these is an experience (noun). But such experience when we look at it closely, is nothing more nor less than a variably complex *condition of the self in action*. There can be no experience apart from an activity. The activity *is* a certain condition of the self, and it *conduces* to some *difference* in the condition between the start and the finish of the action. This difference is a *tendency* in our nature as *involved in the activity*, which tendency may be toward *repetition* more or less of previous activities (establishing of preceding conditions) or toward *variations* therein. Thus, *an* experience is a *condition of the self involving a tendency to repeat old conditions, and so, actions, or to vary them. Experience* in the larger sense of teacher or guide is simply *an organized system of conditions and activities of the self which has all*

sorts of tendencies, now to repetition, now to varia-
tion, in action. The organization probably takes
place in the subconscious self, and its main quality
depends on the subjects of living interest with which
the conscious self is engaged. Of course, we must
remember that the individuality of person is also
involved in the determination of such quality.
This factor, however, is not before us, since the
present book is not a matter of systematic psychology, but is concerned only with business
power. The conscious phase of the self largely
determines those objects of interest, and so, edu-
cates the subconscious phase. The subconscious
organizes conditions, activities, tendencies, into
what we call the individual experience, and reports
in the conscious self, originates impulses which
rise to that phase, and appeals to judgment for
action external, or sways the conscious self without its knowing the fact. Hence, we have as many
sum-totals of experience as there are individuals
living; then, as many *orders* of experience as there
are general interests or pursuits in life, and so, the
experience scientific, philosophical, artistic, social,
industrial, political, pleasure-seeking, religious,
commercial. Each of these divisions analyzes into
specific subdivisions, according to the combination
of individuality with special pursuit, so that in
business all the phases of permanent employment
and of independently conducted operations represent so many kinds of business experience. *This*
explanation shows that every department of commer-
cial activity must rely upon its peculiar individual
and general experience for instruction and instinctive
impulse. It also shows that no instructor can be

substituted therefor, since experience is just an organized system of conditions and activities (the condition *means* activity) obtaining in the subconcious self and reflecting in the conscious self. *But since the subconscious self is to be trained by the conscious, experience itself is a matter to be taken in hand, to be guided and improved.* If we could possibly refuse to do this, we should go back to the state of the jelly fish, or farther.

§ 29. Directive instruction is simply the other man's experience placed to your advantage. *Out of general experience the following suggestions seem to emerge:*

(1) A successful jobber is a good practical psychologist (this is true of every achieving business man). He may be totally ignorant of the word and the science, yet he always fulfils the requirements indicated. *He knows himself—at least, his weaknesses and his strong points—and he controls and uses the self for actual business.*

(2) *He is a constant student of human nature,* and especially of individuals with whom he habitually deals. He buys and sells at the other man's weak point, necessities or business contingencies. Certainly he will not consciously buy or sell at his own weak point, and is always trying to avoid doing business on any particular point of his own necessities or financial contingencies.

(3) *He knows the market,* not in a general way, but in the details of supply, demand, new articles and fields, cost, selling prices, monetary conditions, and the public taste.

(4) He has the *financial instinct* for values and future contingencies. "When I asked him

how much, he answered 'about a dollar.' He simply didn't have any sense of values, and that's the business man's sixth sense." My friend, the mineral dealer, knows the value of any stone at sight, and he manages, by the very certainty of his conviction, to inspire in other people confidence in his judgment, so that he gets prices for his gems that are often remarkable. The value of a thing in business is what you make the other man think it is worth.

(5) This *intuition it is that determines the holding or the unloading of stock* (goods). "These beautiful women," said one, "trained from childhood for the conquest of a rich husband, must have cultivated an extraordinary delicacy of consciousness in such matters. They must have developed for themselves what might be called a sixth sense—a power of feeling in the air what the men about them were thinking of them." That feeling of market conditions and possibilities is one of the most important factors in business power. Its cultivation comes from long and constant attention to the idea itself as involved in practical life. It is a result of subconscious activity.

(6) *He knows where his supplies are to come from and the markets that will take them.* Here also one must carry within himself the ideas corresponding, together with an incessant feeling of alertness.

(7) He has his hand on *transportation facilities*, and keeps front and rear doors open because his business is a "stream" with nothing stale "left over night."

(8) *On his own buying end his attitude* is: "*You sell at prices right to me in your own interest.*"

On the *selling end* the attitude is: "*I sell, you buy, in your own supposed interest, at prices right to me.*" This two-fold attitude should be assumed and the words might well be made perpetual régimes for the education of the subconscious self and conscious activity.

Such are some of the psychic factors obtaining in the business of handling wholesale stocks. The personal qualifications essential to any business, it scarcely needs adding, must reinforce the psychology above suggested.

§ 30. You are, therefore, invited to assume, assert, and practise as realized the injunctions given below:

(a) *Study the business self in its subconscious rather than its conscious psychology;* that is, go deeper in your study than to the every-day phases of self which you know.

(b) *Study human nature through named individuals,* trying to get at their subconscious activities.

(c) *Study the manufacture of your kinds of goods.*

(d) Study *all related kinds of goods,* and *handle only the leaders.*

(e) *Study the market in supply and demand,* and *don't be a follower.*

(f) *Study costs and prices,* between the two seas and over. *Don't be a backyard business man.*

(g) *Study the currents of popular trade notions,* and keep your neighbors informed.

(h) *Study the arrival of new creations and inventions;* then you're not left with yesterday's goods on your hands.

(i) *Study the money world and financial currents,* and *don't play "blind man's buff" with gold.*

(j) Study present *indications of future proba-*
bilities, and *don't prophesy after the fact.*
  If you are not "making," you are losing.

THE BROKER.

§ 31. "The broker is the connecting link between buyer and seller," remarks Sereno S.
Pratt in " *The Work of Wall Street.*" "He is a
middle-man, one who negotiates sales or contracts
as an agent."   For these reasons the broker is here
classed among independent business people.

§ 32. "There are almost as many different
kinds of brokers as there are lines of business.   There
are ' stock brokers,' investment brokers, curb brokers, grain-brokers, cotton-brokers, coffee-brokers,
ship-brokers, insurance-brokers, money-brokers,
foreign-exchange brokers, land-brokers."

§ 33. "Brokers may be divided into two
classes: first, those who do a strictly commission
business and who *are conservative in advice and*
dealings; and, second, those who speculate on their
own account as well as for their customers."

§ 34. Whether the broker acts for himself or
merely as an agent and counsellor, the following
qualifications are evident.

(1) He should be possessed "*with a supe-*
rior endowment of brains."   No fool can last long
on the Stock Exchange.   The broker, whether
he is the office partner or the Board member,
requires.

Alertness;	Ability to take large risks;
A habit of quick decision;	With good judgment;
Accuracy;	Ability to read character;
Promptness;	Power to keep cool;

Wide financial vision; great courage-confidence.

Staying power; instinct for timely re-adjust-ments.

The items should be taken, not as mere factors of analysis, but as suggestions for practical work.

(2) The broker must be narrow in the sense of concentrating to his particular line or field.

(3) "But the broker is broad in another sense. The Wall Street horizon is almost as wide as the world itself."

The above-named writer quotes Horace White as saying: "The operators in the gold-room (in an account of the gold speculation of the war time —1860) should be at the same time the best in-formed and the most intelligent business men in the country. They must have not only the best and latest information, but they must be able to determine at once what is the economic meaning and significance of any given fact which may come to their knowledge. They must be able to resolve the most complicated problems in mental arithme-tic without a moment's hesitation. If the Secretary of the Treasury has decided upon a certain measure of financial policy, or the President upon a certain measure of foreign policy; if there is a short corn crop, or a Fenian rebellion, or a war-cloud in Europe, or a heavy immigration, or a great oil dis-covery, or a change in the tariff, or anything else which can affect the currency or the public credit, they must be able to melt down the mass and weigh the product in terms of standard gold. This is the work of omniscience. No man can do it."

(4) Yet this characterization "serves well to describe the work of the stock-broker to-day. He must keep in touch with every market abroad as

well as at home.   He must know something of the
significance of parliamentary debates and congres-
sional legislation.   He studies bank statements,
railroad reports, crop estimates, statistics of foreign
trade, and the forces at work in domestic and international politics.   As he must give advice which
may make or lose money for his customers, he is
obliged to keep an intelligent watch on everything
of importance that is going on.   As he is not omniscient, he often makes mistakes.   But his grasp
of the world's affairs is firmer than that of most
other observers."

(5)   The methods by which any broker has
acquired the qualities and abilities thus suggested,
from the start, or by which he has cultivated native
endowments, is that which has frequently appeared
in these pages:

Assumption that one surely possesses the factors and will certainly succeed;

Assertion, by the whole personal attitude, of
the traits and powers and of present success;

Action, alert, energetic, confident, compelling
action corresponding to and inspiring assumption
and assertion.   The psychological law here involves the subconscious self.   *What you for long
assume, assert and act, that you will acquire or become*.   But observe:

(6)   If a man's assumption is merely a "think-
so" or a "make-believe," and not a central psychic
affirmation and claim, he can never within himself
and as expressed in his prevailing attitudes, assert
the same with any power; *and unless assumption
and assertion are bona fide deep-seated in a man's
very soul, his action, since it can in the long run*

*conform only to the inner self, will fail to inspire
himself or others or to coerce events in the way of
success.* You see, then, that our reiterated method
is one which must really take hold of the whole
man. If it does this, even feebly at first, it will
come more and more to be vital and to engage
every ounce of self and life. By that time success
has surrendered.

(7) The stock-broker, if acting for himself,
and especially when operating for others, should
know the *nature and the close inter-relations of risk,*
and should never be a *mere imitator and never yield
to the impulse of pure gambling or of panic.* Now,
speculation is not easily distinguished in its legitimate and its illegitimate features. If you pay
actual values for evidences of investment, you may
still speculate, because you are buying for a rise in
value of the investment, at least with the belief
that the investment will not fall in value. Business
power is always doing that sort of thing. But if
you merely guess on a future state of financial
conditions, promising to buy or to sell at a named
figure made by the guess, you are still, again,
speculating; the outcome would be precisely the
same whether your money "takes the goods" or
"takes a mere memorandum," there being not
"goods" enough to go round: you lose the market
difference on settlement. It is just a question of
correct estimation, then. But that simple question
involves great astuteness in the understanding of
the nature and close inter-relations of risk. We
shall see later what this means.

(8) "There is a point, however, where speculation becomes a disease of the mind: it is the point

where it changes into mere gambling. If it is difficult to draw the line between investment and speculation, it is more difficult to draw that between speculation and gambling. Yet there is a difference between the two, although many critics of Wall Street fail to see it. The speculator may be defined as a man who, making a study of business conditions and of the earning power of the companies in whose stocks he proposes to trade, buys because he believes that prices ought to advance, or sells because he believes they will fall; and does so on a margin ample to protect him against any ordinary vicissitudes of the market. He exercises the same foresight and conservatism as does the merchant who places a large order for goods. The gambler in stocks is one who goes it "blind," buys and sells without due study of conditions or of the property in which he invests, but trusts to chance."

(9) Now, the true business speculator, in distinction from the speculative gambler, *bases his conduct on knowledge of the nature of legitimate risk.* "A gambler seeks and makes risks which it is not necessary to assume," as Professor Fisher remarks in "*The Nature of Capital and Income*," "whereas the speculator is one who merely volunteers to assume those risks of business which must inevitably fall somewhere. A speculator is usually fitted for his work by special knowledge, so that the risk *to him*, owing to superior foresight, is at the outset less than it would be to others." The broker, therefore, should base his estimates of values, present or future, upon a real study of financial conditions of all sorts.

(10) Above all, the broker must *be on his guard against the impulse of imitation*, or the tendency of men to run together under certain exciting conditions. There is a market contagion which is as dangerous as any germ disease known to medical science. It is not difficult to play on this trait of our nature and to induce a run in favor or against any commodity or stock, because when a certain "future" is suggested often enough and with sufficient confidence, the suggestion—what someone believes or hopes—becomes more than a suggestion, filling the air as a "sure thing," a real financial fact, and then, unless one is on his guard, this pseudo fact "obcesses" the mind until one is swept off the feet with a multitude of others by sheer force of the impulse toward imitation. "The chief evils of speculation flow from the participation of the general public, who lack the special knowledge, and enter the market in a purely gambling spirit. In addition to suffering the usual evil consequences of gambling, they produce evil consequences for the non-participating public by causing factitious fluctuations in the values of the products or property in which they speculate."

"The evils of speculation are particularly acute when, as generally happens with the investing public, the forecasts are not made independently. Were it true that each individual speculator made up his mind independently of every other as to the course of future events, the errors of some would probably be offset by those of others. But, as a matter of fact, the mistakes of the common herd are usually in the same direction." And then the outcome of yielding to imitative impulses is

apparent in a general collapse which involves all
sorts of related risks and the entire mass of otherwise innocent investors and legitimate speculators.

"A chief cause of crises, panics, runs on banks,
etc., is that risks are not independently reckoned,
but are a mere matter of imitation. A crisis is a
time of general and forced liquidation. In other
words, it differs from any other period in two
particulars, viz.: that the liquidations are more
numerous, and that they are for the most part
forced upon the debtors by the creditors because of
threatened or actual bankruptcy. Neither of these
conditions could exist unless there had been at a
prior time a general miscalculation of the future.
Both creditors and debtors must have made a
wrong forecast when their ill-fated agreements
were entered into. Hence a crisis is the penalty
paid when a previous *general error in prediction is
discovered*. Such a general *error may* be due to the
coincidence of a number of independent mistakes
of individuals; but it almost always *is* due to lack
of independence,—to the principle of imitation."

The broker, therefore, must exhibit what is
called the "*coefficient of caution*" *to a nicety between
timidity and rashness*, studying the real elements of
actual and legitimate speculation in order to determine that nicety, and, so far as possible in the
nature of the case, must take his risks independently, never because of mere contagion, thus avoiding being caught in the rush of imitation which is
always disastrous if carried beyond a certain point
—and the forecasting of exactly that point is the
thing which makes a broker successful; *the ability
to do so is the essence of himself.   There* emerges his

trained and astute subconscious self, and the giving
of correct instruction for the creation of such a self,
beyond engaging in the actual fight of the Exchange, is a task no living mind might essay.

THE REAL-ESTATE MAN.

§ 35. So far as one who handles real property
acts as an agent, the general principles which
should govern representatives are of course demanded. If the real-estate man is practically in
the commission business his personal qualifications
and abilities, and the laws of his occupation, do not
differ essentially from those required in any other
line operating as a medium between owner and
seller of goods. The occupations of real-estate
brokerage, and brokerage in other staples outside
Stock Exchange manipulations, would seem to
concern about the same business field, the main
difference obtaining with regard to the thing
handled and the item of constant stability of
quantity. *In any event the dealer in real property
must know land on sight, as it were, and be able to
appraise its value very closely.*

"Real estate," as Fisher remarks, "in certain
parts of a city where sales are active can sometimes
be appraised correctly within five or ten per cent.;
but in the 'dead' or out-of-the-way parts of some
towns, where sales are infrequent, the appraisement becomes merely a rough guess. Again, in
the country districts, while farms in the settled
parts of Iowa and Texas can be appraised within
ten or fifteen per cent., in the backward parts even
an expert's valuation is often proved wrong by
more than fifty per cent. In some cases, in fact,

where a sale of the article is scarcely conceivable,
an appraisement is almost out of the question."

Valuation often becomes difficult in proportion
as the question of investment for future enhance-
ments comes up. "In a city, for instance, land
may be used either for present dwelling or for
future business purposes, and it often becomes a
question which use is the more valuable. In case
the city is growing rapidly, it may happen that in
certain quarters, although the present use for
dwelling purposes is more important, in a few
years the locality will cease to be a residence
quarter and the land will be needed for business
purposes. In such case, it may 'pay' to keep the
land out of present use entirely and reserve it until
the city has grown so as to make it profitable to
erect a business block. If the land were now
encumbered with a dwelling, either the possibility
of its subsequent use for business purposes would
be cut off, or the profits from its conversion to
those purposes would be impaired by the prior
destruction and waste of the dwelling. Under such
circumstances it would usually happen that speculators would buy up and hold the land. The manner in which the gain presents itself to them is
simply as a prospective rise in value from the
growth of the city; they therefore buy the land to
sell it later at a higher price. Such a speculator is
commonly regarded as keeping land 'out of use.'
He is, however, only *deferring* the use, and, if he
has foresight, is no more to be condemned than the
wise speculator on the wheat exchange, whose
work, as is well known, operates to conserve the
supply of wheat. The speculator thus tends to

bring about the best utilization of the land in the sense that, out of several alternative income streams which the land might be made to yield, that one is selected which possesses for him the maximum present value."

§ 36. If the real-estate business is conducted independently, therefore, the following factors are evident:

(1) *The Real-Estate Insight.* This ability is always an acquisition of some measure of experience. It is the result of more or less extensive knowledge of prices held for land under varying conditions for a considerable length of time. The novice has simply to "prowl" around and dig out exactly this information, *studying neighborhoods and communities, distance from business centres, present and probable use of surrounding land, the movements of population and enterprise,* and so on, and always keenly alert to the personal factors, *intuition and judgment.* All this demands *alertness, observation,* the ability to *absorb information* and to get it by what one might almost call "occult methods," to *sense coming contingencies,* "*size up*" *situations,* the exercise of *practical reasoning and imaginative foresight,* by which financial changes, the trend of events, and the developments of life are made to appear before the business eye. The sketch is rapid, but the words emphasized indicate long régimes for mental and objective practice.

(2) *Courageous Confidence.* " 'Oh, that kind of courage is rare,'" said Thorpe in " *The Market Place.*" " 'When a man has it, he can stand the world on its head.'

" ' But I was plumb scared all the while myself

Courage? I could feel it running out of my boots."

" 'Oh, yes, but that's the great thing. You didn't look as if you were frightened. From all one could see, your nerve was sublime.' "

The real-estate man especially exhibits, if he is more than a musty two-penny variety, great yet sane courage to take hold of big ventures and never waver until the completion of his undertaking. He particularly exploits confidence, both in himself and in the people, that buyers will be furnished and that they will give good values for the land. With these qualities go *indomitable push, inspiring energy, omnipresent and tireless action.*

One whom I know "cleans up" a nice fortune every year in land speculations. His prime attitude is that of confidence that the purchasers surely will be on hand. His courage takes him directly into the home field of local real-estate people. His methods are all planned in detail, and carried out with a ceaseless rush of energy. His advertising is sensational, rapid, convincing. His policy is legitimate business. He knows land, drift of populations,—natural or brought about by his own efforts,—and human nature of the kind to which he appeals. "Offer the people any good thing, and they will take it." He has the external methods, it might be said by local dealers, of the success-robber; but his mental operations are careful and scientific. Not by mere birth did he acquire his ability. He had to develop it; to learn how to do the right thing by doing real-estate things in his head and on the ground for a long period.

CHAPTER XVI.

THE LARGER BUSINESS.

LARGER business power demands all the qualities of the lesser orders, and, in addition, ability to handle men and situations quickly and effectively. The business man is here a manager in the broadest and completest sense. More and more has he called his brain-cells into action and educated them, and more and more has his "great within," the subconscious self, assumed the feeling and attitude of kingship. We are far removed from the origin of such words as "manager," "superintendent," etc., yet never were their "raw meanings" more perfectly exemplified than in the larger business. Thus, "to manage" is to do with the hand of power, and the Sanskrit word, *Ma* (Latin, *manus*), meant "to shape" and also "to think." The managing hand must think. So, too, "to superintend" is to "apply the mind to-above," from *super*, "above," and *intendere*, "to apply, etc." The larger business is something more than mere *busy*-ness; it is *thought, in big phases, comprehensive, alert, swift and conclusive.* It always means the psychic mood of kingship,—

Saxon *kuninge*, German könig, as Carlyle has it,
Can-ning, the Able-Man.

THE MERCHANT.

§ 1.   It is not the meteors that most engage
the attention of common observers and scientific
thinkers. These are a part of "the passing show,"
and they have their day—and reward.   But the
fixed stars and the steadily moving planets have
caught and held the human eye from the days of
Egyptian temples and Phœnician shops and ships.
Large mercantile establishments and huge business
concerns represent immense power, and system,
and harmony.   Such are the factors that attract
and hold trade.   This combination is generated by
the potent practical ability of some master mind.
Yet the laws that govern the big concern are the
laws that operate to build the smaller into the greater.

§ 2.   You are urged to cease thinking of yourself and your business *as inferior*, for we are all poten-
tially alike in powers, every human sharing in the
great psychic forces and nature of the whole humanity, and every successful enterprise involving the
elements of the whole business world.   A live man
in a live world has only big inspiration to deal with.

§ 3.   Our present study, then, merely analyzes
the larger truth suggested.   *Energetic practical
ability embraces the following elements:*

(1)   *A Reasonable Supply of Practical Brains.*

(Your brain-cells may be developed by brain
work involving business action.)

(2)   *The Market Vision.*

(To be acquired by educating the subconscious
self through thought, action, and faith.)

(3) *Alertness Toward the Whole Commercial Field.*

(Objective watchfulness quickens subjective alertness.)

(4) *Adaptation to Changing Neighborhood and Commercial Situations.*

(Intuitions are born of experience and the above qualities, and are cultivated by asking the "soul" for them, together with habitual confidence in them.)

(5) *Prompt Decision of Thought, Judgment, Action.*

(This combination comes of willing it, forcing the sense of inner energy and placing over it rapid but sane judgment.)

(6) *Economy of Details Balanced by Largeness of Operations.*

(The self may be educated by practice to estimate things in relative proportions and in relation to large affairs and outcomes. A small leak or unused waste is important, but a small expense prophetic of greater income is not important save in relation to the outcome of it.)

(7) *Knowledge of Goods and Values.*

(This is a product of experience, but the power expresses through the subjective self, and is acquired by incessant attention and effort.)

(8) *Knowledge of the Public Desires.*

(Of a similar origin as the previous element.)

(9) *Courage to Win Public Confidence.*

(Fear, doubt, hesitation, never develop courage or win confidence. Confidence inspires courage.)

(10) *Confidence in the People.*

(The people will come if you let them know

that you are offering values at prices to their inter-est. The feeling-attitude here considered can be unfolded by the simple régime: assume that you have it, assert its actuality by your mental attitude, and act on the basis of certainty that the public is yours.)

(11) *Magnetic Adjustment to Business and the Buying Worlds.*

(Magnetism is cultivable, and you are referreᴅ to "*Power For Success*" for an exhaustive and prac-tical treatment of required methods. But business adjustment of magnetism, now to the business world, now to the buying public, must be acquired by experience. Nevertheless, you observe that its initiation is largely a matter of feeling, which means a general state of alertness toward the two worlds, and the constant upspringing in conscious-ness of the assurance that such and such is the right time and so and so are the precise conditions and requirements of immediate success. The prac-tical method consists in keeping awake and in con-stantly trying for the feeling, always respecting it, always giving it perfect confidence.)

§ 4. *The gymnasium for practical mercantile ability is the merchant's actual business,* but it should be remembered that *the quality no more comes of mere pushing activity than does a compound steam engine or a triumph of commercial architecture. It is the product of the merchant's directed thinking at his endless best.* The power appears when the whole man is at focus for exactly the end of its development.

§ 5. Said a writer: "Think—think—think! Nothing in the world costs so little and pays so

well as good, hard thinking, study and investigation." *Nothing in the world costs so much while paying so well;* that is the truth. Measure the cost in
time, patience, persistence, courage, confidence,
determination, use of experience, observation,
watchfulness, eternal activity, nerves, actual leisure, ceaseless responsibility, trials, failures
Should a man on a desert island pay all possible
items, he might devise a theory, but he would not
attain practical ends. Practical mercantile ability
costs money: for human contact, for literature, for
experimentation with men, for furniture, goods,
advertising, upholding of markets, maintaining of
positions, and so on almost endlessly.

*Practical commercial mentality is one of the costli-
est things in this world.* It has cost man what
the world of finance is to-day.

For the reasons based in this fact and the laws
of the mind, you are invited, now, to observe the
following suggestion:

§ 6. The merchant will find it a profitable
investment to *dedicate one room* in his establishment
to the development of the dynamic factor—*Commercial Mentality.* Let that room be open to no
human being save himself. *The subconscious self
requires aloneness and the opportunity of silence.* Let
its general appointments be well up to the reasonable limit of his means. Let every article therein
suggest, so far as possible, will, resourcefulness
and success. *Environment immensely influences the
subconscious self.* The pictures and other artistic
features are all of an inspirational character. *Thus
we secure the operation of the law of suggestive uplift.* The color-scheme of the place is appropriate

to the personality of the merchant and stimulating
to his best mentality. *In this way harmony is established for cleanest thinking.* Books abound which
stir thought and are redolent of the large but magnetic will. *Such works call to arms and the success-
moods.* Every important trade journal connected
with the business, and every notable periodical
publication bearing on financial success, are on the
tables. *So is the atmosphere charged with business
incitement.* Other articles suggested by business
temperament or the merchant's line are also in
evidence. *These keep the mind on the chosen track
without the sense of urge and drive.* Into such a
room, now, let the man go, once a day for thirty
minutes, and, mastering his mental activity, concentrate the whole of himself on thought about
improvement of business and resolution to carry
out his plans when thoroughly settled. *Such habituated resort to aloneness and the greater self releases
from distraction and conduces to the freest thinking,
but more, to the strong suggestions and wandering
inspirations which, under the sway of business passion, are of vast power and value in every successful
life.* Surely, if slowly, the merchant so doing will
train his mind and executive faculty to surprising
facility, inventiveness and power. The result will
be infallible. The suggestion involves psychological laws that are as old as man and as deep as the
Infinite.

§ 7. The *practical outcomes*, in addition to
those indicated in the italicised lines above, will
include the following:

You will come to insist upon a *growing knowledge* of self.

You will make *astonishing discoveries* about your business.

You will gather from reflection wider and truer *understanding of human nature.*

You will *analyze and systematise* every department on the place.

You will arrive through directed thought at a closer *knowledge of agents, clerks, managers, all employees.*

The *market vision* will gain the opportunity of the "quiet hour."

The *subjective self* will make objective its *sense of values.*

You will find ideas, schemes, possibilities, crowding upon your attention which will call for *weighing, sifting, experiment and push.*

You will *discover improvable conditions*, management, misfits, leaks, waste, and the like, and the best methods for dealing therewith.

You will come to *out-look your entire business* and its environment in a new light.

You will emerge above the whole *field of advertising*, and perceive that therein alone is a business as complex, as difficult, as important, as the main schemes of your life. And you will in time come to know your part of that business like a map spread plainly before you.

You will thus *get your business under you* instead of above or all around you—and that is the master's position.

You will also surely develop *splendid mentality*, the one prime factor of the merchant's career.

From this room you will *issue orders for all the success-elements* in merchandizing: System * * *

Judgment * * * Alertness * * * Prompt-
ness * * * Courag ? * * * Confidence
* * * Persistence * * * Patience * * *
Energy * * * Push * * * Honor * * *
Reliability * * * Self-control * * * In-
sight * * * Courtesy * * * Tact * * *
Enterprise * * * Adjustment * * * Mar-
ket-Knowledge * * * Sense of Values * * *
Advertising Skill * * * Quick and Profitable
Sales * * * Incessant Improvement * * *
Safe Expansion * * * Solid Building * * *
Permanent Business.

This sanctum is your central power-house. If
the suggestion appears visionary to you, you are
invited to observe that every successful merchant's
skull is exactly correspondent—with these important differences, however: *the room so set apart will
serve you more perfectly, your mind going into it,
because it is larger, ostensibly suggestive and to the
exact purpose specifically dedicated, and so bringing
into operation psychological laws the use of which
you would otherwise miss.*

§ 8. " A property of rubber trees has no real
value so long as there's a wilderness of rubber trees
all round that's everybody's property.   How can a
man pay even the interest on his purchase money,
supposing he's bought a rubber plantation, when
he has to compete with other people who've paid
no purchase money, but just get out as much as
they like from the free forest?"

No real merchant's business can be so badly
placed as that, but it amounts to the same thing
when trade goes all the other man's way, whether
your "rubber trees" are sold just below your limit

or are free, and your own salvation, where competitors try to bring about such a situation, consists in that business mentality which contrives to purchase or control the "free forest." Otherwise, you are in business at what is called the "marginal cost," the highest cost at which the goods can be sold at any profit, and when you do not make more than just enough to keep going, you really lose.

PUBLISHERS.

§ 9. The question first presented concerns the type of publishing business you wish to go into, or have already entered. You may be willing to out-put any print promising profitable sales, or you may decide for a certain dignity of character in the business, or you may combine both dignity and the emphatic financial aim. The qualities of business power demanded by these ideals are not identical. The first order may be coarse, crudely pushing, as purely mercantile as the wholesaling of pork. Witness the auctioning off of a stock of books temporarily thrust in next door to an old-line book-shop; the brutality of the business is evident and the threat to standing trade is commercial only. The second order maintains magnetic resourcefulness tempered by some degree of the finesse of culture. The third order requires equal power, but it exhibits a larger phase of magnetic accommodation. The following suggestions, therefore, may not be amiss:

First, select your type of publishing business, and stand by the choice until you know that a change is demanded. This calls for a clear-cut notion of the type. It is a law of success that the psychic ideal must be distinct and vivid, held

steadily before the mind, and believed in with
great vigor, and that when these items obtain the
practical activity is stimulated and directed by the
ideal.   If you have in mind a luminous picture of
just your kind of business, your thought is inspired, your deeper self broods incessantly on the
best means for its realization, brings to you values
which you would not otherwise discover, and moulds
your conduct of the business to better effect than
can be secured in any other way.   These strange
sounding statements are simply the facts of worldwide experience in practical affairs.

   *Secondly, develop strikingly predominant char-
acteristics* of the book business.   The house that
has none such is not for the twentieth century of
specialized concentration.   If your ideal differs in
no respect from that of other publishers, you are
merely a fighter in the field of common competition.
The value of your conception of your own business
consists not so much in its common features as in
its special differences.   The subconscious "mind"
is never content with ordinary resemblances, but
always seeks to get at the new and the more valuable.   When it is ignored in this respect, it simply
goes to sleep.   When its peculiar and differentiat-
ing suggestions are sought and followed, it then
furnishes the finest values.   Indeed, the danger
then appears of becoming too prolific or too fantastic, and at that point hard-headed objective practical sense must be called in.   It is always a
question, in any business, between ordinary sameness and brilliant but practical leadership.   The
publishing business demands the combination suggested.   It is the striking characteristics and

successes well handled and ever inventive which mark the leaders among those who handle books.

Thirdly, ascertain the financial and literary traditions of your chosen type. Few lines of business have more pronounced backgrounds of tradition than the publishing business, and you should know the traditions of your own field as a possible part of your mental capital. This is not a mere matter of general information. The information warns you against mistakes committed in the line of the tradition, and it gives you more or less the key to past successes in that line. Above all, that knowledge furnishes the soil in which your subjective "mind" may plant its finest seeds of suggestion, and, at the same time, the stimulation from which it may discover—rather, create—those seeds.

Fourthly, at this point will arise the *important question of attitude toward the above rather fixed factors.* Some traditions must be violated; others should be utilized. He who cannot smash a tradition is ruled by it and is a slave—and death has him. He who cannot utilize a tradition is a slave to a notion of progress or freedom, and death has him also. Business Death is not finicky about methods: the end is the same, whether or no. It is altogether clear that when a tradition hampers financial adaptation, it becomes a threat against business and a demand for violation. But some traditions are an integral part of the publishing trade, and others of particular lines. These must be worked into modern commercial life, and this means adaptation to times, conditions, environment. The publisher who remains blind to these requirements has only "luck" on which to count.

The cheapest investment for mere "luck" is a pack of cards, and the best business man at that business is the man who "stacks the pack"—but the tool he employs is not luck—it is brain-experience.

The attitude called for is a complex thing, and is as supple as a wrestler. Generally speaking, it is a compound of courage-confidence, alertness, promptness, tact, judgment, energy, persistence, intuition concerning public taste, demands and values. The shibboleth might well be—"Every day a new thought-impulse!"

Fifthly, the perception of the public taste is the publisher's sixth sense. He must discover what the reading public wants, and be ready to meet the demand when it is on. Warehouses are loaded with belated or premature goods. This perception of public demands embraces seasons and conditions. Some housewives never ask their husbands what they wish for dinner except at the close of breakfast, but the wise cook times her question with appetite. The astute publisher knows when the public will be hungry, and, in a general way, what it will call for. The public is said to be fickle, and that seems to be rather true of the publishers. You have, then, to subordinate your fickleness to the eccentricities of the reading people. They are a helpless lot. They desire mental occupation, or recreation, or development: part of them one thing, part of them another thing; at times all of them the same thing. In the impulse of a certain general appetite, the public may drift to one particular book, magazine, paper,—not necessarily because the kind it happens for the time to take to is just what it really desires, but because elsewhere it gets

what it does not want. A Chinese restaurant on
the Sante Fe railway line was packed with hungry
tourists. No man or woman patronizing the place
desired a single article sold; the eaters wanted rid-
dance of the pangs of hunger, but they desired
nothing that was eaten. Doubtless, the proprietor,
after his place had been swept clean of food (it was
never clean in any other sense), said in self-gratu-
lation: "Gleat chop house! Me show what
Melicans want!" Publishers sometimes mistake
necessity for taste.

It is a psychic law that you can find out what the
people want if you will observe two rules: Practically investigate what they are calling for; and
maintain an alert subconscious attitude of inquiry in
the matter. You can connect with the innumerable wires of the public life, the people who read,
by willing yourself to listen for revelations from
the outside. The great business men rely, it may
be without knowledge of the fact, as much on their
psychic feeling of situations and demands, as upon
objective observation. The two attitudes must, of
course, be combined, for the best results, but it is
beyond all doubt that business power depends on
intuitions no less than on direct conclusions drawn
from external facts.

*Sixthly, the public taste covers the mechanical
make-up and exterior of publications.* Such features
as quality of paper, style of type, arrangement of
page matter, and color and design of the cover, are
vastly important considerations. To these factors
the publisher must bring discernment of the popular art-sense, or educate the sense, and remember
that first impressions may sell or "kill" any kind

of print. The best salesman in every business is
the man who wants the goods. The art-sense of
the people is itself a salesman when its secret has
been caught. And he who tries by practical methods
to catch that sense will educate it. A taste which
you have created always wants your values.

*Seventhly, the publisher must possess the variety
of knowledge which back-grounds his type:* classics,
science, philosophy, education, psychology, art,
fiction, and so on. Even pig-iron demands corresponding information. It is not here intended that
the publisher must be a master of any of these
subjects; that would be impossible. To-day, no
such masters are to be found. But the demands
are similar to those made on the promoter: he must
know his business in a general way (the publishing
business), and enough of the various phases of the
background of his particular line to handle intelligently his own work. Out of this specific knowledge are born a special sympathy with the type
and love for it and the world it represents which
will surely develop the intuitions required and a
kind of general business magnetism of the greatest
value.

*Eighthly, practical psychology underlies all busi-
ness enterprise,* and every successful publisher studies
the psychological peculiarities of human nature, of
human aggregations, of seasons and conditions.
College towns are not summer resorts. Psychic factors determine trade. The publisher, it would seem,
should be master of the fundamentals of mental
science in its practical phases, together with spe-
cializations of advertising, how to handle the crowd,
and so on. Out of such study will in time grow

intuitional power invaluable to business attitudes and conduct.

Ninthly, the nicest huge task confronting the publisher is successful advertising. To this subject an entire division of the present chapter is devoted, and we need not further prolong the consideration now engaging us.

The reading public, like woman, is coarse, or respectably commonplace, or impossibly fine, but, unlike her, is always fickle and uncertain. The publisher has, therefore, three battles on his hands: against himself, against fate, and against that selected class of the people whose response is his business life. Houses have failed because they have refused to fight a lover's war or have lacked the daring that wins the affections of a fast-changing age. John Harkles, in " *The Gentleman From Indiana*" "thought when he seemed defeated: 'To escape the worst that fate can deal, and to wring courage from it instead of despair, that is success; and it was success he would have. He would take fate by the neck.' " The quotation is drenched with the spirit of business power

MISCELLANEOUS.

Other divisions of business noted in the outline given in section 1 of last chapter are sufficiently treated in the foregoing chapters or will be covered by the remaining discussions, and will not, therefore, be considered further, except in two or three miscellaneous paragraphs to follow.

§ 10. Always, of course, ceaseless energy and alert inventiveness are demanded by the very character of modern business. My friend was a

schoolmaster and not suspected of business ability.
He went into a plant that manufactured all articles
used for storing and shipping butter. He soon
literally saturated the place with his quiet, determined personality. Machinery he improved,
material he got more cheaply, employees he utilized
to the utmost, wages he reduced where necessary,
work he combined, waste he stopped, freights he
lowered, products he bettered, prices he met. He
pulled success out of a ramshackle concern. His
will had made sure connection with his brain.

"The thing to do is to make up your mind
what you want, and to put all your power and
resolution into getting it—and the rest is easy
enough. I don't think there's anything beyond a
strong man's reach, if he only believes enough in
himself."

§ 11. *But the man must decide exactly what it
is that he wants.* "The man or woman who cannot decide for himself might as well give up at once,
for he must surely be crushed in the end beneath
nature's most implacable law, the survival of the
fittest."

§ 12. There are two extremes beyond which
success is never found: *excessive cost and mere imitation.* When a man is doing business at maximum
cost, he has against him the whole body of economic
law. "This maximum cost may also be called the
marginal cost of production, because the producer
is just on the point of withdrawing. He neither
makes nor loses. All the other producers—the in-
tramarginal producers—earn a profit. But producing at maximum cost only covers expenses." "In
every business there are always some who are able

just to make both ends meet. Their machinery is antiquated, their capital has been depleted, their business activity and knowledge are no longer what they should be, and their former profits, if there ever were any, have now vanished. They may continue for a time to struggle along, hoping against hope, and may live on their capital, being content to bridge over the next few years without profit; or if they have invested heavily in unsalable buildings and machinery, they may deceive themselves by a fallacious system of bookkeeping, and through a neglect to charge up the item of depreciation of stock or machinery, may figure out a nominal profit. In any case, however, the day of reckoning is sure to come. Sooner or later the producer will find that he is not making money. He will cease producing that particular commodity, and his place will be taken by some more efficient producer."

§ 13. The other extreme is almost as disastrous: mere *imitation*. One who found himself without a dollar at fifty, projected every business qualification into a manufacturing plant which had struggled along on the "marginal cost" plan for years, and in which the usual results had appeared —debts on every hand. The new man's greatest principles were: "I follow no human being, but lead the world in my department," and, "I make good my guaranty first, and investigate complaints afterwards." I believe that all the qualifications mentioned in this volume have all along been exemplified in that manufacturer's business, but the two principles given above have constituted the tap-roots of the success which he built up within ten years. It is now the largest plant of its kind in the world. Especially has it exhibited the fact that "marginal cost," in its influence on business, depends on the quality of the goods represented, for its output commands a higher selling price than that of its competitors anywhere. You can always get a higher price than your neighbor for "the same thing" if it is *not* the "same thing," but a really superior article.

The Advertiser.

As the advertiser is a business man, every section in this book may profit his particular business-exploitation.

§ 14. Advertising is a business. It may be an adjunct, but it is, even as such, distinctively a business to be mastered in the successful conduct of any namable enterprise.

§ 15. It is also a science, not exact, of course, yet involving very definite principles which require understanding in order to the best results. Securing such results demonstrates advertising as an art with rules for the application of the science which cannot safely be ignored. At the start, then, *your will confronts the conquest of a business, a science, and an art.*

§ 16. This particular trinity is at bottom psychological. Its keynote is "suggestion." By suggestion is meant, not intimation, announcement, notification, statement, exploitation; which are merely the external shells or wires for the main thing; the real idea is, *psychic compulsion of desire and action.* It is the business of advertising to compel purchasers. Suggestion is the psychological force resident behind or within external means.

The most artificial creation of modern times is national advertising—and it is forced by that dynamic power: suggestion.

§ 17. *Suggestion by the advertisement must act through (a) the five senses, or (b) the bulk of the physical or mental life, or (c) some phase of either; but it always wins through appeal to personal interest.* In some way, self-interest must be touched by presentations suggesting the appropriate sense or phase of body or mind. And the uppermost fact in all that appeal is this: the possible customer, or client, or patron, or investor, cares nothing whatever for *your* interests; he is ever intent and active on his own interest solely. The people, for an example of suggestion through the senses insuring a purchase, know pianos and desire them, but if your advertisement would read as well for soap, having no hint of music heard by the readers (you have observed such advertisements), or if it fails to convince of finish, durability, permanence and range of tone or price superior to other instruments, it is certainly a failure, and it may sell your competitor's goods. That is being done constantly.

§ 18. The customer is not always alive to your phase of his personal welfare. He has gotten along without you thus far. *You must, therefore, create in him a particular appetite for your values.* But the appetite, to induce action, must be developed in some way into *a cause for decision in your favor.* You have to compel him to desire your goods a little more than he at the time desires other articles or the money involved. His motives are his mainsprings of conduct, and successful advertising confronts the problem: *How to suggest dormant or new motives that will actually impel him to your kind of action for the sake of his own advantage as he conceives it.*

§ 19.   This problem is complex, and space and the design of the present volume permit only very general indication of its elements, as follows:

I.   THE AIMS OF ADVERTISING.   These involve the whole psychology of suggestion.   They have as ends—

(*A*) *To attract attention.*   Here we have the *mechanics of skill.*   Any means or device which accomplishes the object is legitimate.   Where thousands of business men are calling on the public to attend, it is evident that the *deciding factors* must be: supposed *superiority* of article, *extent of effort* with *constancy and regularity* and, perhaps, *variety of suggestion*, and *pre-eminence of arresting qualities.*

(*B*) *To arouse interest.*   Here we have the *psychology of magnetic appeal.*   This factor involves the elements of (A), but its psychic end is not knowledge, but *interest-knowledge.*   I read many advertisements, always first in the magazines.   Now and then one has a life-interest to me; it refers to something I desire.   But some advertisements create a desire, by suggesting relation to my real life, which I had not before recognized.   The considerations are; *what the people are practically interested in;* or, *creation of interest by appeal to the practical individual life.*

(*C*) *To maintain interest.*   Here we have the *law of developed habit through repeated suggestion.*   Desire is an impulse; if you can get the man or woman to have the impulse often enough within a limited time, you have raised a desire-habit. *An unsatisfied habit is a power.*

(*D*) *To create desire.* Here we have *specialized suggestion.* Of course (C) and (D) are co-ordinate in the matter. Nevertheless, the aim in arousing interest is to develop it into active desire of some particular form. The economic factor of "marginal utility" comes now in play. *Your practical desire must spring from a general balancing of a person's income and his desires for ten thousand other things for all of which he is at any one time inadequately supplied with money.* You have to decide the balance of many desires in favor of your own business.

(*E*) *To secure prompt sales.* Here we have all the above factors utilized by *business resourcefulness.* You can, of course, sell your entire stock in time; but meanwhile your expenses are running on; the question, then, is this: will you get a movement on your sales to outrun your advertising expenses? This means such a concentrated focussing of effort that you keep "the iron at white heat," so to speak. The advertising mediums to-day are actually supported largely by the public in a way which should be characterized either as charity or gambling. The fault may not be that of the mediums but there is certainly a large proportion of advertisers who fail to pack results into right lengths of time.

Régime: Investigate your advertisements with these questions: Do they use the above means? Do they embody the aims indicated?

"Advertising is that subtile, indefinable, but powerful force whereby the advertiser creates a demand for a given article in the minds of a great many people, or arouses the demand that is already there in latent form."

§ 20.   II. THE MEDIUM OF ADVERTISING.   This should be—

(*A*) *According to your business.*   If that is local, comparatively local means are in order.   If that is general, you would not advertise a book on Astronomy in a medium supported by Italian laborers.

(*B*) *According to competition.*   The man who will not lead his competitors in advertising is engaged merely in a scramble for trade.   Especially is it true to-day that advertising, because of the element of competition, must resort to methods which a finicky scholarship might find distasteful. My friend, the real estate man, employs the most sensational means because he goes into communities whose local dealers were born on the ground.   He could never succeed in such places were all dealers like himself.   The town would, as a matter of fact, be all sold out.   He leads.   By the time his competitors are ready for action, he has cleaned up his business and departed.

(*C*) *According to Territory.*   The factors involved in territory are, financial ability, staple needs, sectional peculiarities, and amenability to given kinds of suggestion.   You are invited to analyze any specific territory with regard to these factors.   Such study brings into play the psychology of adjustment.

(*D*) *According to Classes.*   Legitimate class divisions as regards advertising are seen in financial ability, education, territorial tastes and predilections, and so on.   *The class-character of some people makes them utterly unresponsive to suggestions of a certain kind.* You may know what they need and ought to desire: all sorts of considerations render them non-suggestible so far as natural bents are concerned. At the same time, *such classes are merely human beings, and, entrenched in superiority or ignorance or prejudice as they are, they are simply powerless, for the most part, when you bring to bear upon them the great laws and forces of adjusted advertising.*

(*E*) *According to Publications.* This and the following elements will be illustrated by reference below to certain statistical maps.

(*F*) *According to Circulation.* It is not always that the extent of circulation should be a deciding factor in advertising. Your article may be of a very special nature, and the big circulations may not reach your people, at least in the true advertising sense of arresting suggestion at all. *Pronounced special desires lead people to look for satisfaction in those publications which really emphasize such desires.* Moreover, the heaviest circulations often represent nothing whatever of life in your particular line. *Always you wish to reach the kind of life which need or may become practically interested in your output.*

(*G*) *According to Publicity.* Reference is here made to sign-boards, posters, and the like.

(*H*) *According to Permanence of Utility.* It is a real question whether you will go into daily, weekly, or monthly or quarterly mediums. There are some articles which do not interest the public as seen in publications which are born but to die. The same readers of the daily will ignore an advertisement which they will read in the monthly. We have here merely a matter of habit: *things are observed in an interested way where habit has induced observation.* Unless you have a fortune already with which to compel a new habit of this kind, you waste your investment when you appeal to people outside of traditional lines.

(*I*) *According to Permanence of Reading.* Reading matter is permanent in an advertising sense when the public preserves the medium because of its matter *and* its advertising character. This element presents the pigeon-hole feature. If your medium suggests a receptacle for this or that interest, to which reference may be had in the future, the medium has the element of permanence indicated.

(*J*) *According to Place, Display, Reader's Tastes, and so on.* This is merely a particularization of some of the foregoing elements.

I have before me a map "showing that most of the circulation of all kinds of publications is confined to the country east of the Mississippi and north of Mason's and Dixon's line."

I have a second map "showing that there are more readers to a weekly publication in the southeastern states than in any other part of the United States."

I have a third map "showing that ten states possess 81.08 per cent of the combined circulation of all publications."

I have a fourth map "showing also that the greatest number of readers to a daily newspaper is in the southeastern states."

The maps show the densest circulation in New York, Pennsylvania, Illinois. But the territory densest in readers-to-a-publication comprises West Virginia, Kentucky, Tennessee, North Carolina, South Carolina, Georgia, Alabama, Mississippi, Louisiana and Massachusetts. Nevertheless, these facts will not decide one to go into the southern field irrespective of other considerations. One of the cheapest and most worthless publications I know is especially patronized in the West and South, and for the evident reason that it appeals to its kind, so that its advertisers are of the same sort. They can live in that territory and through that medium, whereas, it is hoped, you would simply starve.

The ten states which possess 81.08 per cent of the combined circulation of all publications are Maine, Massachusetts, Delaware, Pennsylvania, New York, Ohio, Michigan, Indiana, Iowa, Tennessee.

Illustrative deductions, then, are: If your article is inexpensive and foolish, go into that southeastern territory. If your article is a staple, the last-named states are already open to you by habits of reading. Nevertheless, these facts are cross-cut by all sorts of other considerations, such as kind of product, tastes of people, educational peculiarities, financial ability, specialized tendencies, and the word, "according," therefore represents exactly the psychological problem which the advertiser must solve.

Régime: Study each of these factors and compare your advertising with them by rigid analysis.

§ 21. III. The Purchasers. You have in this respect to consider—

(A) The General Public.

(B) Particular Classes.

(C) Their Moods and Seasons.

(D) Their Specific Financial Conditions.

(E) Their Relation to Your Competitors.

(F) Their Attitude Toward Yourself and your Business.

(G) Their Education in your Line.

(H) Their Suggestibility to your Advertising.

(I) Their Habits of Reading and Observing.

(J) Their Sectional Characteristics and Tendencies.

Régime: You are invited to get the above items, thoroughly understood, in your mind, and to go over your advertising for specific revision and the embodiment of the principles suggested.

§ 22. IV. THE CHARACTERISTICS OF ADVERTISING. These are to be treated—

(*A*) *In general.* "There are just two sorts of advertising: the great general publicity covering the country and cropping out everywhere in favor of an article which can be benefited by such widespread publicity, and the fewer articles of which the advertising must be self-supporting, and of which each advertisement must bring in sufficient returns to pay at least for that advertisement, to pay for the articles and to pay a profit." The general advertiser must plan his campaign and every particle of copy. The psychic factors, without which the money engaged will not move in this direction, are courageous confidence, alertness, energy, invention and initiative which, backed by a persistence never failing is always darting out in new ways and so sustaining the vitality of worldwide suggestion. So far as concerns copy, I hold that the brain that carries on the campaign must be imitated in the preparation of its suggestions, and that no living man can tell "good" copy from "poor" until trial. *The advertiser has really to educate the public to his kind of copy.* Good copy is that which actually contributes to increase of a staying business. A fool *may* write it; but he merely hits off the subtle quality which the man behind the enterprise *originates, creates* right out of hand. The test and the teacher alike is experience. *The artist who achieves the triumph of good copy is the subconscious self which has been educated in the successful business itself.* The only certainty about the matter is the fact that the subconscious self that can build a business can advertise it, *and its ways may violate all the expert laws to be named.* Advertising is a science, but it is really a particular-individual science, not a universal one, except in very general aspects. At any rate, the advertising expert must literally soak in your business if he is to do good work. He has to feel your psychic quality and vibration.

(B) *In planning and preparing copy.* It is a good method to regard yourself as plaintiff, defendant, court and jury. Here are some of the psychic questions that must come "into court:" Advertisements must be correct * * * but not stilted * * * arranged * * * striking * * * but not loud * * * bright * * * but not pert * * * interesting in some permanent way * * * arouse curiosity * * * and not disappoint in the business end * * * aptly phrased * * * avoid slang * * * and overmuch wit * * * original * * * if fitting * * * but sensible * * * never overcrowded * * * not too elaborate

artistic * * * and appropriate * * * exhibit prominently the main ideas * * * specific * * * convey
suggestion through the senses * * * or body or
mind * * * so that readers "sense" your goods
* * * always touch self-interest * * * advertise
your business * * * not the man, unless he is the
business guaranty * * * adapted to the right mediums * * * always just and honest * * * always
adjust to the trade * * * inspire confidence * * *
incessantly changed, except in your particular theme
and device * * * persistently issued in the same
medium * * * convey a sense of business prosperity * * * and confidence in your goods and
business.

Régime : You are invited to study deeply every
item above indicated, and to actually know what
each one means to *you*, to study your business as a
subject for advertising, and your advertisements
for discovery of defects in the regards suggested;
to set your will to realization and improvement.

§ 23. V. THE MAN AND HIS BUSINESS. Some
of the qualifications are—

(A)   *The man and the successful business are one.*
The triumphantly advertised business exhibits the
man:

(B)   As charged with *magnetic energy.*

(C)   As capable of utter *concentration* and *absolute abandonment* to achievement: (Mark the "lacklustre eye" when he is engaged in a problem.
"In it you can see a hundred thousand dead
men)."

(D)   *As indomitably persistent* in forcing the
public to see, think, act, either on ordinary or on
extraordinary motives.

(E) As possessed of *courage adequate* to the surrender of $4,000 for a one-page space or to the expending of $1,000,000 a year in the monumental game of national suggestion,—proportionately, of course, according to business and sane expectation. Your limits would seem to be indicated by the factors—"consumption of article once for all," "consumption repeating itself," "proportion of people who can be induced to consume," and "relation between price of article and above factors." With one White Elephant, no one would expend $100,000 in advertising if the animal's price is $100,000. With a herd, the idea of "purchase once for all," would necessarily determine the advertising output. With a million, the campaign would depend on the probable number of people who ought to desire white elephants. In some cases, it is the *advertising campaign* which is the White Elephant. The aim of the advertisement business is more money than you have to start with.

(F) As marked by *corresponding confidence:* undimmed faith in self, the business, and its advertising.

(G) As endowed with *judgment*, cool, deliberate, wise, emphatic and decisive. Many advertisers are mere gamblers.

(H) As an argus-eyed embodiment of *alertness* for possibilities, defeats, advertising media, and competitors. It is, again, the leader who wins, especially the leader who sells by his advertising nobody's goods but his own.

(I) As, therefore, *resourceful* for the demands of an advertising age, every day of which calls for greater capital and larger and finer brains.

(J) As possessed of wide and true *imagination* for goods, type, display, space, environment, contingencies, situations, the people, sales, improvements, expansion.

(K) As offering actual *utilities and values indispensable* according to point of view.

(L) As a persistent exponent of *system and follow-up*.

(M) As altogether *reliable*.

" Therefore he went after his public and made a continuous performance of the effort."

Régime: Subject yourself to rigid scrutiny until you have discovered how far above or below such a standard of the successful advertiser you are in your own business. Add other distinct qualities to the study as they occur to mind.

§ 24. VI. ADDITIONAL RÉGIMES:

(1) The advertiser should *master some manual of modern psychology*. "Traditionally the practical business man scouts at theory. Psychology, to the popular mind, is something devoid of all practical application, related to metaphysics, and suited only to the recluse and hermit. Such adverse criticism has, however, been the exception. The American business man is not afraid of theories. He wants them, and the more the better."

Psychology should be regarded as the science of self-knowledge for the end of self-development through reaction with the world in which we live. This is the foundation of the author's all-directive work, " *Practical Psychology.*"

(2) He should also study the *psychology of advertising*.

(3) But he should study the *psychology of cur-*

rent advertisements as a matter of psychology as well as of business.

(4) But, again, he should *subject specimens to rigid tests*, searching out misfits, false impressions, failures on the main point, and the like.

Examples may be indicated as follows: A recent kitchen-ware advertisement read, in connection with its announcement of the ware: "POISON never found in the glazing." One's first pronounced impression was of death. A large per cent of the readers saw only the baleful word which was in capitals. A certain table condiment was announced in a single word printed large on a picture of the package, but the desirable substances blended with the condiment and giving it special value were obscured in a perfectly unemphasized statement.

(5) Set to yourself the task of *writing copy for advertisements* of your business, securing as great a *variety as possible*, and embodying the points here indicated, with all additional essentials suggested to you in the reading.

(6) In the meantime, *invent new phrases*, original, sensible, striking, interesting, compelling; and preserve them in a reference-book devoted to that purpose only.

"The idea, resulting in the words, 'Fannie Fern writes for the Ledger,' as applied to the advertising of that famous publication, was the lightning stroke of genius. These words alone were made to fill entire pages in the leading daily papers, and America wondered at the extravagance of space, and bought the Ledger."

(7) Study the *names and varieties of type* used in advertising, and *cultivate imagination for the*

printed advertisement as you look at the copy which you have written.

(8) Re-examine the previous discussion on correspondents, and apply the same to preparation of copy.

(9) Adopt the idea of an advertising sanctum, similar to that suggestion in section 6 of this chapter for the merchant. You are invited to refer to that section and to discover the significance of the psychic elements indicated in relation to the business of advertising.

"Advertising has developed three distinct professions," as the authors of "*Modern Advertising*" remark. "They are the *advertising expert*, the *advertising manager*, and the *advertising solicitor*."

"The expert is the professional man in his own office, who acts as adviser and generally as agent for clients." The advice of these pages is: *Become an advertising expert yourself; become an expert in advertising if you are already in some definite business.* Since the advertising expert is in business for his own interests, every word of his marvelous literature may be taken with the usual business discount. He is just as likely to weaken your own copy as to improve it. He is engaged for all sorts of enterprises, and simply cannot cultivate one style of psychic mood and address, which may be exactly the mood and address your business definitely needs.

"The advertising manager is an advertising expert employed exclusively by one house." Our present advice is: *Become a manager as indicated; manage your own advertising, altogether if possible, but always as "head" of the concern if your business is*

so great that you must have a manager. You have
built up that business, or desire to do so: if success
is or shall be yours, the special mental attitudes and
power behind that success are exactly the elements
required in your successful advertising.

"The solicitor is the man who secures advertising for a publication. In a large sense he is a
creator of business. He makes a study of commercial conditions. He discovers new business that can
be advertised and outlines plans." The advice now
is: *Become an advertisement solicitor; study the sections in chapter XIV which refer to business representatives and the chapter on personal requirements.*

§ 25. The ·following quotations are particularly commended as affording a number of practical
régimes. They take the form of descriptions, but
should be analyzed into specific details, each of
which will constitute direction for study and
practice.

No. 1. "Advertising is a force whereby a *keen-
eyed man,* controlling a *desirable output* from a great
factory, secures for it the *greatest possible market*
by utilizing *every form of publicity,* and *every method
of making an impression* upon the public; who
watches its sales on the one hand and its *publicity* on
the other; who, like a *train-despatcher* in his watch-
tower, keeps *a constant and thoughtful hand* on the
pulse of the market, knows exactly what his *advertising is accomplishing* and what it is *failing to accomplish,* knows *where to strengthen it* and *where to
weaken it;* who, considering the entire country as a
whole, *adapts his advertising to each locality, pushes
his products* where such products may be sold, and
leaves uncultivated the places where no possible

market may be made. He knows *something of salesmanship*, something of the *law of supply and demand*, a great deal of *human nature* and the *best methods of appealing to it;* has a vivid, *instinctive sense* of the *power of repeated impression; knows something* of the force of *striking display*, whether expressed in color on outdoor posters and street-car cards, or in black and white and in type in magazines and newspapers, and uses these as *means to his end."*

No. 2.   "Such a man, realizing that there are in this country so many mouths to be fed, so many hands and faces to be washed, so many bodies to be clothed, so many feet to be shod, makes a breakfast food, a soap, a brand of clothing or a shoe, and then launches out boldly, remembering that just as long as people continue to be born and grow up there will be more mouths, more hands, more faces, more bodies and more feet; and until the sum of human wants be changed, there will be the same steady wants and needs.   He then proceeds to find means for making his article in every home and every mind a synonym for something which will supply one of these needs."

No. 3.   "If you write a thousand words about a certain kind of soap," as an editorial writer has said, "you pay for the thousand words that you put in the magazine or newspaper.   But if you write *ten words* about that soap, write the ten words *cleverly*, make them convincing and interesting, you can perhaps make the reader think *nine hundred and ninety-nine* words more, and then you have inserted that much into the advertisement reader's head *without any cost whatever*.

No. 4. "Don't think for a moment that there is no personality or literary style involved in the writing of advertisements. There is personality in everything that a man does—in his handwriting, in his voice at the telephone, in his walk, his gestures. A man's personality can express itself in his advertising writing, so that no man can possibly take his place, once the public have got used to him, once they have accustomed their brains to taking in statements of facts as he presents them. In no line of work does personality count for more than in advertising."

No. 5. "Business is spreading daily. The individual little shop is vanishing, and the great store (or the hundreds of stores under one management) is taking its place. The manufacturer or merchant who dealt formerly with a few hundred people now deals with thousands or even millions. The business man's ambition to-day does not stop at anything. His effort is to *make the best thing in the world,* and *sell it to all the people in the world,* and there is *no reason why he shouldn't succeed,* if he can do the *right kind of advertising* as well as the right kind of manufacturing."

THE MAN IN HIGH FINANCE.

§ 26. The man in "high finance" embodies this entire volume. Here we have the Promoter, the Syndicate Manager, the President, the Banker, the Big Manufacturer, the Merchant Prince, the Great Broker, and so on. Each of these varieties, in his way, illustrates certain master qualities in the large, as follows:

I. IN PERSONALITY. An English nobleman

had been used and assisted by the promoter, and
had then turned to blackmail the latter before the
Stock Exchange Committee on a charge of fraud,
but had lost track of his one indispensable witness.
The remarks to which he was compelled by the
high-finance man to listen are instructive:

"It was not only a dirty trick that you tried to
play on me, but it was a fool-trick. That drunken
old bum of a Tavender writes some lunatic nonsense
or other to Gafferson, and he's a worse idiot even
than Tavendar is, and on the strength of what one
of these clowns thinks he surmises the other clown
means, you go and spend your money,—the money
I gave you, by the way,—in bringing Tavendar
here. You do this on the double chance, we'll say,
of using him against me for combined revenge and
profit, or of peddling him to me for a bigger profit.
You see it's all at my finger's ends, * * * and your
Tavendar and I are left to take a stroll together,
and talk over old times and arrange about new
times, and so on to your heart's content. Really,
it's too easy. You make me tired!" Of course!
Personality here was strong enough to capture the
other man's only weapon, but it was such personality that enabled the mind back of it to discover
the other man's plans. This personality analyzes
as follows:

(A) The high-finance man possesses certain
characteristics in commanding form: *ability for
affairs of great scope and importance*, vivid and comprehensive *imagination for situations*, possibilities,
combinations, contingencies, outcomes, or, *the big-
brained financial vision*, and *power and skill for the
handling* of men both as assistants and as investors—

with enemies added. *This is Rule Number One, and it covers all other rules given below.* Imitate in your business.

"The promoter," as Meade remarks, "is the outsider who offers to purchase each plant in a separate deal without reference to the price paid for the other mills. By dealing separately with each group of owners he avoids the obstacles of a mutual comparison of valuations, and can attack the proposition with some hope of success. Mr. Flint, testifying before the Lexow Commission for the Investigation of Trusts, explained the necessity for the promoter as follows: 'Q. How can you explain to the committee the fact that combinations of legitimate business enterprises have to be made the subject of promoters' agreement—have to be placed through banking establishments in Wall Street—if they are the normal outcome of a demand of the businesses themselves to enter into combination with each other? A. For the same reason that men of high intelligence are needed to make treaties between the nations, particularly during periods of war * * * Q. You mean it is a delicate diplomatic situation that has to be met? A. It is one that requires the very highest intelligence, and, as a rule, neutral parties—parties not interested, men of the intelligence and reputation to inspire unlimited confidence on the part of manufacturers, are needed to bring manufacturers together in order that they may move with the current of natural laws * * * The advantage of a neutral party, of a banker, is that he is in a position, unlike another in the same trade, to get at the facts * * * to reduce the pretensions—the exaggerated preten-

sions of the manufacturers, and bring their minds
together upon a reasonable and proper basis.'" Of
course the promoters never are perfectly disinter-
ested parties—often receiving immense sums for
their skill and labor, but the order of brains required
is evident, and without that order the business
could not be transacted, as without the high remuneration that order of personal power could never
be enlisted in such enterprises.

(B) *The Giant Will,*—which is one-third
thought, one-third energy, one-third magnetic personality,—like a huge mogul locomotive, modern
and beautifully trimmed and polished, and perfect
in action—leads these indispensables—a vestibuled
train of achievement. This constitutes the *Iron
Rule of Triumph: it is Rule Number Two.* Imitate
in your business!

(C) Whether in cow-hide boots or in dancing-
pumps, the personal bearing of the man of high-
finance fits the occasion. *This is Rule Number
Three.* Imitate in your business!

(D) He is invariably courteous up to the situation demanding drastic measures, and is capable
of employing the latter on the instant and without
necessitating future apologies. He is a practical actor. *This is Rule Number Four.* Imitate in
your business!

(E) Himself and his office exhibit, fairly short
of the overdone, the fine front of prosperity? *This
is Rule Number Five.* Imitate in your business!

(F) But, as he knows the actor's art, he shifts
the front according to demands of business. He
understands the effect of homespun and economy.
This is Rule Number Six. Imitate in your business!

(G)   He possesses and maintains great physical endurance and psychic staying qualities.   *This is Rule Number Seven.*   Imitate in your business!

(H)   He is altogether self-controlled, master of body, mind, emotions and expression.   *This is Rule Number Eight.*   Imitate in your business!

(I)   He is pre-eminently self-reliant: open to aid and suggestion, yet standing solidly on his own judgment.   *This is Rule Number Nine.*   Imitate in in your business!

(J)   Nevertheless, he is rather inclined to give the other man the impression that the thing being done is the latter's suggestion, knowing very well the real source of the idea.   *This is Rule Number Ten.*   Imitate in your business!

(K)   He has acquired the ability to shut out of his mind any environment, to retire within himself, and to concentrate all his powers absolutely on the matter in hand.   *This is the Three-Fold Rule Number Eleven.*   Imitate in your business!

(L)   He possesses, either by endowment or because of intelligent effort, personal force, and business energy and push.   The sense of internal energy may be developed and controlled, and merely requires willed attention to the thing itself, summoned at stated intervals.   See the chapter on " *The Energy of Success.*"   *This Rule is Number Twelve.*   Imitate in your business!

(M)   He maintains unbroken inner determination to bring his plans to a successful issue.   *This is Rule Number Thirteen.*   Imitate in your business!

(N)   That is to say, he has inexhaustible persistence and patience.   The only method for the acquisition of these qualities consists in enforce-

ment of growth by practical effort, but this may be
assisted as follows: By the resolute appropriation
of the idea—"Every needful thing which I wish to
avoid because it is disagreeable, or difficult, or
apparently hopeless, I do now, on the instant,
for exactly those suggested reasons; and every
strain or impulse for present gratification that will
or may interfere with my final goal I now refuse, on
the instant, simply because yielding would gratify."
This is the Rule of Stoicism, and is Number Fourteen.
Imitate in your business!

(O) He never permits present gain of any
sort to interfere with or defeat his ultimate purpose;
but holds the long-run aim in a vice-like grip
through all minor advantages. *This is Rule Number Fifteen.* Imitate in your business!

(P) He has the ability of rapidly marshalling
facts, situations, reasons, for and against any
proposition, and of prompt and final decision on
demand. *This is Rule Number Sixteen.* Imitate in
your business!

(Q) The disease of double-mindedness he does
not know. "I am of two minds about one thing,"
said the Virginian ("*The Virginian*"), facing his
wedding with a woman in the throes of a New
England conscience and her personal fears, and a
duel with Tampas on the spot. "I'd sooner have
a sickness than be undecided this way. I reckon it
would make me sick." *This is Rule Number Seven-
teen.* Imitate in your business!

(R) He is an enthusiastic and tireless worker.
This is Rule Number Eighteen. Imitate in your
business!

(S) He is never discouraged, except after the

thing is done—perhaps not then. A railway builder traveled the length of the road which he had built through the Blue Ridge mountains, and went sick at sight of the difficulties which he had overcome. During operations every frowning obstacle had merely hitched his determination a notch higher. The spirit is self-hypnotizing, but it is indispensable. *This is Rule Number Nineteen.* Imitate in your business!

(T) And he acquires the art of concealing nervousness and fear, of covering disaster, of making good any seeming defeat. *This is Rule Number Twenty.* Imitate in your business!

(U) He is, therefore, a man of resourceful courage; his soul is sometimes daring, but always foresighted, sometimes bold, but always wise, and while confident forever, is never ostentatious. *This is Rule Number Twenty-One.* Imitate in your business!

(V) But he is alert, watchful, keenly observant. *This is Rule Number Twenty-Two.* He has his hand on every factor of his enterprise, and takes no chances which will not pay largely. Imitate in your business!

(W) He believes in himself, in his plans, in his success; and experienced failures seem to enhance this triple faith. *This is Rule Number Twenty-Three.* Imitate in your business!

II. § 27. In Business Action. Certain other master qualities appear in the business action of the high-finance man, such as the following:

(A) He is an inveterate student of human nature. *This is Rule Number Twenty-Four.* An uneducated "handy-man" said to a writer on psy-

chology: " There is very little difference between
one man and another; but what there is is very important." Be such a student!

(B) He cultivates the art of adaptation, and
would be called in the West a " good mixer." *This
is Rule Number Twenty-Five.* Cultivate in your
business!

(C) He studies the art of using third persons
for ends he cannot reach himself by direct methods.
This is politics, and is *Rule Number Twenty-Six.*
Cultivate such business politics!

(D) He is, hence, a diplomat. He wears the
mask of reticence or the open countenance of
frankness, but he keeps his own counsels, learns
those of other men, and meets every situation with
skill invariably turned to his own advantage. *This
is Rule Number Twenty-Seven.* Practice diplomacy
in your business!

(E) He handles men as tools, honorably, of
course, but for the business in hand. *This is Rule
Number Twenty-Eight.* Master men in your business.

(F) He manages, in some way, to inspire confidence in himself and his plans. *This is Rule
Number Twenty-Nine.* Imitate in your business!

(G) He is a winning pleader, but is, if the
fact were known, advocate, court and jury, for it is
his business to decide every question, yet convey
an opposite impression in many instances. *This is
Rule Number Thirty.* Imitate in your business!

(H) And the times and the words of any surrender never can be used against him, for they are
always in the last analysis favorable to himself and
his purpose. *This is Rule Number Thirty-One.*
Imitate in your business!

(I) But he secures assent to his propositions, not as in his interest, but always—such is the appearance—in the interests of investors or of other properties. *This is Rule Number Thirty-Two.* Imitate in your business.

(J) He contrives to know, ferret out, defeat, and use, his enemies, personal or financial. *This is Rule Number Thirty-Three.* Imitate in your business!

(K) He knows, not only his plans in the large and in detail, together with the probable outcome, but the ways and means of reaching every step of progress. *This is Rule Number Thirty-Four.* Imitate in your business!

(L) And so, he utilizes the firm hand and the steady discipline, which factors control forces, punish blunders and hostilities, reward fidelity, service, success—lavishly. *This is Rule Number Thirty-Five.* Imitate in your business.

(M) He is always possessed of business sanity and mental balance. *This is Rule Number Thirty-Six.* Cultivate in your business!

(N) Yet he develops the gift of the gods—financial intuition. *This is Rule Number Thirty-Seven.* Develop in your business!

(O) Above all, he is incessantly engaged in acquiring the magnetic will. *This is Rule Number Thirty-Eight.* Acquire in your business!

III. § 28. AT CLOSE QUARTERS. The mastery of high finance demands, at close quarters, definite values such as the following:

(A) Omnipresence, in the thick of specialized action, capturing and holding men and forces, and concentrating them for the final scene—completion of the business. *This is Rule Number Thirty-Nine.* Live this rule!

(B) The master business man utilizes every modern instrumentality: rail, boat, wire, phone, and so on, without stint of time, patience, money, and grants no opportunity for "slumps" or withdrawals, because he covers a state, a continent, or a globe, and the one important thing is control to the finish of what he has in hand. *This is Rule Number Forty.* Live this rule!

(C) In order to the above, he must thoroughly understand the mental and practical art of combination. *This is Rule Number Forty-One.* Of reconciling conflicting interests, *Rule Number Forty-Two.* Of inducing sacrifices for larger or surer gains, *Rule Number Forty-Three.* Live these rules!

(D) And so, he is compelled to know plants, properties, stocks, markets, territories, their resources and certainties. *This is Rule Number Forty-Four.* Live this rule!

(E) He must know labor, materials, wages, cost, market conditions, and prices, according to the business in hand. *This is Rule Number Forty-Five.* Live this rule in your business!

I do not mean that the promoter must understand the practical, hand-to-hand working of every property he manages as a promoter. This business is a business by itself, just as the properties he is dealing with are businesses in themselves, and no man could engage widely in miscellaneous promoting and possess such a fund of knowledge. But he must understand his propositions sufficiently to foregather them and see their possibilities. "The

professional promoter, in the course of his business,"
as Meade remarks, "and from his association with
technical experts, must necessarily accumulate a
great store of practical information. His ability to
make a technical judgment should constantly increase; but if he devotes his energies to the
promoting business, it is next to impossible that he
should master all the sciences and arts whose conclusions and rules are put at his service by the
experts whom he employs."

(F) He must know all assets involved, available, improbable, and the values in question. *This
is Rule Number Forty-Six.* Illustrate this rule!

(G) He must understand and have a hand in
legislation. *This is Rule Number Forty-Seven.*
Act this rule when needed!

(H) He must anticipate the ultimate kinds of
his stock or shares, their final allotment to those
who come into his project, his own proportion,
their transfer and exchange, their sale at a pre-
mium, and, if desired, the final closeout. *This is
Rule Number Forty-Eight.* Realize this rule in
your business so far as it applies!

(I) He must acquire the skilled ability to
quiet men who are dissatisfied, and to hold off and
control men who are elated with success. *This
is Rule Number Forty-Nine.* Acquire in your
business!

(J) The Napoleonic financier is absolutely
absorbed in the one undertaking—although he may
have many projects on his mind from time to time.
This is Rule Number Fifty. Actualize in your
business!

§ 29. The man who promotes financial enter-

prises is absolutely indispensable in our time.
Without this order of intelligence the industrial
resources of the world could not possibly be utilized
to anything like their limit. "It is the promoter
who organizes new companies and places their
prospects before the speculative and investing
public. His organizing energy usually, although
not of necessity, follows the line of largest immediate advantage to the community. If there is
an opportunity for new industries or new combinations of industries, the promoter organizes companies to take advantage of the opportunity. Noting the most promising outlets for industrial
activity, he capitalizes the new opportunities and
markets the securities while the public is in the
humor for buying shares. If we go back to the
earlier years of our industrial history, we find the
promoter organizing banking and land companies.
At a later period, railroad schemes were put on the
market.   Public-service corporations, mines, and
street-railways have each had their share of attention. Whenever an opportunity is presented for
the exploitation of new resources or new conditions,
the promoter is on hand with his prospectuses and
his propositions to be submitted to the approval
of the investing public."

Such "enterprises are constantly being promoted throughout the country, not only on mines,
but on real estate, manufacturing enterprises, water-
power, irrigation, and timber.   The details of each
may vary a bit, but the essential principles are the
same: (1) The securing of a right to purchase an
opportunity to make money; (2) the capitalization
of that opportunity at a higher figure than the price

to be paid the original owner plus the funds required for development; and (3) the sale of the certificates of this capitalization to the investor either directly or through the agency of middlemen for a sum of money exceeding the amount necessary to purchase and develop the resource which it is intended to exploit. The difference represents the promoter's profit."

"The promoter performs an indispensable function in the community by discovering, formulating, and assembling the business propositions by whose development the wealth of society is increased. He acts as the middleman or intermediary between the man with money to invest in securities and the man with undeveloped property to sell for money. In the present scheme of production, the resource and the money are useless apart. Let them be brought together, and wealth is the result. The unassisted coincidence of investment funds with investment opportunities, however, is fortuitous and uncertain. The investor and the land or patent or mine owner have few things in common. Left to themselves they might never meet. But the promoter brings these antithetical elements together, and in this way is the means of creating a value which did not before exist, and which is none the less a social gain because much of it is absorbed by the promoter and the financier."

§ 30. The aim of these quotations is suggestion for the development of business power. Opportunities are occurring in every direction which only financial alertness can discover and business skill and energy can develop. You are urged to scan the horizon of your world, big or small, for such opportunities.   The external field for business growth is unlimited and is constantly revealing phases which look perfectly simple when once discovered, but which are altogether opaque to the ordinary unobserving man in business for others or himself.   Moreover, there is an inner field awaiting your discovery which is of prime importance to advancement in the external field.   I refer to the used areas of your brain.   Here are territories that are as unoccupied by yourself as were now-irrigated but formerly desert lands of the West.   You can only awaken these possibilities by irrigating them with alert and strenuous thought.   Without thought the human mind is a desert indeed.   The only methods for securing larger brain areas for action and growth are those which I have attempted to sample in this book.

§ 31.   But Business Power requires wisdom in the matter of investment no less than skill in securing it.   The psychic attitude of the investing public would seem to demand instruction by way of warning not to place unlimited confidence in the promises of high finance.   "A minister or a physician has a few thousands laid by, a woman has either saved or inherited a small amount, a workman or a farmer has managed to scrape together something for a rainy day.   Such people are found by the thousands in every part of the country. From their accumulations they draw a small rate of return, often so small that they are constrained to add it to the principal, and do not venture to apply it to expenditure.   Their lives are hard, monotonous, and barren.   Before their eyes are constantly flaunted the luxurious extravagance of the wealthy

leisure class. To such people the prospectus of a
new enterprise is wonderfully attractive. In exchange for a few thousands it offers them a fortune.
The offer dazzles them. Their desires benumb
their judgment. The risk of the undertaking is
forgotten. Few of those who put their money into
a speculative scheme enter it with the thought of
risk. The calm balancing of chances is the exercises of a superior order of mind. The speculator
does not buy a chance, he buys what he thinks is a
fortune. He has had a vision of a vein of ore or a
great reservoir of oil. He has seen a populous
town arise around a factory in which he has invested. He has forsaken the difficult paths of
reason for the flowery fields of imagination and
conjecture."

"Hundreds of these companies are floated every
year, and their promoters often find good markets
for their wares. Most of these promoters are
honest. They expect to spend a large part of the
funds intrusted to their care in the exploitation of
the resource or opportunity which they control.
A minority are fraudulent. But, one and all, they
must, in order to float their schemes, appeal to the
imagination and the cupidity, and blindfold the
judgment of the people who buy their shares. All
that they can properly offer is a chance in a lottery
in which there are few prizes and many blanks."

"The line of speculators is very ancient. In
1720 there was printed for W. Bonham, in London,
'an argument proving that the South Sea Company is able to make a dividend of 38 per cent for
twelve years, fitted to the meanest capacities.'
This was one of the first prospectuses ever issued,

and the succession has been worthy of its ancestor:
Spanish Jackass Company, Louisiana Bubble,
South American Bonds, American Improvement
Bonds, South American Railways, Australian
Railways, Rand Mines, American Industrials
—John Law, Hudson, Barnato, Hooley, Gates,
and Lawson. The line runs true. The Jackass
Company still lives." And while this is writing
a Boston broker whose name indicates his sover-
eignity (King) is earnestly wanted by investors who
slipped their savings into his accumulating hands!

So far as the caution here indicated is
concerned, it makes no difference whether the
"scheme" be purely speculative or apparently industrial and legitimate. The one method is sensational and the other is as dignified as a Mahogany
desk. The one "throws a sprat to catch a whale,"
and the other throws a whale to catch a sprat—in
either case to catch a sucker. Of course there are
strictly legitimate investments, but always is it the
big return for small outlay which marks the business as a sprat-whale affair. "There is no real
difference between the argument of the syndicate
manager of the trust and that of the oil or town-
site 'boomer.' The first is more dignified, that is
all. The method of the appeal and the class to
whom the appeal is made are the same in the case
of either proposition."

CHAPTER XVII.

MASTERY FOR THE LARGER BUSINESS.

YOU possess all the power you live for. This is the universal law. Into an atom or an ion power has poured itself to the limit of the receiving field. No more is true of that System which amazes us in the Galactic Circle. To every existence all the power required, is the fiat of Nature. Requirement is measured by reciprocal interaction. Were it demanded that a molecule of matter should balance the Universe, adequate power would instantly make the equation good. If the molecule might be acted upon by the whole System, it would needs react with effectiveness equal to balance. Reciprocal interaction in such a case must call for power which shall express the fact of equilibration. For the Universe is self-bound, and thus all the power it needs it has. No existence within the Universe is self-bound in the same sense, and hence the history of power in the lesser fields is not merely the history of conservation of energy and correlation of force; it is a history of transfer of *internal* energy according to reaction to *external* force. The law here is that reaction is equal to action, a law

which holds good in all things during ages, from an
atom in crystallization to a neuron in the human
brain.   The atom and the neuron can only react
equivalently to outside force-action.   The moment,
however, that the something called intelligence—
"the chooser between"—appears, that moment it is
demonstrated that the self of man may react une-
quivalently to external force-action.   *Man can be
and do less than the outside activities that rain upon
him call for.*   Observe that, for we all agree to the
proposition!   In that case he possesses little if any
power.   But—now the logic comes in from the
former statement—*man can be and do more than the
outside activities call for.*   It is not important that
you can be the less thing, but it is vastly important
that you can be the greater thing.   In this case the
man possesses power sovereign over external force.
In the one instance he lives for little and he gets
little.   In the other instance he lives for much and
he gets much—even beyond the call of his living.

§ 1.   The important question in any field of
work a man may choose is, then, precisely this:
*Shall I not or shall I get out of life all that's coming
to me?*   If you interpret this in terms of big wages,
short hours, and easy work,—of large return for
small outgo,—you wholly miss the point.   The
question signifies: long hours, hard work, and
therefore large returns.   It now becomes: *Shall I
live, in amount and quality of effort, so that all that
belongs to me on that basis shall surely come my way?*

§ 2.   If you live for all the power you ought to
possess, you have that power now.   To-morrow, on
this rule, you will live for more power—and infallibly receive it.

§ 3. By so much as you increasingly become possessed of more and better power, you will compel corresponding reaction on the part of the business world. You will have your reward—infallibly.

§ 4. This law cannot fail, and no man can prevent its operation, because it works automatically—is a part of the Universal Government.

§ 5. The foundation of these propositions seems to be one of the deepest truths man knows; the tendency of all things to come to equilibrium. Such a tendency is evident in the material world and climaxes with all things in system: the ions in the system of atom, the latter in that of·molecule, the latter in those of compounds and crystals and cells, the latter cells in physical functions, the former compounds and crystals, in planets and universes, and the physical functions in the system called the human body, whose chief glory is the brain system, as the latter's highest expression is a complex of psychic activities known as "mind.' The goal always is equilibrium through harmony. In any physical system both tendency and goal are evident. "Mind" exhibits this peculiarity: it demands a non-material system in which balance means increasing development without limit (not true in the physical field, where balance signifies limit and so, equivalence, of interaction), but especially means inter-relations (mind with mind) making such limitless development possible.

In "*Balance: The Fundamental Verity,*" Orlando F. Smith defines balance or equilibrium as "*that principle or order*—manifest in action and reaction, cause and effect, antecedent and consequent; in harmony and antagonism; in attraction and

repulsion; in the law of averages; in correspondence; in correlation—*through which comes universal
adjustment.*" This statement is illustrated on every
hand in the physical world.

§ 6. The tendency to equilibration is observable in the business world because it is a phase of
all human life. If your reaction to life—to business—is weak and inefficient, the tendency drives
you into and settles you in an inferior position.
You receive what you live for—what your living
calls for. If your reaction is potent, balance puts
you on a higher plane. Your reaction disturbs environment and compels re-adjustment in which you
get the benefit. Felix Le Dantec said, in "*The
Nature aud Origin of Life:*" "While it lives, a
living substance by the act of living creates in the
environment around its semi-fluid body whirlpool
movements which count for a great deal in the determination of its own form. Thus, just so long as
it survives, the living being carries along with it,
not only its own substance, but also a certain system
of movements which it imposes on the medium in
the immediate environment of its body." So long
as you really live in the business world—live po-
tently, steadily, effectively—you "carry a certain
system of movements which you impose on environment." You see, then, that *environment must reckon
with you.* It is for you to determine whether those
movements shall be large and important or small
and worthless. If you will that the latter shall be
so, you can compel business environment to react
and reckon practically with yourself and your work,
and to reckon in a large and remunerative way.

§ 7. Exactly this is what general business has

accomplished—compelled the world to reckon with
it and to yield it large returns. When business is
small, it must itself do all the reckoning that's done.
The peanut vender must hustle in order to live.
But as business expands and lives for large control,
the day is prophesied when every huge department
of life has to give an account of itself to business
about as business determines. It is with individuals
in this respect as it is with trade. In the last of the
progress from small things to great we have this
truth exemplified: "The advantage of the capitalist
is further enhanced by the tendency toward monopoly. The result is a most interesting circle, constant combination at the top in order to force
down the commercial price of the risk (attendant on
any business), and monopoly of the upper field
which pays tremendous profits, resulting in still
greater increase in the financial power of the risk
takers. To this there is no end, save in the divorce,
through heredity, of ability and financial power."
The more a business lives for big things, and the
greater its reaction on industry and wealth, the
more certain is it of becoming monopoly when
reaction means control; and, similarly, the more
the individual lives for big values and the greater
his reaction upon business in general, the surer is
he of becoming in the personal meaning a monopoly
of high position and salary and income. In the
sense here indicated, monopoly is simply equilibrium: a president or general manager at balance
with a railway system, a merchant prince at balance
with the local dealers in a dozen chained department
stores, a United States Steel Corporation at balance
with the entire iron industry of a nation.

In the business world you receive what you practically live for.   The business world, like Nature, is forced to give you all that your reaction makes imperative.   The bargain is always forced, but it is none the less inevitable.

The Master Régimes.

§ 8.   Now, the phrase, "living for," has a double significance.   That reaction to the business world which induces large return-action, and so, large rewards, involves practically effective conduct of affairs, of course, but as well, certain superb psychic factors which every great business man exhibits and which are really the secrets of the ancient saying—*mens molem movet*—"mind moves the world."   It is not mere mental activity, even of the best sort, that can move this world in the long run of the centuries.   It is a master spirit in which courageously confident will, like a huge dynamo, is ever at work behind such mental activities.   For the most part, these psychic factors have already been indicated, but it now remains to suggest for them larger proportions and a deeper meaning.   Indeed, if you have worked yourself into the preceding pages, the factors have by this time assumed in your thought the suggested greatness through subjective operations.   This result has come about in the author's mind: the main things seem vaster and more financially important than at any preceding moment.   The ideas which I have tried to handle have been unfolding for many months.   For thought grows.   Fact, law, truth disclose more and more of their content as the objective "mind" studies them and the subconscious self assimilates the results of such study. It is for these reasons that the work of all the foregoing pages closes with what we may call The Master Régimes.

§ 9. Business men frequently use the words, "tireless work." When they write essays on success, "hard work" becomes a frightful god (or devil), held solely responsible for fine residences and notable enterprises. This is one-half sheer nonsense. Without the essential elements already indicated, hard work digs failures out of life's best possibilities. Deified work is a golden calf. Adaptive persistence, alert as lightning, infusive as air, unyielding as granite, deathless as death, is merely the outer circumstance, for example, (the insulator), of the real power of success, and that power is wholly and profoundly psychic. For the larger phases of that power the master régimes are now suggested.

§ 10. FIRST MASTER RÉGIME: EFFICIENCY OF BUSINESS ASSOCIATIONS. It is vastly important in business life that you should associate with those who do not discount your strong points and who do make up for your weak points. To associate in business with a man whom you do not thoroughly know—know his past, know his financial standing, know his business habits and power, know his personal traits and characteristics, is rank folly. Assuming these elements to be understood, how does this man supplement or complement you? If you add two holes, you do not make a mound. If you add two mounds, you do not make a hollow. The other man's defects must be balanced by something in your make-up, and, *vice versa*, the other man's powers must be of such a nature as to "make good" against your failing points. Moreover, associates must be mutually magnetic. Such harmony multiplies every ability and lessens every defect. If, in addition, mutually magnetic associates can mass into one persistent force psychic courage, confidence, and will-power, the compound becomes well nigh resistless. The régime concentrates, then, to this unvarying attitude: *We, each in his strength and skill, all together, achieve to the limit whatever we undertake!* Well said Andrew Carnegie, in "*James Watt*": "He who proves indispensable as a partner to one man might be wholly useless or even injurious, to another. Generals Grant and Sherman needed very different chiefs of staff. One secret of Napoleon's success arose from his being free to make his own appointments, choosing the men who had the qualities which supplemented his and cured his own shortcomings, for every man has shortcomings. The universal genius who can manage all himself has yet to appear. Only one with the genius to recognize others of different genius and harness them to his own car can approach the universal. It is a case of different but coöperating abilities, each part of the complicated machine fitting into its right place, and there performing its duty without jarring."

Such a "fitting in" demands psychic alertness in all associates to the nature and moods of the others, secured by the thought, "*I am trying to adjust to you for what you are at your best.*" For there is an inner feeling, an inner attitude, of coöperation which is to be attained by thinking it, trying to realize it as a fact within. When such adjustment is sought, invariably will unfold a mutual harmony for the main thing, business success. If every associate harmonizes with every other for that goal, and always conceives the business in its largest possibilities, success is assured, other things, of course, being equal. This is the method of all the great financial associations of the modern world.

§ 11. SECOND MASTER RÉGIME: MAINTENANCE OF COURAGE. James Watt encountered innumerable difficulties: drunkenness on the part of employees, unskilled workmen, the acquisition of foreign land guages in the search for latest information, lack of capital, and timid partners. Watt's characteristics were indomitable push coupled with occasional fits of despondency. When you become despondent, you remove no difficulty, you assume an extra burden—despondency. Why take another, if one is already heavy? I *know* that persistent will can banish every desponding mood. Here is a ghost which, unlike Banquo's, will surely "down" in time, if forever you thrust every suggestion of the kind aside. One of Watt's partners, Matthew Boulton, was in resources and personality exactly the kind of man needed in the business of enabling Watt to complete the stationary engine. "Boulton's mind partners," says Carnegie, "no doubt were amazed that he was so blind to the dangers which they with clearer vision saw so clearly. How deluded they were. We may be sure neither of them saw the danger half as vividly as he, but it is not the part of a leader to reveal to his fellows all that he sees or fears. His part is to look dangers steadily in the face and to challenge them. It is the great leader who inspires in his followers contempt for the danger which he sees in much truer proportions than they. This Boulton did, for behind all else in his character there lay the indomitable will, the do-or-die resolve. He had staked his life upon the hazard of a die and he would stand the cost. 'But if we fail,' often said the timid pair to him, as Macbeth did to his resolute partner, and the same answer came, '*We* fail.' That's all. 'One knockdown will not finish this fight. We'll get up again, never fear. We know no such word as fail.'" This is the spirit which the larger business requires. Any man can acquire that spirit. One who is engaged in a business that has always made heavy demands upon him, financially and mentally, writes to me in regard to a volume in The Power-Book Library: "'*Power for Success*' showed me for the first time in my life, and I'm over sixty years of age, that I could be 'just as good' as any other man— and brought me that confidence in myself, and my self-ability, to be a success in any honest endeavor. In other words, my diffidence and uncertain feeling in regard to myself has changed to confidence and this confidence has helped me through the most severe test of strength and endeavor of my life, to a gratifying success."

Such confident courage may be a matter of temperament, but it is as certain as natural law that you can build it by incessantly striving to realize or feel it, and meanwhile endeavoring *to conceive the dual quality in a large way, as having to do with large affairs*. It is a universal fault that men think constantly of small affairs in a small way. This habit shrinks the whole nature. The little tobacco-and-paper shop-man permits his brain cells to work over petty doings and pennies and dimes until the cells become two-penny neurons, and his business courage is horrified at the vision of a pin-head lawyer who lives, like the gadfly, only to sting.   The picture holds up to the mirror millions of men.   The publisher of one of the most widely circulated magazines or papers of America had the courage to plunge $200,000 in debt to an advertising agency, and then to say to the latter: "Unless you help me another $100,000, you lose all." The daring of the man at least was commendable, but we may be sure that this daring was the product of a broad sowing of big ideas. Such ideas familiarize the mind with the spirit of faith, so that always the larger self inhales more and more the very breath of power.   The psychic origin of this kind of courage hides always in such a sentence as this: "*I shall stand forever for greater things than I have achieved, and I possess every minute the confidence demanded by the situation.*" The sentence is like the Count of Monte Cristo, who cried, on escaping from a political prison-fortress, "The world is mine!" Observe: the real Monte Cristo said these words under his breath: they signified certainty, not the boast.

§ 12.   THIRD MASTER RÉGIME: HOLDING THE RESERVE.   This régime bases in the financial fund kept good for special emergencies.   "A small balance on the right side performs wonders.   This recalls to the writer how, once in the history of his own firm (the Carnegie company), credit was kept high during a panic by using the identical sum Boulton raised, $70,000, from a reserve fund that had been laid away and came in very opportunely

at the critical time.   Every single dollar weighs a
hundred-fold when credit trembles in the balance.
A leading nerve specialist in New York once said
that the worst malady he had to treat was the man
of affairs whose credit was suspected.   His unfailing remedy was: 'Call your creditors together,
explain all and ask their support.   I can then do
you some good, but not till then.'   His patients
who did this found themselves restored to vigor.
They were supported by creditors and all was
bright once more.   The wise doctor was sound in
his advice.   If the firm has neither speculated nor
gambled (synonymous terms), nor lived extrava-
gantly, nor endorsed for others, and the business is
on a solid foundation, no people have so much at
stake in sustaining it as the creditors; they will
rally round it and think more of the firm than ever-
because they will see behind their money the best
of securities—men at the helm who are not afraid
and who know how to meet a storm."

But the present régime refers also to the
psychic account which every man should hold with
himself.   At any instant your personal capital is
x-energy x (knowledge + courage + confidence +
practical ability + self-mastery + psychic intuition)
together also with x-energy x (muscle + nerve + endurance + elasticity + recuperative powers).   The x
is, of course, unknown, but experience has taught
you more or less of its value, and this must be relied
upon in employing the present régime. Experience
is an acute or a dull teacher according to the attitude of reception which you have cultivated.   It is
commonplace to advise you to draw on this psychic
resource.   It is valuable instruction to say that you

can develop psychic intuitions in regard to "reserves
on hand" of the above psychic possessions. If you
insist upon knowing approximately the value of x, you
can acquire the ability to do so. As you go to your
bookkeeper for a balance-sheet showing your net
capital and your reserve, so you can turn to your
subjective self for a fair knowledge of your psychic
reserve fund of power. The method consists in
quieting down, now and then, giving your "mind"
time to "settle," and in then trying to feel how your
reserve of energy, nerve, mental fruitfulness, and
so on, stands. If the "reports" prove vaguely
disquieting, assent, but with perfect confidence in
yourself, and *stop the expenditure*. Better lose ten
dollars than one nerve, one phase of mental deftness, one iota of reserve power. As certain as law
is it that you can teach yourself to respect and conserve a special fund of all-round power, by feeling
for it, asserting it, and claiming it, so that, when
the time of dire emergency comes, you have that
fund with you to master the day.

§ 13. Fourth Master Régime: Maintaining
A Low Level of Risk. All business ventures are
motived by a desire for improvement in returns.
"What the financial writers call 'pure interest' is
the return," says one, "upon investments from
which the element of risk is absent. For example,
take the English consuls. These bonds, which
represent the credit of the British Empire, yield in
interest the holder only 2½ per cent a year. Now,
if there is a security anywhere in the world which
may be considered as absolutely safe, it is this.
'Pure interest,' therefore, may be said to be in the
neigborhood of 2½ per cent to 3 per cent, and any

interest or dividend which is in excess of that figure represents greater or less risk. For instance, any investment yielding 6 per cent may be said, other things being equal, to stand for 2½ per cent of 'pure interest' and 3½ per cent of risk." This statement is somewhat conservative. The meaning of "investment" would perhaps vary the proportion. As Professor Fisher says: "United States Government bonds are not used for investment purposes, except among those in whom the element of caution is unduly strong, but are held for the most part by national banks. It is therefore misleading to cite, as some have done, the rates of interest realized on government bonds as an indication of the true rate of interest." Nevertheless, the risk element advances as the rate of return advances above a certain point. Evidently there are no really riskless investments, and the safety of a risk is a question for practical business power. Above the sane convictions of "the street," interest or return ceases to be legitimate and becomes a sign of hazardous risk. The general law is, of course, high dividends, high risk. It is, therefore, a master business policy to keep the element of risk down to its lowest level consistent with a going enterprise. "There are five principal ways in which risks may be reduced, viz. :—

"(1) By increasing guaranties for the performance of contracts;

(2) By increasing safeguards against incurring losses;

(3) By increasing foresight and thereby diminishing risks;

(4) By insurance, that is, by consolidating risks;

(5) By throwing risks into the hands of a special class of speculators."

The present régime requires that the performance of contracts be safeguarded, and this means an *alert, investigating, forefending psychic mood and habit of mental action*. The habit may be acquired by examining all sides of any proposition, present or future, and making sure that you know the terms, contingencies and outcomes. If the practice is observed in small details, the mood will enhance and the habit will settle for larger affairs. The thing must never be done in a state of mental confusion. The suggestions also apply to safeguarding against losses. Understand a transaction, inside, outside, top, bottom, all around, before you go into it. Get at the facts yourself. Have the real facts stripped to the skin. Do not presume, assume, believe, or guess;—know—and for sure. These practical considerations are placed here for their psychic value. They signify development of psychic acumen in the business self. Increasing foresight relates to similar mental processes. The word, "foresight," is almost always misinterpreted, being made to mean *sight before, sight beyond, a vision of things yet to occur in the future*, when it means, and can only mean, *now-seeing things in present operation as determining things to come under natural law*. The man of financial vision foresees because he *sees now* what is going on. The mood and habit suggested above will furnish the basis on which a sound foresight can draw its logical conclusions—its conclusions determined by natural law in the business world. Such mental attitudes of caution and exacting investigation are in themselves insurance,

and constitute inevitably a psychic demand for
institutional protection.   Of course, insurance is an
investment, but it represents, if secured by attitude
and action here suggested, a greater investment,
the will and effort and time necessary so develop
the business instinct and judgment of adequate
protection.   No more contenting statement can run
through a business man's "mind" than this: "It's
all cared for," and that contentment both releases
and stores energy and wisdom, as phases of the reserve fund already called for.

§ 14.   FIFTH MASTER RÉGIME: MAINTAINING
THE PASSION FOR BUSINESS.   That love of a man's
work which we have seen to be essential to the
craftsman is imperatively demanded by the larger
business.   One reason for the dislike which some
men feel for their business is its *pettiness.*   This
book advises the abandonment of all small and
narrow notions about yourself and your work, and
the substitution therefor of the largest ideas you can
imagine, thinking of yourself daily as *power* and
conceiving your business in mental pictures of
greatness and victory.   This effort will in time shed
a kind of romance over all you do, and will develop
an inspired passion for your business in its practical
conduct.   I append here two paragraphs from Prince
Kropotkin which are pertinent.

"Very often the idler is but a man to whom
it is repugnant to make the eighteenth part of a pin
all his life, or the hundredth part of a watch, while
he feels he has exuberant energy which he would
like to spend elsewhere.   Often, too, he is a rebel
who cannot submit to being fixed all his life to a
work-bench in order to procure a thousand pleasures

for his employer, while knowing himself to be far the less stupid of the two, and knowing his only fault to be that of having been born in a hovel intead of coming into the world in a castle. "

What is the help for all this state of things? The Prince says: "Give the workman who is compelled to make a minute particle of some object, who is stifled at his little tapping machine, which he ends by loathing, give him the chance of tilling the soil, felling trees in the forest, sailing the sea in the teeth of a storm, dashing through space on an engine, but do not make an idler of him by forcing him all his life to attend to a small machine, to plough the head of a screw, or to drill the eye of a needle." But there is no one to accomplish this for the workman, for the clerk, for the small merchant. *He must help himself!* And the way to help himself is the way of courageous energy, set on freedom from small things, and forever dreaming of and "hustling" after larger things. By this dream and struggle will come a love for effort and achievement which will mightily stimulate every power the man possesses. The second paragraph is now in point.

"On the other hand, he who since his youth has learned to play the piano (anything) *well*, to handle the plane *well*, the chisel, the brush, or the file, so that he feels what he does is *beautiful*, will never give up the piano, the chisel or the file. He will find pleasure in his work which does not tire him, as long as he is not overdriven."

The secret of masterhood is mastery, and the great lure of mastery is larger achievement, and the very breath of utter devotion to work conceived in the large is a passion for business. A fine illustration of this régime is seen in one of the employees of the Carnegie Company, who began at two dollars a day and died receiving an immense salary. He had earned the army title of captain. "Once he was offered an interest in the firm, which would have made him one of the band of young millionaires. His reply was, 'Thank you, don't want to have anything to do with business. These works (steel rail mills) give me enough to think of. You just give me a "thundering salary."' All right, Captain, the salary of the president of the United States is yours." This man's "business" was making steel rails. His ideas and the work were of the larger sort, and he therefore loved what he was doing with a passion too great to be diverted by the mere commercial side of "business." It was that devotion of passion which made the United States Steel Corporation. You are invited, then, to *think of your business in the greatest imaginable way*, and to *work for the heavier affairs and rewards of the business world*. The effort will infallibly breed in you devotion and passion.

§ 15. SIXTH MASTER RÉGIME: CREATING INSPIRATION BY IMAGINATION. Said Ralph Waldo Emerson: "Human labor, through all its forms, from the sharpening of a stake to the building of a city or an epic, is one immense illustration of the perfect compensation of the universe. The absolute balance of Give and Take, the doctrine that everything has its price, is not less sublime in the columns of a ledger than in the budgets of states. I cannot doubt that the high laws which each man sees implicated in those processes with which he is conversant do recommend to him his trade, and though seldom named, exalt his business in his imagination."

This is the foundation bed-rock—that the Universe is Balance, and that a man may exalt his business in his imagination; that is, not merely think of it in large visions, but *make his imagination the architect of a great concrete structure.* Why build mole hills? The pyramids call! We see what the alert imaginative business man can do in this description of James Watt's partner, Matthew Boulton: "He had a genius for business—a gift almost as rare as that for poetry, for art, or for war. He possessed a marvelous power for organization. With a keen eye for details, he combined a comprehensive grasp of intellect. While his senses were so acute that, when sitting in his office at Soho, he could detect the slightest stoppage or derangement of the machinery of that vast establishment, and send his message direct to the spot where it had occurred, his power of imagination was such as enabled him to look clearly along extensive lines of possible action in Europe, America, and East. *For there is a poetic as well as a commonplace side to business; and in the man of business insight genius lights up the humdrum routine of daily life by exploring the boundless region of possibility wherever it may lie open to him.*"

"This tells the whole story, and once again reminds us that without imagination and something of the romantic element, little great or valuable is to be done in any field. He 'runs his business as if it were a romance,' was said upon one occasion. The man who finds no element of romance in his

occupation is to be pitied." It is the devoted passion
of business imagination that discovers by anticipation the larger and more splendid possibility of
inventive, industrial and commercial application.
"Be king in your dreams."

§ 16. SEVENTH MASTER RÉGIME: MAINTAINING
ACTIVITY WORTH WHILE. To hoard energy and to
waste it are extremes of one evil. Preceding master régimes suggest action, continued night and day,
but action that is demonstrably worth while because
alert imagination has always worked with practical
ability. Assuming that your effort is well directed,
you are invited to believe that the phrase, "keeping everlastingly at it," means vastly more than
mere relentless activity. It means that the human
mind roots down into the Infinite, and must infallibly bring forth ideas, plans, methods, propositions,
visions and judgments, a very swarm, related to
business, and of the greatest value, *provided the
business man holds his work always in mind*, thus
sustaining the compound attitude of resolution and
interrogation: *This business must surely succeed!
How shall I make it a success?* Such is the present
régime. You are urged to bring your "mind,"
that is, yourself, to the attitude indicated. By this
kind of psychic attitude you constitute yourself a
powerful magnet attracting from the "great within" and the open world a constant stream of values,
both in the way of thought, and in the way of
external forces drawn in your direction. If this
sounds "occult" to you, I reply that every successful business—creation—has harnessed the occult.
But there is no real occult. There is only the "now
unknown," the "just beyond."

The fact is, business is a kind of life. Life grows. It grows by attraction: things needed are drawn into its field. The subconscious self broods over any fixed idea, and then a process of growth occurs which makes everything in the neighborhood contributory. This is what men mean when they say, "At last things are coming my way"

§ 17. EIGHTH MASTER RÉGIME: GOING ALOFT FOR VISION. It is absolutely necessary, if a man would succeed in a large way, that the "mind" should acquire ability comprehensively to over-see his business, aloft, as it were, in a clear bird's-eye view. Some men are always in the whirl of their business, and they are, at any time, psychically only where they chance to be in bodily presence. A man should be immanent in his business, but this task one cannot accomplish in a physical sense. The present master régime calls upon you to get out of your body in some way and be "all over the place" at once. The method consists in knowing every inch of place and detail of the work *as the head of the concern*. On such a basis, the method expands to the assumption of a *willed mental attitude of being everywhere*—seeing all things—listening to all things—feeling the whole business in all its parts. In order to achieve the method it is necessary to *realize yourself as aloft above the place*, as though you were standing on the roof, that and the floors being transparent. Here, also, the apparently miraculous confronts us. The ability is an acquired one with most men who possess it, though an endowment with some; nevertheless, the power is actual and the outcome of natural law, I believe. "He seems to be omniscient," is said of one. He

is.   By one faculty or means or another, the king
aloft knows the busy-ness of the kingdom. You are
invited to practise the method for long.   The
results will be gratifying.

The régime has a further phase in actual and
accurate knowledge gained through objective observation of every department of the business in
hand.   It is not enough to guess, presume, assume,
believe, take for granted.   Business power *knows*,
knows *how* it knows (for the most part), knows that
it *can* know.   It knows that every man in the
undertaking is doing the right thing, that every
demanded thing is being done, that every department is working as organization for specific results
and annual increase of business.   Modern facilities
for organization, system, celerity, perfection, reports on and dispatch of business, are so numerous
and so skilfully devised that this exact information
is now altogether the normal thing. The king aloft,
like Peter the Great, of Russia, who forsook his throne
temporarily for a Holland ship yard in order that he
might learn how to build ships for himself, must
frequently come down into the confusion and detail
of his own business. All the better will be his
view if he do this from time to time.

The final phase of the present régime consists
in *assembling activities and outcomes for practical
results.*   You can "view aloft" and work in the
midst of your place of business, but you must put
the products together, start them in transportation
or transition, and secure their sale at your figures.
McClellan could "see" his army from the altitude
of commander, and know his regiments by inspection. Grant had these powers, but he possessed the

eye of genius for companies and corps in the chaos of battle, and his was the hand of mastery for assembling all the resources he had, at the right time, in the right way, for the right purpose. It is valueless to be even an adept up to this point. The goal is to turn your business effectively and continuously into *more money to-day than you expended on it yesterday*. The matter is practical, and requires practical ability. Nevertheless, business experience develops the ability, and auto-suggestion unfolds the psychic phase of the power. Our method, then, consists in actually working to that end—assembling all your business unceasingly for the disposal of your values at a profit—but as well, in persistently *conceiving precisely that end as realized*, in your whole business body of thought—the thing as actually and now accomplished.

§ 18. NINTH MASTER RÉGIME: UTILIZING THE LAW OF DEMAND. You wish success in business life. Then *demand* success, with deepest emphasis and surest confidence, day after day, month after month, and, if your work is as effective as the preceding chapters should make it, your demand will be splendidly realized. I affirm that the Universe is a fund of force, and that you are a centre of force-creation and force-attraction. Your mental and practical demands induce power-currents your way. Remember this! Believe in this! Do not toil less, but affirm more: "*I demand that measure of success which my personality and my thought and my work call for. I am a centre! I receive power! I shall gain my goal! I shall make good my demand!*"

And, observe! In this mental affirmation the psychic factor is to *lead*, not follow, the practical phase of your efforts. Set the dynamo of your soul to the task! Develop power by *demanding* it! Work, but think! And behind all thinking, *demand!*

So comes our task to its end (yours?). I be-grudge the faults of this book—all its incomplete-ness. Business! Vast as the world! Complex as the billion-celled brain of man can make it! Who might expect to surround, know and exploit the science of business? My own task has been less—to instruct for psychic power in business enterprise. Even in this undertaking, imperfection confronts the would-be helper. Yet, be it thus: I write the final words with the conviction that "*Business Power*," like all the Power-Books, is the best of its kind thus far, a pioneer, and will surely prove "good value" to those who really achieve the demanded exchange: *the book into the "mind" for the "mind" into the book.* May such exchange be yours—and all good fortune.

> Sincerely, for Real Success,
> A Brother Co-operator,

Printed in the USA
CPSIA information can be obtained
at www.ICGtesting.com
LVHW011956121223
766149LV00005B/551